59-13842

1/26/60

600

As Others See Us

As Others See Us

The United States

through Foreign Eyes

EDITED BY FRANZ M. JOSEPH

WITH CONTRIBUTIONS BY

Raymond Aron	Luigi Barzini, Jr.
Denis W. Brogan	Morris Broughton
Pura Santillan Castrence	Daniel Cosío Villegas
James Eayrs	S. N. Eisenstadt
Jacques Freymond	A. D. Gorwala
K. A. B. Jones-Quartey	Mohammad Khalafallah
Amanda Labarca H.	Mochtar Lubis
Jorge Mañach	Julian Marias
Ömer Celâl Sarc	S. R. Shafaq
Marija Vilfan	Peter von Zahn

PRINCETON, NEW JERSEY
PRINCETON UNIVERSITY PRESS
1959

Introduction

O wad some Pow'r the giftie gie us
To see oursels as others see us!
It wad frae monie a blunder free us,
And foolish notion.

—ROBERT BURNS: TO A LOUSE, ON SEEING ONE
ON A LADY'S BONNET AT CHURCH

ROBERT BURNS'S famous wish has sometimes been amplified to include a wish that others might be endowed with the gift to see us as we see ourselves. Both gifts are needed in our close-knit world, and tokens of both are offered in this book.

Visitors from twenty nations throughout the world show how the United States looks to them and their countrymen, and in doing so they tell much about their own nations. Anyone who has lived through the developments of the past two decades knows the significance of these efforts at portraiture. In scarcely more than a single generation the United States has become an influence throughout the world: it is felt everywhere, and opinions about it are held everywhere. The value of the contribution this country can make in the world role in which it now finds itself depends crucially on the relation between what it thinks about itself and what others think about it, and between its views of them and their own views of themselves.

Because the essays in this book are concerned with these two faces of a single coin, each approaching the subject in its own way, they form a unity, with every part contributing to every other. Certain specific aspects may be of first concern to individual readers: the contributions from particular countries or writers; the critical remarks or the indications of esteem; factual description or discussion of major issues; vivid narratives of personal experience or thoughtful analyses of underlying and countervailing forces. But all such variations are parts of the whole, like the separate movements in a symphony. It is as a totality that these essays serve their purpose of making the United States and the rest of the world better known to each other.

There is wide variation in the nature of the essayists' American experience. Of the men and women, young and old, who speak

in this volume, some have been in the United States on many occasions, others only once, some for long periods of time, others
for short visits. Several are acquainted with more of the country
than most of its citizens ever see, while others have visited only
limited parts of it. Most are concerned primarily with the present,
but a few concentrate their attention on impressions formed years
ago, even though they have since returned on other trips. All such
variations are essential aspects of the mosaic that represents the
world's views of the United States. Observations from brief trips
are communicated to fellow countrymen at home as readily as the
knowledge gained from years of close contact; in fact, it is mainly
in brief encounters, and in limited areas, that foreigners know any
country and its people. And memories of past experiences may
influence current feeling as strongly as an encounter within the
past six months.

It is striking that in spite of the variety of these observers and
their ways of thinking, they show a large measure of agreement
with one another in what they say about the United States. The
forcefulness of this agreement is not diminished by the fact that
many of their reflections have been emphasized by other commentators, both foreign visitors and native analysts, and are sometimes
acknowledged even in our private thinking about ourselves. What
gives substance to these essayists' observations is not only what
is said but how many say it, with what emphasis and what insight.
In the way a nation appears to the world there is significance in the
very fact of majority opinion. It is the shadings of that opinion,
the variations on a common theme, that lead to a deeper comprehension of what is involved in living together.

In recent years the social scientists have given much attention
to the "images" that each nation has of other nations. This book
has been planned and carried out on the basis of an extensive study
of this literature, but in several important ways it departs from
the usual work in this field: by gathering together a wide variety
of visitors from many different countries; by attempting to assemble thoughtful observers interested in a civilization as a whole
rather than in isolated features of it; by asking the visitors to express themselves fully, with no structure assigned except the suggestion that they look at their experience from the point of view
of the broad questions mentioned in the letter of invitation; by

presenting their responses in full depth without attempting to abstract them or correlate them. It is hoped that this approach, though it consists in presenting the material rather than analyzing it, will provide suggestive insights to those who are interested in the problems of "image" formation and change. A brief discussion of their work is appended to the present volume.

Although the letter of invitation, which was identical for all contributors to this book, prescribed nothing about the approach the essays should take, it asked that they include a consideration of these three questions: First, in what respects has your stay in the United States changed your former ideas about the United States and its people? Second, how does your present view of the United States and its people compare with that held in your country, by the population in general and by its main social and intellectual groups? Third, what, in your opinion, can the people of your country and the United States learn from each other?

The letter continued as follows: "You are free to deal with the questions in your own way and to include a discussion of any other problems that may appear relevant. For example, in what respects do the people of the United States, in your opinion, have a distorted image of the people of your country? What common interests have your country and the United States? What similarities do you find between attitudes and institutions in your country and the United States (social behavior and relations, economic and political attitudes, legal principles and practices, standards in the arts and forms of entertainment)? What is your opinion about past efforts, and what specific suggestions can you make for future efforts, to bring about a better understanding between your country and the United States?" No other suggestions were made regarding the content of the essays.

The contributors wrote their essays at approximately the same time, and the manuscripts were received at the end of 1957 and early in 1958. Because of unavoidable space limitations, it was found necessary to omit whatever was expendable without injustice to the authors or detriment to the value of their contributions within the prescribed aims of the work. As a result some of the essays had to be reduced in length and a few had to be omitted entirely. Let it be said most emphatically that editorial agreement or disagreement played no part in these decisions. The book is based on the firm conviction that the reader alone should decide on the validity of the points of view here expressed—and that if he does so with due reflection, both in dissenting and in concurring, the nations of the world have been brought closer together.

ACKNOWLEDGMENTS

THIS BOOK results from a project of the American European Foundation, Inc. Many people have made valuable contributions at various stages. My sincere thanks go to all of them. I must especially express my profound gratitude to two members of the New School for Social Research: Dean Hans Staudinger of the Graduate Faculty and Miss Elizabeth Todd of the Research Division. They have given generously of their experience and their wisdom, and have actively participated in every phase of the project from its conception to the final completion of the manuscript. I should also like to acknowledge my indebtedness to the other members of the Advisory Committee of the Foundation: Ambassador Benjamin Cohen, formerly an Under-Secretary of the United Nations; Dr. Ralph C. M. Flynt of the US Office of Education; Professor John N. Hazard of Columbia University; Miss Marguerite Higgins of the New York *Herald Tribune*; President Kenneth Holland of the Institute of International Education; Dr. Hugh L. Keenleyside of the United Nations; President George N. Shuster of Hunter College; Dr. Shepard Stone of the Ford Foundation; and Dr. Kenneth Thompson of the Rockefeller Foundation.

New York, May 1, 1959   F.M.J.

Contents

As Others See Us

from England

DENIS W. BROGAN

The author: born in Scotland (Glasgow), 1900; studied at Glasgow, Oxford, Cambridge, and Harvard. Dr. Brogan, Professor of Political Science at Cambridge and a Fellow of Peterhouse, has also taught at several universities in the United States (Washington, Illinois, Yale) and has written numerous books and articles about this country. He has reported five Presidential campaigns for British newspapers, and has delivered frequent broadcasts concerning the United States. His writings also include several works on France. Dr. Brogan is the father of three sons and a daughter. His many trips to the United States since 1925 have taken him throughout the country.

I

I AM going to concern myself here with changes—changes in my own, and particularly in the British, view of "what is America." It is now nearly thirty-five years since I first visited the United States, and in that time I have returned repeatedly (three times even during the late war). In the course of these visits I have been more than once in every region of the country, and have lived for stretches of time in all of them except the Deep South. Thus my view of the promise, achievements, and limitations of American life has changed continually over the past generation or more, as the United States itself has changed.

When I first visited America in 1925, my ideas were those of most of the young "liberal" intellectuals of that time in Britain and in Europe. On the one hand, there was the immunity of America from the shock of the First World War. True, the United States had participated in that war, but for a brief time, with comparatively little loss, and had walked out of the peace settlement. The European, contemplating the United States at that period, suffered from divided feelings. One was envy and to some degree a spirit of emulation. This was "America the Golden." Another was something very like contempt for a country that had ignored so many problems, that had allowed a world whose historical destiny it had so profoundly affected to go its own way, that professed to believe itself immune from most human ills, to have conquered most hu-

3

man problems, a society that was soon to adopt and believe in the Coué slogan: "Every day and in every way we are getting better and better." To a young student who had seen the devastated regions of France, who had lived in Rome in the "anno primo" of Fascism, whose home town, Glasgow, was one of the British cities most badly hit by unemployment and contraction of markets, this optimism seemed indecent.

Moreover, like most young "intellectuals," I was predisposed to see American problems in European terms, to condemn the American political system for its division of powers, for its toleration of judicial review, for its consequent slowness and conservatism. Above all, America seemed to be a country uninterested in politics, in asking fundamental questions, in contemplating the ineluctable demands of the modern world, like those presented by the survival of the Soviet Union, whose existence official American policy ignored but whose reality could not be denied. My opinion (a representative one I think) was that American society, except in the field of economic production, had a great deal to learn from Europe, while, except in that field, we had little to learn from America.

The success of the United States was limited, so the critics thought, to the more crude forms of material advancement, to central heating, a car in every garage, the creation of a mass market supplied by crude if popular artifacts like the Model T Ford. The life that was satisfied by these material achievements was drab and spiritually uninteresting. And this view was reinforced by the character of American literature and art. It was an old story that the American artist was destined to be an exile, whether in the body, like a Whistler, a Sargent, a Henry James, a T. S. Eliot (his reputation among the young was just beginning a rocket-like ascent), or in the spirit, like Mark Twain as depicted by Mr. Van Wyck Brooks.

Even the growing prestige of American literature reinforced this judgment, for the books that won most readers and most prestige were highly critical of the American way of life. *The Jungle* made for Upton Sinclair a reputation that he never lost, and his cutting socialist criticism of the United States (for example in *Oil*) buttressed the "liberals' " hostile view of America. So, in a more dra-

4

matic form, did Jack London's *The Iron Heel* (an important influence on Mr. Aneurin Bevan), which suggested that American democracy was a sham and that the rulers of America were the great business magnates. Some of the most savage critics of American life, like Dreiser, were read and admired in England before they really established themselves in America. The dead "culture" of Boston was condemned either in the terms of Mr. Eliot's early poems or in the wave of bitter hostility that swept all Europe after the execution of Sacco and Vanzetti and found popular expression in Upton Sinclair's *Boston*.

Sinclair Lewis was widely read, and the term "Babbitt" passed into the language; Mr. Joad, the English popular philosopher, called his anti-American diatribe *The Babbitt Warren*. The debunking practiced by H. L. Mencken was much admired, and "highbrows" (the term was just coming in from America) read and treasured the "Americana" section of the *American Mercury*; even when this was copied, as in the "This England" feature of the *New Statesman* of London, it was felt that the English entries were merely fruits of eccentricity while the items of "Americana" were deeply representative. Unconsciously representative, it was thought, were popular periodicals like the *Saturday Evening Post*, whose praise and exemplification of American life were its most effective condemnation.

It was permissible to admire some popular American arts, above all that of Charlie Chaplin (noting that he was not an American), even to welcome, in a superior way, such refreshing novelties as the American-style musical comedies like *No, No, Nanette* and *The Girl Friend*. But many highbrows were or professed to be alarmed at the effects of the movies on European culture. There was a determined plugging of European art films, like the Russian *Potemkin*, the German *Siegfried* and *Caligari*, the early René Clair. There was less to point to with pride in British film production, but with the coming of the talkies there were hopes that the allegedly "intolerable" American accents would drive the British masses to see films spoken in English rather than in "Amurrican." In general, American popular art, like American popular civilization, was regarded as shallow, naïvely optimistic, barren, without ideas—as all the best American authors pointed out.

5

II

The first impressions of America both confirmed and refuted this view. A great deal of popular American art was just as naïve and infantile as had been thought (whether it was any more so than the same types of folk art in European industrial society was a question seldom asked and still more seldom answered). The average American city still had few examples of the works of great or even of competent masters. Even the great museums, New York, Boston, Chicago, were rather undiscriminating in their methods of exhibition and in the assessment they put on their possessions. And Richmond, Kansas City, Washington, Toledo, Columbia (South Carolina), Williamstown were still innocent of the rather sophisticated art exhibits in which they can take rational pride today. The great collectors were conservative in their tastes; the great collections were still private. The "ashcan school" was thought to be rightly condemned by the very title.

But an openminded visitor could see the growth and fostering of more sophisticated tastes in places like Harvard's Fogg Museum; and in such magnificent, if in detail unoriginal, works as the great railway stations, the great bridges, the stadia and ball parks, it was possible to see the marks of a society that a Roman would have admired and envied, if an Athenian would have thought it excessive and barbarous. These art forms were the proofs of an energy that was visible in the Detroit assembly line (to which I paid pious pilgrimage); in the great locomotives; in the fantastic spectacle of New York; in the astonishingly athletic character of so much American popular entertainment as purveyed in the still flourishing vaudeville houses; in the ease, optimism, competence, confidence of the average American, often a recently transplanted European to whom the move to America had been a real liberation.

It was possible too to see, or think one saw, signs of a liberation of American life from many of the shackles that had constricted its movement and growth. Structures like the Woolworth Building were no longer universally admired in America, and the traditional Chicago Tribune Building was soon to be savagely criticized in the light of the alternative plans submitted by Saarinen but not accepted. Eyes were turning from the Beaux Arts to the Bauhaus or even to Frank Lloyd Wright, and since architecture was the most conspicuous and important American art, its liberation was the first sign of a new spring, a new "golden day," to borrow an evocative title from Mr. Mumford.

The past "golden day" of New England was looked upon in a new light. Emerson was seen as a revolutionary force, not as a pietistic moralist with essays in place of his ancestors' sermons. Hawthorne was seen probing far more deeply into the nature of the human situation than his more complacent admirers had admitted. And the revival of Melville, which had begun in England just after the First World War, with the publication of *Moby Dick* in the Oxford "World's Classics," admitted an almost forgotten name to the American canon. Henry Adams in *The Education*, through his conscious and unconscious exposition of the limitations of the traditional New England culture, was a liberating force. Of the classic Americans of today, only Henry James was still under a cloud.

Defenders of the old order, such as Stuart Sherman, were beating a retreat. What was called "Ku Klux Kriticism" was laughed out of court, and with it the traditional taboos that had led (so we learned from Mr. Van Wyck Brooks) to the emasculation of Mark Twain and the ignoring of Dreiser. The efforts of the "Boston Watch and Ward Society," the occasional and temporary triumphs of local censors over such works as Bourdet's *Captive* or O'Neill's *Desire Under the Elms*, were obviously pyrrhic victories. It was no longer necessary to pretend, even in Boston, that the hero and heroine of *La Dame aux Camélias* were "engaged" (as Henry James assured us was once the custom) or for New York critics to pretend that they thought adultery meant "putting sand in sugar." Freud had brought down the walls of the Puritan Jericho and, as was said by a resigned elder, "Young people not only can talk of anything, they can't talk of anything else."

Even what was the great American scandal in the eyes of the censorious outer world, the "Monkey trial" in Dayton, Tennessee, seemed to underline this victory of "the Enlightenment." If it was comic to think of a sovereign state in the year of grace 1924 seeking to exorcise by law the devil of Darwinian evolution, the practical outcome of the trial, the discomfiture of William Jennings Bryan, seemed to show that the days of "the old-time religion" were numbered, and that hence a powerful force of obscurantism and bigotry was weakened.

7

The visible failure of prohibition, more and more seen as a defeat for the Protestant and fundamentalist mores of the "Bible Belt," seemed to teach the same lesson. With their accustomed political ingenuity and absence of dogmatism, the American people were nullifying what Mr. Hoover was to call the "experiment noble in purpose." And if the whole project seemed to the sophisticated European proof of contemptible innocence about the nature of man, the results of the nullification, the rise of the great gangs of the booze barons, recreated the legend of the Wild West, strengthening European feelings of superiority and gratifying the European need to know that there existed, *somewhere*, a life of dramatic and almost legitimate crime. It is not a paradox to assert that Al Capone made a great deal of American smugness tolerable and comic.

Not all of American crimes were seen in so tolerant a light. The long ordeal and final execution of Sacco and Vanzetti provoked more than feelings of smug superiority. This episode reinforced a very general belief that, to preserve the American social order, crime, crime by the state, by the possessing classes, was tolerated, was thought to be necessary. Millions knew nothing of Harvard but that it produced A. Lawrence Lowell, and of him nothing more than that he was one of the Pilates who condemned Sacco and Vanzetti. Indeed, inside and outside America, the line-up over this case was a precursor of the bitter schism caused by the Spanish Civil War. I shared the orthodox "liberal" European view of the case (I still do), but I had the good fortune to come across evidence of the ambiguous and callous use made of it by the American Communist party, an early initiation into the realities of the "party line" that later stood me in good stead. Sacco and Vanzetti, like the encouragement of racial bigotry, of which the Ku Klux Klan was only the most dramatic example (others were some of the defenses of that great and negative event in world history, the new American immigration policy), were dark blots on the scutcheon, but that was all.

Even the international role of the United States could be defended and perhaps admired. As in the case of prohibition, American deeds were wiser than American words. True, the United States avoided the League of Nations like a virtuous matron snubbing a fallen woman, but how much the United States did that the League didn't do! There was the Dawes Plan; there was soon to be the Young Plan. If American tariff and immigration policies were causes of world unrest, American bankers, it was thought, showed more sense and more courage than the Department of State (although that had the Washington naval treaties to its credit, with their realistic acceptance of the role of Japan in East Asia). Some Wall Street activities, like the support given to Mussolini after the Matteotti crisis, might be criticized, but the recovery of Europe was thought to be largely due to the sagacity of the rulers of the American financial system. And the same contrast between political futility and business competence was shown in the official refusal to recognize the palpable fact of the Soviet government and the help that American firms, for good business reasons, were giving to the industrial plans of that government.

With all its imperfections thick upon it, the United States was the healthiest member of a convalescent world, and even in the fields of art and thought it was rising to the challenge of its economic triumph. Here for all but the doctrinaire, was "the last, best hope of earth," and residence in America made me, as it did many others, highly skeptical of European dogmas, often, it seemed, invented to cover up a deep feeling of guilt and incompetence.

III

Then came the great debacle. No event, not even the American role in the Second World War and its aftermath, has so colored the European view of the United States as "the Depression." The first news of the crash of 1929 was not ill received. There was not only a marked feeling of *Schadenfreude* at the snub that destiny had given to the over-confident masters of the new world, but also a widespread belief that the extravagant gambling of the New York market was one of the chief causes of our ills. A sharp purge of America's dangerous economic humors and the discovery of new sources of gold to induce some sage inflation were popular panaceas between 1926 and 1929. But as the extent, depth, and duration of the American depression began to be appreciated, as its impact on all the world, especially on the dangerously unstable political and economic *status quo* of Germany and Austria, became more evident, as the old wound of unemployment was made to bleed more deeply in Britain, the tendency to blame the United

States became overwhelming. Gone were the illusions about the "secret of high wages." If ever found, it had now been lost.

In the depression years more people fled America than entered it. The emigrants were embittered, disillusioned. Their stories of bread lines, of apple sellers, of the savagery of the police (including Ford's muscle men), of the cruelties of the primitive social services, revived all the old suspicions of a country in which the rich, ruthless, callous, savage, ruled. The belief that it was American bankers' pressure that brought down the second British Labour government; the French belief that all Mr. Hoover's moves were designed to save the assets of American investors in Germany; the decline in the American demand for European exports; the defiance of European needs and rational policy that marked the Smoot-Hawley tariff—all were taken as proofs of the unfitness of the American people, above all their leaders, for the role in which history had miscast them.

American politics was seen as not only sterile but positively immoral and dangerous. Criticism of the existing political order and of the Republican party grew to a great height outside the United States. Mr. Hoover's moralism was as much disliked as his positive policy. Even before the depression there had been, in the Presidential election of 1928, a great deal of revealing sympathy for Al Smith. American business and its political arm, the Republican party, had been tried in the balance and found wanting. And it is safe to say that the election of F. D. Roosevelt was welcomed in every country of Europe as good news almost overshadowing the nomination of Adolf Hitler as Chancellor of the German Reich.

Nothing was known, it is true, of the President-elect. Nothing but that he was not Mr. Hoover. Nothing was known of the Democrats but that they were not the Republicans. The "New Deal" started in the minds of most British observers with these two great advantages. But "FDR" and the "New Deal" soon acquired another advantage: they were unlike the drab, dreary, impotent government of Ramsay Macdonald and Stanley Baldwin. Not much might be known of Mr. Cordell Hull; too much was known, however, of Sir John Simon (and of M. Pierre Laval). As the New Deal mounted the American horse and rode off "in all directions," the British spectators cheered. Contemplating the British depressed areas, the curious pinned their hopes to the stories they heard of the TVA. Even the incoherent experiments of NRA seemed better than the resignation with which the British "National Government" contemplated the state of Britain.

For many, FDR replaced Henry Ford (once greatly admired, and now deeply damned in public opinion by his anti-labor policies as well as by his anti-Semitism) as the representative of the hopeful side of the American problem. Of course, to the increasing number of real or alleged Marxists, the New Deal and FDR were corks on the surface of the tide of human destiny. The folly of hoping for anything from such reformist efforts was preached by confident doctrinaires like Mr. John Strachey, not yet chastened by war and failure. But for millions who had no wish to be remade by ideologies, and who had a shrewder idea of what Communism meant than had frivolous men of letters like Shaw or disappointed pedants like the Webbs, America was again a land of hope, of example, of originality. The President of the United States was the only democratic leader to be compared, for a moment—in courage, relevance to the age, power of mass appeal—with Stalin, Mussolini, and above all Hitler, whose dark star rose with his. FDR acquired in Britain (and not only in Britain) an appeal that he never lost, an appeal that was increasingly to anger the American conservatives who detested him and who, to the outside world, did not know when they were well off or how little they deserved their luck.

There were blots on this New Deal scutcheon, too: the failure to cure unemployment, now seen as the Achilles heel of capitalism; the excessively empirical character of the administration's program which, some thought, explained the continuance of mass unemployment. If the representative American book of the twenties was *Babbitt*, the representative book of the thirties was *The Grapes of Wrath*. In very different ways John Steinbeck and William Faulkner and Erskine Caldwell made the European picture of the new America—much more so, I think, than the urban novels of "social significance" (often written by party-liners) that were popular in America.

And this society, with its limited success in remaking its economy, seemed doggedly determined to contract out of the world situation. The New Deal was, or so it seemed to me, originally very isolationist in temper, and even when the President began to shift—as in his Chicago *ballon d'essai*, the "quarantine" speech of 1937—his own followers definitely refused to follow; the President's interest in the Navy was seen by many (including myself) as a mere hobby. The American public was lavish in sermons and advice, was all in favor of "standing up to Hitler" or Mussolini, but also firmly in favor of "letting George do it." The advice was often good (or so I and a great many more thought), but it lost much of its weight by the accompanying barrage of denials of any possibility, under any conditions, of American armed action.

In these circumstances it was comparatively easy for the Baldwin and Chamberlain administrations to write off American support and to pursue their own idiotic dream of a "sensible" deal with the dictators. At the same time, passionate support for the Spanish Republic became the mark of a good "liberal" in both America and Europe, and the support given by the Roosevelt administration to the non-intervention policy of Britain and France alienated many. Conservative elements in Britain resented American criticism of the China policy of Sir John Simon or the European policy of Sir Samuel Hoare. Left-wing elements, while retaining much interest and some trust in the New Deal, noting with approval the rise of the CIO for instance, had not recovered from the disillusionment of the depression, the suspicion of Big Business (Henry Ford had passed from hagiography to demonology with no intermediate state), and were tempted either to overlook the realities of Stalin's Russia or to call a plague on both their houses. USA and USSR were both too big, too crude, too inhuman to be models or leaders.

During this period I made repeated visits to the United States and formed (and tried to disseminate) a different view. I had been much impressed by the zeal, openmindedness, energy of the young men and women who saw in the New Deal the beginning of a new era, the ending of the domination of American life by business, and by incompetent business at that. This attitude contrasted with the inertia of British Conservatism and with the credulity and doctrinaire prejudice of so many Labour intellectuals, who, despite abundant evidence, persisted in seeing in the Soviet Union the pioneer state.

For many this illusion was finally shattered by the Molotov-Ribbentrop pact, but the disillusioned could offset the treason of the Soviets by the neutrality of the United States. During the "phony war" the American attitude mattered little (the importance of the repeal of the Neutrality Act was underestimated), but with the collapse of France, American attitudes became of overwhelming importance and the role of some Americans of serious consequence. FDR was more and more a focus of trust, the role of Mr. Hoover, Senator Taft, Colonel Lindbergh difficult to make intelligible to a people fighting for its life and, as it believed, for a cause dear to Mr. Hoover and to Senator Taft.

It is possible that if Pearl Harbor (or its equivalent) had occurred before the German invasion of Russia, the contrast between the friendliness of the United States and the hostility of the Soviet Union might have made a permanent impression on the public mind. But the resistance of the Red Army, and the belief that it was causally connected with the cessation of the attacks on London, bred an attitude of respect and gratitude for the Soviet power which the disconcerted Left gladly exploited. There, in "the Socialist fatherland," was the secret of victory. If Britain did not win as many victories as Russia, it was due to an inferior social system. If the United States won victories—but few knew that she was winning them. With the fall of Hong Kong and Singapore—each thought of as inglorious defeats by the home-front warriors—British interest in the Pacific war ebbed. Few knew of the importance of the battles of the Coral Sea and Midway. The war in Africa, then in Italy, then in France absorbed all or nearly all attention. And as the great American naval war, the greatest in history, was nearly ignored, so the merits of the American social structure as revealed in that war were ignored.

What was *not* ignored were the merits and defects of the American social system as revealed in the GI invasion of Britain. This arrival of millions of soldiers did much good and surprisingly little harm. There were few really dangerous incidents. The opulence of the American way of life, as represented by the pay, equipment, and feeding of the American soldier, bred some ironical comment, but that was all. American vainglory usually shriveled before British irony, and American friendliness, as much as American lavishness, won many friends.

Yet there were difficulties. The marked race prejudice of many Americans startled people who thought themselves, sometimes

13

rightly, above such absurd attitudes. There were one or two public scandals that angered the average man and alarmed people like myself who had responsibilities for maintaining good relations. Discipline varied from district to district, from unit to unit, and where it was bad there were squabbles and worse. (Thus the condemnation of an American Negro sergeant for "rape" of a notorious rural prostitute provoked violent British indignation and resulted in the quashing of the conviction. And a very popular story concerned a farmer in the same region who replied, when asked what he thought of the Americans: "They're very nice fellows. Such good singers and so kind to the kids. But we can't stand the white bastards they've brought over with them." This story was traced to a humorist in the American embassy, but its popularity was significant.)

There were other discoveries: the comparatively helpless state of the sons of the pioneers when they were away from urban resources like piped water; the contrast between the blasphemous but rarely obscene language of the American soldier and the obscene but seldom strictly blasphemous language of the British soldier. The American was often shocked by the candid and often venal sexuality of the English women (although not to the point of actual repulsion), and by the visible minority status of the practicing, church-going Christians. The British were startled by the innocence of many American farm boys of the character of great cities, and by the political naïveté, not to say political "idiocy," of most American soldiers. But victory was sweet to both, and few allied commanders have known, in any age, the universal popularity of General Eisenhower.

IV

Victory brought more problems than war. There was much moral smugness over the dropping of the A bomb and over the alleged excessive sacredness of the life of the American "boy" (the use of the term "boy" to describe grown men was thought to be significant). There was a widespread belief, held in high quarters, that the new Labour government would find it easy to deal with its "socialist" brethren in Moscow while the American capitalist government would not. The death of FDR was felt as a personal blow and a great political loss; no other American politician was much known, or if known (and few were) much trusted.

But the clash came with the discovery that the two countries had come out of the war in very different shape. Many in both Britain and America anticipated a crisis of unemployment in both countries (I was one of them). What occurred was a crisis of over-employment, but one producing very different results. With mirac-ulous rapidity, American swords were beaten into more and better plowshares; the "American way of life" was a great "party." The English way of life was austerity, the sacrifice of the home market to the need for exports to pay Egyptians, Indians—and Americans. Rationing continued on a scale more severe than in wartime; bread was rationed for the first time. The English housewife, if she was lucky, got "export rejects," goods not finished enough for the over-seas customers; if she had American friends or knew visitors to America, she got occasional gifts of nylons. In one country victory brought an intensification of the state of siege, in the other a para-disc of consumption, the provocation, by skilled promoters, of artificial needs.

It was easy if foolish to contrast these two destinies. The Eng-lish had only their pride to keep them warm; it did not keep them very warm. It was easy for the confident Americans to blame all this on "socialism," for the soured English to believe that American wealth had in some way been stolen from a common pool in a war to which England gave all. "Why," Napoleon was asked, "do your brothers and sisters, whom you have made kings and queens and princes and princesses, quarrel with you so much?" "Because they think I have cheated them of their share in their inheritance from their father the late King." So felt the English. It was unjust that America should be so rich; it was infuriating that she should be so powerful, so indispensable. It was all very well to say with the Labour lawyer, Sir Hartley Shawcross, "We are the masters now," but the real masters were in Washington or, as Socialist demonology insisted, in "Wall Street."

The freedom of action of the Labour government was severely limited; it had to pay for food and raw materials, and to do it in an unkind world where the Americans, for doubtful reasons, proved ready to help and the Russians most manifestly could not and did not want to aid their "Socialist brethren." I think that a great deal

15

of importance should be attached to the *déception d'amour* that the Labour intellectuals now felt. There was the deception with the Soviet Union, as the harsh realities of Stalinist rule became more and more obvious. There was another and deeper deception. The British working classes proved scandalously avid for the material gains of the American way of life.

English society was economically more egalitarian than it had ever been. The Labour government carried out with fidelity and skill its announced program. The new day had arrived. But the tastes of the emancipated masses were not what the intelligentsia had hoped for. There were few Morris dancers, vegetarians, spiritually minded workers, and still fewer culturally docile workers' wives. The decline of the old-time religion had not bred an avid desire for new forms of spirituality. The old idealism of the Labour "movement" gave way to more practical concerns. The unions showed less and less sense of community obligation as the living standards of their members rose. They became more like American unions, unideological business organizations. And the workers wanted American gadgets, TV, washing machines, even cars and "contemporary" furniture. When the Conservative government gave them a choice between the edifying programs of the BBC and the largely American and nearly all lowbrow programs of commercial television, they plumped for "I Love Lucy." An enthusiastic Labour woman politician had innocently anticipated a day when England would be "a Third Programme country." That day did not come. Popular pap was in ever greater demand; the Third Programme died.

It was easier to find a scapegoat than to question the edifying vision of the good, uncorrupted taste of the workers which had so long been an article of faith. And the scapegoat was and is America: no doubt the Americans *have* so many things, but their life is empty, their society unattractive! This was an article of faith, and a necessary one. It was easier to hold to it, however, on a bourgeois farm in the Home Counties than in one of the vast new housing settlements, the English equivalents of Levittown, where the more spontaneous reaction to the "American way of life" was not contempt for the spiritual vacuum that it notoriously concealed, but "nice work if you can get it."

But could you? In the first place, there had never been a time since the start of mass emigration in the nineteenth century when firsthand knowledge of America was scarcer. Emigration had dropped to a trickle, stopped entirely in wartime, and, even allowing for the limitations of the quota system, was curiously slow to revive. All other forms of direct contact with the United States were rigorously rationed. Not until 1957 was the ordinary tourist allowed to take any money to the United States (then he could take $275). Only officials, businessmen with expense accounts, journalists, and some privileged "intellectuals" could see and feel America at first hand.

The physical exile from the United States was not adequately compensated for by other contacts. The prestige of American literature slumped. Paris was again the chief supplier of cultural gadgets. Sartre and Sagan met most demands. Mr. Faulkner still had much prestige, and the American theater, especially in the offerings of Mr. Arthur Miller and Mr. Tennessee Williams, was much admired; but they represented an America that gratified the irritated vanity of the English, an unhappy, fear-ridden, thought-killing America. News from the lynching, rape, and incest belt was always welcome (as it was in France, where the Prix Goncourt given to *Les Mandarins* rewarded more than literary merit). Not only was there no respectable demand for novels dealing with the moral and professional problems of the business executive; also the more serious American cultural exports, the music of Mr. Copland, the mobiles of Mr. Calder, the poetry of Miss Marianne Moore, were all neglected or given tepid praise. It was smart to ignore America. There were exceptions: the *Partisan Review* still had its admirers; the same people regarded Mr. Edmund Wilson and Miss Mary McCarthy with respect. But Miss McCarthy, Mr. Trilling, Mr. Jarrell, to choose names almost at random, built up the picture of an America with much to give but little to teach.

Even in those fields of American cultural endeavor where admiration was in order, it was tainted with envy. The protection and subsidies given to "resident" poets and critics, the subsidization of literary research, the great achievements in publication—Walpole, Jefferson, Boswell—all aroused self-pitying reflections on the death of *Horizon*, the absence either of a market or of patronage. At best, the American intelligentsia was seen as in the same leaky boat as the English and French.

17

At best—but at worst? Over the picture of America as painted by the most friendly artists lay the shadow of McCarthy. The alleged reign of terror imposed by the Senator, and by sinister if comic henchmen like Messrs. Cohn and Schine, was the Sacco and Vanzetti case of the postwar years. All the traditions of the American hatred of freedom, of the domination of American life by vicious big business, the lessons taught by Jack London, Theodore Dreiser, Upton Sinclair, were recalled to sinister life. There was quite enough fire to account for the prodigious amount of smoke. And the news out of America was welcomed by men and women who had to explain away their infatuation with Communism, their generation-long trotting at the heels of Russian policy and performance.

Thus it was convenient to pretend that McCarthy and Yagoda were much the same kind of monster (as later that an American illiberal businessman was the same kind of tough guy as Nikita Khrushchev). Even Korea, even Hungary, even Burgess and MacLean did not shake the desperate partisanship of men who had staked their all on an ethical solution of economic problems and discovered that they were betting on a race not being run—above all, not in the Soviet Union. A wicked, belligerent, selfish America, cheating the workers with corrupting benefits, barely restrained from lynching Negroes, was a necessity for a whole generation of deeply insular "liberals." If Mississippi, if McCarthy, had not existed, they would have had to be invented. But alas, they did not need to be invented; they were there, and a great deal of the panic search for traitors in America seemed as foolish and base in the Vatican as in Oxford, the execution of the Rosenbergs as much an error as the execution of the Duc d'Enghien.

The case was not so bad in England as it was in France. Far more English than French people knew something of America (though far fewer than was desirable); the wiles and ways of the fellow-travelers were better understood; a certain traditional and just indifference to the political views of the intelligentsia made the moral problems of the mandarin class uninteresting for the average man, or even for the intelligent common reader. But this very indifference alienated the remaining unreconstructed "left." If the philistine indifference or bourgeois appetites of the workers were one ground of disappointment, the apolitical attitude of many of the new members of the intelligentsia was another. Was it for this that the Workers Education Association had labored, the Fabians had intrigued? Aging and neglected prophets found it hard to accept this situation; they needed an explanation—and it lay, if not at hand, not impossibly far away across the Atlantic. Every American foolish word, every American preposterous action (and there were plenty), was made to resound.

But—and it was and is an important but—not many marked them. England was smug, isolationist, wrapped up in her own problems. And the news from America was not all bad; there was news of supermarkets, of nylons, of plastics, of washing machines, of new styles in hairdos, new styles in popular music, new stars like Marilyn Monroe. Outwardly despised, America was, in England as in the rest of the world, from China to Peru, the successful materialist society to be imitated, with whatever gestures of moral repulsion. The truth was slowly sinking in that American wealth was America's doing, not a mere matter of luck, of natural resources, of immunity from invasion. American "know how" was accepted as part of the secret. That the American worker was not the downtrodden helot of *The Iron Heel* but a middle-class type, with low ideological content but high economic well-being, was noted with less horror by the young than by the middle-aged. When it was reported in shocked tones that the Americans had no labor party, the young Britons, apolitical themselves, were prone to answer "So what?" Neither of the British mass parties excited such enthusiasm as to make the absence of their like in America an absolutely damning mark against American society.

And that society was regarded as in some ways interesting, even admirable. The social mobility of America, the absence, if not of class lines, at least of the visible, painful, and resented class lines of England, was noted. Leftists who could see no other good in America envied the school system, which was idealized. The somewhat inexact picture was painted of a society in which the children of rich and poor went through the same free schools up to college stage, mixed socially, received a common and relevant education. The American "comprehensive high school" became the remedy for many real or alleged English educational ills, just at the time that it was being violently attacked in America and more effectually undermined by the growth of the "private" preparatory schools.

19

In academic circles the Great American universities had long been fully accepted, and every year a high proportion of the brightest British college graduates attempted to enter their doors. It was smart to admire American popular culture, and there was an increasingly brief time lag between the crest of a wave of juvenile *engouement* for a singer or film star in America and the crest in England. James Dean was as much a symbol in England (and in France) as in America. No doubt, rock 'n' roll, the sillier vulgarities of imported television, the vogue for Mickey Spillane and the like, were all chalked up against American life by the censorious, but few marked them.

Another aspect of American life was thrust into prominence by the sudden emergence of the problem of desegregation in the Southern public schools. The Supreme Court decision had been welcomed in England and prematurely accepted as "solving" the problem of racial discrimination in the South. The Montgomery bus strike had been widely reported; the ambiguous resolutions on "civil liberties" in the Republican and Democratic conventions had been studied, if not wholly understood. But the explosive potentialities of the situation were fully appreciated only after the beginning of the Little Rock crisis. And the apparent slowness of the President's reaction, combined with some of the uglier revelations of racial temper, awakened a never deeply slumbering suspicion of the true character of American "democracy" and a resentment of sermons on the iniquities of imperialism coming from such a suspect source. There was temptation—and it was promptly succumbed to—to call the kettle black.

V

Meanwhile there were increasing doubts in England about America's political maturity in its dealings with other nations. Britain had bowed to the inevitable and had abandoned India. Why should not the Americans do the same in China, with far less strain, far less loss? The Generalissimo had never had, in Britain, the carefully constructed place he occupied in America; his wife had never been mistaken for Joan of Arc. "Liberals" and "old China hands" alike were skeptical about the virtues of the Kuomintang; there was no equivalent of the China Lobby, of the Yale-in-China missionary bloc. The American refusal to recognize the completeness, the finality, and the inevitability of Chiang's defeat—emphasized by wild talk of "unleashing" Chiang, made by Mr. Dulles and other spokesmen of the new Eisenhower administration—confirmed the suspicion of many that Americans were children in world politics.

The Americans were seen to be taken for a ride by many adroit propagandists, with disastrous results that were not confined to the United States Treasury. At the same time, the "brinkmanship" tactic angered many, and for some was the cause of ostentatious if not always genuine alarm. If the most popular act of President Truman (apart from his coming up from behind to win the Presidency in 1948) was his dismissal of General MacArthur, the support given by President Eisenhower to the policies and, still more, to the tactics of Mr. Dulles did more than anything else to dim his popularity. The old "Anglo-Saxon" habit of preaching was not liked when the English were at the receiving end of the sermons. Threats of war over Indo-China, over the "Offshore Islands," sulks (as it seemed) at Geneva, brash talk of an "agonizing reappraisal" that many thought might well begin at home, all diminished the limited stock of trust in the Secretary of State and of respect for the judgment of his chief.

The Suez adventure was the last effort of the old, dominating, adventurous Toryism, and it failed, mainly because the United States objected (for the public, Russian threats did not count). On the Right, all the suspicion of the irrelevant "idealism" of American policy was then inflamed. On the Left, opposition to the policy of the Eden government made most of the Labour party reluctant bedfellows with the Secretary of State. It is safe to say that the majority of the British intelligentsia were hostile to and alarmed by their government's policy, and since the President seemed to be speaking for an old British tradition there was for a moment a willingness among them to suspend the usual skepticism of American judgment. The bitterness on both sides, for and against the government, recalled the Spanish Civil War and the disputes over appeasement. But opposition to the government over Suez did not entail admiration for the role of the Texas oil industry, and many were persuaded that there was nothing to choose between the White House and Downing Street.

The same resentment of American leadership or the absence of it was revealed in the reaction to the launching of the first sputnik. That the Russians should beat the Americans to it was not totally ungratifying. Nor was it totally surprising, since it was not an article of British faith that all scientific and technical progress must originate in the United States; a lot, it was thought, originated in Britain. But the *Schadenfreude* that the Russian triumph provoked was sobered by second thoughts, especially after a number of American statements revealed that one American asset was the possession of bases within fifteen hundred miles of the Soviet borders, thus menacing the USSR—from British soil. The complacency with which Americans reassured themselves about their bases—after all, concessions from the countries where they were situated—reminded too many people of the Irish landlord who wrote to his tenants that "if you think you can intimidate me by shooting my bailiff, you are much mistaken."

Doubts about American leadership mounted, and are mounting, as they are in the United States. The revelation of how closely the interests of the two countries are intermingled is a not totally comforting thought. For the peoples of the two countries, united by so much, the relationship is often one of more or less friendly competition; for the two governments it is one of imposed cooperation. The problem of the statesmen is to combine the driving force of emulation with the necessary modifications imposed by the need for cooperation. It is a task of great urgency and difficulty, and one that has been neglected too much and too long.

Yet a survey of Anglo-American relations in the past thirty-five years suggests that it is not an impossible task. When I first knew America it was becoming an unexamined article of American faith that the United States had been trapped into the first war, and the national temper was summed up in "Don't be played for a sucker." The old complacency that was the parent of that isolationism is now dead. "River stay away from my door" has no meaning as a slogan today. The United States government, with the deep if reluctant assent of the American people, has ceased to play Canute. As the implications of Russian technical power are digested, there will be less and less belief that the United States can "go it alone." Indeed, the boot has at times been on the other foot, and Britain has seemed to be the truly isolationist country, preferring to wear blinkers rather than face the realities of Soviet aims.

Some anti-American feeling in Britain has been indulged in

22

largely to justify an attitude of indifference to the Russian danger; it is for this reason that anti-Americanism has been a necessity for many elements of the Left. Equally it has been a necessity for many elements of the Right. Faced with the decline in British imperial power, with the visible weakness of the British economic position, and with the world power and mass wealth of the United States, many British Conservatives (some inside the Conservative government) have been prone to blame the policies of the United States for a great and disagreeable change in the British position. Both sides have justified their resentment by criticisms of the "American way of life," identified by them with the most common, vulgar, and unintellectual American material and cultural exports. And both sides have been reluctantly forced to notice that the very aspects of the American way of life that they despise are those most treasured, envied, and emulated by the mass of the British people.

Indeed, this popular reaction reinforces a lesson of history. The closest links between Britain and America have been in the masses of the two peoples—the masses that provided, on the one hand, the emigrants, the "uncle from America," the living links with the new civilization, and, on the other, the servicemen and tourists who acquired at first hand a greater knowledge of Britain. A further development, important but not decisive, is the fact that the academic respectability of America as a field of study has been transformed out of mind in the past thirty-five years. Willingness to study the United States seriously, although a desirable novelty, is not necessarily the same thing as willingness to learn from it, but study usually breeds more understanding and more willingness to learn. Fortunately the studying and learning have not been a mere matter of academic exchanges. Delegations of employers and workers, of schoolteachers, of newspapermen have been given a chance to see American society at work, with generally beneficent results. Also, American studies of many aspects of British life have been received as useful contributions to British knowledge of Britain. The intellectual relationship is now too complicated to be described in terms of parent and child, teacher and pupil. There is a constant interchange of ideas, techniques, fads.

But the basic relationship is not to be reduced to mere exchange of ideas and projects and persons. It is to be found in the

23

ineluctable fact that in the United States is to be seen the model modern progressive society—fluid, comparatively classless, technically enterprising, materially rewarding—that all the free world envies, copies, admires, and fears. *Odi et amo* is the reaction of all the old European societies to the sight of this dominant child.

And faced with this inevitable "Americanization," the European spectator, British or French or German, naturally wishes to preserve as much as possible of what he treasures in his own culture, and in adopting what is good to accept as little as possible of what is evil in the American society and way of life. He may regret that his relatively declining continent is being dominated by that way of life; but the thought of the alternative to American domination daunts him. The USSR is often the most effective propagandist for the United States. Three decades ago M. André Siegfried said the world would have to choose between Gandhi and Ford. Today it has to choose between a more civilized and a less civilized version of the world of Henry Ford, between Washington and Moscow.

from Spain

JULIAN MARIAS*

The author: born in Spain (Valladolid), 1914; studied at University
of Madrid. Dr. Marias is a director of the Instituto de Humanidades in
Madrid, which he founded in 1948, with José Ortega y Gasset. Of his
numerous books, two have been published in English—*Reason and Life:
The Introduction to Philosophy* and *An Approach to Ortega y Gasset*—
and several have been translated into other languages; one on the United
States, *Los Estados Unidos en escorzo*, was published in Buenos Aires
in 1956. He has lectured in many countries of Europe and South America, and several times has been Visiting Professor at the University of
Puerto Rico. During 1951-1952 he spent a year in the United States,
teaching at Wellesley and, during the summer, at Harvard. He subsequently returned to this country for shorter stays and taught at the University of California at Los Angeles (1955) and at Yale (1956). In
the course of these trips he lectured at about twenty-five other colleges
and universities throughout the country.

I

IN 1951-1952 I spent a year as visiting professor at Wellesley—
my first contact with the United States. It happened that the
year before, in France, I had attended a lecture on the women's
colleges, their beginnings and workings, by a professor from another of the most distinguished of these New England institutions,
a native of France but a lady of long teaching experience. What I
discovered in Wellesley, from my first day there, had so little connection with anything she had said, was so distinctly *otherwise*,
that I discarded everything I then knew or assumed I knew, and
prepared to find out things for myself. All of my subsequent experience has only served to increase that divergence between my
preconceived image of the United States and the one I have formed
through direct contact. Since my information on North America
was not exclusively or even principally Spanish, but European, I
can only conclude that the European view is, by and large, deficient and confused.

Some European misconceptions about the United States are based

* Translated from the Spanish by James F. Shearer.

on outright errors, as when it is assumed that things exist or occur there that in fact do not. Sometimes it is a question of the survival of facts or information that ceased to be so thirty years ago, perhaps ten or five—because in the United States things change rapidly. (It is incredible to what an extent the picture of the Prohibition years persists in Europe, a picture more or less deformed by literature, the movies, and the accounts of past travelers.)

It is true that present communication is uninterrupted; everyone comes and goes; droves of journalists and correspondents relate immediately everything that happens and even what is going to happen. But even so, almost all the information that reaches Europe is misleading. I mean by this that it concerns isolated aspects of American life which, even when they are transmitted faithfully, are interpreted in Europe divorced from their actual contexts, and consequently falsified. Any fact, torn from the frame in which it normally appears, becomes another. The elements in these accounts are understood in European terms, and thus have very little to do with the reality of the United States.

And even more important, there is a dominant assumption in Europe today that "the American" represents only a modification, an amplification—many people would say a corruption—of "the European." Implied here is a lack of *originality* of the United States, an incapacity for *creation*. This in turn implies—and the assumption is widely held—monotony, vulgarity, "colossalism," intellectual inferiority. In certain respects the greatness of the United States is undeniable and is not denied, or at least infrequently. But this is understood to be merely a quantitative greatness and so suggests nothing really new or compelling. At most the United States is viewed as the country of the masses, where the superior individual has no role and rarely exists: the intellectual or the artist, be he American or foreign, is always an exile there, lost in a strange land of Philistines.

When I accepted an unexpected invitation to go to the United States, I was sure I would find many surprising things, different from the European, perhaps even valuable ones. What I did not anticipate was that those things would prove personally attractive to me. It seemed only a remote possibility that American living would prove enjoyable and interesting. I was convinced that I was going to feel completely alien. The enormous cities, the mechani-

26

zation of life, the complete uniformity, haste and lack of tranquillity, the utilitarian spirit and the pressing desire for wealth, constant innovation and the lack of a traditional past, how could all this interest me except superficially? Grandiose perhaps, but inhuman, is how I imagined the world of the United States. On the other hand, there was ancient Europe, poorer to be sure, less pretentious, less prosperous without doubt, but lovable, full of beauty and significance, easygoing and, above all, "made to man's measure."

It turned out, however, that scarcely had I arrived in the United States when I felt myself keenly attracted. Frequently I was amused, charmed, deeply and unexpectedly moved. Why? Simply because I discovered something that I had never been led to expect: in the first instance beauty; secondly poetry; and finally the charm of everyday life. The rest began to emerge a little later.

Why has so little been said about the American countryside? How does it happen that a person going to the United States scarcely ever knows that he is going to discover, almost upon arrival, scenes of distinctive and at times overpowering beauty? So little does one expect to find them that he runs the risk of missing them, the opposite of what occurs with the traditional, "officially" beautiful sites. Everyone speaks of the national parks, the Grand Canyon, Niagara Falls. But what of the more modest, perhaps even unassuming landscapes of so many nameless places, of so many states without any special renown? What of the forests of New England, which in the fall of the year are changed into an unbelievable chromatic delight? What of the monotony, at once severe and tender, of the plains of the Middle West; of the greenish, lazy rivers of the South; of the deserts of California and Arizona, at times set against the bluish line of the mountain ridges in the background?

And then there are the cities, and especially those small towns that hold the secret of the United States—with their frame houses, their adjoining gardens always open to the view, their grass of a succulent and hospitable green, their tall, powerful trees, their modest and silent intimacy, softened in the whiteness of the snow or expressed passionately in the floral effusion of the springtime; their hospitable and secluded churches, their bustling schools, their solitary streets along which there shine at night, among the trees, the lights of so many open windows; and the business streets with the bank, the gasoline station, the tempting and ingeniously arranged shop windows, the market, at a far end the fire station, the brightly lighted and friendly drugstore that shines late into the night. "Here, precisely here," I said, "is where one would have to compose the poem of everyday life."

In the United States this is a way of life that is clearly defined by virtue of having a definite *form*, that is to say, by being channeled into a system of solid and effective norms that do not impede movement and change, but on the contrary permit them, just as the river bed is what makes possible the rapid flow of the waters. These norms result in a general moral level that is not surprising if one has any appreciation of the basic conditions requisite for effective coexistence: kindness taken for granted, at least relative love for one's fellow man, pleasure in dealing with him, a predisposition toward benevolence, infrequency of envy to a degree that it is possible to live without taking it into account (although, as is obvious, it *also* exists here, as do the rest of the sins and defects of this world); mutual confidence, veracity, and understanding. And finally those things that are at one and the same time the basis and consequence of all this: the primacy of private over public life, limited preoccupation with politics, widespread good health and well-being—not only economically but in everyday life —and participation in a gigantic historical enterprise of which the Americans, without too much or perhaps even enough rhetoric, are more or less cognizant.

Ordinarily it is feared that life in the United States will be hectic, and it turns out, rather, that it is calm. People speak of the crowds, and actually the great danger that continually threatens is loneliness. There is the myth of the country's noise, but in two years I did not hear a radio in an adjoining house, and not infrequently I cocked my ear avidly to catch the sound of footsteps in the street.

When one really understands the situation, what he finds deficient in the United States is not private life but, rather, social gatherings for conversation and the exchange of ideas. Instead of instability, he finds that what changes occur are not always, through a lack of imagination, profound enough. Far from seeing "imperialism" in the Americans, one discovers that they have but scant talent for leadership, insufficient in present circumstances;

and also that they display too narrow a concept of themselves—a trait quite compatible with a certain annoying and disturbing self-sufficiency in directions where it is little justified.

My personal "discovery" of the United States consisted then, from the beginning, of a rectification of the ideas prevalent in Spain and, in general, in Europe; of a progressive interest in those aspects of American life of which people don't even speak. One might say that the change of viewpoint was a radical one, because it did not consist precisely of thinking "otherwise" about the same subjects, but in turning my attention to other subjects. It is for this reason that I venture, without any flippancy, to speak of a "discovery."

When I resided for a second and third time in different parts of the United States, when I came to know larger areas of the country and to frequent different circles, when my command of English became more proficient and allowed a more commodious and intimate contact with Americans, to what degree was the impression I had received during those first months revised? Very little. I might best express the situation by comparing it with that of a person who, having heard much indirectly about another, finally comes to meet him. If friendship ensues, the variations that may occur in it can in no way be compared to the change effected in the mind at that first point, when the living person replaced the abstract notion of him. When one has personal contact he does not know the entire person, but what he does know is authentic. It must not be forgotten, however, that human reality, individual or collective, is opaque, though its intimate meaning may filter through expression and gestures; that no knowledge completely exhausts it, and therefore dealing with it is a process of advancing along a road full of surprises. What one knows continues to be the same, but with myriad variations.

II

To understand the prevailing opinion in Spain concerning the United States, one must examine a little of its history. Spain is the only European country (except for England) that has had a "private" war with the United States, one that was not a part of a general world conflagration. The Spanish-American War of 1898 was, moreover, a decisive event in the domestic life of Spain; and it is not without significance that the generation that caused the most profound change in contemporary Spain is called precisely "the Generation of '98." From 1898 dates what we might call *our period* or, if you will, present-day Spain, while everything that goes before strikes us as essentially *another time*.

One might therefore conclude that the resurgence of the Spanish conscience dating from the Generation of '98 was characterized by hostility toward the United States. This would be, if not entirely false, at least decidedly inexact. It cannot be denied that the Spanish-American War was considered unjust, unequal, and fatal for Spain, and that, as a consequence, it provoked some rancor toward the American government and even the country. On the other hand, there was a very widespread discontent with Spanish political policy of the time; the war was considered by Spaniards to have been a national blunder, the historical consequence of our inept policies over a period of many years. Nevertheless, one aspect of the war—and this strikes me as significant and interesting— did engender indignation and enmity: the American imputation that the blowing up of the *Maine* in Havana harbor had been the handiwork of the Spaniards. It was always held in Spain that the accusation was false, a deliberate slander, offensive to Spanish honor. That aspersion, which probably no one believes any more, did more to alienate Spanish opinion than the war itself and contributed incredibly to a lack of regard for North Americans.

During the next two decades, when the memory of the war was gradually fading, the United States was of only passing concern to the Spanish: very little was known about it, and the prevailing impression of it was schematic and elementary. But after the First World War, especially after 1920, the presence of things American throughout Europe became more common. The movies, jazz music, the Ford car—these three factors were of paramount importance in a growth of interest in the United States. And, as might be expected, this *rapprochement* was in general a positive and friendly one. The themes of the Far West, the epic of the twentieth century, became immediately popular; Hollywood was converted into the great myth and *then* functioned as an American force. Although it was known that Greta Garbo was Swedish and Marlene Dietrich German, for everyone their pictures were American; Charlie Chaplin was born in England, but when one thought of

City Lights one knew that this was New York, where the engaging tramp moves, suffers, and laughs with the Kid (Jackie Coogan, whom they call *Chiquilín* in Spain). All these were grouped together with Douglas Fairbanks, Mary Pickford, and countless others to form that unreal world which Hollywood projected over all of the European continent, as on an immense screen, and which was supposed to be a virtual representation of the United States.

The first wave of hostility came some years later. For one thing a more somber picture of the United States fixed itself in the minds of Europe: Prohibition, which struck many as an insane and Puritanical measure; the increase of smuggling and gangsterism (remember the associations suggested for so many years by the name of Chicago); the end of prosperity and the serious economic crisis around 1930. To all this there must be added a political factor, one to which Spain was especially sensitive: North American "intervention" in Central America and the Caribbean, the Nicaraguan incidents during the time of Sandino, all of which began to be called North American "imperialism." At that time the influence of Hispanic-American writers and journalists was greater in Spain than elsewhere in Europe, a fact that provoked an even sharper reaction. Certain political groups of the extreme left nourished this climate of hostility, and some thirty years ago the conviction took root in many Spanish minds that the economic well-being of the United States depended in large measure on the "exploitation" of the poorest countries of Hispanic-America: fruit from the Caribbean, Chilean copper, the general oppression of Puerto Rico, were considered at least a partial basis for North American prosperity. It is amazing to what an extent these ideas have survived.

After 1936—and even earlier, with the mounting tension that erupted in the civil war—Spanish life was brought within the sphere of politics in an increasingly profound and far-reaching manner. Thus the prevailing attitude in public opinion regarding the United States was dominated above all by political motives. Friendliness was confined to the intermediate political zones—the non-Fascist conservatives of the right, the liberal groups, and the adherents of moderate socialism—but during the years of violence and passion associated with the civil war, this moderate zone had scarcely any voice or influence and was throttled by every sort of political extremism. Most seriously, the coincidence of the Spanish civil war

31

and the Second World War had the effect of unduly perpetuating attitudes and positions that normally would long since have been replaced by others. For example, from 1939 to 1952 the official curriculum for the bachelor's degree included the following description under the third-year history course: "The United States of North America. The materialistic and inferior spirit of American civilization. Lack of fundamental principles and moral unity. Immoral financial practices. Their unjust aggression against Spain and the Hispanic-American countries, Nicaragua, Haiti. Moral superiority of Hispanic-America over North America" (Official Government Bulletin, May 8, 1939).

Despite this—and in part because of it—from the last years of the Second World War there developed a current of interest, admiration, and friendliness toward the United States. There was an appreciable increase in information on that country; the presence of things American—supplied through news media, books, industrial products, personal contacts—was enormously intensified; many eyes were hopefully turned in different ways toward the United States. In the years immediately following the war, when one began to detect an anti-American feeling that alarmed both continents, Spain was an exception. Americans visiting Europe noted the difference between their cordial and friendly Spanish reception and the cold, reserved, rancorous manner in which they were received in other countries.

But progressively during the last few years a current of aversion and hostility toward the United States has arisen, not so strong as in other countries, but definitely noteworthy if one compares it with the previous situation. What can be the reasons for this change? One might assume a major cause to be the presence in Spain of Americans in much greater numbers, as a result of military bases and other factors. Actually I believe that this is one of the least important considerations. First of all, their presence is a limited one, in the sense that the American military personnel and technicians are not very much in evidence. (Rather, Spaniards resent their isolation, their tendency to live in districts by themselves, their limited contact with the Spanish people.) Secondly, when contacts are established one notes a reciprocal display of friendliness. It is not rare, of course, to hear pejorative comments on the Americans in Spain. But almost invariably these concern either what "people say," rather than things the speaker has actually seen, or insignificant details. Nor is it true that the presence of Americans on Spanish bases is viewed by the great majority of Spaniards as an affront to Spanish sovereignty.

Nevertheless, it is a fact that there is a general, one might say mute, hostility toward the Americans, an antipathy whose rapid development is matched only by its lack of solid foundation. Its most striking characteristic is what I would call its "apriority": the tendency to *assume* that the Americans behave badly, that the United States is wrong, that its political policies are benighted, that its leaders are stupid and naïve. A taxi driver, on seeing a car make a wrong move, will exclaim irritatedly, "Those Americans!" without taking the pains to notice that the car is German, Portuguese, or simply Spanish; a university professor asserts as unqualified facts that Puerto Rico is impoverished by American exploitation and politically oppressed, that Negroes in the United States live like slaves and are detested by the whites, that the United States dominates and exploits South America and is trying to destroy the power of Europe. This attitude is characterized by a tendency not to get the facts and by the omission or rapid overlooking of all that "doesn't fit"; by the generalization, on the other hand, of many insignificant details provided they do fit and support the predesired image; and especially by ignorance or ignoring of the role played by all these details within their contextual framework, and consequently missing their true importance.

The real causes of this new point of view are in my judgment to be found in two different but connected areas: the increased weight of certain European and also Hispanic-American attitudes; and certain national political positions. Spanish communication with Europe was practically nil from 1936 to 1948 or 1950, but since then it has greatly increased. Today many thousands of Spaniards travel in Europe, and other millions of tourists visit Spain. The exchange of newspapers, magazines, and books has multiplied; European movies, because of disagreements with American producers, have invaded the Spanish screens to a degree never before equaled. Prevailing points of view in other European countries have thus rubbed off on Spain, and critical sentiments and attitudes have been implanted that have little or no resemblance to the real situation.

This is combined with political repercussions (of necessity very confused in the light of the Spanish situation) whose obscurity and frequent incoherence are accentuated by the fact that it is scarcely possible to talk about them publicly. The role played by Communism throughout the world in the formation of public opinion regarding the United States is so obvious that it needs no elaboration. What does need to be kept in mind is its influence in countries where it is not easy to determine what lies behind appearances. The Spanish public receives very little information about the United States, and for most of the country this comes only from the press and the radio stations, strictly controlled. To be sure, one hears frequent praise of the States, but this is very generalized, protocolar, and perhaps self-defeating ("friendly countries," "free peoples," "the common struggle for human dignity and Western civilization"). On concrete, day-to-day matters, hostile comments are very frequent in newspapers and on the radio, with insistence on unfavorable aspects, insinuations that the United States is responsible for many of the world's problems today, and unflattering comparisons of it with other countries.

One or two examples are worth mentioning. The standard of living of the working classes in the United States cannot be compared with that of any other country. The United States represents the only case in history in which a large people has been able to overcome poverty as a condition of life, reducing its existence to exceptions due to some particular condition or circumstance. North America exhibits a minimum of economic and social inequality and, moreover, the lower level is relatively very high. It has no masses of the population living in subhuman conditions, or suffering the degree of want frequent even in other prosperous countries. In view of this, one would presume that the workers in other nations, and especially the "laborites," would have a high regard for the United States. Actually, however, this is not at all the case. The propounded and prevailing picture is that of a "capitalistic" country, which in Spain connotes a country of "the rich" (this, of course, is seen as a result of fortuitous circumstances, pure good fortune, and not as the result of an enormous, intelligent effort) that cannot possibly be considered an example of social justice. It is as if the American workers were not actually workers, as if they

34

should not be regarded as workers when one contemplates their position in society.

Then there is the Spanish attitude toward Senator McCarthy and "McCarthyism." The "avant-garde" or "progressive" groups (without necessarily being Communistic) considered that the United States was dedicated to witch hunting and an inquisition, that all vestiges of freedom had been obliterated, and that a new kind of totalitarianism was in command. The reactionaries, on the other hand, showed an indescribable admiration for McCarthy and his political philosophy; they made him a symbol of American patriotism and tried to identify Catholicism with him. To this point both positions, while debatable, are at least coherent. Incoherence sets in with the decline of McCarthyism in the United States, which ended with the virtual disappearance of McCarthy from the political scene, well before his death. The groups I have designated as "progressive" have given no indication that they are aware of the dissipation of McCarthyism. They continue in the same attitude they had at the height of its influence, and have failed to take cognizance of the fact that this eclipse of the liberal American spirit was very transitory and superficial in nature. On the other hand the reactionary elements have carefully seized on the disappearance of that influence, interpreting it as a triumph of Communists and fellow travelers.

Up to this point I have referred to prevailing Spanish attitudes in the great mass of the population—to what we might call diffused public opinion, and to the sector of that opinion that manifests itself through the normal media of communication, accessible to all and subject to the direct intervention and control of the state. It is necessary now to consider the more complex positions of the select minorities, especially persons of intellectual professions, who are the most influential and who in large measure initiate changes in mass thinking.

At the outset it should be said that those who have been in the United States usually have, notwithstanding their specific reservations, an extremely favorable attitude, reflecting not merely admiration but pleasure, not only friendship but—especially if they have lived there for some time—profound affection. Much greater in number, however, are those who do not know the country directly, and it is this group that I shall here consider.

The Spanish upper classes, though well acquainted with some foreign cultures, are not really familiar with even the thought and literature of England, much less with those of the United States. The principal consequence is not so much that there are so many unknown things as that there has not been an accurate appraisal and understanding of the place that what is *known* occupies in the whole picture. As a case in point, the image conveyed by certain extreme books of the "lost generation," generally read long after they were written, has done much to deform opinion on the United States and, specifically, on American intellectuals. Present-day readers of *1919, The Sun Also Rises, The Grapes of Wrath*, or *Tobacco Road* frequently take such works as actually representative of American life today; and in general those readers who would never think of taking literally such works as *Nada* or *Der Steppenwolf* frequently forget what literature is and take *Sanctuary, A Streetcar Named Desire*, or *The Postman Always Rings Twice* to be social documents. Then one must add the influence of books about the United States—or those that have been interpreted as such—from the *Scènes de la vie future* of Duhamel to *The Loved One* of Evelyn Waugh, on through such books by Aldous Huxley as *After Many a Summer Dies the Swan* and *Brave New World*.

Against this general background, many of the Spanish elite have assumed, since 1953, an increasingly negative attitude toward the United States, something they did not display before. They are predisposed to find things American bad, and to consider good what is in one way or another opposed to the American. A rather simple but very clear example of this is seen in connection with the cinema. The "cognoscenti" and educated fans have long since decreed that American movies totally lack quality, while French, English, and especially Italian and Japanese films are deemed excellent. When they are forced to concede that an American picture is splendid, they point to it as an "exception," and it matters little to them that the exceptions are numerous. On the other hand, once it has been established that the Italian cinema is a marvel, it makes little difference that the vast majority of its examples lack any merit whatever; they are not taken into account. Similarly, though it is true that European cars are easier to park and use less gasoline than the larger American ones, and are thus especially suitable for the cities and purses of Europe, people are not content with this, and argue that American cars in general are very inferior to the European—that a Peugeot or a Volkswagen is preferable to a Chevrolet or a Ford; that American cars are ugly and in bad taste, while the French, the Italian, or the German are "mechanical marvels." Nothing is said about airplanes—an understandable fact since ninety percent of those used by world airlines are American.

In the question of strictly intellectual values, the attitude most favored by the Spanish upper classes is a certain scorn. They assume that the United States has boundless financial and technical resources but few achievements of real quality; that its highest values are European and that in general these become sterile when transplanted to American soil (without stopping to think whether the change is due to simple expatriation and uprooting). Nevertheless, a few American writers enjoy a profound respect in Spain, and in general it is conceded that the contemporary novel and part of the theater in the United States are of genuine interest. And it should be added that competent Spanish intellectuals know and respect American attainments in their own fields, even though this does not dispose them to draw conclusions about the whole country.

Finally, in the matter of political problems and the role of the United States in the world today, some of the principal suppositions of the select Spanish minorities are the following: first, the United States has no idea of what is going on in the Old World; second, its intent is to destroy the power of France and England, and it is provoking chaos with its "anti-colonialism"; third, the American government is not very intelligent and its foreign policy is completely stupid; fourth, the Americans' financial greed makes them seize markets and exploit the weaker nations, like those of Central and South America; and fifth, in trying to "encircle" Russia with military bases they are compromising the other countries and endangering the peace of the world. Whether or not facts or reason confirm these points of view is a question of secondary importance. For example, the reflection that in order to "destroy" England and France, it would have been simpler and cheaper not to spend many billions of dollars to aid them does not occur to anyone, or if it does it is not taken into account. The simple calculation is never made that the whole volume of United States trade with South and Central America is negligible when compared with its foreign aid, and that therefore, even though it results in benefit and profit, it is scarcely enough to justify the accusation of such greed. Either it is not known or is immediately forgotten that American business is almost totally "domestic," that American industry rests on this fact, and that as a result foreign markets, vital for other economies, are a secondary consideration for the United States. And similarly in many other things.

All of these points of view are not in any way peculiar to my country, but are common to Western Europe. The Spanish reaction to the Suez incidents, to the events in Hungary, to the launching of the Russian artificial satellite, to Hollywood, or to the talents of John Foster Dulles represents nothing essentially different from the French or the Italian reaction. The distinctive aspect of the Spanish position is that it is less *motivated* and is *very recent*, while in the rest of Europe it has been developing for a number of years.

Spanish reactionary elements feel a deep-seated antipathy for the United States because the foundations of American life and politics are diametrically opposed to those they support and defend: tolerance, multiplicity of religions and political parties, freedom of speech and of the press, a democratic system of government, private enterprise, and a minimum of government intervention. So antithetical is all this that "friendly" relations between the two nations must of necessity be very vague and abstract, without entering the realm of details and much less the area of true *rapprochement*. The Communists and those who follow their line, without being card-carrying members of the party, are in Spain as elsewhere opposed to everything American. And the zone of more enlightened public opinion—that of liberal orientation in the broad sense of the word—is becoming more and more alienated, not only because of the factors I have already mentioned but also because of disillusionment in realizing that cooperation with the United States has not led in the smallest degree to the correcting of conditions that are causing discontent.

III

In the United States, knowledge of Spain is very limited and vague. Naturally, this is nothing exceptional; the ideas of all countries about others are extremely fragmentary. Moreover, Spain is generally little known everywhere, and almost always badly understood. One reason for the lack of understanding in the United States is that Spain is frequently confused with Spanish America, despite its important differences in structure, problems, and population. Another reason is the Spanish civil war of 1936-1939 and its present-day repercussions.

That war was followed in the United States with a passionate interest wholly unsuspected in Spain. But the Spanish civil war was extremely complicated. Its positive and negative elements were inextricably intermingled; initial positions changed several times during the very course of the war, and then after its termination. There has been scarcely a word of truth written about the war anywhere, either in Spain or outside. A thick cloud of partisan propaganda, falsehood, and disfiguration envelops everything touching on the Spanish situation since 1936. This, plus the "clandestinity" that affects everything that has to do with Spanish politics and public(!) life, makes almost everything different from what it seems, frequently makes apparent political positions quite different from the real ones, and makes it imperative to take everything that may be said about these matters with extreme caution. Such caution is lacking among Americans, because their country is characterized by approximately opposite conditions.

For all of these reasons, acts directed specifically toward Spain by the United States are ordinarily not effectual and frequently produce the opposite of the desired end. For example, a great many official or semi-official American activities have an air of "propaganda." It is my belief that propaganda is one of the great curses of the present world, and that it has come to replace rhetoric in the indispensable business of managing people. But besides this general consideration one must keep in mind the fact that Spain is a country that for the last twenty years has been saturated with propaganda, and consequently is one where it has been completely discredited. (This is precisely the cause of the success of propaganda favorable to Russia. Since Russian propaganda is in principle prohibited—and I say in principle because the matter is actually much more complicated—it is not so presented and is accepted almost automatically.) Moreover, the publications that official American agencies send to the Spaniards are at once too elementary and obvious for the educated classes and lacking in any power to attract the masses; they arouse no interest and at times even a certain aversion.

Errors in the realm of personal contacts are also very frequent. American officials usually spend only a little time in any one country; they are replaced at the end of two or three years, in other words, at about the time they begin to know their way around. In a country as complex as Spain—where, moreover, almost nothing (and almost no one) is what it appears to be—confusions and misunderstandings are more than probable. Thus at times the American government itself expresses in some way, through invitations, honors, or the like, its esteem for people who enjoy very little respect throughout the country. The impression this makes is that the Americans are completely off the track, that they are working on the basis of certain received standards of values—perhaps the inverse of those prevailing among private opinion, the only opinion that exists—or that they have had some personal briefing that is not too trustworthy. Moreover, and this is more serious, one can scarcely imagine how American prestige in Spain has declined through the association of some representative Americans with individuals who not only enjoy no esteem whatever but are fundamentally hostile to the United States and are against the groups in Spain who are presently or potentially friendly to that country. The general comment has been, even in the most favorable instances, that the Americans "do not distinguish," that they do not understand European matters. In other cases it is asserted that they favor groups in which Spaniards detect the gravest danger for their future.

Not long ago, for example, an important American magazine expressed its hopes concerning a certain group which, for the great majority of Spanish intellectuals (those, after all, who read the magazine), represents the eclipse of the country's possibilities. The journal's loss of prestige has been sudden and complete; more important, in a country accustomed to detect the government's hand behind all publications, the adverse opinions have redounded to the discredit of the United States itself, on the ground that if it is going to move in this direction, we can expect nothing of it or of its friendship. Naturally such an inference would not have been possible had the incident not been preceded by a whole series of similar occurrences, though they were of a less precise and explicit character. The important thing is that minorities which are now and, especially, are going to be influential, and which a few years ago looked with hope toward the United States, are today alienated and are leaning toward other connections. This they are doing not through a direct interest but because they project to the international plane certain aspects of American conduct that they know well, and assume that in all the dealings of the United States there is the same mistaken support for what does not merit it. The criticism caused by the whole Suez matter and its implications has been, in my opinion, unjust toward the United States, but the foregoing question has been one of its principal roots.

People speak a great deal in Europe of the isolation of the Americans, their impermeability, their incapacity for getting to know the countries in which they live. I do not think this to be entirely the case. I know of few foreigners who have reached to the core of Spanish life so quickly, so cordially, and so wisely, who have scrutinized and nosed about with so much curiosity and friendliness, and perhaps also with so admirable a critical spirit, as have certain Americans. But these were people thoroughly attentive to the life of the country, people with independent attitudes and knowledge of the language—perhaps professors and scholars doing research in Spain, perhaps twenty-year-old college girls who viewed everything around them with fresh and curious eyes and who, after three months in Spain, knew more about the country than many diplomats.

On the other hand, the alleged impermeability is frequent in the three classes of Americans who are most in evidence and who perhaps carry the most weight: the tourists, whom the ultimate perfection of the travel agencies surrounds with a kind of American wrapping that virtually isolates them from the country they are visiting, with the result that they pay more to travel less; the government officials, who almost always live together, who deal principally with other Americans (the diplomats with other diplomats, in other words with other foreigners), and who, moreover, are always laboring under the constant preoccupation of their official status as "representatives"; and the journalists (although this seems a paradox), who are so intent on *getting information* that they rarely find out about what is most important, not the "news item" itself, but the news-behind-the-news and its background, who pay primary attention to what is told them, forgetting that the most interesting part is almost always what is not said (because it can't be or simply because, as the Spanish saying goes, "since it is known, it is not mentioned").

I should like to know whether the Department of State ever bothers to obtain any information on Spain from the American students who spend a school year there, from the scholars who engage in research, from those who, with a good knowledge of the language and a sensitive intelligence, have mixed with the country, have made friends, have had private discussions with Spaniards, have read the books and magazines that here are judged worth reading (and perhaps some others), have gone to public entertainments as one normally goes to them, to be amused, and have been alert to perceive how the audiences respond. Through them it would be able, perhaps better than by means of expensive special "missions," to find out what to rely on in the question of "who's who" in Spain; what Spaniards believe, fear, and hope for; which among them feel friendship toward the United States, and for which of them it is an unknown country; which of them misinterpret it or perhaps simply hate it. "Missions" move in "official" environments, in what I call "the world of official objects," in which everything is conventional and has nothing to do with reality.

A final factor that is disturbing to a clear image of Spain in the United States concerns political emigres. Many Spanish expatriates living in the United States, principally those who are in academic life, exert an extremely favorable influence on the relations of the two countries. But I would not be inclined to say the same of certain purely political, partisan publications, managed by emigres of very dubious reliability, which issue as many falsehoods and misrepresentations as analogous Spanish publications and engage in polemics with the official representatives of the Spanish government. The American spectator has a tendency to believe that all this is significant, when actually the parties involved may be most unimportant in Spanish life, and completely unimportant for its future.

IV

In view of all the differences between the United States and Spain, can the two countries learn anything from one another?

For anyone who is not envious or resentful, it is obvious that Spain —and any other country, for that matter—can learn a great deal from the United States, a country in which a great historical undertaking is being carried out and, moreover, at so rapid a pace that one can actually contemplate the process, a thing that would not have been possible, for example, during the slow constitution of the Roman Empire.

My allusion to the Roman Empire is not fortuitous, because it is the only historical reality that in some measure clarifies the role of the United States in the world today. In a certain sense the United States is the opposite of the Roman Empire. The latter was the result of the expansion of a city, Rome, the urbs; it was the creation of a minuscule social "head," and as a matter of fact the great problem of the Empire and its decline was, more than anything else, the incapacity of the Romans to surpass the idea of the *city* and to articulate the social and historical reality that they themselves had fashioned. The Roman Empire was essentially "exterior." The United States, on the other hand, is "interior," almost "headless," with a minimum of influence emanating from the capital city. It is an immense ambit, a colossal interiority such as never existed before in history, and it acts in the world *from that interiority*. The United States is practically self-sufficient, except in the case of a few products; its foreign trade is of secondary importance; the thing of prime importance for it is the interior.

I have always been struck by the adjective used by Americans to designate what in other places is called national: this word is "domestic." The airlines, for example, speak of "domestic" flights, the post office of "domestic" mail. Can it be that the Americans view their great nation as an enormous house, an immense home? Can this perhaps be the explanation of many of the peculiarities of the American attitude as it is revealed throughout the world? I have the impression that the basic sensation of the American when he is abroad is that of being "outside," in the sense that he is outside the "within" of his country. On that account, say what they will, he is not "imperialistic," he is perhaps less imperialistic than the present situation demands. United States leadership in the world today is not what it should be—because leadership is indispensable and other nations are not exercising it—and possibly the reason is that Americans feel themselves easily overcome by a profound homesickness; by a nostalgic longing for that great, habitual interiority that as tourists they try to preserve in their travels. Perhaps the explanation—and this is at best a wild guess—lies in the preponderant role of women in the organization and ideals of American society.

Moreover, this homesickness for the United States is not strange; I believe that it is experienced even by foreigners, if their American experience has been more than superficial. I personally feel it whenever I leave the United States, even though I have a deep sense of belonging to a European nation and do not feel myself to be American at all, not even Americanized. In spite of this I cannot escape a nostalgic feeling for the United States, precisely because of its home-like qualities and the forms of its daily life. The characteristic thing about the United States, and the thing about it that reminds us of the old order, is that life there has retained certain definite forms, as was formerly the case in Europe. As a result it furnishes the individual, not happiness—this is a personal and delicate matter, and no social reality can itself produce it—but what elsewhere I have called an alveolus, a snug compartment where each distinct individual can find his place and thus where happiness is made normally possible and statistically frequent.

Therefore in considering what can be learned from the United States, one must take care not merely to point out those features that are excellent in that country. The thing is not that simple. What one might call "direct translation" is not possible. One cannot take isolated elements from American life, because these immediately become untranslatable; when they are placed in other surroundings they frequently cease to be valuable. This is one of the reasons why certain virtues of the Americans are criticized when they are abroad, and with some justification: what is a virtue in the United States, joined to many others in a complex configuration, may cease to be admirable when divorced from that whole and projected on other forms or ways of social life. In order to transplant ingredients of American society to others, one cannot proceed directly. Rather one must go by way of social structures, and seek out in the other society the element that would be homologous to the one to be adopted.

In consequence, what is ordinarily understood to be "Americanization" is not that at all. Its results are usually the least American thing imaginable, the farthest removed from the basic temper of the United States. This is observable, for example, in South America, when it is attempted there to assume appearances similar to the North American. And again, to cite an extreme case, nothing is less American than the publications that the United States itself prepares for foreign consumption, attempting to express itself through an adaptation to the foreign milieu—nothing, unless it be those foreigners who, once in the United States, try to "Americanize" themselves come what may. These I think of as "plusquam" or "super" Americans, because they never succeed in becoming simply Americans.

The internal form of American life strikes me as profoundly admirable, but unfortunately inimitable. It is not a question, for example, of institutions. American institutions are admirable, without doubt, but they are neither unique nor too original, nor can they be transplanted to other places. What is interesting is not the institutions themselves but the effective social forces that make them possible. Underlying the institutions, underlying the state itself and the political principles that govern American life, is the regulation of society by a system of patterns or governing norms (beliefs, ideas, opinions, customs, programs of individual and collective living). These give American society stability, solidity, and fluidity for change, and make possible the establishment and functioning of institutions that, without them, would be just so much useless apparatus.

Americans usually think that when a foreigner reaches their country, especially if he comes from one where freedom does not abound, he feels he has been transported to a system of perfect institutions and can now at last breathe freely. But this is not exactly the case. A certain rigor that characterizes the entry process, ordinarily heightened by subordinate employees, beginning with those in foreign consulates (frequently not Americans, let it be said in passing), does not produce exactly an impression of well-being. In particular, requirements regarding minute declarations and medical examinations carried out by specified and not always estimable doctors, while they may have some hygienic justification or may be necessary for security purposes—which I doubt—have certainly alienated the friendship toward the United States of a large number of people whose opinion means something. The elimination of these proceedings or their more discreet application would be a simple means of improving attitudes toward the United States abroad. Some of us feared that the centenary of Freud in 1956 would be the occasion for adding psychoanalysis to United States entry requirements; fortunately, however, the centenary has passed without such fears being confirmed.

Does this mean that the foreigner gets no impression of freedom in the United States? He surely does, but it comes a little later and is not derived directly from government or institutions. (Even in nations that are particularly anti-liberal, the visitor does not come into too great contact with government. Political pressure, save in extreme cases, and in their acute phases, has little or no effect on appearances. One runs head-on into the state when one wishes to *act* or to plan a personal or professional pattern of life. In consequence a visitor to a country supposedly oppressed often sees nothing to indicate that it is; everything is perfectly "normal." And from his point of view he is right; what happens is that this point of view is not that of those who have to live their lives there, seriously and for all time.) As I was saying, the splendid well-being of American life and its real freedom, while safeguarded by its institutions and its system of government, come not from these but from American *society* itself, and the forces and norms operative in it: from the generally assumed confidence in matters of dealing and living together; from the friendly attitude toward one's neighbor, although he is unknown; from the hope in the future, the basic conviction that reality taken as a whole, despite all its evils, is essentially good.

The American smile, which has been so ridiculed by those who believe the intelligent thing is to know everything already—without, of course, knowing much of anything at all—seems to me to be the expression of love for one's fellow man, of the basic fact that in the United States it is firmly believed that living together is a blessing. This is derived, in my opinion, from the historical make-up of the United States and from the American spirit, from its loneliness and the fact that for so long the presence of other men was an occasion for joy. This, strangely conserved despite social transformations, seems to me one of the most fabulous of American riches. Envy does exist in the United States, but in such small measure that one need not count on it; life is not set up on the assumption of its existence. Pleasure at the good fortune of one's neighbor is the normal thing, and I know of no other country of which this could be said. Hostility among men in the United States is minimal; many gestures that elsewhere cover a generous dose of rancor, antipathy, and hate are almost cordial in North America.

Many things about the United States are given a bad interpretation in Europe because Americans tell everything about themselves and even insist on the disagreeable aspects of their country, which others would conceal: statistics on crime, reports on juvenile delinquency, full accounts of any immoral act whatever, complete details on racial difficulties, and so on. One need not go to foreign sources for information on the defects of the United States because Americans themselves relate them, comment on them, and at times even exaggerate them.

When the subject of race struggle is discussed, the European or South American usually believes that it is based on a ferocious hatred that might easily lead to a war of extermination. And, indeed, if the outward manifestations were the same in other countries, the internal situation would be as they imagine it. But in the United States hostility is rather slight, limited to inflamed groups, condemned by large segments of the population, and offset by much stronger currents of understanding and friendship. It is carefully emphasized abroad that this or that abuse or injustice has been committed, even that a reprehensible crime has gone unpunished (reprehensible, but still *one* crime). What is not said is that the same thing is publicly proclaimed in the United States, that people there have the same opinion of that crime, that the power of the federal government is used against its own citizens—and even against those of the "first class"—to protect minority rights and to impose, at the risk of disturbing internal peace, the law of the land. The United States takes upon itself its vices and crimes; it does not have recourse to the convenient expedient of attributing them to the enemy or to a portion of the country that can be ignored by the rest, as though it had no connection with it.

This is what I believe Spain could learn from the United States, and not only Spain, of course: those configurations of society and of the form of ordinary life that produce the superior well-being by which American political institutions are nurtured. Without that

47

condition not even those things that seem most easily transferable are fruitful—for example, technology and industry. The installation of apparatus, devices, and technical procedures serves little purpose if it is not accompanied by the moral support of efficiency and seriousness, punctuality and respect for standards, a sense of cooperation, helpfulness, and veracity. The spirit of enterprise is an excellent thing, and the desire for profit also, providing there is not lacking the positive form of "utilitarianism" that prevails in North America: that is, the sense of social life and the sporting attitude toward rivalry and competition.

American life rests on the principle that if something is proposed to a person that is advantageous for him, he normally accepts. In other places this is not the case; rather, one thinks first whether it benefits others and if so declines it. The saying "to cut off one's nose to spite one's face" is rather expressive of what I have in mind. The Americans' desire for profit is very genuine and most efficient. But it is not, as is ordinarily supposed, either sordid or especially "materialistic," because it depends to a large degree on the spirit of effort and on putting personal qualities into play, and it does not end in avarice or hoarding but rather in generosity. The American likes to earn money, especially because in so doing he sees a demonstration of his merits, but perhaps he likes even better to give it away.

A consequence of all this taken together is a characteristic of American life that is perhaps the one most lacking in Spain: the *team* spirit, continued and indispensable collaboration. In other times it was possible to get out of trouble with inspiration, courage, and a little good luck. Today all of these are necessary but they are not enough in themselves: if Spain does not succeed in developing team spirit in all its forms, it will be left irreparably behind, impoverished and on the periphery of history. Spain can learn from the United States not in building skyscrapers where they are not needed, in places where in America it would never occur to anyone to put them; not in replacing our cafes with cafeterias (I would propose that the reverse be done in the United States); not even in filling the houses with electrical gadgets without first assuring the production of electricity—but precisely in adopting certain forms of conduct, certain essential vital forces, and especially those at the basis of social life.

V

And what can the United States learn from Spain? Very little it might seem, for Spain's present situation is far from brilliant: economically it occupies one of the lowest stations in Western Europe; its political difficulties are well known and of long standing; its scientific and technological development is rather modest; the volume of its culture today, if compared with that of the four or five first countries of the world, is limited.

Nevertheless, Americans who really come to know Spain feel strongly attracted to the country. Almost all of those who have lived here more than six months wish to return, and many do; some stay indefinitely. Those who leave have that nostalgia, that homesickness of which I have spoken before, in an inverse sense. Some Americans soon acquire a kind of "Spanish patriotism" that is both amusing and moving; sometimes this occurs among Hispanists who have penetrated the intimate depths of our culture from afar, without having ever been in Spain. I do not have the impression that this occurs when they come in contact with other European countries, or at least not with all. How does this come about?

What Americans find in Spain could be called the taste of life. At times this taste is not good, but it is always particularly intense. A certain monotony of life, a certain opacity, frequent in the United States and perhaps more frequent in some of the most prosperous and comfortable European countries, is unknown in Spain. This has an immediate tonic effect. That zest, that intensity, is due to certain profound forces that operate in a lively and energetic fashion in Spanish life, despite all its vicissitudes. At times distressing circumstances have made it seem that these forces have disappeared, but after a while they have come back in full vigor. And some of them are precisely what is lacking in American life. By a strange coincidence Spain, which otherwise has very little to offer, produces the few things in which the United States is deficient. A commerce in cultural and historical items would convert the United States into an importer of strange Spanish products that are not found, or at least not in such vigorous state, on other soils.

Above all, the frequency of friendly intercourse. For some years I have wished to make a statistical calculation, which I recommend to those having the resources to do it well: take a piece of paper divided into columns and at the head of each write "once a day," "twice a week," "once a week," "twice a month," "once a month," "once every three months," "once a year"; then under each of these headings enter the number of persons you see with that frequency (excluding, of course, those with whom you live or work). The result will be what might be called a table of friendship frequencies. If such a calculation were carried out carefully, with people of different classes in different countries, I have the impression that Spain would head the list. This is the principal item of Spanish wealth, the only one that is really important: that of friendly human intercourse. Political hatred, insecurity, mutual distrust, and fear of denunciation have endangered this marvelous commodity; but it has always overcome and survived every difficulty, even if with some loss.

Since the American soul is shaped by loneliness, since this is the great danger that threatens at every moment, the effect of this density of Spanish sociability is, when it is first experienced, almost intoxicating. Its end product is conversation. Spain is one of the countries in which people talk most (in others there is more shouting, but not so much conversation); although in a state of decline, the social gathering for conversation still exists, where intelligence or simply wit is lavished and lost, or perhaps not lost, who knows? One could as well say that the rain is lost that "falls mainly in the plain." In the United States the habit of conversation does not exist. It is not that Americans are incapable of it, or that they don't take delight in conversing; on the contrary, one can pass hours and hours talking with an American or a group of them. But one has to provoke them to it, stimulate them, in some way justify that "exception" for which there exist no established and spontaneously indulged forms. This occurs in part through a lack of imagination —one thing that is not abundant in the United States—and in part also because of a certain inferior form of practicality that consists of a fear of "losing time."

I should like to persuade Americans that losing time is an excellent investment, that it has a utilitarian justification as one of the most productive activities. The Spaniard has always harbored a certain shame about his duties, though he is losing it and this worries me. Today the Spaniards, including those of highest social rank, work a great deal. But even so, one still finds that it is considered somewhat inelegant to be too busy, and chores are hidden a little. It is rare that a Spaniard, unless he is very inflexible, will refuse to see you for a little time of talk. After losing a couple of hours, he goes to bed later, perhaps sleeps less, misses an entertainment or some sport. But he finds a compensation. After a good period of friendly conversation *he produces more.* Toned up by human contact, excited by the witty remarks of the other, his ideas flow more quickly, his thoughts are better articulated, his attention is more alert, he misses fewer details: the intellectual cooking takes place at a much higher pressure, and consequently in less time. "To lose time" in a generous, friendly, and intelligent fashion is one of the best ways to save it.

There is something else that seems to define profoundly the differences between the structure of life in North America and in Spain: the distance to which it is projected. The Spaniard projects his life over minimum and maximum distances, that is, *extreme* ones, and his foresight for medium distance is wanting. He decides this very moment what he is going to do this afternoon, making up his mind while the thing is white-hot, when it really appeals to him, when he really wants to do it, or thinks he does. He does not have the vaguest idea what he will be doing next week, and if one proposes an appointment for next Wednesday he will hesitate, he will be ill at ease and will suggest telephoning again on Tuesday to confirm it. Rather than set up a plan of action that has to last two or three years, he prefers to live right now. On the other hand he has probably accepted a position, a "career," for his whole life, one that he will not change even though he becomes tired of it and bored, even though he realizes that he has missed his calling and that his work is comparatively unremunerative. By the same token he will feel himself bound to many things that perhaps he does not really want. The American is exactly the opposite: he projects to *medium* distances. He knows in detail what he is going to do next week and, a little more vaguely, what he is going to do during the next two years, but he does not plan for tomorrow, for this afternoon; he has already determined somewhat in advance what he is going to do, and there is no room for improvisation, for this bothers and displeases him. And if an American felt himself irrevocably tied to a predetermined future for the next thirty years, the prospect would seem like a millstone around his neck.

This I believe is the explanation for the marvelous stability of American *society*—because the medium distance is precisely that of social relations—and for the instability and inefficiency of Spanish collective life. We find here also the reason why, despite all I have said, there is a greater stability to *individual* lives in Spain, why there is a minimum number of cases of maladjustment, of mental unhinging, of personal fracture of the pattern of life, while these are frequent among the splendid, prosperous, secure North Americans. The capacity for acting on the spur of the moment, immediately, gives life a certain flexibility, a means of adapting itself to the change of circumstances. This capacity is frequently missed in the United States, where everything is planned, anticipated, carefully foreseen; and where, by the same token, the future is mortgaged and in a measure ceases to be the kingdom of freedom that essentially it is. An integration of these two extreme tendencies, the Spanish and the American, each of which has its limitations, would give results of an almost inconceivable fruitfulness.

Another area in which I believe the United States could learn some important things from Spain is that of intellectual life. Spanish tradition in intellectual endeavors was very unimportant from the seventeenth century—and in some fields from before that time —to around 1900. Then a group of men began to be active in these fields, and in doing so they were moved by an energetic intellectual urge, without stimuli of any other kind, such as those based on economic gain or social esteem, or those coming from educational institutions; in this sense they approached their task with an authenticity of purpose comparable only to that of the pre-Socratic philosophers of Greece. This is the only explanation of the fact that during the first half of the present century, with a limited total production, without benefit of team or group collaboration, the Spanish contribution to the field of ideas, to the literary and artistic forms of the West, has not been inferior to that of any other European nation. A few names are the best proof of this fact: Unamuno, Ortega, Baroja, Azorín, Valle-Inclán, Antonio Machado, Juan Ramón Jiménez, Lorca, Menéndez Pidal, Ramón y Cajal, Picasso, Juan Gris, Manuel de Falla. And these, to be sure, are not the only creative spirits of this period.

Precisely because of the deficiencies of the period that ended in Spain around 1900, the Spanish intellectual renaissance was less burdened than similar movements in other countries with the ballast of the past, and had freer hands to attack future projects. When one notes to what a degree these Spaniards anticipated ideas that fifteen or twenty years later circulated throughout Europe, and how full their works are of possibilities not yet known or exploited, one ponders what this could mean for a culture like the American: a culture still fresh, free of restrictive shackles. With even a little help from fate during the next twenty years, the forcefulness with which American culture approaches reality can produce an effective, original, and creative intellectual life that would hitherto have been premature, and consequently false and fruitless.

And there are other aspects of Spanish intellectual life that may be worth consideration. Spanish culture has been characterized by a minimum of esotericism; it has been in close contact with the country; the daily papers have always published articles by the most important writers; and the latter have seen fit to treat even the most serious subjects, including philosophy. I am not referring particularly to present-day papers, whose limitations are well known, although even these frequently publish articles of excellent quality. I am thinking rather of what *El Sol* was from 1917 to 1936, when it published articles, poems, and essays that today are the important books of one generation and of a good part of another. The result has been a sharpening of the sensibilities of a considerable segment of the Spanish public for serious, thoughtful subjects. It is a public now capable of an interest in philosophical, sociological, historical, and poetical works; capable of attending courses or lectures of considerable profundity; of exhausting editions of books that in other countries of greater splendor cannot be printed or perhaps have been translated twenty years after appearing in Spanish.

I often reflect on what American life would be on the day that the publishers of magazines, newspapers, and books stopped underestimating their public by mulling over old ideas of fifteen or twenty years ago, and set themselves the task of really giving their public challenging ideas, good literature, inspiration, and fewer texts predigested by teams of experts, fewer trivialities. My own experience as a lecturer and professor in the United States leads me to believe that there are very considerable numbers capable of following the discussion of a difficult and rigorous subject with interest and intelligence—provided the lecturer does not assume that if he treats the subject thoroughly they are not going to understand it, as so many Europeans seem to assume, who speak in the United States in a way they would not venture to do in their own countries.

It is in the fields of the humanities and philosophy—precisely those in which the United States will be most deficient during the coming decades, if it evolves a program of collective life appropriate to its historic role—that Spanish thought of the last half-century has made its most original and fruitful advances, not only in details but in the very manner of understanding. Ortega described himself in his youth as "not at all modern and very much twentieth century," and it is this attribute that has characterized the truly vital and contemporary in Spanish thought of this period. The United States has to posit its problems from this historical level, and here it might well profit from Spain, which has been characterized by a relative insensibility toward what has been most specifically the "modern period"—the source of great evils and limitations in Spanish history—and by an early realization of the horizons leading beyond it.

VI

That Americans and Spaniards—essentially so different—have some resemblance is seen in the speed with which they are capable of establishing mutual relations. *Person to person*: this might well be the formula for friendly relations between the United States and Spain. When the American and the Spaniard meet, there is usually comprehension and frequently a lively congeniality. In unknown American surroundings, the Spaniard, after a few moments, feels himself to be among friends; at the end of some months of association, a close friendship is possible. Heaven knows how much time and effort would be required to attain a little intimacy with people of other countries, including "Latins."

For this reason I believe that the most effective element in relations between Spain and the United States is direct, actual contact. The one who visits the other country, and really lives in it, understands and loves it at the end of a short time, its citizens, its people; he becomes attached to their way of life, he feels "at home" away from home. But I said really lives in it—not wrapped in any sort of cellophane, which may take the form of his "official" status, fear of germs, political partisanship, or an insurmountable resistance to the language. And not for too short a time. Those trips of a few weeks in the United States, when the traveler sees cities, factories, newspapers, observatories, universities, waterfalls, and mountains, are likely to produce a sensation of dizziness and a thick residuum of commonplaces. In Spain the short trip involves less risk, for many reasons: the smaller size of the country, its greater age, a more closely knit society, but especially because the American ordinarily comes with fewer preconceived ideas and is more disposed to change them; the great danger for him is that of not actually entering into the life of the country, but remaining in that no man's land of tourist and international organizations.

But there are, naturally, other tasks— especially that of presenting the other country to the millions of Spaniards and Americans who have no reason to cross the Atlantic. This is a difficult and complicated undertaking. I can indicate here only a few principles that strike me as useful. The first, without doubt, would be the adoption of a "methodical pessimism": not to assume that things are already known, but the contrary. It cannot be taken for granted that the names of the politicians who took part in the Spanish civil war mean anything to Americans, or that Spaniards know where Connecticut is (where I say Spaniards and Americans, one can substitute any pairs of national names). There is no idea about the true plane of life—only isolated details that in a majority of cases are misleading.

In the second place, everything must be referred to the whole, to what one could call the social structure or pattern of life. This requires seeing the place and function of each element within a totality that precedes every one of its details. It also requires considering each country "in movement," in other words in the true reality of its program of collective life, keeping in mind the *plot* (without this actually being fully known) on which its history is based. And in the third place, one cannot lose immediate contact with real events; they must be presented as they appear, without ever replacing them with preconceived ideas or mental constructions. I once defined this method as *impressionism and analysis*. If the first is lacking everything becomes abstract, the result of a fleshless speculation operating in a vacuum; without the second everything, even the truest and most exact, becomes deceptive.

Alongside these principles that we might call "theoretical" I would place others, which it might not be inappropriate to call "moral." The most important of these would be respect for the secret of a country, a people: a recognition that it is never possible to know deeply and completely any country save one's own, where every flick of an eyelid is meaningful, clear as a bright morning, while in the foreign country everything is clothed in mystery, is recondite, is a question. By dint of time, love, and intelligence, a foreign country gradually begins to be less foreign. This is one of the deepest emotions, one of the greatest delights man can enjoy, an unexpected extension of his life and personality, something vaguely similar to the loving conquest of a woman, equally problematic, difficult, and uncertain.

The present state of the world does not allow for choice, either for Americans or for others. Today the United States is the country that must be taken into account, like it or not. This fact, which must be accepted as a condition of historical reality, makes it a modern version of the "Black Legend," evident in its bad press throughout the world. Moreover, the United States, whether it likes it or not (and naturally it doesn't like it, because it is more comfortable to be "at home"), is *in the world*. And to be in the world, not simply in one's own part of it, means the necessity of coming to grips with it, with each country and with the whole. This and no other is the destiny of our hour.

Whether the future of our world is going to be fruitful and meaningful, or whether stupidity and violence are going to rule, depends on many things. One of the most important of these is the relation of the United States with the rest of the world, and most particularly with the Western countries. Implicit in that relationship is a preceding idea about these countries, and the degree to which this idea is adequate will determine how far the United States can know *what to depend on*. It should not be forgotten, however, that to know what to depend on does not mean to "know everything," but the contrary: it means to keep clearly in mind that reality always outdistances our ideas, to recognize that reality lies there indomitable, enigmatic, and always hidden behind outward appearances.

56

from France

RAYMOND ARON*

The author: born in France (Paris), 1905; studied at the École Normale Supérieure. Before World War II Dr. Aron held several teaching positions, primarily in social philosophy, but after the Battle of France he joined General de Gaulle in London and became Editor-in-Chief of the monthly *La France Libre*. Since 1947 he has been editorial writer for the newspaper *Le Figaro*, and he is also Professor of Sociology at the Sorbonne. In his dozen or so books, some translated into English, his main concern has been to interpret the social and political trends of our century. His first visit to the United States, in 1950, has been followed by a number of other brief trips, which have taken him to several major cities of the country.

I

IN the course of half a dozen trips to the United States since 1950 I have never had time to linger there for long. I have stayed in New York, Washington, San Francisco, Cambridge, and have passed through Detroit and Montgomery. I know America's streets better than its homes. I know opinion-makers better than the common man. In that country that prides itself on not emulating its intellectuals, I know the latter better than the big businessmen. I have not explored the scamy side of American life, the areas of shadow and unhappiness.

Is this to say that my visits have taught me nothing I could not have learned in books? That would be going too far. Something essential is lacking in our view of the United States if we have not seen the people, the sky, the houses; if we have not dined in private homes, visited the national shrines; if we have not elbowed citizens in the street, in the trains, in the subways. Only experience enables us to sense how the institutions, the values, and the habits that we had come to know through books actually come to life. Only experience helps to place in proper perspective ideas that are at once true and apparently contradictory. Concepts, whether scientific or superficial, remain abstract, without flesh and blood, unless "one has seen for oneself."

* Translated from the French by Anita Tenzer.

For example, direct experience in the United States emphasizes certain economic considerations of which one is not unaware but which there is a tendency, from a distance, to underestimate. The hostility of the French workman toward "American capitalism" stems to a large extent from ignorance and ideological prejudices. Actually, it is the non-privileged classes, the workers, who profit most from American-style capitalism: a high standard of living changes their lot much more than that of the privileged; the middle class in the United States lives no better than the middle class of an averagely developed European country, and in certain respects it has a more difficult existence. And although the benefits of American wealth are less unequally distributed than many French leftists think, for many Americans, particularly for the young people, life is not so easy as is often imagined. In the United States, as everywhere else, one must work, and work hard.

American wealth manifests itself in two ways that are equally striking to the visitor. On the one hand, people speak of dollars, of price, more than anywhere else in the world. In France a suspension bridge would be singled out for the tourist's admiration by reason of its length, height, possibly the difficulties of construction and the genius of the architect; in San Francisco and elsewhere people rave about the sixty-million-dollar bridge. On the other hand, though everything is reckoned in dollars and cents, primary commodities such as electricity are squandered with a prodigality that scarcely ceases to surprise one. Strict economic calculation based on abundance of material and scarcity of manpower—this abstract formula found in all the books becomes a concrete reality.

After a few days this reality combines with numerous other impressions that converge toward a controversial proposition: American society was built by Europeans but is today, in many of its principal aspects, different from European societies. In a word: while I was with Americans in Europe I was above all struck by the European background to their way of thinking, feeling, and living, but in the United States I was above all struck by the originality of American society.

The first reason for this impression stems, it seems to me, from the scale of natural phenomena. Europe, from Saint Andrews to Naples, from Brest to Warsaw, exists within certain norms: the rivers, the plains, the fields seem to be on the same scale. American norms are different. It takes one night to go by train from Paris to Berlin, three days and three nights to cross the American Republic from east to west. The airplane was necessary to make it possible to go from New York to San Francisco as one would go from Calais to Marseilles. Assuredly, if one thinks of it, the agglomeration of Paris or London is as excessive as that of New York —in fact even more monstrous, when considered in relation to the size of France or Great Britain. Nevertheless, in New York the vertical architecture, in Washington the distances from one section of the city to another, give you the physical sensation of this "difference in scale" between the European nations and the United States.

There has been so much emphasis on the conformism and at the same time heterogeneity of American society that I hesitate to take up this theme. One has the feeling that there is greater religious, moral, and family diversity in the United States than in any European country. But superimposed on the national and racial differences, which depend on the origin of a family and the length of time it has been in the country, is a homogeneous façade. It is created in the first instance by the diffusion throughout the country of certain tools of technical civilization—drugstores, milk bars, service stations, and the like. The large-scale standardized production of objects in current usage spreads a uniform social veneer on the surface of American life; it is this technique of the "American way of life" that separates the majority of American tourists, in uniform or in civilian clothes, from the peoples among whom they live or visit. Also, a certain typical manner of behavior in social relations is shown you—by waitresses, gas-station attendants, salesgirls. A stereotyped smile greets you that at first delights, then irritates, and finally leaves you indifferent. In American society everyone contrives to wear a happy expression and to disguise the impersonality of social relations by greeting the stranger as though he, and he alone, were the only one expected. Adaptation to the environment is a virtue taught in the schools. Obedience to social demands becomes a necessity whose acceptance gives a feeling not of constraint but of merit.

This dialectic of plurality and conformism lies at the core of American life, making for the originality of the social structure, and raising the most contradictory evaluations. One speaks of a classless society while finding aggravated in it all the conflicts that tear European nations apart. Americanism assures the maintenance of the national community because this Americanism, while denying the reality of class struggle, admits as normal the rivalry between individuals and groups and accepts a hierarchy of money and prestige that is never definite, never crystallized, but at the same time never absent. In France, Great Britain, Italy, Germany the sense of nationality takes different forms, but all the European countries seem to me to belong to the same general order; American society belongs to a different order. Its colonial history, its vast territories, the varied backgrounds of its people have given it characteristics that make it seem essentially different today from the nations of the old continent.

Let me make myself clear. One could easily enumerate a great number of phenomena, institutions, amusements from across the Atlantic that have acquired citizen's rights in France, elsewhere in Europe, and even throughout the world. This process of "Americanization" is looked upon by many with horror. But in some respects the battle is not so much against Americanism as against the universalizing of phenomena linked to the development of material civilization. If the effort toward increased productivity and the subordination of all usages to the imperatives of greater output is termed Americanization, then the whole of Europe, including France, is indeed in the process of becoming Americanized. In this connection it has to be remembered, though, that not all the secrets of American productivity are transferable.

II

International politics, for the first time in history, embraces the five continents. The United States is the first authentic world power. Since it is also the richest and most powerful country, it cannot but inspire mixed feelings—envy and resentment combined with admiration or fear.

I myself belong to the group of Frenchmen described as pro-American. In my view, American diplomacy, which seemed to me deplorable during the Second World War, has been fundamentally sound during the postwar period, at least in Europe. Reconciliation with a reconstructed Germany seemed to me in the best interests of France, and therefore I had no reason to agree with those who accused the leaders of the United States of a plot in favor of defeated Germany and against victimized France. But it was not so much in Europe as in Africa and Asia that American policy was irritating to French public opinion. The chief reproach leveled by many Frenchmen at the Americans in the years following the second war was their anti-colonialism, their intervention in the French empire against French sovereignty. The fate of the Indians and Negroes has become the weapon used against the United States to counter the accusation of French colonialism.

I shall not attempt to investigate here in what proportion the defenders and the indicters are justified. It is true that the French are less race-conscious than the Americans, and that the latter are more impatient to grant self-government to all peoples, whether developed or underdeveloped. In certain areas there are real and often well-founded differences of interest or of feeling between the two countries. On the other hand, contact with the United States shows not only these differences but also the inevitable contrast between the attitude of a European or Asiatic country and the attitude of one that is of necessity global.

Glance at the map: the east coast of the United States faces toward Europe, the west toward Asia. In Washington the Secretary of State, the President, the journalists, feel just as much sense of responsibility toward South Korea or the Philippines as toward Berlin or Greece. Inevitably, those who are responsible react to news from a continent not only in terms of their friends and enemies on that continent, but also in terms of their allies on the other side of the world. During the Suez crisis in 1956 the positions taken by India or Burma weighed as heavily as those of Great Britain or France. The two latter countries were friends and allies of the United States, while Burma and India belong to the "unaffiliated third party," the vast group that, having acquired independence a few years ago, is passionately anti-colonial and wants to retain an active neutrality between the Soviet bloc and the free world.

The visitor to Washington gets a physical impression of the United States' world-wide mission when he consults the list of distinguished guests received by the President. The Austrian Chancellor succeeds the President of Indonesia; the President of South Vietnam or the President of Tunisia succeeds the Premier of France.

One visitor is reminded that the United States has always sympa-
thetically followed the struggles for independence of the peoples
of Asia and Africa, which is true. The other is solemnly assured
of the traditional friendship that exists between his country and
Americans, which is not false either. Thus American leaders are
convinced that their point of view on the world is less unilateral,
more complex, than that of any of their allies. They are sincerely
shocked that a tendency toward excessive simplification is attributed to them when they are consciously striving to encompass the
whole earth.

There is no doubt that they have a global perspective, but the
criticism of their penchant for simplification is not refuted because
of it. In Europe, as in Asia, many observers face American leaders
with the same reproach: that of bringing everything back to rivalry with Communism. And I think there is another more profound explanation for this oversimplification criticism. In politics
Americans—average Americans even more than their leaders—
seem to me to apply a method of "technical" thinking that expresses itself in terms of problems to be solved and a search for
means to reach an end. Every situation is a problem; every problem admits of a solution. In the eyes of a fair number of Frenchmen
every problem is a situation, and situations admit not of solution
but of clear perception, a gradual inurement, possibly a transformation effected by man—above all by the great master of man and
things, time. The allies of the United States are often much more
perturbed by the manner and the language of American leaders
than by their acts. Members of Congress, generals, journalists,
sometimes express themselves as though the Communist problem
could be taken care of by a radical solution—whereas for years,
for decades, perhaps for centuries, it will be a reality with which
we shall have to live, avoiding both "shooting war" and "appeasement."

This tendency to confuse political thinking with technical thinking
sometimes leads Americans to assume implicitly that they can change
the world at will—as if they were able to manipulate men, their
feelings and their aspirations, on command. And it may be granted
that the technical method of approach, while it risks impatience
and oversimplification in analysis, is not without its advantages,
for it is at least a stimulus to action. The French tendency—to

analyze a situation, to note that each possible decision clashes against insurmountable obstacles, to wait until time wears away the obstacles or events remove them—is quite the opposite: it has the virtues of apparent lucidity, of real subtlety, but it risks the confusion of action with awareness.

Something that strikes a foreigner and has often impressed my compatriots is the spectacle offered by the capital of the United States, where the policy of the leading world power is elaborated. Washington, unlike London or Paris, lives only through politics. Federal capital though it is, it has practically no theatrical productions or concerts. Nothing there distracts the professional politicians from their vocation. The inhabitants of Washington, civil servants, diplomats, politicians, journalists, have nothing to do outside business hours but to meet for cocktail and dinner parties. Inevitably, they talk. President, Secretary of State, members of Congress, generals, admirals, talk among themselves and from one group to another, talk to journalists and before radio or television microphones. News released in the morning has made the rounds of the city by sundown. Exclusively political, it is the most gossip-ridden city in the world. As for the innumerable statements that are registered by press agencies each day and reverberate through all corners of the earth, they form part of the political game. The spectacle includes competition among the interest groups, factions within the parties, factions within the civil service and the military. Washington never speaks unanimously. One always wonders who speaks in the name of the United States. In periods of crisis these contradictions among the American voices lend themselves to interpretations that may be sincere or insincere but are rarely favorable: "war mongering," "men of straw," "lack of unified action." One must step back to acquire perspective; one must have had direct experience with the "American way of conducting politics" in order to discern—beyond the spectacular episodes, the delirious polemics, the great debates—the continuity of a moderate policy that is neither imaginative nor grandiose but does not lean toward war or toward capitulation.

Let me add that three categories of Frenchmen cannot share my view: professional diplomats; champions of certain French national interests that American policy ignores or vehemently attacks; and those who see the United States by way of categories

63

(capitalism, imperialism) that in themselves inspire hostile judgments. No experience will change judgments that stem less from
raw facts than from the historical and moral interpretation they
are accorded.

III

While the concept the French have of the United States as a
political power depends essentially on their individual political
bent, it is entirely different in regard to American civilization. Here
the admirers and detractors are not distributed in a parliamentary
hemicycle, one group to the right, the other to the left. The American way of life inspires liking, indifference, hostility, according
to criteria that seem not to be political.

Since 1944 the relationship between French and Americans has
been closer than at any time in the past. Thousands of American
soldiers have lived in France, thousands of French people have
had contacts with them, and other thousands have themselves been
to the United States. But let us remember that partial knowledge
does not necessarily carry with it deep understanding. Even if
French and Americans were to exert themselves to be fair to each
other, they would not reach a good understanding unless they accepted each other's differences. If one ponders what the two peoples have to learn from each other, the first answer, the most
banal and perhaps the most important, is that each, through the
discovery of the other, should learn that it is not alone in the
world and that its own sense of what is obvious is not necessarily
universally shared.

The Frenchman does not always regard as charming the American child whose parents apparently grant him complete freedom;
frequently he considers him insufferable. He is not always aware
of the meaning of the collective life that Americanism develops,
but is struck by what he considers a mediocre level of intellectual
development. The optimism of Americans sometimes seems to him
an attractive sign of youth, at other times a sign of puerility. The
refusal to think of death, to make room for it in the awareness
of human destiny, seems surprising and almost pitiable to many
cultured Frenchmen. But the well-brought-up French child surprises and shocks American parents a little. The American observer does not regard as necessarily admirable the abstract, theo-

64

retical, sometimes encyclopaedic nature of the training received by French students. The American soldier is too affected by the discomfort of the houses and the dirtiness of the street in French villages; the French visitor in the United States is too affected by the facile smile of the salesgirl, the abundance of cars, the vulgarity of the television. Each makes the mistake of comparing the worst of what he sees abroad with the best he knows at home.

What types of Frenchmen manifest the most lively hostility to the American way of life? Without laying claims to exhaustiveness or scientific precision, I shall enumerate four types. One is the "cultured Frenchman," enamored of a certain style of living, who detests big industry, mass production, the lowering of standards in favor of the masses. (Georges Duhamel in *Scènes de la vie future* seems to me to epitomize the ideal of the "craftsman civilization" versus "industrial barbarism." His picture of the United States is a caricature, but M. Duhamel is also less the picture than the caricature of the Frenchman hostile to American life.) The second type, of which M. Etiemble is an example, is above all struck by the race-consciousness that Americans condemn but have not yet surmounted. A third type is not unaware of industrial barbarism and race-consciousness, but lays greater stress on the character of human relations, and on the impersonality of most of these relationships in the United States, the tendency to be satisfied with the superficial and to ignore the deep ties of love and friendship; thereupon unfolds a description of the boredom and emptiness of American life, and the reaction to it—violence, speed, sexuality, and so on. A fourth type is struck above all by the intellectual fodder offered to the American masses, from scandal magazines to digests of books, even of great books.

These four types are not absolutely distinct, one from another. It goes without saying that the representative of the first type also invokes race-consciousness, impersonality in human relations, and cultural poverty. But those of the second and third groups do not lay the blame on "industrial barbarism," for most of them are aware that economic progress is indispensable to the raising of the standard of living. The exponents of the last three types make free use of the same arguments, but they do not place emphasis on the same aspects of American life. Race-consciousness, pragmatism and superficiality in human relations, or the vulgarity of mass culture appear as the major and characteristic factor, depending on the psychological makeup or attention of the observer.

Are these critics of American civilization typical of French opinion? There is no dearth of enthusiastic descriptions of the United States, the latest being that of Renée and Pierre Gosset. It is probable that the French lower classes, the laborers and *petits bourgeois*, would be more impressed by the advantages of the "American way of life" than the middle class and the intellectuals, since the European middle class already enjoys most of the advantages of industrial civilization and, in addition, certain of the advantages of incompletely industrialized countries. Nonetheless, a good number of the French who actually visit the United States, especially among those who express their views and offer them to their compatriots in book form, belong to the pessimistic rather than to the optimistic school of thought, to the critics rather than the admirers.

The picture of the United States held by a great many Frenchmen who have never crossed the Atlantic—probably a vague picture, and perhaps constituted or deformed by prejudice or political conviction—is neither false nor true. A young dynamic country with a high standard of living: the description is insufficient but not untrue, not an obstacle to mutual understanding. On the other hand, the antipathy manifested toward the United States by many French intellectuals who have been there is a reality that must be taken into consideration and that cannot simply be eliminated on grounds of prejudice, emotionalism, or misunderstanding. It is not enough to know each other in order to like each other; this axiom is no less true for peoples than for individuals.

No argument invoked by the critics is without a certain weight. It is true that race-consciousness exists in the United States, and not only in the South. It is also true that the attenuation of class distinctions has been countered by the accentuation of national or racial differences. The hierarchy among national groups is subtle, and it thins out slowly as the latest arrivals, the Poles, the Italians, the Balkan peoples, gradually, in their turn, move up the social scale. It does not disappear completely, because the desire to be distinguished by virtue of the length of one's American roots, by religion, by nationality of origin, combines with the ideology of human equality. With regard to color, the barrier continues.

Many Europeans have a fantastic conception of the lot of the

Negroes in the United States. Actually their social and intellectual level is continually rising. There are universities for colored people, a Negro middle class. An increasing proportion of Negroes live in the North, where race-consciousness takes different forms from those in the South. Compared to the majority of the world's Negroes, those in the United States are probably the most highly privileged, at least in the material order, for they participate in the country's exceptional standard of living. But when the myths have been brushed aside, the main fact remains. The contradiction has not yet been resolved between what the American ideal demands and what American society's actual attitude is toward the Negroes. Would those people who pride themselves on not being race-conscious succeed in avoiding this contradiction if, in their own countries, they had a proportionate percentage of colored peoples? Should the inability of the Americans to put their consciences in order be indignantly denounced, or should one sympathize with their efforts to regulate their conduct according to their principles? Each will decide for himself.

By the same token, the other French criticisms—the impersonality of human relations, mass culture—are not, and cannot be dismissed as, the result of ignorance or bad faith. The fact is that many French people, especially in the cultured class, believe that human relations in the United States are deformed by pragmatism, emptied, so to speak, of all intensity and depth by concern with self-adaptation and immediate unqualified cordiality. Is the victim of half-knowledge worse than the victim of ignorance? Is he deceived by the surface of American life and thus unable to discover the friendships, the love—just as singular and rich in the United States as elsewhere—that are cloaked across the Atlantic under apparent absence of reserve and openness toward strangers, as they are cloaked in France under the seclusion of family life and reticence on first acquaintance? I shall not attempt an answer, but shall only suggest that this Franco-American colloquy contains certain elements of well-founded criticism, founded not necessarily on the real situation in America but on the reality of certain French reactions to the United States.

Perhaps the decisive question concerns what is termed, on both sides of the Atlantic, "mass culture." Delight is taken in confusing this with American culture in general—and isn't this culture-for-all, this bargain culture, the very antithesis of real culture? Productivity, industrialization, rise in living standards, do these terms that are associated with modern civilization conceal a drift of the rich and in certain respects democratic societies toward barbarism? A Frenchman who visits the United States cannot fail to be struck by certain facts: the style, which seems vulgar to him, of much of the radio and television, the sordidness of the sensational and scandal-oriented press, the provincialism of much of the news, the widespread use of rewrites and digests, the mediocrity of many of the films. But these facts would be acknowledged by the majority of Americans. Once again, it is a question of the place they occupy in the whole of American life, the significance they assume. Are they typically American, or are they linked to some degree to phenomena typical everywhere of modern civilization?

It must be admitted that the mass-circulation papers in France or Great Britain have no need to look to the United States for their ignoble proceedings. Not that they haven't borrowed a few from American models, but they have found quite enough on their own. Such French and English publications have proportionally as many readers as the American. The French love-stories press is perhaps of a higher caliber than the American crime or sex press, but this is not altogether sure. Soviet censorship eliminates excesses of crime, sex, and sentimentality, but this puritanism has, as a counterpart, an edifying literature of "positive" heroes and idylls in the shade of a tractor. For the time being, the fact that everyone knows how to read has resulted in the creation not of a single world of culture, but of two, perhaps as far apart from each other as were formerly the world of unwritten popular culture and that of the select.

Is the American case exceptional because the duality is more marked? Personally, I am inclined to reply that the duality is less marked. What most shocks the European intellectual is a certain continuity between the two cultural worlds. The kind of entertainment that the American child absorbs daily, even in intellectual families, the kind of literature he devours, in other words the vulnerability of cultured circles to the masses' lack of culture—this is the phenomenon that strikes so many European observers and occasions their condemnation. The practice of producing résumés of masterpieces is another example of this admixture of the two worlds that shocks and disquiets them. (In addition, of course, there is the problem of differences of opinion—the occasional refusal of the average American to subscribe to a hierarchy of values that seems obvious to the Frenchman.)

The observer favorably disposed toward American life replies that never have so many Americans (and young Americans) frequented the museums; never have there been so many good orchestras and good concerts. In the last analysis the amount of live art (music, painting) offered in most American cities far surpasses that offered in French cities or provinces. Never, thanks to radio and "hi-fi," have so many Americans heard good music. Never, thanks to reproductions, have they admired so much great painting. The indictment denounces the sliding of higher culture toward mass culture; the defense shows how a growing number of average Americans are reaching the higher world. I do not think one can entirely reject either thesis. American life supports both this risk and this opportunity. Depending on his sympathies or temperament, a person will stress the one or the other. At the moment, the allegation of American lack of culture, very widespread in French intellectual circles, is based on two aspects of American life.

The first of these is that in the United States the scale of values of the "highbrows" is not officially accepted by the general public (even the cultured public). The French, even when cultured (except for literary quasi-professionals), are far from being convinced of the genius of Baudelaire, Claudel, or Kafka, but for the most part they do not hesitate to appreciate the avant garde. Whether in literature or in painting, the pseudo-enthusiasts tend to subscribe to the judgments of the authentic enthusiasts. The heretics have become orthodox. In France one may try in vain to cause a scandal or to provoke the philistines. By way of intellectual comfort, the middle class has apparently become converted to the values of bohemia or of maligned authors. Perhaps there are still some unrecognized geniuses, but never has there been such fear of not recognizing genius. The United States has not yet reached the indisputable reign of the avant-garde.

The second basis of criticism is the indifference manifested by Americans to cultural values, especially aesthetic values, in the course of everyday life. Concern with beauty is apparently ignored, or at least subordinated to utility, to preoccupation with income.

The beauty that stems from the functional architecture in American structures strikes a discordant note in a harmony whose inspiration seems entirely different. The suburbs of European cities, especially in France, are not beautiful; the sense of town planning is too often absent. And nevertheless the cult of form, of aesthetic values, remains inseparable from the spirit of French culture—as it is in Japan, where concern with beauty touches every incident in existence, every piece of work, every garden, the fish-platter, the house. This cult seems, in the United States, to be superimposed on a radically different spirit.

Will an industrialized France, concerned with productivity, become a mediocre replica of the United States? Will the qualities that enchant so many foreigners in French life be irreparably destroyed by the modernization of the economy? And on the other side of the Atlantic, will the United States go ever farther in its own direction—production, pragmatism, awareness of the future rather than of the past? These are, I believe, the two questions that dominate the Franco-American colloquy, a dialogue of men and of cultures, the background for the polemics of the public square.

Barring ever possible catastrophes, I myself think that the charm of the French provinces is less linked to the slowness of economic development than it is said to be. It is not the low yield of labor but the art of living that is exemplary in France, and industry will not ruin the art of living, provided the French keep faith with themselves. And in the United States the growing expansion of the economy is, as of now, attenuating rather than aggravating the obsession with income. Since it has become the world's leading power, by force of circumstances rather than voluntarily, the United States has been forced to overcome that insularity in which all peoples delight. In the principal universities the number of professors and students devoted to the study of other worlds has multiplied. General culture has assumed a wider place in the curriculum, even in the technical schools. The younger generation wants to explore the world, and it seems to me is more interested in the arts than were former generations. According to my way of thinking, American society is maturing, and little by little broadening the pragmatism of the colonists resolved to conquer rebellious natural forces. It is acquiring a sense of history.

70

Is this to say that France modernized and the United States grown up will meet each other halfway? It would be ridiculous to substitute this new mythology for the old ones. The Franco-American colloquy originates not only in the supposed French refusal of technical civilization, the supposed youth of the United States, indifferent to the past and without experience of suffering. The soil, the sky, the dimensions, the population, the religion, are different on the two sides of the Atlantic. French culture is conspicuous for its catholicity, its profound pessimism, its undefined tension between faith and skepticism. National consciousness in the United States is pragmatic and moral; it will stay that way in the foreseeable future, at whatever stage of economic progress.

Alexis de Tocqueville thought he saw in American democracy the common destiny of all peoples. Many observers—with enthusiasm or with dismay—think they see in the technical civilization of the United States the picture of the industrial society that will be the common destiny of all peoples. Undeniably, we are all caught up in the same adventure, condemned to push ever farther in the direction of industrialization, urbanization, rationalization. Will ways of living and thinking, social relations, and ideologies tend in like manner toward uniformity?

I should not like to reply either yes or no. There are certain general implications inherent in technical progress. On the other hand, when it comes to attitudes toward life, death, the social hierarchy, or society, to questions of philosophy or of religion—here I have not seen the picture of our future in the United States. I think I discern there, beyond a transferable Americanism, the traits of a national community in process of formation that will be neither the ruin nor the salvation of the whole of humanity, but one among others.

from Italy

LUIGI BARZINI, JR.

The author: born in Italy (Milan), 1908; studied at Columbia University in New York. During the decade of the 1930's he was traveling correspondent for *Corriere della Sera*, an important Italian daily, and covered the outstanding international stories of the time. He was on the *Panay* when that ship was bombed by the Japanese in the Yangtze Kiang, and was awarded a medal by the United States Navy for his help on board and ashore. In 1940 the Fascist government condemned him to forced residence in a village for five years, but in 1944, when Rome was liberated, he resumed his journalistic career, as editor-in-chief of daily and weekly publications. At present he devotes his time only to independent writing, his works including a book on the United States and a study of the Italian Communist Party. He is the father of five children, and lives on a small farm near Rome, where he produces his own olive oil, wine, vegetables, and fruit. Since his first stay in the United States (1925-1930), when he became acquainted with the East and parts of the Midwest, he has returned repeatedly to this country for short trips.

I

I WAS sixteen years old when I first landed in the United States, as an immigrant, in August 1925. And if I could add up all the things that struck me as important, interesting, or significant, the result would be less an accurate picture of the United States than a conception of what was lacking in Italy in the twenties, according to a boy of college age.

Italy, then, was a very old, tired, uncertain country, torn by civil strife, still exhausted by the war effort, dominated by a new dictatorship that tried to hide all contradictions and defects of the national life under pomp and rhetoric. Italy was definitely not a "modern" country. She was wary of experiments; her superimposed social classes were as distinct as different races. She was not, like England, changing her ways covertly under the cloak of the old forms ("plus c'est la même chose plus ça change"); rather she was putting on a show of Potemkin-like modernity under which the old decrepit habits went on undisturbed ("plus ça change plus c'est la même chose"). Italian aristocracy had style, but was dis-

72

credited; the Italian bourgeoisie had power, but was new, raw, greedy, irresponsible, and without style.

What interested me in the United States, therefore, was the "modern" concept, in which all things seemed to be done in a revolutionary "modern" way. Everything was the product of fresh thinking, from the foundations up. Everything had been "improved," and was continually being "improved" from day to day, almost from hour to hour. The restlessness, mobility, the unceasing quest for something better impressed me. I had come from a country that found consolation for its many shortcomings—poverty, unemployment, obsolete production methods—in the exaltation of spiritual factors. I was irritated by this line of reasoning, bored to hear my countrymen say, "We may be starving, we may be weak, insulted, despised, and sometimes dishonest, but Italy is the mother of civilization." In the United States I disregarded spiritual factors, which I learned to be wary of and to discount as rationalizations, and I sought truth in the concrete, scientific, materialistic, technical aspects of the country.

I was pleased with almost everything, from the new gadgets in the bathroom and kitchen to the taste of the chemical substitute for vanilla. I liked the Americans' pride in their country, their commonsense acceptance of obvious ideas, their admiration for their old bourgeoisie, the style of their lives and of their houses. I thought American girls were more beautiful than any in Europe. I could put up with American coffee and liked home-cooked American food. I loved American architecture, music, literature, jokes. I was charmed by the lean, silent men who smoked pipes, lived outdoors, wore tweeds, and said disagreeable ironic things almost without opening their mouths; they charmed me, of course, because there were no such people in Italy. I liked the obvious waste of precious materials, the heavy bronze doors of banks and movie theaters, the bronze cuspidors, the excessively heavy steel beams supporting bridges, the large bumpers on automobiles, all the unmistakable signs of wealth—even to the use of cream instead of milk in tea.

I listened impatiently to older Italians' lamentations about their life in America. We lived in a middle-class Italian milieu in New York, one not officially recognized by Americans, for whom Italians were either counts or illiterate peasants. The older Italians' complaints included almost all the differences between life in Europe and in the United States. They grumbled that it was difficult to carry on a conversation with Americans, that servants were hard to find and not good when found, that life in New York was a mad scramble, a rat race, in which competition killed all the finer feelings and joys of life. They deplored the absence of cafes (the existence of lunch counters and places where one could eat standing up seemed to me not defects but conquests), and said that American coffee was bad (this meant nothing; Italians complain about the coffee everywhere they go, and talk endlessly about it). There were the usual complaints about crime (it was the age of prohibition and gang warfare), political corruption, and the starry-eyed belief of Americans in magic formulas that would change everything overnight (Italians believe in the fundamentally immutable quality of human life). The religious and medical cults were deplored, and also some ridiculous aspects of even the best American qualities, like excessive trust in human nature and naïve humanitarianism. I saw the same things, or practically the same things, but instead of deploring them I admired them. Did the Italians say this was a materialistic, utilitarian country? I was an eager apprentice of materialism and utilitarianism. Were cultural values regarded in the United States as inferior to money matters? I directed all my plans, work, and dreams to amassing fabulous quantities of future currency. Was American literature designed only for big sales? I was a worshiper of success. I was going to write only the biggest bestsellers, which could be sold to the movies, and would disregard everything else.

The American secret became open to me, after a while, and I applied it to everything: all things were to be produced with the least effort for the comfort and satisfaction of the largest number of people. Anybody who tried to travel his own way, to follow his own private ideas, was the object of my contempt. And the American road was not difficult, for there were tested formulas for everything (like the ready mixes for cakes)—even for things that in older days had been considered the product of magic and genius, and were still so considered in backward Europe and other unenlightened continents. Anybody with a few dollars could go into a bookshop and buy books that taught him "How to Make Money on the Stock Exchange," "How to Write a Novel," "How to be

Popular," and how to perform triumphantly a number of other human activities. If the book was not enough, one could take an extension course in a university and be taught the correct and scientific way to reach one's goals. I bought the books, I took the courses, I worked hard, and waited for success to come to me— with the candid trust of a buyer of flower seeds watering his little pot.

After two years in college I spent two more years in the Pulitzer School of Journalism, and was graduated in 1930. There I acquired the illusion that I knew everything in my chosen line and that writing of any sort was merely a matter of technique. I traveled a little, and took odd jobs now and again. In the summer of 1929 I was, for a few weeks, the youngest reporter on the New York *World*. My duties consisted mainly in getting the names of all the people who had died during the day, writing them on slips of paper, arranging them in alphabetical order, and typing them for the composing room. I could see some of the most famous by-lines in American journalism walking through the corridors, talking among themselves, and looking through me as if I were transparent. Later a small Long Island newspaper asked for a willing young man (willing above all, apparently, to accept a small salary for working hard). I took the job. There I learned many things and suspected the existence of many more, which nobody had mentioned in the School of Journalism.

Though I often felt defeated I thought, like all young men of my age, that it was my own fault. But for me this difference between inexperienced expectations and harsh, humdrum reality was aggravated by the difference between my Italian interpretation of America and the human, everyday actuality. It never quite managed to be exactly what Americans of my age hoped, and it was even more profoundly different from the imaginary country of my desires. I could see the paradise all around me. It was documented by advertisements, magazine articles, pictures in newspapers, books, tales of friends, glimpses of gay people going by in automobiles, famous restaurants, beautiful houses of the rich along Fifth Avenue or on Long Island. The paradise was there all right, but it so happened that wherever I was it vanished.

In 1930, after graduation, I decided to go back to Italy to live and work. The reasons that dictated my decision were many and complicated. America as a dream had finally shown itself unreachable, like the pot of gold at the end of the rainbow. My college friends probably felt the same way, in those months. It was perhaps the inevitable discouragement of young intellectuals emerging from a sheltered life into the wide open world. But my case was different, I thought. I was Italian. I was tempted to think that my difficulties were due to my nationality and could never be solved. In the twenties there was enough prejudice against my countrymen to justify my conclusion. Now I know it was not justified in my case, but at the time it was an alluring alibi, a plausible reason for trying the easier climate of Italy.

II

My distorted picture of America was not peculiarly my own, or, turned upside down, my countrymen's alone. It was a mosaic of the things Americans also believed of themselves at the time, a composite picture of many pre-1929 convictions, the ideal America of the end of the nineteenth century (rugged individualism, free initiative, the devil take the hindmost, boundless opportunities for all) and of the Coolidge and Hoover eras. The two Americas, the golden nation of immigrants' dreams and the great optimistic empire which its countrymen were invited not to sell short, somewhat overlapped.

The illusion that all human activities could be improved and taught by means of "how to" books or college courses, until success was open to all men and not only, as in Europe, to an aristocratic minority born with a special talent, was part of every American's credo, often supported by verifiable reality. The belief that success was the one goal in life, not alone because of the wealth and prestige attached to it, but also because it was the proof of one's usefulness to society, was held by Americans and immigrants alike. Faith in the dogma that technique could do all things I learned in the university, from American professors as hopeful and optimistic as I. If I traveled completely enclosed in my mental cocoon, seeing only the things a young man from Italy wanted to see, Americans were likewise wrapped within cocoons, seeing only the things that perpetuated their own image of their country, an image that kept them working hard and hurrying ahead.

The prosperity of the 1920's really gave the impression of being due to an American formula, one that had for the first time defeated history and might annul Adam's condemnation in the Garden of Eden, an ingenious, clever gimmick that foreigners could learn and apply to their own problems. If I had stayed on in New York through the early thirties I would probably have changed my ideas about America, or at least corrected them. The sight of the depression, the unemployed queuing up for soup, the poverty, fear, and hopelessness overtaking the land would have taught me that the American magic formula was good for most but not all times; that something had gone wrong in the impeccable mechanism that produced more goods, more jobs, more wealth, and more successes; that Americans were, like all men everywhere, possible preys to unfathomable forces. The depression obviously could not be explained by saying that too many people stopped studying the right books and developing the correct virtues.

But I was in Italy at the time, and kept alive a picture of the country I had seen with my own eyes and thought I knew intimately. The fact that I could consider myself morally one part American prevented me from adapting my memories to what I was seeing in the newspapers. Even my quick professional trips to the United States did not help. I was too busy studying facts, gathering material, interviewing people, to understand anything deeply enough. Even today, when dealing with Americans, I get along well with New Yorkers of my vintage, educated in the twenties, imbued with the same hopes and superstitious beliefs, and find myself uncomfortable with younger people from other parts of the country, whose experiences I have not shared.

After the second war things had changed so much that there was only a superficial resemblance to the America of my imagination. My Americans, I thought, were stubborn individualists, who loved to struggle, take risks, go their own way, and accept the consequence of their acts. The Americans I met after the war sat for hours in conference rooms to take the smallest decision, which often had to be unanimous in order that nobody in particular could be blamed for an eventual mistake. My Americans were jealous of their own finances, saved money, insured themselves and their houses according to their own judgment, hoped for success but knew how to accept failure. Apparently the new Americans looked for security, avoided hard choices, liked state insurance schemes and pensions based on savings by organizations. My Americans had been rebels, hard to be persuaded of any leader's real superiority; they loved to consider their President a man like themselves, or a little worse. The new Americans were eager to put their trust in one, two, or three Great Men who would lead them to salvation and relieve them of the anxiety of the unknown.

To my mind the two Americas (both, I am sure, simplified cliches only vaguely resembling reality, but important, like all cliches, because people tend to behave according to an accepted pattern) were symbolized in the automobile models. In the twenties it was the ungainly, puritanical, ugly, but cheap Ford, whose color, design, and structure were determined purely by function and price. Now the cars were baroque, decadent, made for psychological and moral reassurance rather than for transportation; expensive, often impractical, and too complicated for one man with pliers and a wrench to fix. The Ford had been a brave, stern, rebel automobile, which despised frivolous hypocrisies and did not give a damn for appearance. The keynote of the modern models, it seemed to me, was fear, fear of not being conspicuous, fear of poverty, insecurity, and mediocrity. These were no longer machines made for transportation of men, but anthropological specimens, like totem poles. Had fearlessness disappeared from the soul of the younger Americans, that fearlessness that I had envied and admired? (To be sure, the older Americans' fearlessness was perhaps partly due to their ignorance of the risks they were running as a nation and as individuals, but it was also grounded in their upbringing, traditions, moral outlook, and national history.)

Since the new Americans had not sprung from the ground from sown dragons' teeth, they and their ideas must have been there all the time, in the twenties. I never saw them. As I said before, I had been misled by both the foreigners' preconceived notions of America and the Americans' own description of their country. This, I consider, is very important. Many of the world's recent catastrophes have been due to these misconceptions. Perhaps some of the world's future troubles will be caused by similar distortions.

My personal experience is insignificant. Nobody paid any attention to my American point of view in Italy, in the early thirties. My training helped me, of course. People tolerantly put up with

78

it, colleagues teased me, and superiors benevolently overlooked it. People thought I was insolent and too sure of myself, but felt that I would forget my prejudices in time. While American friends considered me a thoroughbred Italian, Italians considered me for many years almost a foreigner, "l'Americano." I was one of very few Italians educated in the United States, a rarity.

But there are countries where "American returned students" and the graduates of local American institutions have formed a strong and decisive minority, even a fateful one. In China, for instance, at the time of the Chiang Kai-shek regime, I met many of them, or their counterparts who had studied in Western Europe. Like their predecessors under Sun Yat-sen, they wielded great power and tried hard to reshape their country in the image of their ill understood ideals. They filled Shanghai and other cities with American skyscrapers, hotels, and apartment houses, filled their houses with ugly Western furniture and their minds with undigested slogans and wisdom tablets of all kinds. They believed in science, they were always swallowing pills, killing germs, and taking cures. They thought the new ideas they had learned, the modern scientific ideas, would sweep the fog of the past away from their country and renovate it from its very foundations.

The Chinese were, of course, extreme illustrations of this distorted point of view. I merely use them for didactic purposes, and because their mistakes helped to provoke one of the greatest tragedies in history, the disappearance of Chinese civilization in the totalitarian concentration camp, with its blaring of loudspeakers and its barking of policemen's orders. The Chinese built a tragic and impotent imitation of America, pathetically thinking that the shell would somehow fill itself with the spirit that animated it in the United States. Now we know it is easy to destroy an old culture but almost impossible to transplant an alien one. In the vacuum left by the ruins of the ancient structures there is room only for totalitarian dictatorships.

The Soviet Union is now making enormous and successful efforts to catch up with American industrial, technical, and scientific progress. Since the early twenties the Russians have admired and imitated the United States and dreamed of reconstructing their own country as a Marxist America. They too have accepted only the

79

materialistic final results of their model, the industrial power, the financial concentrations, the material wealth, and ignored the real sources of American strength. This tragic and bloody travesty of the United States is now threatening our civilized life and the very survival of humanity in this world.

The mistake is not in trying to apply *real* American ideas to foreign scenes, but in applying what foreigners, and many Americans, regard as the American ideas. The greatness of America is not due to the superficial formulas taught in the universities and printed in most magazines, which returned students try to teach their countrymen. All formulas are misleading. The empirical approach (get all the facts, pay the experts, and you get an answer to any question) is not infallible. Technique does not produce works of art. Science does not have all the answers. These are tools and not recipes. It takes men educated in the American tradition to use these tools, and even they sometimes make mistakes.

Take Hollywood movies, for instance. Their past greatness and universality was not due to what producers and directors thought. They were fables of childlike, Homeric quality, which told all men elementary tales as simple as those the mediaeval storytellers had spun for centuries. They were the legends of modern man, in which women were beautiful and pure, virtue was rewarded in the end, life was wonderful, and hope was never disappointed—legends for long winter nights. Once the magic vanished, once the movie makers were no longer naïve but, conscious of their limitations, became ambitious, the American movies went into a decline. Books by the thousands and innumerable college courses taught young men how to make a movie, and went into intricate details of every phase of the craft, how to write scripts, how to direct, photograph, act, cut, and add music. In reality, the books could teach little that was worthwhile and created a lot of misfits. They could only be diligent guides to yesterday's experiences, the codification of yesterday's genius and inventiveness. Just as staff officers always know how to fight the last war, readers of "how to" books and students of specialized college courses, in the end, can only make a movie of ten years ago and cannot, as a rule, make the good movie of today. When they do, it is only because they bring to their work something beyond the simple recipes they have learned, something that is inside of them, like talent, tradition, candor, faith, or ingenuity.

Intelligent Americans know these things. Foreigners in the United States rarely do. No great American playwright writes according to formula. No successful Wall Street speculator buys and sells according to "expert advice." No decision of peace and war is taken on the basis of the opinion of technicians. When Harry Truman gave the order to drop the atom bombs, or to resist on the 38th parallel with no weapons and no troops, he questioned his soul, his conscience, his American moral tradition, and not the opinion of experts alone. The secret of America is the American moral heritage. This, of course, is an obvious fact, not by any means an original discovery of mine. But it took me years to understand it, and my studying and working in the United States during the twenties did not help me greatly. The time, perhaps, was not propitious.

It is not a mistake (let me make it very clear) for foreigners to go to America to learn advanced techniques, production processes, and scientific progress. It is not a mistake for them to study and adopt some of the best features of American society, a modern democratic, progressive society in which men find work, shelter, satisfactions, security, and prosperity. Far from being a mistake, this process of transfusion of knowledge and experiences from a wealthier and more advanced country to others, less fortunate, is necessary and fruitful. There should be more foreign students in the United States, and there should be more American students abroad. The only mistake is to attribute to American "know how" a magical quality it does not have. "Know how" does not solve man's problems. It is a tool that can be used well or badly. It can be used as it was by the returned students in China, or by Communist founders of industrial organizations in the Soviet Union. On the other hand, it can also be used, as it is now in many places in the world, within the local spiritual framework, to increase production, to defeat disease, to give happiness to millions.

One thing must be made clear to foreigners who think about the United States: it has developed some new and useful techniques, points of view, capacities, which can be imitated but must not be worshiped; they are not panaceas. There are not many shortcuts, and all men and all nations must work their own solitary way. American democracy is not just a way of running a country in the least unsatisfactory manner. What animates the American scene and makes American miracles possible is the American spirit, the inheritance of centuries of religious faith and culture, with deep and ancient roots. When I finally learned these things—it took me several years and several trips back to the United States—my old American experiences and ideas became useful and meaningful.

from Switzerland

JACQUES FREYMOND

The author: born in Switzerland (Lausanne), 1911; studied at universities of Lausanne, Munich, and the Sorbonne. Since 1955 Dr. Freymond has been Director of the Graduate Institute of International Studies at Geneva, where he is also Professor of History. Earlier he taught modern and diplomatic history at the University of Lausanne, and during 1946-1955 he was, in addition, diplomatic chronicler for the *Gazette de Lausanne*. His first trip to the United States, lasting about a year, was in 1949-1950, as a Rockefeller fellow. At that time he spent five months at Yale, partly as a guest of its colleges and partly living in a private home; made an extended tour of the country by car, with stopovers in the Midwest and Far West; and had four months in and about New York City. He returned to this country in 1955, for two months in New York and Washington, with short trips to New England and the West.

I

WHAT forms the visitor's picture of America? What combination of "pre-fab" ideas, personal interests, individual memories? And what relation has this picture to the country as it is?

The first impression is that of an international America, no more American than its European equivalent: America of the big hotels, of Pullmans, of tourist agencies, of luxury, comfort, abundance, expert organization, but of mediocre food and very high prices. Then, alongside, is America the symbol of the up-to-date twentieth century, of the brave new world, commonplace because so much described: the airfield with its swarm of planes, the amazing perspective of skyscrapers, the parkways coiling and recoiling with their double and triple lines of cars running nose to tail.

Behind this display of conventional ideas, so satisfying for lovers of stereotypes, file one after the other the projections of individual travelers according to their interests or their prejudices. So many travelers, so many Americas. The America seen by the bankers, the businessmen, the industrialists: realm of free enterprise, pressed on by competition and forever seeking new procedures for produc-

83

tion and distribution. The America seen by the doctors, rationalizing to the utmost limit the fight against disease. The America of the universities, a world in itself and sufficient unto itself, become a hierarchy of power by reason of the demands of an intellectual elite. The America seen by the lecturers, left with scarcely time for thought by organized tours that fill the mind with fleeting pictures of railway stations, hotels, lecture halls, nameless listeners, receptions, interviewers courteous or too persistent; no free moment for any original summing up. The America seen by the novelists, interrogating their colleagues and scanning the world through their over-critical eyes. The America of the trade unionists, representing a redoubtable state within a state, its leaders engaged in an everlasting struggle on two fronts to retain the obedience of their vassals and to wring a still larger portion of profits from the employers. The America seen by the Marxists, full of contradictions, with only one exit—or seen by the political scientists, trying to reconstitute, behind the processions and the colorful electoral campaigns, the more subtle struggle of the pressure groups.

And to each of these Americas corresponds a picture with some memory attached, memories of operating rooms, laboratories, cyclotrons, of library stacks wherein to lose oneself, of the quiet charm of some shady campus, of gigantic factories, Wall Street at the end of the morning, the rush hour in the subway, the dull tranquillity of evenings in small provincial towns. Houses, districts, neighborhoods, all seeming alike yet all presenting their social distinctions: East Side, West Side; suburbs of inexpensive houses, gardens of less than one acre, the more affluent quarters with grounds of two acres, ten acres, thirty acres or more on Long Island, in Tuxedo Park, in Fairfield County. But also the Bronx, Harlem, and the Puerto Rican slums. The America of wealth and luxury, the America of the middle and lower-middle class, the America of poverty and racial strife.

But what of the America of the Americans? For such a one does exist, embracing all these partial conceptions, comprehending and surpassing them. This America of everyday life is simple and accessible, though not discerned from Europe. It is a modern land where technical ingenuity is apparent at every point, in the equipment of a kitchen as well as of a car, but at the same time a land of gardens, of flowers, of home activities, where a man, away from

84

his office or his work-place, enjoys tinkering at his bench, making a piece of furniture, repainting his house, repairing a fence, or mowing his lawn. A land of luxury but also of simple pleasures. There is an America that strolls in the parks in its suburban Sunday clothes, or cavorts on the beaches, and plays baseball everywhere, in the college squares, in the smallest of fields, even in the streets. It is a land of skyscrapers and of towns far too symmetrical, but a land also of timber forests and willow-bordered lakes; a land of parkways but also of lanes winding through a peaceful countryside. And there, close to some big city, a house stands alone in the twilight, surrounded by its farm. The walls of its library are lined with books bearing familiar titles. Two children with tousled hair are busy at their homework, pencils between lips. Horses just brought into the yard are seen through the window.

This America of the Americans is as much the land of the countryman as of the town-dweller, paradoxical as that may seem. It has remained close to nature while struggling unceasingly with it. The towns, even the biggest, are in fact—the airplane shows it well—nothing more than small islands, lost in an immense continent where fields, prairies, and forests predominate. This contest with nature, so difficult to win, offers the only explanation for a manner of life and living that excites so much astonishment when it is looked at from outside or transplanted to another continent. The sharp contrasts of a harsh climate, the extreme heat and cold, in some regions the constant dampness, explain the measures taken for protection against them: the search for comfort, the ever-present refrigerators, the increasingly pervasive air-conditioning. In the same way mechanization arises out of the unceasing effort to conquer distance and thus permit man to dominate a world that is not of his stature.

This omnipresence of nature at its most powerful, generous and terrible at the same time, is felt progressively strongly as one goes ever farther toward the West. For the European the West is a discovery in itself. Without direct contact with it, no understanding of America is possible. In the East, in spite of the Atlantic, the Old World seems to live again as a Greater Europe, attached to its dethroned homeland by too many ties, both new and old, for the rupture ever to be complete—attached too by a community of interests that would reduce the War of Independence to the level of an unavoidable family quarrel. Only by himself going toward the West can the European, wherever he may come from, measure the limits of his influence and realize the mistake, so frequently made, of regarding America as a prolongation of the Old World and assuming the right to judge it by exclusively European criteria.

The most ordinary terms have different shades of meaning on the two sides of the Atlantic. Take the word democracy. For the Swiss it means the priority of communal rights, embodied in the state, over those of the individual. It would perhaps be a surprise for them to learn that to an American the same word conveys an affirmation of the rights of the individual as against the state. And how many misunderstandings have arisen during the last ten years, in Switzerland as well as in other parts of Europe, from references to American capitalism? Most Europeans knew nothing of the evolution that took place in the United States after the Wall Street crash in 1929, palpably apparent though it was, or of the changes brought about in method as well as in the whole economic structure. Here too, only by direct contact, which places the capitalist myth in its economic and social setting, can the true facts be appreciated.

It is not surprising that the European view of the present situation in the United States does not tally with the facts. In Europe, or at least in Western Europe, society evolves so imperceptibly, with such strong resistance to every change, that it would appear to be crystallized were it not for the havoc wrought from time to time by revolution and war. Switzerland has not experienced any serious revolutionary crisis for more than a century; it has remained outside the great European and world conflicts since the early 1800's. Although the enterprising spirit of individuals has imprinted a remarkably dynamic character on the country in the realms of science and technology, the weight of tradition and custom is still greater. American society, on the contrary, is continually evolving. It has not ceased changing for the last century and a half, and it continues on its course, interpreting every slackening of speed as the beginning of atrophy and a premonitory sign of decline.

This need for change, this desire for new experience, is very much in evidence. It is manifest in all branches of art as well as in science and economics. For instance, before my first visit to the United States, about ten years ago, I had no idea of the place that orchestral, choral, and chamber music takes in American life, or of the evolution of musical taste. This transformation, which came about in the period between the two world wars and has gathered speed during the last ten years, is explained not only by European influence and the improved means of diffusion and reproduction. Its explanation lies also in the spirit of curiosity and the susceptiveness of people who seek unceasingly to extend their knowledge, and who know how to devote their time and strength to doing so—as is evident in the systematic musical education provided in schools and colleges throughout the country for many years past.

Another example is the striking contrast between European and American universities. In Switzerland, as in most other countries of Western Europe, universities have the appearance of being guardians of century-old traditions. They go forward at their own rhythm along their chosen path, watchful for any intrusion that might disturb their intellectual life or deflect them from the line of scientific research. Thus they can sometimes appear bereft of the power of movement, and therefore incapable of responding to the needs of the community. Universities in America, on the contrary, give the impression of undergoing constant change. For foreigners the record of their repeated experiments is in the highest degree instructive. The audacity is at times almost disconcerting. It is not without a shade of anxiety that one learns that some great university has altered its study program from top to bottom and effected a kind of minor revolution. Europeans wonder if it is really necessary. But at the very moment when I was tempted, in observing spectacular experiments, to criticize some concession to an intellectual fashion or some manifestation of instability, I would find in the dynamism itself a proof of the vitality of leaders who do not forget that a sense of anticipation and a readiness to take risks are necessary for leadership. The universities of Europe could benefit from this continual search for new procedures.

In short, nothing can replace seeing with one's own eyes. In contact with the United States and the American people the picture I had when I started out became more varied and was even deeply transformed. One cannot remain insensible to the attraction that the country itself exerts. Space—which for the Swiss has a tonic effect—and movement combine to open up perspectives and to induce a sense of adventure. And one who lives an everyday life with Americans at home cannot help but find his point of view changing. Attitudes and habits that can be disconcerting in single individuals away from their own country are easily understood. Intimacy grows, friendships are formed. The kindness of the Americans, their natural gift for hospitality, leads to lasting ties. Henceforth it is from the inside and through the eyes of the Americans themselves that one will look at them. Criticism may not be less severe because of this, but it will be directed toward America as it is, with its strength and its weaknesses, and not toward that caricature of America that has been the target of so many attacks from parts of Europe for more than ten years past.

II

What is the European, and particularly the Swiss, picture of America—that picture that is so in need of deeper knowledge? More specifically, what enters into its formation?

Certainly one factor that must not be overlooked is the slight emphasis given America in educational institutions. In Switzerland, as in most Western European countries, the teaching of literature and history is centered on Europe itself, on ancient Greece, Rome, the civilization of the Middle Ages and of modern Europe. Through secondary school the history of the United States is touched on only indirectly, as it has affected that of Europe, with quick surveys of major events, geography, resources. At the university a few courses deal with America: from time to time one on American literature; occasionally a more intensive study of the history of the American people; historians and economists give more attention to the United States as they enter into the twentieth century. But on the whole there is very little systematic study of either the United States or its people.

Thus the picture is fragmentary from the beginning, and it is not greatly filled out by the fleeting impressions gathered casually from reading. Criticism of American civilization, frequently enough expressed, is often based on the books of American novelists. Not so very long ago Babbitt stood for the whole of America. Today it is from the novels of Faulkner—or perhaps the plays of Tennessee Williams—that the reading public tends to build its picture of American life.

And also of course from contacts with Americans, irregular and complicated by language difficulties. Exchanges between intellectuals, which have become more frequent of late years, are still too rare, limited to members of a somewhat restricted group. To be sure, there are many students from the other side of the Atlantic in Swiss universities, but their presence there does not necessarily imply contact with Swiss students or with the people of Switzerland—whether because of the difficulties of language, the instinctive tendency to remain in national groups, or the American habit of holding to a certain way of American life even when abroad. This way of life, taken out of its natural setting, causes surprise, amusement, or irritation. And then there are the tourists who pass through Switzerland every year. Do the Swiss people, and others, build up a truer picture of the United States because of the great number of individuals that they thus meet? An American tourist is not more representative of his country than is any Swiss who travels abroad. He may be wholly untypical of even his own section of the many-sided American society and nevertheless he contributes his share to the picture formed of his country.

To these impressions derived from personal contacts, others of quite a different kind may be added. Certain aspects of American advertising conflict with established Swiss custom and are considered shocking. Differences of methods in trade or business have sometimes been so acute as to cause disagreement, though it is probably in the business world that the interpenetration of interests is most marked. And let us not forget that the great majority of Swiss people base their ideas of life in the United States very largely on movies, picture magazines, newspapers, and reporting of every sort and description. Everyone knows what they find there: an America of great wealth and luxurious cars; an America full of contentment and health; a capitalist and materialist America— everything necessary to strengthen the old prejudices. No one asks whether this corresponds to the real America, or realizes that a great many Americans themselves do not accept the picture of American life painted by Hollywood or by certain periodicals of wide circulation.

Furthermore, the view of American life and civilization is more or less explicitly connected with the view of American international policies. And on this subject Switzerland, despite her traditional neutrality, tends to share the general European, particularly the French, way of regarding the United States, an opinion that is primarily critical. The combining of political and cultural strictures has served to fix even more firmly the distorted picture of the United States. Even those who could have, and should have, evinced enough curiosity to inquire into American intellectual and artistic developments have been held captive by a negative attitude toward United States policies abroad. The emotional atmosphere generated by political strains and crises is scarcely favorable to intellectual exchange.

In view of all these considerations it is not surprising that the view of America held by an average Swiss or other European is quite different from the life that Americans actually lead in their own homes. The same thing happens in regard to other countries as well: the mania for simplification, whether for its own sake or for argument or to facilitate action, leads to caricatures also of Germany, Italy, France, England. But with neighboring countries continual exchange gives each the possibility of correcting an untrue picture and making its outlines more exact. This possibility does not exist for countries that are farther away. Stereotyped views are long-lived and persistent, and distance is all in their favor.

It is quite possible that the inaccurate picture of the United States held by the Swiss, in common with so many other peoples, would be more easily rectified if they did not, in turn, feel themselves victims of a certain amount of distortion. When misunderstood, collectivities react very much the same as individuals. Just as the inability of a great many Swiss and other Europeans to understand the United States can hurt the feelings of Americans, so can the sense of being misunderstood and ignored give rise to resentment in Switzerland. For example, how is it possible to confuse Switzerland with Sweden? Why should every Swiss be looked upon as a watch-maker or a yodeling shepherd? Has this country nothing more to show than Lucerne, Interlaken, the Jungfrau or the Matterhorn? Has it not its technical colleges and universities, its scientists, writers, musicians, painters? The ignorance displayed about themselves leads the Swiss to believe, rightly or wrongly, that their already-formed opinion of America's lack of

90

culture is confirmed, and thus they find new reasons for holding on to their stereotyped views. They are encouraged in this also by occasional frictions between the two countries, occasioned for example by American attitudes toward the Swiss policy of neutrality, or by American restrictions on Swiss imports. Economic, political, and cultural relations are bound together more closely than one usually thinks. An economic crisis, which could have been easily settled, served not only to stiffen certain attitudes and assessments already formed, but also to weaken convictions among people who, better than others, could have corrected inaccurate conceptions.

It is said that Switzerland, of all European countries, is the most like the United States. Perhaps Americans who hold this view have found in Switzerland a prosperity and a comfortable way of living that closely resemble their own. Perhaps they have gone further and have found some resemblances in the political institutions, which indeed is not inexact; certainly it was on the American model that the Swiss based their legislative organization when they drew up the constitution for a federal state in 1848. Perhaps, again, American travelers who observe our political manners and customs and our practice of democracy find some analogies there, in the behavior of the citizens and their attitude toward the national community.

But this kind of comparison, however seductive, does not lead very far. The better way is to recognize the radical difference between the geographical and historical conditions under which the two countries and the two societies have grown up. On the one hand, a settled population occupying a small portion of European territory, its division into compartments favoring the maintenance of traditions and leading to a certain social conservatism and to political prudence; on the other, the swift and boisterous occupation of a vast continent of apparently unlimited resources by a people constantly on the move. The one country conscious of the limitations imposed by a nature that is imperative and grasping; the other, on the contrary, having the feeling of space, which provides imagination with all that is needed for expansion. This contrast in dimensions emphasizes the fact that for the Americans frontiers are now formed by the sea and are therefore ever open, whereas Switzerland has for many centuries been shut in by Europe.

And this difference in scale is manifest, directly or indirectly, in the life of the two peoples, whether it be in the organization of work, in means of transport, in production, or in human relationships. Where bicycles serve the Swiss, cars are indispensable for the Americans. In the one country, limited possibilities of markets have contributed toward a maintenance of artisan traditions, of precision industries, and of high-quality manufactures, while, in the other, almost unlimited demand has necessitated mass production and standardized manufacture. The tendency of the one to division of labor is partly explained by the need to protect itself from a neighbor that is too close or a competitor that is too enterprising—for the space meted out to each is limited. But in the United States there is room for everyone, and there seems to be as little fear of proximity as of new experiments. With such vast perspectives and such apparently inexhaustible resources it is possible to start out on an enterprise without knowing what it will lead to. But a Swiss cannot enjoy this luxury. He has to know exactly where he is going, for his daily life, his neighbors, and the very restricted circle from which he must move out are all there to remind him how limited are his possibilities. He is afraid of letting his fundamental optimism as a man of action be seen too clearly, and at the height of his most striking prosperity he will still feel curious twinges of anxiety.

I have not as yet laid any stress on community of interests, for its basic elements are sufficiently obvious. Switzerland, notwithstanding her neutrality, belongs to the Western community of nations—a rather vague term, but the peculiar circumstances of this revolutionary twentieth century make it precise enough. She cherishes those values on which the Western world claims to found its existence, and serves the same cause that the United States has at heart. But ties of common interests need to be given the more attention as they are the more threatened by propaganda aimed unceasingly at exploiting every possible source of discord. We have seen how many obstacles there are, how frequently tension arises! What then is to be done, and how? We should be wrong to go too far in search of remedies that are at hand. There is already in existence a whole network of exchange, which has given proof of its value and could be enlarged to even greater scope.

In the first place, exchange of individuals. As I have said, nothing can replace this direct contact, which nearly always has positive results. Sharing the daily life of Americans gives rise to friendship, which cannot fail to be reciprocated by Americans who have the same experience in Switzerland. This exchange should take place between persons in all ranks of society, should not be exclusive in any way. Its results may carry farthest, however, when it occurs among members of universities and other intellectuals, particularly those who are concerned with teaching. Not only do students benefit from the teaching of a professor from overseas, but when he returns to his own country he can share something of the experiences through which he has passed.

Since exchange of individuals cannot be increased indefinitely, efforts should also be made to develop cultural relations and, in a more general sense, means of communication. Because of the difference in the scale of the countries, this problem is more difficult for the Swiss in the United States than for Americans in Switzerland, but its importance should not be underestimated. The slackening of the American program of information in Switzerland a few years ago had repercussions that were all the stronger because it coincided with the restrictions on the import of Swiss watches and with the McCarthy crisis. Perhaps our best chance lies in finding some modification of the way in which far too many newspapers supply information—an old problem indeed. Here it is not the instruments that are inadequate, but the use we make of them, concentrating our intellectual curiosity on the casual rather than on the more permanent.

However difficult it may be to overcome prejudices, especially collective ones, some progress is evident. Contacts of various kinds have helped to allay some of the Swiss distrust and to convert an America wrapped in the mists of fantasy into something more human and more accessible. Quite recently, for example, an important Swiss firm, of an international character, obtained the patronage of one of our most traditionally minded universities for a training institute staffed entirely by Americans—an interchange that will be profitable to both sides. Paradoxical as it may seem, it is toward the Harvard Business School that one looks for help in a country that prides itself on a certain amount of experience in matters of education and commercial knowledge. It is by no means certain that such a venture would have been possible a few years ago without running into the obstacles created by an atmosphere of suspicion. That it is possible today may be looked upon as a promise for the future.

Throughout this discussion I have not been sparing in my reservations or criticisms on both sides. Perhaps it will be thought that I have insisted too much on the influence of prejudices, and on our tendency to accept without question our untrue pictures of others. But is there not abundant proof of the seriousness of political consequences arising from misunderstandings, most often the fruit of ignorance? Communist propaganda has often been endowed with greater power than it actually possesses. Its influence would be singularly restricted if it were unable to exploit those misunderstandings which are sustained by the stereotyped views of which I have written. Men, as we know, act on the basis of the images in their minds of the situations to which they address themselves, and for their actions to have some validity, their images should correspond to the reality. International cooperation depends on our capacity to attain this correspondence.

from Germany

PETER von ZAHN

The author: born in Germany (Chemnitz), 1913; studied at universities of Vienna, Jena, Berlin, and Freiburg i.B. Peter von Zahn, who received his doctoral degree in mediaeval and modern history (1939), served during World War II with the German Signal Corps and later as a war correspondent on the Russian fronts. After the war he helped develop the programs of the largest German radio network, coedited one of the first monthly magazines in postwar Germany, and as a roving reporter covered the reconstruction of the Ruhr and the beginning of the European Steel and Coal Community. Since 1951 he has broadcast from the United States several times a week, giving listeners in West and East Germany a running commentary on daily life and political developments in this country. He has also produced a series of half-hour documentary films for the German TV network, showing the non-sensational aspects of life in the Americas, and has written two books about the United States. With his wife, five daughters, and four dogs he lives in a farmhouse in Virginia, near Washington, D.C., and has traveled in many sections of this country.

I

AMERICA played a very small role in the education of those who grew up in Germany between 1910 and 1930. We were taught almost nothing about its history, and nothing at all about the role it was beginning to assume with World War I. Of course, information reached our minds through other media than the schools, but it was highly filtered. There were many moving pictures, and Upton Sinclair, Sinclair Lewis, Ernest Hemingway; also a great many photographs and magazine and newspaper articles, showing us the new skyscrapers of New York, the floods of the Mississippi, the lynching of a Negro, automobile races and gangster fights, the Oakies in battered Fords, again and again the canyons of Wall Street.

That stockbrokers in America usually jumped from their windows was impressed on our memory. We knew that there was immense wealth and the most appalling poverty, but about the middle class we knew only through Babbitt. We learned little about American domestic politics and a lot about the double standard of life during Prohibition; little about art collections and a lot about the ostentatious castles that millionaires had taken over from Europe, stone by stone; nothing about the thinking of Harvard and Princeton, but in great detail about Jack Dempsey and Gene Tunney. And then there was jazz, bringing something of the rhythm of America's life unadulterated into our bourgeois rooms. A composite picture of the American as seen by the contemporary German in his most receptive years would contain Lindbergh's boyish charm, the square chin and gray hair of a businessman (Rotary pin, two-tone low shoes, straw hat), Charlie Chaplin's little stick, Tilden's tall figure, the puffed-up cheeks of a Negro playing the saxophone.

In most German eyes America was a country strangely composed of prejudice, dream, and reality, a country where you could make your fortune, but a material fortune only. It was the country of mass production, skyscrapers, and a fast buck. It was boundless, but completely uniform in its thinking and acting. It was as simple as the questions asked by American tourists, as violent as the exploits of Al Capone and Dillinger, as generous as the presents from the emigrated uncle, as exciting as jazz, and as funny as Buster Keaton, but actually no more real than a Hollywood film. It was a collection of unrelated oddities.

What was completely missing in this picture was the message that the United States was undergoing a profound transformation from a highly capitalistic country to a welfare state. Of Roosevelt's New Deal the Germans became aware only after his death; and that America had undergone a bloodless revolution while everything in Europe went topsy-turvy was learned by most Germans—if they learned it at all—only after 1945.

Only rarely in peacetime do peoples come to know each other intimately. It is through war that their good and bad qualities are brought out clearly—frequently in extreme form. The Second World War and the ensuing occupation period put Germans and Americans into deep and far-reaching contact, and this supplied each nation with a wealth of concrete notions about the other.

As far as the Germans were concerned, they first of all came to know the strength and power inherent in the United States, of which, up to that time, they had had but a hazy idea: the air fleets that cruised in full daylight over the German cities; the number of vehicles that emerged from the bellies of landing craft; the well-equipped, well-fed, and well-rested divisions that relieved each other so frequently; and the extravagant amount of explosives that broke up any resistance before the GI climbed out of his foxhole. All this made a deep impression on a people that was proud of its technical skill and for many years had listened to the praise of a policy of strength.

This impression was stamped into each German Fräulein who compared the extravagance of an American PX with her own meager ration. The German, educated on notions of thrift, wondered why the officers of the Occupation Army left the lights burning in their private homes, left doors and windows open even in winter, and the radio going night and day, as if heat and electricity cost nothing. He saw the big upholstered cars glide at moderate speed over German potholes while consuming enormous amounts of gasoline. All this allowed of no other conclusion but that the Americans had reached a standard of living at which material well-being had become a matter of course and its costs unimportant.

The generosity practiced by the Americans in Germany contributed to the picture. Most soldiers seemed to forget in no time that they had just faced the Germans in a war. The ban on fraternization was like a sieve whose increasing permeability was the aim of diligent work, especially on the part of the German distaff. Private and official relief work, CARE packages, and finally the Marshall Plan, all these together shaped in the minds of the Germans an image of the American as a being from another world where sincere cordiality reigned and envy and pettiness were unknown.

Even the political measures of the occupation period, the schematic procedures of denazification, the baffling administration of justice at Nuremberg, did not leave the impression of pettiness. On the contrary, they strengthened the German in his conviction that the American's conceptions about right and wrong were simple, sometimes primitive; that he did not know political compromise, the nuance, the shades; but that he attempted, with the greatest determination and complete disregard of precedents, to make his views prevail. This misjudgment is excusable. By their behavior in Germany the Americans did not indicate that in their

97

homeland political compromise had been raised to the dignity of an art, and precedent to the rank of an idol—even though, to be sure, they are prone to crass simplifications, to extreme and fast measures, prefer action to lengthy consideration, and are quick at judging and punishing.

Not without admiration the German recognized in the American an idealistic vein, a missionary zeal, hoping to eradicate the evil in this world. And where this energy appeared comical the German recognized—without always admitting it—a certain kinship of souls. The American program of reeducation was basically an attempt to graft the ideals of a Midwestern town on German conditions. German local commandants in the Ukraine had failed in similar experiments. But the American missionaries of a Jeffersonian and Jacksonian democracy left behind a significant legacy: with their sermons on free competition they spurred strong German instincts; they confirmed the Germans in their veneration of achievement and efficiency; they uncovered a propensity, lying dormant in Germany, to challenge governmental authority; and thus they helped to reestablish organs of public opinion that defended freely and aggressively what they considered to be the rights of the people.

While prewar contacts with the American way of thinking were restricted to a small circle, those who survived the war were now exposed to a broad and mighty Mississippi of American self-testimonials. Tennessee Williams, Thornton Wilder, Eugene O'Neill conquered the German stage. Bookshops were suddenly full of novels in which no heed was paid to literary rules. Hollywood exported to Germany what for ten years had been detained at our borders. Since most of these testimonials prefer extreme and pointed situations, there sprang up a tendency to equate America with extreme situations. There is no doubt that the stream of German visitors and exchange students that has flowed to America, on invitation by the United States, has acted as a corrective; presumably the exchange of visitors—competent visitors, if possible—is still the best way to obtain a clear insight into one another's circumstances, especially if the guest is offered the opportunity to look around for himself. But one has to realize that few Germans come to the New World as entirely unprejudiced observers. Their experiences with Americans are of a special kind; their view of the United States, shaped in distant Bavaria or Hesse, has already been imprinted so strongly that it is not easily coated by reality. The New World and its inhabitants contribute to a certain confusion which no visitor escapes.

II

If my stay in the United States has taught me more than merely a superficial knowledge of the Civil War generals and the jargon of teenagers, it is a distrust of the simplified patterns in which Americans are seen by others and also by themselves. There is a widespread attempt to reduce America to simple formulas—as if the conflux of so many peoples and races, traditions and civilizations, were of little importance when compared with the formative force of a new beginning. It is true that the surface is smooth and simple. But for that very reason it is deceptive: it frequently conceals more than it reveals; almost every phenomenon has a false bottom. American authors are the best witnesses to the fact that the American carries with him many secret drawers.

There is nothing strange about this. A French expert on Germany has said that if you think you can see the Teuton in the German he will suddenly turn out to be a Latin, and if you react accordingly he reveals himself as a Slav. Something similar could be said of the American—but with him everything is a little more complex.

Whatever your preconceived ideas may be when you arrive in America for a visit, by the time you leave they will all be nicely confirmed. When I set out on my first trip there, I was highly skeptical about the descriptions of the country as an ultra-modern, streamlined machine. Promptly I discovered a cozy America: a country of gaily colored frame houses, sleepy towns, farms à la Grandma Moses, and young couples who, on a Saturday, build a fireplace behind the house for the barbecue. This has developed into a fixation, and even today, after many arrivals and departures, I don't succeed entirely in freeing my ideas about America from the cover pictures on the *Saturday Evening Post*.

It is confusing to think that America can confirm hundreds of the most contradictory preconceived ideas without bursting into a thousand pieces. Maybe it is true, as has been said, that America is as large as life: in it everything can be found, if only we search long enough. Another reason may be that the "New World"— as it likes to call itself—being an experiment of mankind, calls more vigorously for judgments, and thus of course also for misjudgments, more vigorously in any event than, say, Chile or Norway. Whoever returns from America is asked whether things over there are indeed what American magazines or Soviet Russian broadcasts claim they are. These questions are asked of people who, far from being sociological analysts, have simply wanted to conclude a little steel deal, but they require a well-reasoned reply.

Furthermore, Americans themselves continually challenge the visitor to comment on America. No sooner has he put his foot on the ground than he is assaulted with the question, "How do you like our country?" And my compatriots, with the thoroughness that distinguishes them, will in general expound to the amazed questioner the judgments they have formed—judgments that are strengthened and hardened by the very fact that they are forced into expression. One is inclined to call on all Americans: if you wish to help create calm judgments and abolish prejudiced ideas about your country, for God's sake don't ask everybody how he likes it. But this may be expecting too much. The question is an echo from the past, even though it has long since been made obsolete by history. It echoes the uneasy hope of hearing the visitor from the older and more distinguished continent, Europe, confirm to the children of the poor immigrants that they have made something impressive out of the New World. We need only turn the tables in order to understand the nature of the question. Could we for instance imagine a Parisian asking a man from Kansas City, "And how do you like France?" Rather, he would ask, "How do you like Kansas City?"

I am mentioning these things here merely as a kind of warning— a warning not to accept the following statements without a grain of salt. Physicists claim that certain physical experiments are slightly deflected from their genuine course by the very fact of being observed; similarly, there is the suggestive power that emanates from the patient to the physician observing him. America, in this sense, is a huge guinea pig, and precise descriptions of its nature cannot easily be achieved.

100

Peter von Zahn

III

Above all, the United States has a double face. Now one of them is turned toward us, and now the other—without either the Americans themselves or their visitors always being aware of that peculiarity. Diametrically opposite traditions or tendencies exist together, and somehow the fabric is not torn apart. As Will Rogers remarked about the drinking habits of his countrymen in Oklahoma, "They'll vote 'dry' as long as they can still reel to the polling station."

Consider, for example, the question of violence. Certainly it is not easy to find a common denominator for the American attitude toward this. Since the day that John Foster Dulles attended the Hague Peace Conference as the secretary of the American delegation, there has been hardly another country that has put forth so many fruitful ideas on how to outlaw violence in international relations. The League of Nations and the Kellogg Pact and the United Nations and the Organization of American States are as many attempts of the American spirit to catch violence in a network of agreements and treaties and render it harmless. At the same time, however, a mild tolerance of the system of violence prevails in various aspects of American domestic life.

In the big cities gangsters are able to hold meetings at which questions of professional training are discussed, probably in much the same way as at the Annual Convention of Retail Clerks in Chicago; the police look the other way. With a grin the newspaper reader takes note of the fact that obvious criminals before investigating committees of Congress are treated with a kind of ironic reverence. And on another level there is the widespread glorification of self-help in situations where legal means fail to produce results. A native American is likely to see no conflict between his efforts to educate his children to become citizens of a country governed by law and his tolerance when such important educational means as television and moving pictures praise the shortcut procedure of self-help as practiced in "Westerns." To be sure, the good and the evil, represented so impressively, eventually get their fitting rewards—but these rewards can be distributed only through the impatience of the masked hero who does not wait for the normal procedure of civilian life to take its course.

Thus one's conclusions on the American's attitude toward violence will be diametrically opposite, depending on the point of observation. He who watches the steadfast fight of Negro organizations in the courts of the United States, and contemplates the majesty of law, as it progresses slowly and with resounding paces of reason, to open parks, busses, restaurants, and schools to the colored man in the Southern states, sees a system that favors peaceful change and a society capable of adjustment and flexibility. On the other hand, he who looks at the far-reaching system of force that prevents the Negro from exercising his rights, and considers the Ku Klux Klan parades and meetings of White Citizens' Councils, sees a form of society based on violence and believing in the use of violence for the defense of its existence.

In America the tradition of self-help with violence is almost as old and hallowed as that of the Saturday evening brawl in an Upper Bavarian inn. Its development is commonly explained by the spaciousness of the country, the thin distribution of legal authorities as the frontier moved westward, the special conditions of frontier living. There is still, however, the unexplained fact that a tradition of violence can be maintained in a country whose political leadership is drawn mainly from the legal profession.

The situation in the South is especially confusing, because there the muscles and tendons of violence have been covered by the ruling circles with the flesh of legalistic justification. An opponent of these circles may be tempted to say that the passionate study of constitutional law in the Southern states is the tribute paid virtue by vice, but this does not sufficiently explain the peculiar attitude of Southern society. Where else in the world is there a society that for over a hundred years has resisted with all means, including violence, giving up forms and privileges that constantly require thinking along double standards and measuring with double yardsticks?

It is difficult for the outsider to do justice to this double face that America shows her observer. In Germany it is frequently assumed that the future relationship of the white and the colored worlds depends above all on how the leading power of the West, the United States, finds a solution to its race problem: interest in events such as Little Rock and the bus strike in Montgomery could hardly be keener in Seattle than in Düsseldorf. But those who want to form a judgment about the processes involved in this solution can hardly do more than scratch the surface. They are confronted now with one, now with the other, face of American evolution, and cannot put them into meaningful relationship. And this confusion promotes a onesided selection of facts that confirm a preconceived opinion.

There are other traditions in America that coexist unmixed although one would expect them to be mutually exclusive. Thus Puritan tradition fights valiantly against all the symptoms that show up where adventurers and fortune-hunters assemble to get rich quick. But it does not get the upper hand, even where success and wealth are consolidated: as if by agreement, Puritan instincts keep open a loop-hole—Las Vegas or Miami. If the first Americans one meets are modest, educated, and polite specimens, a credit to their New England Alma Mater, and never miss a parent-teacher meeting, it is all the more surprising to encounter so many people in the expanses of the country who do not fit at all into the picture of the Pilgrim Fathers. Of course they form a minority as compared with the broad layer of respectable middle-aged married couples who live in $14,000 homes between the church and the Elk Lodge. But there they are, giving the lie to the preconceived notion that Puritanism bears heavily on American society like a leaden veil. At times one is led to recognize in certain pronunciamentos of prominent Americans something of the spirit of self-complacency that is attributed to the successful Puritan: the world is divided into good and evil and the citizens of the New World are engaged in the struggle of Light against Darkness; proof that they are chosen are the material goods and achievements that the Lord has graciously heaped upon them. But nowhere is this attitude subjected to more caustic criticism than in America itself.

To an outside observer Americans are one way one moment and entirely different the next. Within the same person the most diverse traditions coexist. A man may condemn the colonialism and imperialism of the British, but accept as just and equitable the occupation of Haiti in the 1920's or of Okinawa in the 1950's. It is his deep conviction that Soviet Russian totalitarianism is bad. Trujillo's prisons, seen from the inside, look much the same as Stalin's, and Big Brother pictures on the wall resemble one another perfectly in their intentions, whether they appear in Spanish of-

103

fices or in Russian, but somehow Latin-grown dictatorships are considered excusable, the Communist variety not. Frequently the distinctive criterion is their position with regard to the Christian Church; their attitude toward religion itself plays a minor role. Neutralism based on religion, as in Burma, is objectionable; neutralism motivated by politics, as during the early years of the United States, is cited with pride.

The visitor arrives in America ready to deduce from hundreds of conversations with businessmen and trade unionists that it is a country of free enterprise. Soon, however, he comes to know about a bewildering maze of government regulations; he hears entrepreneurs advocate in the same breath the free play of economic forces and vigorous protectionism for the distressed textile industry; he listens to other entrepreneurs railing against government subsidies at the same time that they are loading their goods on ships, sending their mail on airplanes, and doing their research in laboratories, all heavily subsidized by Uncle Sam. One meets many people, intelligent people, who predict a terrible end for the European welfare state and, without turning a hair, approve of federal appropriations for veterans which would make any European Minister of Public Welfare turn pale with envy.

To the observer from abroad the double faces shown by each of the major American parties appear completely incompatible. Proudly his acquaintances call themselves Democrats, but for opposite reasons: one because he thinks he belongs to a party of progress, another because he is determined to stay put on the same historical spot he occupied several years or decades ago. The same party unites what the European would call classical left-wing liberalism and classical ultra-reaction. If the observer looks for the unifying center of the Democratic Party, what does he find?—its opponent, the Republican Party. And this party, too, is split, in a different but hardly less conspicuous way.

The list of such contradictions could be continued at will. It could be compiled also, of course, for other countries—especially for Germany. But there it is rather the result of contradictions between theory and practice, with practice tolerating what theory condemns, whereas in America many instances of the "double face" represent two ideals vying with each other. Frequently the two are incompatible. For example, the ideal of preserving the purity of the white race exists alongside the color-blindness embodied in the Constitution. In no other country could these opposing principles coexist in such a manner in the twentieth century. Imagine a nation in one half of which the equality of its citizens before the law extends into the remotest corners of club charters, and in the other half of which the inequality of castes is established by law; within a short time such a nation would break up.

Not the United States. The categorical and radical utterances of which Americans are capable tend to make one forget that nowhere else in the world are contradictory ideals being reconciled by such wise and lasting compromises. The radicalism of the American is a radicalism of the tongue. It takes a long time for this to be understood by the observer of the American scene, and Americans themselves can give him but little assistance, since they have grown up with their contradictions and consider them the most natural thing in the world.

IV

A word about American conformity is now in order. The United States is frequently regarded as a country of tedious uniformity, and as frequently it is described as having great variety. Both views, of course, can be confirmed. Drugstores everywhere are alike; hotel rooms give the visitor no indication whether he is in New Jersey or Oregon; the business centers of the big cities are as alike as peas; the dishes in small-town restaurants everywhere could very well have been prepared by the same unimaginative cook. The apparel and war paint of young ladies in American colleges completely lack individuality; forms of greeting and polite phrases do not vary between Boston and Los Angeles; evening conversations in the recreation rooms of the $20,000 homes always touch on, and steer clear of, the same subjects; everywhere the same magazines are read; Book-of-the-Month Club selections are binding for almost all readers. Only the answer to the questions, "Scotch or Bourbon?" "Episcopalian or Baptist?" varies from region to region.

On the other hand, what a wealth of variety in a country that lets the Amish live their own way, driving with their horses and buggies through Pennsylvania and Ohio, and until recently looked in the other direction when fundamentalist Mormons indulged in a little polygamy. Is it indeed possible to maintain that America has flattened all differences when the wealthy residents of Fifth Avenue, with their roof gardens, charity bazaars, and Renoirs, are scarcely more than a block away from Puerto Rican immigrants who live eight to a room and, after many years in New York, still don't speak English? The clothes and makeup of the young ladies on college campuses may be very much alike at a given moment, but woe to him who thinks that the rather free social forms of American college life in the thirties would be acceptable to an American girl today—a girl whose ardent desire seems to be to "go steady" and get married soon. Tomorrow it may again be different.

What a distance between the seething and funny nationalism of Texas and the metropolitan indifference of New Yorkers, whose most turbulent manifestations of parochial patriotism concerned the Dodgers and Giants—and proved relatively mild when the two teams moved to California. How to explain the fierce jealousy between San Francisco and Los Angeles, or the rivalry between Dallas and Fort Worth, between St. Paul and Minneapolis—all of them cities that are equally young by European standards and have nevertheless been able to develop their own climates, which change from one mile to the next as fast as the weather at the Golden Gate? Between the rancher on his cow pony in Arizona and the sharecropper behind his mule in Georgia—what a difference. Between the philosophy of life of the feudal barons of the Southwest and a town meeting in Vermont—what a world of difference. Nothing holds them together but the same brand of cigarettes and a mutual faith in the mission of the United States—and even this faith is frayed in those who indulge in the works of nonconformists such as H. L. Mencken and E. B. White.

The German visitor who tries to harmonize these two American aspects—conformism and variety—cannot fail to be bewildered if he considers the phenomenon of McCarthy. In Germany interest in it was great, for several reasons. Whoever grudged the eminence of upstart America in world politics would point to the Senator's anti-intellectual witch-hunt with a feeling of self-justification; whoever had not forgotten the American attempts to reeducate Germany said his *tu quoque*; and whoever regarded the preservation of American democracy as a paramount necessity of our times was

106

genuinely alarmed by McCarthy's activity. Furthermore, there were of course quite a few who saw in McCarthy's warnings and in his success a belated confirmation of their own anti-Communist past, however pro-Hitlerite it may have been. All these observers from afar saw in McCarthy the reincarnation of the religious fanatic— a man who wanted to reestablish the community of the pure and the holy and, if necessary, to compel conformity of the individual by means of the inquisition. This was the only role that seemed to fit America.

Watching McCarthy in action, however, one felt almost disappointed to find a man who had absolutely nothing of a Savonarola. Shrugging his shoulders, the Grand Inquisitor made use of the material that offered itself to him: the fear of spies and conspiracies that obviously visits the American continent at regular intervals. He did not preach "mend your ways, change," but seemed to say "everything can become again what it used to be when nobody threatened us, if only we get rid of a number of scoundrels." The mood of the country met this extremely simple recipe halfway. Historical events and sudden revolutions—as for instance the replacement of American influence in China by Communist influence—were interpreted as the result of a fantastic conspiracy. If it was to be unmasked in all its ramifications, a close watch had to be kept on each one who was different, who stood out because of his nonconformist ideas, who stood out at all. But to be no different from your neighbor in the country club, the office, and the church community means to meet on the level of the lowest intellectual denominator—where there is nothing left to discuss. McCarthy, for one, regarded as superfluous the intellectual effort required to refute the Communist or liberal ideology. To him, that did not appear desirable at all: it was sufficient to follow the ceremonials, taboos, and rituals (at least in political meetings and before the press) that are considered to be the marks of patriotism.

All this had nothing to do with religious zeal. It did not exclude the most transparent kind of political intrigue. The man who made use of the prevailing suspicion of one against the other was not nearly disciplined enough to build up a disciplined following. While he was not averse to an occasional violation of the rules of the political game, he was not bent on reforming the Constitution and society. He was an eminently practical politician who

107

enjoyed the publicity that the times afforded him so abundantly.

In spite of his crusade against nonconformists, McCarthy certainly did not fit into the pattern of American uniformity. If a German had been given the task of selecting from the U.S. Senate the man whom American conformity would choose as its tool, his guess would probably have been one of ninety-five others rather than the stubborn, arrogant, and hardly engaging Senator from Wisconsin. Germans who followed the Army-McCarthy hearings on television were utterly confused by the human contrasts that the American scene is capable of producing: to listen to McCarthy, Welch, Jenkins, and Cohn arguing with one another was enough to dispel any suspicion that in the country of conformity the individual would be the loser.

As for any similarity between McCarthyism and National Socialism, it was confined to the recklessness with which those who thought differently were denounced. The other aspects of Hitlerite philosophy were lacking: neither should orders be given for the sake of giving orders nor was anybody encouraged to be more efficient, more vigorous, more brutal, or more obedient than those around him. A full acquaintance with the rise and fall of the Senator could allay the fears of anybody who was concerned about the accessibility of American democracy to dictators. Seldom has it happened that a would-be dictator was disposed of so elegantly. Indeed, it was absorbing to witness the self-cleansing of a democracy, and to find that public censure by his colleagues was sufficient to cut the political ground from under the Senator's feet. This was remotely reminiscent of ancient procedures: no criminal offenses had to be construed; it was the breach of moral standards, of public decorum, that caused the downfall of the ambitious man. He was not punished—as a methodical German public might have demanded he should be. Instead, people turned away from him.

This would not have been possible if two institutions of the New World had not functioned correctly. For one, the courts put up barriers against McCarthy over which he could not leap: the regulatory power of American legal thinking is little known to the European, especially the German. The other institution was the press, the media of public information. For the first time in modern history there was achieved in the McCarthy case, through television, something like the atmosphere of an Athenian market place, where the citizens themselves could take a close-up look at their leaders. McCarthy had developed political exposure into a method of seizing power. He fell victim to his own invention when the people were able to watch him every day. Here too, however, the double face of many American institutions is evident, for it was the press, radio, television, that made McCarthy what, for some time, he was. In that period it was copy when he sneezed; what he wanted to be reported was loyally reported; publishers and reporters smelled an attraction and made the most of it. The reporters saw through him at a relatively early stage; the editors-in-chief and publishers occasionally took longer. Nevertheless, the point is that eventually a unanimous opinion formed about him, and that was his doom.

I cannot recall any similar episode in Germany. There the formation of public opinion—always a mysterious process—follows different laws: rarely does it happen that the tone is not set from "above," by the teachers, public officials, good families, those whom the majority considers to be notables and whom it honors by listening carefully when they pass judgment. In the New World, judgment depends on the response that comes from a broad and hardly articulate general public. Those who formulate public opinion listen to the outside, to the large masses, to the "below," and wait for reactions; the fact that they occasionally dress up their own opinions as public reactions only tends to confirm this thesis.

The system, though, has its shortcomings. If there is no compelling reason for submitting complex matters to the judgment of public opinion, the results of unawareness may be serious, as for instance the relative decrease in the quality of American education. Such matters do not cross the threshold of public consciousness until a dramatic event, a Russian rocket perhaps, thrusts them into the center of general discussion. Clearly this system presupposes the existence of a certain number of determined dissidents and nonconformists who have at their disposal enough media of public opinion to serve a corrective function. McCarthy strove to stamp out this gang in the news media and in education and research, and he was supported in his endeavors by public indifference toward intellectuals. Retributive justice saw to it that this Goliath was killed by such a nonconformist David as Senator Flanders.

V

If a foreign visitor lives for some time with Americans he discovers other ways too in which they deviate from the conceptions that are held about them, both by themselves and by others. They are regarded, for example, as a people "without forms," without established procedures for social relations. The fact remains, however, that they have developed a pattern of social intercourse in which all rough edges and sharp corners are avoided precisely because of its finely perfected forms. Public education, from kindergarten through college, is essentially an education for living with one another, getting along with one another, through well-defined formulas—formulas for teamwork, for public discussions, for the meetings of the sexes. What is discussed on a date and what, in departing, remains unsaid and undone, is governed by laws as strict as those governing a parent-teacher association.

These rules, though unwritten, are in effect from San Diego to Boston. They change—and suddenly—but nobody can foretell when and why. In the attitudes of young people, for instance, they have changed in the course of one generation from stressing the importance of variety in friendships with the opposite sex to concentrating on one partner only. Whatever the reasons and the consequences of such changes, the rules are adhered to, by a strange tacit agreement. Emily Post and Amy Vanderbilt can only ratify what has long since happened in the realm of forms and ceremonies. It is useless to sneer at the fascination of American schools with child adjustment (what German teacher would think of scribbling on a report card "Jean is such a happy child"?). In a New World of immigrants education toward common patterns of life arises not from a whim but from a necessity.

Many Germans, believing in the myth of American "formlessness" in social life, accept at face value various gestures of Americans that are actually nothing but social cliches. It starts with the smile of the receptionist or the waitress. The visitor from Frankfurt, familiar with the businesslike appearance of these ladies in Europe, believes the smile to be aimed personally at himself, and his ego is inflated. At his first cocktail party on American soil a charming young lady calls him by his first name. Important figures of public life tell him, as he takes his leave, that it has been most

110

interesting to talk with him, that they hope very much to see him again, that they would be happy to be of service at any time. The visitor is sorely disappointed if he takes the smile, the intimate address, the cordial invitation, as more than a specific way of simplifying social intercourse. It is some time before he realizes that the friendliness of his American hosts is not directed especially to him but comes from a wish to be friendly to everybody. Frequently the realization leads to a pronouncement that Americans are false, superficial, and incapable of real friendship. It is a repetition of what the Germans said about the French in the eighteenth century. Polished forms of social intercourse, rules covering all situations arising among people of the same class, always impress outsiders as insincere.

On the other hand, the German frequently overlooks the generous and instinctive readiness of neighbors and strangers to be of help—the characteristic that makes life in America so easy and agreeable for every newcomer. You are left to your own devices, to be sure, but a hint, and sometimes less than a hint, is sufficient to set flowing a warm stream of practical help. It has often been noticed that the American asks "What can I do for you?" whereas the European says "What do you want?" American society in a neighborhood, a city block, a farm community, is a fabric of practical assistance. Mutual aid is practiced quietly, without asking questions and without expecting a *quid pro quo*. It is more than a mere matter of good manners; it has to do with the active way in which the American wants to prove his Christian faith, and with the frontier traditions that are still present to the citizen of the New World.

The feminine influence in American life is hard to describe. Word has spread, of course, that in the New World the role played by women is different from what it is in the Old World. But that they play first fiddle, nobody thinks possible—neither the German man, who has his own ideas as to the place due a woman, nor the German woman. What distinguishes American and German men from each other is not their attitude toward politics, business, card games, and duck hunting, but their attitude toward their wives and mothers. Even so, they at least understand each other. Between German and American women, on the other hand, there is so complete a misunderstanding that they feel sorry for each other, and for opposite reasons: the German woman is pitied because she lives in bondage and without freezer, the American woman because she has to be so independent and does not enjoy culling and washing fresh vegetables or chatting a little at the baker's. It is also believed that the tyranny of the husband, familiar to the German wife, is replaced for her opposite number in the New World by the tyranny of the child—and there are many more similar misunderstandings. If it is really essential for the relationship of two peoples that their most important groups understand each other, an exchange of ambassadors between the female elements of the United States and the Federal Republic would be of great consequence.

It is worth while to deal a little longer with this subject, and to note to what extent the Germans err in their evaluation of the American woman. She is considered tyrannical, demanding, and spoiled. The prototype of this myth is obviously a certain stratum of city-dwelling ladies whose bank accounts are kept well stocked by their overworked husbands and whose afternoons are spent at the bridge table. In a certain way the life of the wives of American officers and government employees in Germany has helped confirm that impression. Cut off from their accustomed surroundings, and equipped with a maid in the kitchen, they possibly allow those virtues to wither which are so conspicuous in any American "suburbia": the inexhaustible energy with which the average American woman shuttles back and forth between her house, the school, the PTA, the store, the church, and her job; the great interest with which she throws herself into every cooperative venture— from the car pool to helping with the school lunch to the collection of clothes for refugees, blood for the sick, money for the poor, and signatures under a protest against the felling of old trees that stand in the way of a new street.

My compatriots view the emancipation of the American woman as a successful attempt to invade the traditional domain of the man: big politics and business. But it seems to me that these are the fields for which the average American woman shows the least interest. There are not that many independent business women competing with men; percentagewise, the number of female members of Congress is smaller than in Germany.

But feminine influence on the close-by and simple spheres of life is tremendous. The participation of women in the public life of the church community, neighborhood, city block, farm community, is much larger than in Germany, and in the majority of cases is the result of a freely taken decision. Another significant difference: speaking in Germany of a teacher, one thinks of a "he," in America of a "she." True, American men are reluctant to accept positions in elementary schools, because they are so poorly paid; but this only helps to strengthen an already existing tendency of American society to entrust the education of the new generation to women—with all the frequently analyzed consequences that such a state of affairs entails for the authority of the woman over her future husband. Growing up and studying, social gatherings and entertainment, guiding stars and hopes are molded by women: the cultural climate of the country depends on them. It is therefore amazing that American womanhood has not been able to produce an "ideal type" that would influence the conceptions of the outside world.

An important aspect of this development is the consideration given by the American economy to the woman's world. Beer is brewed in accordance with the requirements of the slender line; automobiles are loaded with gadgets that make driving easier for women, the cars becoming dinosaurs whose main purpose is extravagance. In Germany women seem to be the protecting and preserving element of the economy. In America (where they cannot be addressed by the title of their husbands, as Madam Ministerial Counselor or Madam Doctor) they are prodded by publicity into showing their income level by the amount of chromium on their cars and, for that purpose, anticipating next year's income. This happy confidence of the American woman in the future and in the continuance of the economic boom makes her the main pillar of capitalism in the twentieth century. It is assumed that eighty percent of the American national income flows through the well-groomed hands of American housewives. Should they one day collectively decide to stop buying air conditioners, washing machines, cars, and television sets for one year, and to be satisfied with the old model, the Western world would face a crisis of unimaginable proportions.

There is still another widespread misunderstanding. The American woman is supposedly frigid, possibly even asexual—a notion

113

prevailing among Europeans of male sex, traveling in America, especially because they don't know the rules of the game but find in movies and magazines a cult of the bosom that in no way corresponds to reality. May it be that the American woman appears frigid because she is surer of her cause—or rather, of her prey— than the European woman? And that therefore she has less recourse to feminine stratagems? There are certain indications that this theory may be tenable. Agents I have dispatched into the female camp have returned with the report that American women show a remarkably low degree of jealousy of one another; that friendship exists among women; that good comradeship among working women is all but uninfluenced by the presence or absence of a man. This cannot be explained by frigidity, but only by a consciousness of possessing immense power over man, a power that the female sex in the New World receives as a gift in the cradle. In contrast to the customs of Arab civilization, the husband in America may consider himself a possession. But it is one of the basic errors of casual German observers to draw the conclusion that because American men wash dishes and change diapers, the women in the New World do not handle their possessions with great warmth and caution.

VI

Anyone who gives some thought to the future of German-American relations within the next fifty years must expect such misunderstandings to play a certain role. They will not easily be corrected, especially since so many intrinsic differences between these two nations are concealed under a deceptive cover of outward similarities. And Germany, unlike Great Britain, has no old diplomatic tradition that tells how to get over alleged similarities and real differences without suffering shipwreck. The strong contrasts which in America go hand in hand with a remarkable uniformity— they will continue to fascinate and fool the German. A continuous critical study will be needed if the contradictions within America, the competing, unconnected ideals, are to receive well-balanced judgment. And this process would be made easier if Americans ceased judging peoples according to their stand for or against America.

To the German people the privilege of riding in the same boat with the United States will appear desirable only so long as common interests are clearly evident. Should this not be the case, or should the compass be obscured, they will become fearful of being left in the lurch by the big partner. This fear may subside. The younger generation—with its bobby socks, crew cuts, blue jeans, rock 'n' roll, with a developing flair for publicity and inclination toward easy credit, tranquilizing pills, and do-it-yourself—has absorbed not only American externals but also a fraction of the American sense of life. This may eventually strengthen the feeling of belonging together. For some time, however, it will be wise to rely more on common interests than on a common liking for Louis Armstrong.

But although common interests are a strong link—as should be stressed again and again—they alone are not enough to improve the climate characterizing the relationship of two peoples, or their mutual understanding, and to an even lesser degree is this achieved by periodical professions of faith in common idealistic goals. Peoples actually come close to each other only when they believe that they agree in their political methods. Between the United States and Germany this area of agreement is small, if we disregard the fact that roughly the same conceptions of rational organization prevail in the business worlds of Frankfurt and New York. It is therefore of the greatest importance that each should acquire some understanding of the political means used by the other.

In this field what the Germans should not necessarily take over but come to know is the barriers erected by Americans against any concentration of public power; the means by which a minority is protected against the tyrannical will of the majority; and also the way of thinking that tends to transform political into legal conflicts. Then too, the moves from planning to preparation to political action often follow other laws in America from their course in Germany. This difference in procedural habits is well illustrated in the area of sports. It can be seen in the difference between the favorite European sport, soccer—where the teams and the object of their struggles are in constant movement, constant action—and American football, baseball, and golf. In these peculiar varieties of New World games, long periods of apparent inaction and serene calm alternate with short sudden spurts. They have been planned long in advance and press a maximum of energy and resources into a brief period of time—with the result that the situation in the field is abruptly and radically changed. Long preparation alternating with sudden action—this is typical of American political methods. And the Germans would be well advised to familiarize themselves with this peculiarity, not only in the library, but also in the stadium.

It falls within the subject of political methods—and also is part of the philosophy of the New World—to take people as they are, taking into account their weak and strong points without expecting that they can be changed by a wonder drug or the stroke of a magic wand. In the mind of almost every German when he meditates on his country is a vision—a vision that has been variously called the "other," the "real," the "covert" Germany. It is the platonic idea of Germany, waiting just below the unsatisfactory and dreary surface to be conjured up to the light: perfect, redeemed, cleansed of all the stains of the past and present. This perfectionist vein shows time and again in my compatriots—now as disgust with politics, now as an exuberant chiliastic hope for the millennium. The world around senses this, and is afraid of it. Not the least of the reasons why Americans feel that a man like Adenauer is reliable is that he enjoys politics immensely and is nevertheless sober enough to believe that perfection is not of this world.

In this he agrees with the citizens of the New World. Their Constitution draws its impulses from a recognition of the weakness of man. It divides and balances powers in order to deprive the sinful and frail human of the opportunity to taste too much of the sweetness of power. Man is a deceptive instrument. That is the reason why—as far as he is of importance to the public—he should be subject to constant correction and replacement. Thus elections are frequently held in America. They do not purport, however, to confirm the good but rather to choose the lesser among several evils. Political methods as they have developed in the United States are not propitious to the idea of an "other," a "real" America; they do not aim at creating heaven on earth. On the contrary, they leave it to everybody to find his happiness pragmatically, by experience, trial and error. It is an experiment with liberty, in a framework set up by conservative skeptics. It would be well for the Germans to understand this. The common future of the two nations does not depend on whether the Americans learn from the Germans how to do mental arithmetic and how to hike—nor does it depend on whether they follow exactly the same political aims. But it does depend on their achieving understanding and agreement on political methods.

from Yugoslavia

MARIJA VILFAN

The author: born in Yugoslavia (Ljubljana), 1912; studied at the Arts
Faculty in the University of Ljubljana. After her graduation from the
university in 1935, Mrs. Vilfan taught French and English and worked
as a journalist. She also participated in left-wing activities and in the
national liberation movement. After the war she continued her journalistic activities, in Trieste, and later became Deputy Director of the
Yugoslav Information Office in Belgrade. Since 1953 she has served
as Secretary of the Commission for International Relations in the Socialist Alliance of the Working People of Yugoslavia. She is also a
member of the Yugoslav Commission for UNESCO and of the editorial board of the monthly periodical *Nasa Stvarnost*. Mrs. Vilfan is
the mother of three sons. Her husband, now Secretary General to President Tito, was formerly Yugoslav delegate to the United Nations. In
1947-1950, when he was serving in that capacity, she spent two and
one-half years in the United States.

I

MY VIEWS, feelings, and judgments arising from my experience within the United States have never been entirely
personal, not only because I lived there as a diplomat's
wife but much more because I am a Yugoslav. I belong to a nation that has gone through very difficult and bitter struggles to
win and protect its independence, and I can hardly think and act
in a purely personal way in matters where my country's relations
with other nations are concerned. My experiences with the US have
always been colored by the entire complex of collective Yugoslav
experience with America.

The interplay of a whole series of political forces and circumstances impelled Yugoslavia and the United States toward cooperation at a difficult stage of postwar history. In this situation the
United States, basing itself on its national interest, developed a
positive approach toward a small nation that desired to be treated
as an equal member of the international community, to develop
economically, and to build up its own socialist way of life. Experience has thus shown that the relations between the United

118

States and a small nation may be of mutual benefit to the two countries and to the world at large.

Lately Yugoslav-American relations have not followed an even course. Will the differences between the two countries prove too great to be bridged? Were the good relations we had in the past a coincidence, or were they a promising beginning of a mutually beneficial cooperation that may prove permanent? What can we do to help promote this positive development if it is really there? These are questions I often ponder over.

I arrived in America in the middle of 1947, when our mutual relations were fairly bad. In contrast to those Yugoslavs who are at present traveling to the USA I had but scarce knowledge of American history and contemporary problems. I had my opinions on some matters, but I found out later that they were wrong. I thought that the labor movement was similar to those of West European countries, namely an independent political factor directly opposed to the Democratic and Republican parties alike.

I slowly began to realize how vastly the US differs from the industrialized countries of Western Europe. The US is a country that developed without feudal traditions, one in which liberal democracy took strong roots from the very beginning, a country whose colonization and subsequent expansion to the West were acts of bravery requiring generations of courageous and able men and women. The fact that, as distinct from Europe, labor was always expensive led to the rapid development of labor productivity. The traditionally high purchasing power of the people not only attracted immigrants but also created a rich home market that made possible a rapid industrialization. The USA is a country in which people remember the Great Depression with a horror equal to that provoked by memories of the war among us. All these things are of course familiar to all Americans, but I had to "discover" them.

I was pleasantly surprised by the American people, their democratic manners, the American readiness to hear another's opinion. This impression is felt by all Yugoslavs who arrive in the USA. I think it is a pity that many Americans lose these qualities once they appear as spokesmen of their nation. Then they are frequently unable to understand the way of life of other people, and tend to

119

propagate the American way of life as the most suitable for other nations as well.

I lived in America at the time when the first waves of McCarthyism began sweeping over the country, and I was able to observe its effect on many people I knew. It was a depressing experience to see people losing the faith in the future that they had at the time of the New Deal, to see them becoming passive. I felt that those who had the courage to oppose McCarthy were privately admired by most Americans. McCarthyism has been officially buried, yet I doubt whether the whole lesson has been drawn from it. Anti-Communism, on which it was based, continues as its heritage. It hampers the Americans in the reappraisal of the international situation, and makes it difficult for them to approach those nations that have chosen a different way of life.

My knowledge of American literature and culture in general was slight when I arrived in New York. In 1947 the myth still prevailing in Europe was that America has no cultural traditions of its own. I confess I was surprised by the hosts of brilliant intellectuals, writers, artists, musicians, and scientists. I was amazed to see how the organization of scientific research work in the USA had emerged from the individual artisan phase, which still predominated in some countries in Europe. I liked the books and magazines that popularize science, and I think they are among the best. I liked the American theater. I now often think of the perspectives the adoption of shorter working hours opens up for the cultural enrichment of the American people, and wonder how the needs will be met.

I was surprised by the discrimination that still exists in the USA, not only toward the Negroes but also toward other groups of US citizens who are not of Anglo-Saxon origin. Afterward I became acquainted with the efforts made during the New Deal and World War II to put an end to such practices. I also saw groups of Negroes who visited Hyde Park, and the enthusiasm with which they acclaimed Mrs. Roosevelt, who happened to be there. Yugoslavs who have lived in the USA, by contrast to the average Yugoslav, are aware of the US government's efforts to solve the Negro problem. The average Yugoslav citizen was pleasantly surprised by the decision to send federal troops to Little Rock. US prestige depends to no little degree on the faster solution of this internal problem.

120

I was impressed by the complicated procedure of reaching political decisions at top levels, a procedure that sometimes makes it difficult to know what American policy consists of and certainly contributes to the feeling of perplexity about America's relations with other countries.

I arrived from a socialist country that was seeking new roads of development and rejecting many old dogmas. Therefore the trends of social development in the US were a matter of paramount interest to me. Before arriving there I thought that in the transformation of American society the American working class could play a role similar to that of the labor movement in Great Britain. Today I believe, as do many of my friends, that the New Deal represented for America the same stage of development reached in Great Britain by the postwar measures of the Labour Party Government. We consider the New Deal important because it made the economy the object of calculated state intervention and introduced the gradual redistribution of national income. Increasing purchasing power became one of the main instruments of the functioning of the economy, bringing about an improvement in the living standards of the broad masses of people. The New Deal also laid down the achievement of full employment and complete social insurance as objectives of national policy.

The New Deal is significant to me also because it expanded civil rights, primarily those of the working class, through the recognition of the trade unions. American labor has not developed its class consciousness in the conventional European sense. Yet with its numerical growth and firm orientation toward the improvement of living standards and security of workers, it represents a force that is driving America toward planning and regulation of the economy. It also exerts a powerful check on capital, which although constantly restricted by taxation and controls, nonetheless constitutes the strongest economic force in the USA.

The Tennessee Valley Authority attracted my particular attention, not only as an attempt at a comprehensive planned development of a region but also, as noted by Mr. Lilienthal in his book, because it enlisted the workers employed on the project as advisers, which is close to some of our ideas.

I am keenly interested to see how the USA will solve some of the problems that confront American society. I have the impression of a certain stalemate. Will the USA succeed in solving the problem of inflation, and to what extent will state intervention as practiced so far prove an efficient means of preventing recession? When and how will the USA devise a system of social control over corporations, which, as shown by Congressional hearings, is becoming an increasingly urgent problem? Has not the time come in the USA when a step beyond the New Deal should be made? How will the USA resolve the problems ensuing from excessive government centralization and bureaucracy, and bring about a more efficient functioning of the state administration and the restoration of grass-roots democracy, which according to many American authors shows signs of deteriorating? The successful tackling of many social problems in the USA, which are receiving so much attention and publicity in the American press (education, family life, corruption in the trade unions, loss of political idealism, indifference, conformity), probably hinges on the solution of these issues.

I have the feeling that the USA has been far more successful in resolving the problems of production and labor productivity, the development of science and promotion of living standards, than the problems raised by the adaptation of society to its material foundation. New concepts of values, which according to American writers themselves are now being reduced to individual prosperity and success, seem to me another urgent problem.

This is broadly speaking my outlook on the internal problems of America, which I am following with keen interest. Yet the USA is not limited to the American continent. It is felt almost everywhere. Fifty percent of world industrial power is concentrated in American hands. US relations with the individual countries, including Yugoslavia, will primarily depend on the degree of accord that will be achieved in the understanding and solution of the fundamental international problems.

It seems to me that the USA is hypnotized by its chief antagonist, the Soviet Union, and cannot discern the fundamental processes in the world to which all countries, including the USA, will ultimately have to adjust their policies. The USA aims at organizing the world on the basis of the antagonism between itself and the Soviet Union, while leaving a series of burning international problems unanswered. The Yugoslavs are deeply convinced that the economic development of the underdeveloped areas is the crucial issue that will brook no delay. People in the underdeveloped countries are awakening, and they demand an improvement of the standard of living that can be achieved only through economic development. They want independence and refuse to be involved in bloc combinations, for this would hamper them in the accomplishment of their basic task.

II

Comparatively little was known of the USA in Yugoslavia during the period between the two world wars. At the end of 1943, with the arrival of an Allied military mission, along with liaison officers and journalists, new US-Yugoslav relations were inaugurated, but in the immediate postwar period those relations were not exactly happy. The only bridge of understanding between America and Yugoslavia was then built by the US citizens of Yugoslav origin, who organized campaigns for the collection of relief, sent equipment for hospitals, financed the building of schools, and sent medicines. It was only after 1951, with the beginning of economic and military aid to Yugoslavia from the USA, that the process of mutual acquaintance began.

The Americans were then interested in Yugoslavia as a country to which they were extending aid. The reporting of the American press became fairly informative. The American approach to Yugoslavia began its positive evolution, although the aggravation of ideological struggle in the USA itself constituted and still constitutes an obstacle to the full understanding of Yugoslavia.

Our public opinion became more interested in the USA—what it looks like, how it emerged from the Great Depression, how it is developing its economic potential, the difference between the Democrats and the Republicans, how the Negro problem is being solved, how the US trade unions operate, why the American working class is without its own political party. It was through our newspaper correspondents who traveled in America and described the country that our citizens gained their first systematic acquaintance with America. Our economic and social science institutes also felt the need to study the American reality and analyze it. The change of relations with the USA was a problem for the Yugoslavs. Our citizens were not satisfied with the mere statement that the US

123

policy toward Yugoslavia was changing and that the US government was extending aid. The strongest capitalist country in the world was giving aid although we were a state in which the Communist Party was in power. Our citizens wanted an explanation.

What does the average Yugoslav citizen think of the USA today? In order to answer this question I carried out a little poll in ten cities located in various parts of our country. I interviewed workers, peasants, students, and politically active persons.

From this poll it is clear that the Yugoslavs' opinion on the USA is molded primarily by their reaction to the US foreign policy. Those polled emphasized the present-day problems and passed over the positive contributions of the American foreign policy after the war. The answers given are fairly like-minded and self-assured, but they are representative. Consensus concerning foreign policy in nations like ours is characteristic of modern life. Those polled were fairly critical of the present US foreign policy. None of them considered it to be entirely good. The main objections referred to inconsistency and lack of principle, reliance on blocs, the US attitude toward the Near East and Eastern Europe, toward China, toward the small and non-aligned nations, the policy of military alliances, and the waging of anti-Communist struggle.

The people asked were not so ready with their answers when requested to state their views on the internal developments in America. Several of them were reluctant to say anything, because they "do not know much of this development." Most were acquainted with US economic capacity. "One should pay tribute to the great achievements in the field of economic development and technical progress. This also ensures a pleasant life for most Americans." "The problem of the specific conditions that made the USA the foremost technical nation, with an above-the-average standard of living, is of special interest." Some even cited details related to US agriculture.

Here are a few opinions on the relations that prevail in American society. "The factories and shops belong to the owners, who decide how one will live and work." "I know that capitalist relations prevail in production, that there is exploitation of labor." "I think it is a matter of some concern that the strong capitalist circles, of course reactionary, are succeeding in hampering the good intentions of President Eisenhower." "I know that capitalist working conditions prevail there, so that the magnates are the ones who profit from the sweated labor of the workers." A worker declared, however, that the "results accomplished in the field of labor legislation and labor relations are not to be underrated." A peasant: "I think that the attitude of the factory owners is honest, and I like that very much. The owners earn much, it is true, but they also let the workers live well. I know it is hard for the worker if he falls ill. Then he loses everything he earned. The US should arrange this somehow." Several remarked that the inadequacy of the health and social insurance system is a weak point in the American way of living.

A Croatian peasant said that he could not "understand many manifestations of the American way of life, but if this suits the American people, let them live so." Some limited themselves to statements that are a result of their contacts with Americans: "The Americans are a busy and industrious people. From my personal contacts with some people from the USA I know that they have much less spare time than our people." One answered that he liked US family relations, in which all members lead an independent life. He considered it good that each member of the family becomes independent as soon as he begins earning his living. One said: "It is known that America is a country where there are divorces, murders, and suicides, robberies and blackmail. This permits us to draw certain conclusions." Several recalled the late Senator McCarthy, and one considered him a product of social relations in America. One said he could not understand why even distinguished scientists were persecuted.

Had the poll taken place several years ago, all these people would have reacted most violently to Senator McCarthy. Today their attention is focused on the Negro problem, as a sequel to the events in Little Rock. As a people that fought for freedom for centuries, the Yugoslavs are sensitive to problems of national or racial discrimination in other countries. All readily gave their opinion on this problem in the USA. "I seriously reproach American society for not having done away with all forms of racial discrimination more resolutely and boldly." "In the eyes of the man in the street this problem compromised the US most. Such an attitude is an anachronism. Notwithstanding certain positive legislative acts, segregation still exists, owing to the unreasonable policy of some Southern governors. It would be a good thing if the responsible men in the USA would be fully aware how much their prestige would be increased by the solution of this problem."

Very few said that they are not acquainted with American literature. "I know American literature, as our bookshops are filled with translations of US authors." The best known include Ernest Hemingway, Jack London, John Steinbeck, Theodore Dreiser, Sinclair Lewis, Upton Sinclair, William Faulkner, Arthur Miller, Pearl Buck, William Saroyan, Tennessee Williams, Thomas Wolfe, Erskine Caldwell, Robert Sherwood, Mark Twain, Sherwood Anderson, Edgar Allan Poe, Margaret Mitchell, Irwin Shaw. "American literature, generally speaking, is positive, it is even abreast of many other significant achievements." "It is my impression that this is a great humanist literature and that it is in no way inferior to the leading nations in the field." According to one, "American literature is a peephole through which the contradictions in US society may be observed. It reflects the intellectual vacuum caused by industrialization and exaggerated business spirit. The American theater is highly interesting in this respect."

Opinions varied where US films are concerned. It was generally considered that the acting and photography are good, "yet the substance is frequently flimsy, as if US cinematography were in the throes of a crisis." "They have many great achievements, such as *Glass Menagerie, Death of a Salesman*, etc. It seems to me, however, that sentimental, superficial, and mediocre films are increasingly frequent. Perhaps the subjects and themes of their motion pictures correspond to their mentality, however." Attention was called to the commercial aspect of this problem, as "the market demands a lot of cheap goods." Some liked "Westerns"; according to others they have a negative influence. Some objected to the insistence laid on the American way of life. "The luxury we see on the screen would testify to the fact that life in the US is ideal. Yet we know from other films that life there is not ideal."

The poll indicates that Yugoslavs are not inclined to make apriori judgments, as for instance that everything is bad in the USA because it is a capitalist country. They are willing to assess every action of the US and every phenomenon there on merit; there are good and bad things in the US approach to us, and American foreign policy, too, is not devoid of favorable aspects, although, in their opinion, the negative predominate at present. I think that such non-apriori reasoning stems from our foreign political conception, which is basically optimistic, believing in the world trend toward closer cooperation. It helps people to notice positive facts wherever they are to be found.

The press and other media of mass communication play a tremendous role in this respect. They can inform or misinform, and ease or aggravate strained relations. My opinion is that in regard to Yugoslavia the American press should be less of a means of propaganda and more informative in character. It should not depend so much on momentary moods. It should strive to provide an objective analysis of Yugoslav foreign and internal policy.

And how does the Yugoslav press report on the US? I put the question to the editor of a responsible Belgrade daily who knows the USA well. He answered: "I think we can justly claim that at present the Yugoslav press correctly and regularly informs its readers on all the important events in the USA. Consequently it provides the basis for a picture of the USA which more or less corresponds to reality. This by no means implies that there are no weaknesses in Yugoslav press reporting on the US at present. A certain disproportion is noticeable at times, when shortcomings receive greater publicity than the achievements of the American society. But the editorial offices of the big dailies have drawn the attention of their US correspondents to this fact. The Yugoslav press has also published its comments and views on US foreign policy and individual concrete foreign political problems. These comments have frequently been critical. It may freely be said, however, that taken as a whole this was an analytical criticism, which never degenerated into anti-Americanism." The editor's answer adequately expresses, I think, what our press aims at. I criticized freely the writing of the American press on Yugoslavia, and I would welcome an American opinion on the Yugoslav press coverage of America.

I inquired in the editorial office of a big Yugoslavian daily newspaper about its readers' wishes with regard to reporting on the USA. Since this particular paper had for a time published a lot of material on US economic capacity, letters began arriving that requested information on the sphere of social relations, educational problems, social insurance, youth life, the status of factory workers, and the like. Another kind of letter received by the editors of this paper is also worth mentioning. The USIS Reading Room in Belgrade organizes photo exhibits, and many of the correspondents objected to this "ostentatious showing off of US achievements." "It is a custom here," wrote one reader, "that a rich man deliberately behaves modestly when in the society of those less fortunate than himself, so as not to offend them by his wealth."

The interest in and the basic sympathies for the USA in Yugoslavia have not yet lessened as a result of the major friction that has developed between the two countries. Yet American public opinion has already been influenced by the present state of affairs. If this attitude toward Yugoslavia continues in the United States, it may in the long run also affect the sympathies of the Yugoslavs for America. Thus the handling of the intended visit of President Tito to the USA at the end of 1956 gave rise to strong feelings over here. The US government invited President Tito on a state visit. Instead of a normal welcome we heard an uncontrolled display of ill manners. Some voices were heard in favor of the visit when it was obviously too late, and it was clear that under such conditions the invitation could no longer be accepted.

III

We must not let things drift. People who influence American public opinion should try to understand Yugoslavia as it is, without continuously making it fit one or the other preconceived scheme. In such a case US foreign policy toward Yugoslavia would find a solid foundation to our mutual advantage. As I have said, the communication media are here of great importance. So too are the various possibilities of cultural exchange.

In the field of cultural exchange the picture is as follows. Since the war hundreds of American novels, short stories, and other books have been translated into Yugoslav languages. Many American plays are in the repertory of our theaters. Yugoslav music lovers have heard Stokowski, the Minneapolis Symphony Orchestra, have seen *Porgy and Bess*, the New York Ballet Theater. We have seen among others the exhibition of Contemporary American Plastic Arts, that of contemporary American lithographs, prepared by the Cincinnati Art Museum, the photograph exhibition "Family of Man," which pleased us very much. A great many American films are being shown in Yugoslavia, and US papers and books are sold freely.

But US-Yugoslav cultural exchanges are one-track. No work of Yugoslav literature has been translated in America. Only the Janigro Zagreb chamber-music orchestra and two folk-dance groups have given successful recitals. There are no exhibitions of our painters and sculptors. While American exhibitions in Yugoslavia are being organized with at least partial state assistance, US official circles have never extended an invitation or offered their assistance for the organization of Yugoslav cultural activities in the US; apart from the interest of private US citizens, this is left entirely to commercial channels. In the case of small nations reciprocity in cultural exchanges cannot be achieved through the initiative of private managers. I think the US government should help in promoting exchange and acquainting its citizens with foreign cultures—which is already the usual practice in Europe.

On the "labor front" the situation is bleak. The American trade unions are among the very few in the world that have no contacts with the corresponding Yugoslav organization. Allegedly our trade unions are not free but state-controlled, "an instrument of the Party," and besides, they advocate the policy of cooperation between trade unions of different countries in the international labor movement. This is denounced by the representatives of US labor as the "Trojan horse of Communism." American labor representatives repeat slogans that have lost the power of persuasion outside the USA. This prevents them, to their own detriment I think, from getting acquainted with the problems of the Yugoslav working class, which played a leading role in the struggle against fascism and later took over responsibilities of economic development. It partly sacrificed its standard of living in order to make possible the implementation of the overstrained investments, but now enjoys the broadest possible democratic rights in a system of economic management based on the material incentive of the individual worker.

The Yugoslav trade unions have sharply criticized the cold-war policy of the representatives of the US labor movement. But this has not prevented them from reporting objectively on labor activities in the US. Moreover, many magazines are publishing studies

129

and surveys of the present status of the US trade unions, their substantial achievements, their aims and their problems.

When I asked a number of my friends who had visited America what the Yugoslavs could learn from the Americans they suggested: to be industrious and practical, to be economical and rational, efficient organization of work, inventiveness, independence in work, to be systematic, and to simplify problems. American Technical Assistance provided many Yugoslavs with an opportunity of traveling to the USA and learning what my friends suggest we could learn from America. We are studying the American technological achievements and applying them; we learn from many spheres. What the Yugoslavs dislike is that their willingness to learn from America is interpreted by some Americans as an admiration for all things American; and they dislike the procedure necessary to obtain American visas.

In America Yugoslavia is known as a Communist country. We always refer to it as a socialist state. We believe that we have followed an original road of development during both our Revolution and our postwar development. We were inspired by Marx and Lenin, but we solved our own problems in our own way. Objective studies on our country would enable Americans to realize that in Yugoslavia "Communism" is a way of life of a nation. They would understand why we feel so keenly about the significance of independence and our socialist way of life. They would realize that our socialist orientation is a historical necessity, a result of all our former sometimes tragic experiences. It is at the same time an expression of human faith in progress toward an era of happier relations among nations and fuller individual life.

In our socialist development we have encountered problems that are today inherent in all societies, such as that of the relation between the individual and the state, which under present conditions of technological progress grows ever stronger. We have found solutions in a special type of grass-roots democracy that would perhaps be most aptly described to the American reader as a modern version of a New England Town Meeting, extended to all spheres of contemporary social activity, factories in particular.

All this is an integrated experience. If America would look at us objectively then it would be easier for her to understand the Yugoslav foreign and domestic policy. Many irrational ideas evoked in American minds by anti-Communist myths would be dispelled. Americans would also discover what many of them who have visited Yugoslavia as tourists have discovered for themselves: that we do not have the American way of life, but are a normal country in spite of this, a country in which people like to have a good time, with half of the male population ready to undertake a long journey to see a good soccer game; that the kids wear blue jeans and grab the daily papers from their parents to see the comics first; that the trade unions are exerting an unflagging pressure for increases of wages and salaries and improvement of living standards; and that an increasing number of families are purchasing electrical appliances on the installment plan. They would discover many things that are familiar to them. We should understand each other better because there is a kindred streak in the Yugoslav and American temperaments.

from Turkey

ÖMER CELÂL SARC

The author: born in Turkey (Istanbul), 1901; studied at Robert College in Istanbul, and at the University in Berlin. Dr. Sarc has taught economics at the University of Istanbul since 1926. During 1949-1951 he was Rector of that university, and since 1951 he has been Director of its Institute of Statistics. His books are in the fields of economics and statistics. In 1948 he represented his university at the installation of General Eisenhower as President of Columbia University in New York, and he was again in this country in 1950, visiting universities from the East to the West coast as a guest of the State Department. During 1954-1955 he was Visiting Professor at Columbia, and in 1955-1956 he served as Chief of the Middle East Unit in the United Nations' Bureau of Economic Affairs. Thereafter his work with the United Nations brought him again to this country, for shorter stays.

I

ONE of the distinctive traits of the American people which the foreign visitor remarks is the prevailing democratic-folksy spirit. In contrast to some other countries, class consciousness among higher ranking persons is weak if not absent. People are not ashamed of a humble origin, but rather tend to be proud of it if they have made headway in life. The tone adopted toward the small man is neither paternal and condescending nor cool and reserved, and his own attitude is characterized by a total absence of servility and of any inhibitions or aggressiveness arising from a sense of inferiority. Persons in the higher layers of society usually like to chat about weather and sports events with lower-ranking people, such as shopkeepers and waiters, and handshakes are often exchanged.

Not only is the small man not disdained, but some of his standards seem to gain ground at the expense of those of the elite. Thus in many fields demeanor appears to have become increasingly less formal. Persons are often addressed as "Mac," audiences as "folks." Even bosses and subordinates are soon on a first-name basis. On her latest visit to the United States the Queen of England was greeted, I hear, with cheers of "Hi, Liz." Dressing also becomes more and more informal. The top hat and the white tie are almost obsolete. In summer a growing number of men renounce neckties and wear short-sleeved shirts, an attire for which American tourists in more sophisticated Europe have sometimes been criticized. The trend manifests itself in language too. In many countries the speech of the elite is the model that the majority strives to follow, since it is regarded as a mark of high social standing. In America, on the other hand, the speech of the masses appears to have a greater appeal. I had the impression that the elite, instead of attempting to defend its way of speaking, tends to flirt with the popular idiom, by readily adopting neologisms and often using slang. There are of course groups where formality still prevails, rank counts, and attention is paid to descent, for example to the length of time since the family's first acquisition of wealth or since its arrival in the United States. But the numerical importance of these groups is slight and decreasing. It appears that by reason of the country's history and political structure this democratic spirit has always been inherent in America, but that in the decades past it has become stronger. This may be because the growing purchasing power of the masses, combined with their enormous voting power, not only makes it mandatory to take their preferences into account in business and politics but contributes to a diffusion of their standards in other domains as well.

Of course this democratic spirit does not imply a general recognition of the equality of all human beings. Racial prejudices still exist in parts of the population. In the South some people tend to regard the Negro as inferior, while others, though recognizing his equality, do not wish to associate with him in everyday life. Even in the North, apparently, there is sometimes a reluctance to have Negroes as neighbors, and I understand that real-estate prices ultimately fall in quarters into which Negroes move. I think, however, that the extent of racial prejudice in America and the difficulties in the Negro's situation are usually exaggerated abroad. The regrettable incidents that sometimes occur are easily generalized, while certain other facts are overlooked. In the first place, there is no country that is entirely free of some such prejudices. Second, the problem is particularly complicated in the United States by its relatively high percentage of Negroes in the total population. Furthermore, anti-Negro feeling is declining. Great efforts are being made toward overcoming racial prejudices, efforts that can be said to reflect the American people's strong sense of right and wrong. Considerable progress has been made in assuring Negroes equal treatment in most fields, partly by resorting to legislative measures. The material situation of the Negro population, though not so good as that of the white, especially with regard to dwellings, is by no means bad compared with other countries. Its income has increased with rising general prosperity. In the parts of America I visited— the northern and western states—Negroes in no way left on me the impression of a persecuted race.

The attitude of the American people toward work and business is remarkable, especially in comparison with that in my country under the Ottoman Empire. Among the Moslem population of the Empire there was a marked predilection for government careers, while trade and industry, and of course manual work, did not enjoy high prestige. Conditions have now greatly changed. Low salaries have much weakened the attraction of government careers, and a class of Turkish traders, bankers, and industrial entrepreneurs has come up. But some vestiges of the old mentality can still be noticed. There are occupations that continue to rate low (such as that of the waiter), and quite a few people find it perplexing to see anyone who, though well off, does not stop working. In America, on the other hand, all kinds of work appear to be considered dignified. To work as waiter, dishwasher, newspaper vendor, for example, seems not to impair prestige but rather to enhance it, since even children of rich families sometimes perform such jobs and are proud of it. Work is apparently not regarded solely as a means of making a living—and of course much less as a necessary evil—but has become an end in itself. It is believed to make life richer and to give it content. This attitude may be traced back, I think, to the spiritual heritage of Calvinism and Puritanism, and has probably contributed largely to America's stupendous economic development.

The American pattern of diversion is strongly affected by the fact that work is much more strenuous in the United States than in other countries. In factories the worker has to adjust himself to the fast rhythm of the machinery in operation, while in offices and shops the large volume of business to be handled calls for uninterrupted activity. Furthermore, many jobs are monotonous

134

and unattractive, because specialization has reduced them to very simple operations. True, paid holidays have been introduced, and the number of working hours has been reduced; the forty-hour week is now a general custom, and most places of work are closed on Saturdays. But the time not spent in the establishment cannot be entirely devoted to relaxation and rest. Because of the acute traffic problem many persons lose much time and energy in commuting between their homes and their places of work. More important, the lack of servants necessitates extensive chores for the household. This restricts the time available for entertainment, particularly for entertainments outside the home. And the need for such diversions is weakened by television, which enables one to follow events or to enjoy shows and music at home, without wasting time in transportation or spending money for tickets and perhaps for a "baby sitter."

It is natural, therefore, that some types of relaxation, prevalent in my country and others, are practiced to a much smaller extent or not at all in the United States. One of these is strolling, either for looking at shop windows and watching the movement in streets or for admiring beautiful scenery. I think the need for this is not felt widely in America. In cities strolling is hampered by frequent stops for red lights and by the haste of most walkers, and there are few scenic walks for pedestrians.

And American relaxation habits do not include the frequenting of coffeehouses, a custom that is widespread in Continental Europe and in my country. One of the functions of these establishments is to enable customers to while away time, while enjoying a refreshment, by looking at a beautiful view or observing the bustle in the streets or—if they are not in the open air—at least watching the comings and goings in the coffeehouse itself. Often they serve also as a kind of club, offering the possibility of reading the papers, meeting and chatting with friends, or writing letters. Their absence in the United States is mainly attributable, I think, to the fact that "whiling away time" is hardly compatible with the pulse of life there. In addition, coffeehouses in America, like any other establishment, would have to strive for a high turnover and could not allow customers to linger too long.

Stronger than in various other countries, and perhaps also than in Turkey, seems to be the predilection in America for the lighter

135

types of musical and theatrical entertainment—for jazz and operettas, or for comedies and thrillers rather than plays that have a pessimistic note or are centered around philosophical and social themes. Although there are signs of a change in this respect, it would seem that the percentage of people who devote much of their leisure to artistic and intellectual entertainments, even including plays and concerts followed on radio and television, is lower in America than in Western European countries. Radio and television could be very effective means of cultural edification, but the little I saw of them in America did not impress me as of high standard, though they do seem to have contributed to an interest in American and world politics.

II

Americans are generally characterized as materialistic, in contrast to other nations, particularly those in the East. The meaning of this word is not very clear. It seems to be used mostly to mean that material welfare is given priority over spiritual interests. Several indications appear to support this contention, but reflection shows that important qualifications are needed if the charge of materialism, so defined, implies fundamental differences in this respect between the United States and other countries.

Among the indications of American materialism is the widespread tendency to evaluate things in money terms. Thus people like to speak not only of $40-million bridges or of the $100-million damage caused by an insect but also of a $300-thousand El Greco painting and of a $100-thousand-a-year man. A second factor that may appear to support the contention is the extreme cost-consciousness one remarks in the country. In all fields it is customary in decision-making to evaluate with the greatest possible accuracy the probable costs and returns, and to compare them carefully with each other, a tendency that is much less pronounced in many other countries, especially in mine. Moreover—to use the slogan of a well-known American department store—it is smart to be thrifty, while for a great number of people in my country, even for many in the lower income groups, lavishness still rates higher than thrift.

But to a large extent these American attitudes represent manifestations of rationalism rather than of materialism. Cost-consciousness is entirely attributable to a rationalistic mentality, and if it is very marked in the United States this reflects in no way the primacy of material interests—even a person who prefers temples and museums to factories may be cost-conscious—but solely the fact that people there have learned to think more sharply. And thrift, which is more pronounced in some European countries than in the United States, is again a phenomenon of rationalism since it denotes careful foresight.

The same is true to a certain extent of the tendency toward monetary evaluation. One of the main trends in modern civilization is to translate qualitative phenomena as far as possible into quantitative terms, in order to make them measurable. Perhaps it has rendered the world less colorful, but it has contributed to great advances in science and technology. Thus the American's inclination to "price" all values can denote a materialistic attitude only if he neglects to distinguish market prices, costs, incomes, and the like from intrinsic values, such as a person's usefulness to society or a painting's aesthetic value. It is wrong to assume that the practice of putting price tabs on all values necessarily implies a failure to make this distinction. True, the failure may well be more common in the United States than in other countries. Prestige in society depends there to a greater extent than abroad on wealth and income. Thus businessmen apparently rank much higher in people's eyes than scholars, while the reverse is probably the case in Turkey. But I think one easily overstates the differences in this respect between America and other countries. It is often overlooked that everywhere social scales of value seem now to be evolving toward the American pattern. Moreover, even in the United States higher income by no means always confers higher prestige; it would be totally wrong, for example, to suppose that scholars rank there lower than the wealthy Frank Costello.

Another factor indicative of materialism in America is the strong impulsion in the masses to improve their living standards. Despite the remarkable rise in real wages, no opportunity is missed for making additional money. Thus wives frequently work to supplement the income of the husband, while children perform occasional jobs in their spare time, to contribute toward the cost of their education or to earn the money needed to buy something they particularly desire. In my country the chase after money, so

137

far as it exists, is often camouflaged, but in America it is manifest, since standards of social ethics sanction it. And parallel with this, the sums spent for improving material welfare show a progressive increase. There is a continuous scramble for better dwellings and for all the new devices that promise to ease work in the household, to increase comfort, or to provide new forms of diversion. Such devices soon become necessities. To the motorcar have been added, in the course of time, the refrigerator, the radio, and now the television set. People strive increasingly to partake in pleasures that were hitherto reserved to the privileged few. More and more persons take trips to Europe and visit fashionable American resorts, a movement that has been aided by the system of paying fares in installments, by guided tours and similar arrangements of transportation agencies. This high standard of living has come to be greatly cherished. Americans are proud of it, and are strongly apprehensive of anything that may lead to its reduction. Excluding a war, perhaps no event is more feared than an economic depression.

All this is clear, but certain other points must be considered. Three questions are relevant in this context: the driving forces behind the chase after higher living standards; the extent to which this preoccupation is peculiar to America; and how far it implies a neglect of spiritual interests.

Regarding the first point, it should not be taken for granted that the tendency is solely the reflection of a growing addiction to secular pleasures and comforts. A genuine addiction to comfort undoubtedly exists, and it can indeed lull people unduly and make them reluctant to sacrifices when the necessity arises. But I doubt that it is so strong in America as to have become dangerous to society. Experience has hitherto shown that Americans are ready to give up important material advantages whenever their ideals are at stake, and I strongly doubt that this attitude has changed. The unpopularity of the Korean conflict might be cited as an indication of change, but I feel that the basic reason for that attitude was war tiredness, coupled with the natural pacifism of the American and with the failure to make the masses realize the connection of the Korean situation with the country's security. The reaction of Americans to the sputniks shows that they are still basically the same.

As for the second point I have mentioned, it is doubtless true that in comparison with other countries, at least with Turkey, the urge to raise living standards is appreciably stronger in the United States. In Turkey there are probably more people who are satisfied with an income that is sufficient to maintain accustomed standards of life, and do not strive for more. Thus we sometimes find—though now rarely—that Turkish agricultural workers respond to wage increases by working a shorter time. This attitude may of course be related to the limited availability of certain goods that have a strong appeal to the people; in fact, experience shows that where such goods are more readily available there is a strong inducement to earn more. And another consideration certainly carries some weight. A price must generally be paid for increased earnings—for example by moving into another locality, letting the wife work, renouncing leisure. In other words, one has to incur a loss in so-called "psychic income." In Turkey, as a result of stronger conservatism, greater appreciation of leisure, contentedness with cheaper, contemplative forms of pleasure, and similar factors, this price probably appears too high to a large proportion of the population, even though they lack most of what are regarded in America as necessities.

On the other hand, it is obvious that higher incomes are greatly welcome everywhere, and that in general they are also actively sought, even though not always openly. Besides, the pursuit of higher material welfare appears to have become more intense in recent years. In Turkey, particularly since the improvement in the network of roads, the peasant increasingly seeks not only foodstuffs of which he previously consumed very little (coffee, sugar, and the like) but also durables, such as bicycles and radios. Some authors mention an awakening in underdeveloped countries of a sudden appetite for such accessories of a higher standard of living as motorcars, refrigerators, and better dwellings, a phenomenon they designate as the demonstration effect. Since limitedness of needs has often proved a serious impediment to economic development, the upsurge of interest in material welfare, though at present creating some acute economic problems, must be regarded as highly salutary in the long run. In general I would say that differences between America and other countries with respect to the emphasis on material interests are not fundamental but only a matter of degree. In addition, these differences are definitely decreasing.

And now the third question I have raised: the relative positions of material and spiritual interests in American society. While formerly the fine arts were much less regarded in the United States than in other countries, it appears that they are now receiving growing attention, a trend that has probably been furthered by the large increase in incomes; in fact, material and aesthetic interests are not mutually exclusive but are to a large degree interdependent. Interest in the social and natural sciences has always been strong in America, and here she has great achievements to her credit. Furthermore, Americans are strongly religious, and have a very pronounced philanthropic spirit. In allegedly less materialistic countries one often finds a certain indifference toward the lot of other countrymen, but in America one is struck by the great interest people take in the conditions of others. Many persons devote much of their time and energy to charity and to activities aimed at providing some betterment to their community, their country, or humanity as a whole. Large donations are made for schools, research, museums, churches, hospitals, and similar projects, in the country itself and abroad. Not only the rich but also the lower-income groups are never thrifty when it comes to help. Some drives for humanitarian purposes are financed mainly by the small contributions collected from the general population.

I am aware that in politics most of what is attributed to idealistic motives has an economic background, and nevertheless I think that purely moral motivations have influenced government policy in America to a larger extent than abroad, as is exemplified by Woodrow Wilson.

In short, material welfare is probably more strongly appreciated in America than in other countries, but this in no way implies also greater selfishness. Rather, there are indications that there is generally less selfishness in the United States.

III

It was a great surprise for me not to find in America marked class differences, allegedly a fundamental attribute of a capitalistic society. Some poverty certainly exists. I know of the "Tobacco Road" conditions in the deep South and the hillbilly regions in the Appalachians, and have seen destitute quarters in cities. Before the Second World War about forty percent of the population appears to have had only enough income to make possible bare subsistence—measured of course by American standards. But since then the amazing increase in national income has mostly benefited the poor, and there has been a sharp decrease in the percentage of families unable to provide more than mere subsistence. At the same time the very rich have become somewhat poorer, mainly because of sharply progressive income and inheritance tax rates and to some extent through a decline in the interest rate. As a result, a large-scale equalization has taken place, which manifests itself in the tremendous absolute and relative expansion of the middle class. At present the income of perhaps two-thirds of American families appears to be above the level necessary to assure adequate diet and clothing, some medical and dental care, and a certain amount of entertainment and comfort. Many enjoy in addition the benefits of social security.

Of these families only a very small proportion are really rich, say with a yearly net income of $15,000 or more, and among the remainder, constituting the bulk of the population, differences in living standards are slight. The families in this large group can afford neither servants nor custom-made suits, but practically all own a motorcar and a refrigerator, and have lodgings that are adequate in at least certain respects, for instance well heated in winter. In this immense middle class the main difference in living standards seems to be that certain durables (television, air-conditioning sets, movie cameras) and certain possibilities (trips to Europe, college education for children) are available to some but not to all.

This relatively equal distribution of income constitutes at present one of the distinguishing features of American society. Turkey does not belong among the countries with the greatest inequality in income distribution; the masses there are poor, but their poverty is not so great as elsewhere (they are at least not undernourished and do not lack footwear), nor is the wealth of the rich comparable with that in some other countries. Nevertheless the range of differences is much larger than in the United States. In America the difference between a university professor's standard of living and that of a factory worker is one of degree, but in Turkey it is fundamental, affecting housing, furniture, clothing, and medical care, not to speak of the education given to children. In fact the worker in Turkey does not belong to the middle class. Since marked disparities in living standards are an important barrier to genuine fraternization between individuals, it can be said that the equalization of income distribution has greatly consolidated democracy in America.

Moreover, this has been achieved mainly by an upward leveling. Though the average income of the very rich has somewhat declined, the increment in that of the masses has come very little, if at all, from taxes collected from the rich. Its principle source has been the large increase in national income; both legislation and trade-union action have provided labor with a growing proportion of this increase.

It is noteworthy that the greater equality in income distribution was brought about without giving up basic principles of capitalism. To be sure, capitalism in the United States today is something greatly different from what it was in the nineteenth century. "Rugged individualism" has been harnessed and the "laissez faire" principle to a great extent abandoned. Very strong controls exist with regard to such activities as railroad transportation, banking and finance, monopolistic combinations, while extensive regulations govern working conditions and wages. The government incurs large welfare expenditures and levies very heavy taxes on high incomes. But basic principles of capitalism have been maintained. The principle of private ownership is largely intact. Direct economic activity by the government is very limited, consisting of the postal service and the operation of some airports and water, gas, and electricity works. There has been an expansion into production of hydroelectric power, but not into manufacturing. Military plants built during the war were later sold or leased. In this respect there is a sharp contrast with Turkey, where 55 percent of the net value of large-scale manufacturing was derived from public establishments in 1954, and some fields, such as iron and steel and sugar production, are de facto under government monopoly.

Moreover, despite all government regulations the American economy is not a planned economy. Its functioning is governed to a large extent by decisions of individuals, though these are of course indirectly influenced by government measures, for instance in the field of monetary policy. Thus some major targets of socialism have been attained without much damage to the mechanism of the free-market economy, and society continues to enjoy certain benefits this mechanism provides, particularly those arising from competition.

Some characteristics of the American economy and of American production methods are remarked even by visitors who are not professional economists. The enormous turnover in shops and the uniform standardized type of most merchandise sold are indicative of mass production. One not only hears of the high level of wages but soon sees many of its manifestations. In the huge amount of consumer purchases it is striking that everything with a large wage component in its costs (particularly services, such as repair of watches, custom-made suits, doctors' fees, even shoeshining) is much more expensive than abroad, while the reverse is true of goods that are produced mainly by machinery and thus have a low labor component. But there are also some aspects of the economy which are puzzling to the foreign visitor. The huge sums spent for advertisement appear wasteful, as does the lavish use of various materials. Packaging, for example, is very elaborate, but practically all containers and wrapping material go to the wastebasket as soon as the merchandise is unpacked. Stockings and shirts are rarely mended, because new ones are cheaper than the time mending requires. Only a deeper scrutiny reveals that some of these phenomena are explainable by the immense natural resources with which America has been endowed, and that others entail advantages outweighing in importance the waste incurred.

Visiting foreign economists are puzzled by the farm policy, which has led to an enormous accumulation of stocks and will probably contribute to their further increase. They wonder about the outcome of labor-union efforts to continuously boost wages. They ask themselves whether latent inflation is inherent in the American economy, and of course particularly whether economic depressions will recur. But American rather than foreign economists are entitled to treat these questions.

IV

Until recently Americans generally tended to be engrossed in their domestic affairs, but there is now a considerable change in this respect. Today Americans are eager to learn about foreign countries, particularly of course those that constitute serious world problems, such as Russia, China, and India, but also others. Thus the number of American tourists to all countries has greatly increased, and there is indication that a growing percentage of them are less in search of pleasure and relaxation than of a deeper insight into the countries they visit. But though curiosity and knowledge about the world abroad appear to be much greater than before, the majority of the population still knows little of foreign countries. To a certain extent this is of course inevitable, since everywhere the majority of people are concerned mainly with their very immediate interests.

More serious than inadequate knowledge of facts about foreign countries is, I think, a certain failure to understand the psychology of foreign nations. Many Americans, I found, easily assume that all peoples have the same standards and attitudes as they. Thus America was very slow in detecting the Machiavellian element in the policy of some countries with which she came into close contact, an element that her own policy has generally lacked. Americans appear particularly to overlook the weight of irrational and emotional motivations in the conduct of some foreign nations, and to incline to think that difficulties can generally be overcome by material means. Insufficient comprehension of the often dissimilar mentality of foreign peoples has, I think, occasionally led to mistakes in policy and to bad feelings in personal contacts.

The average Turk has probably come to know more about America than the average American knows of Turkey. By reason of her political and economic importance, America receives great attention in the Turkish press. Moreover, the interest of the masses is aroused because many highly appreciated technical devices for work and entertainment are of American origin. It is true that most of these are still accessible only to the few, and on account of foreign-exchange shortages appear on the Turkish market, if at all, with a considerable time lag; thus cinerama and television have not yet come to Turkey, and only a small minority is acquainted with dacron, tape recorders, and high fidelity sets. But some devices, such as cinemascope films, the bulldozer, freezers, tractors, are widely known and greatly esteemed. Then too, there is a considerable number of transient and resident Americans in the country (tourists, businessmen, teachers, officials, and others) and for

144

many decades there have been American educational institutions. Finally, for more than a generation American films have dominated the Turkish screen, and movies are in Turkey perhaps a more popular type of entertainment than in most other countries.

But the general knowledge about America is somewhat distorted. The fact that in Turkey even Americans of lower rank own cars and live in good dwellings leads easily to the belief that everybody is rich in the United States. And movies leave some strange impressions. The prevalent type of American film reflects the United States as a world of fun and frolic. Detective films give an exaggerated idea of the incidence of crime, and "Westerns" exaggerate the extent of lawlessness. The compulsory happy ending pleases the masses by showing that ultimately right always triumphs over wrong and all problems find their solution, but it is regarded by intellectuals as unrealistic and as indicating a certain Philistinism. Few people have an adequate notion of the hard work and the strong civic spirit that underlie American society, or of the upsurge of intellectual and artistic interests in America in recent years. The unparalleled achievements in raising the level of welfare of the masses and in fulfilling the requirements of social justice also escape the attention of most persons.

The Turk's attitude toward the American is influenced in part by specific social and political factors. One is the consciousness that America is a powerful and reliable friend and ally, and has extended considerable economic aid, which has greatly benefited the country even though most people believe it inadequate in comparison with the needs. Also, America is now the leader of Western civilization, toward which Turkey has chosen to head. A tremendous effort has been made to appropriate not only its technology but also its content, even going so far as to replace the Arabic script, in use for centuries, by Latin characters. Some of these reforms are perhaps not yet firmly rooted in the whole country, but a great transformation has taken place. There are distinct changes in the position of women in society, and in general outlook, particularly in the attitude toward work, business, and material welfare. Considerable headway has also been made in democracy, even though it is not yet so solidly anchored as in the West. There may of course be some concealed opposition to Westernization, but most people realize that the trend cannot be reversed and that it will inexorably follow its course. Moreover, the prevailing tendency is to evolve not toward the socialistic type of Western society but toward the type based on private enterprise, as represented by the United States.

In addition to these circumstances that make for a sympathetic attitude toward the United States there is the good will arising from the purely human factor: the Turkish people's appreciation of certain American attributes. While Americans as individuals are regarded as simpler, less reserved, and less sophisticated than some other nationals, the common man likes the American's democratic spirit and anti-colonialism, and admires his technical ingenuity. In certain countries feelings toward Americans seem to have been affected by resentment of their higher living standards and by the too ostentatious behavior of some American tourists, but this does not appear to have been the case in Turkey to any appreciable extent. Though one occasionally hears complaints that the higher paying capacity of Americans in Turkey serves to raise rents and the wages of domestic servants, the great majority of the population does not seem to find anything abnormal in the fact that Americans in the country live better than themselves. And Turkey has been largely spared the too ostentatious type of tourist. Incidents between Turks and Americans occur, but they are very rare.

The appeal of the American way of life seems strongest among the young generation in cities. Many youngsters greatly appreciate American music and dances, allegedly because of their dynamic rhythm. The American way of dressing and other American usages are often imitated. What attracts youth most seems to be the informality of Americans, the practicality of the devices they use, and the liberty teenagers enjoy in the American family; some aspects of this are of course overlooked, such as the fact that American youngsters often work very hard in their spare time. The attitude of the upper classes and intellectuals, though generally pro-American, can be said to be more reserved. These classes have been greatly influenced by the standards of the French, the first Western nation with which Turkey had intensive cultural contacts. But the critical tendencies of this group—referring for example to the American's informality and his alleged aesthetic inadequacies—have been modified by closer contacts. Many American playwrights and novelists are now known in Turkey, and their works

146

have clearly demonstrated the high level attained by American literature. Also, it is increasingly recognized that criticism of some American attributes is inspired by values belonging to an era now definitely past.

Among these groups, and among the masses as well, sympathetic attitudes toward America do not mean a yearning for the American way of life and a desire to imitate it. The few aspects of it that people know are impossible to reproduce in Turkey under prevailing conditions. More important, methods that work admirably in the United States may fail to do so in Turkey if they are not adapted to the totally different conditions there. Turks cherish their own pattern of living and seek improvement only within its framework. This pattern has considerably changed in the decades past, and will probably change further with increasing industrialization, but it preserves some of its distinctive features. And it should continue to do so, since most of these features are compatible with progress whereas indiscriminate imitation leads to shallowness.

I think that each country, without imitation, can learn from the other, and thus Turkey, in her contacts with the United States, need not be solely the receiver. Perhaps her experience can be helpful, for in her nearly seven centuries of statehood Turkey has gained a knowledge of problems and prevalent attitudes in areas adjoining her present territory. And though she cannot give technologies to America, she may have something of wisdom to offer, a wisdom that may help the American to attain fuller relaxation and a more intense savoring of life.

from Egypt

MOHAMMAD KHALAFALLAH

The author: born in Egypt (Suhag), 1904; studied at Dar-el-Olum College (Cairo) and the University of London. Since 1942 Professor Khalafallah has been at Alexandria University, where he is Dean of the Faculty of Arts and Head of the Arabic and Oriental Department. He is particularly interested in a psychological approach to the study of Arabic literature and literary criticism, and is the author of several books and articles in these and related fields. In Alexandria he delivers weekly radio broadcasts on Arabic culture, and also serves on the councils of youth organizations, on ministerial committees concerned with education, and on various university and government delegations. His wife is English; they have two children. He visited the United States in 1953, spending some time in Princeton and Washington, D.C., and then traveling throughout the country for about six weeks. The author obtained the permission of his government to write this essay.

I

PERHAPS my earliest impression of America dates back to the Armistice after the 1914-1918 war, and the announcement of President Woodrow Wilson's Fourteen Points. These were acclaimed with enthusiasm and admiration by our leaders and public speakers, for they advocated guarantees of political independence and territorial integrity to great and small states alike. And this early association of America's name with my country's efforts toward self-realization remained vivid to me through the succeeding years. In that period the American War of Independence, and the valor of its leaders and commanders, stood as inspiring examples to the Egyptians in their national campaign against the colonizing power.

My visit to the United States in the fall of 1953 came about through two invitations: one to attend a Colloquium on Islamic culture, sponsored by Princeton University and the Library of Congress; and one from the United States government to visit places and organizations of interest. The Colloquium afforded a direct and stimulating contact between the Islamic world—with its long-established spiritual and cultural heritage—and the modern world

148

of America, with its material progress and its scientifically planned and organized life. (The conference also revealed a certain American desire to discover, and perhaps encourage, Islamic attitudes favoring a secularization of the legal systems and a modernization of the classical Arabic language and writing—two fundamental problems that Muslims and Arabs prefer to tackle on their own initiative, guarding against suspected suggestion and enticement from outside.) And my subsequent tour of the country—east, west, north, south, and middle states—had many interesting points to offer, in the form of new friendships, closer contacts with people from widely separated parts of the country, correction of hasty impressions about American life and people, and sympathies gained for modern Egypt and her legitimate aspirations.

A month and a half of traveling, halting for one or two days in a city, and then off again to another, with clockwork regularity and a hustling speed! Streamlined efficiency was evident everywhere: in the airport, in the hotel, and in the city. To be efficient, to get the maximum results out of every undertaking, to reduce waste of material, time, energy, and thought to the least possible, and to secure the highest standard of living for each of the more than 150 million citizens seemed to me a generally adopted philosophy of life in the United States. But a visitor to America also receives plenty to stimulate his mind and aesthetic taste. He finds there not only inspiring beauty, natural and man-made, but also a whole new world, originally of different races and cultures, forming one big progressive nation, building a new social structure, creating novel forms of literature, art, and philosophy, and possessing unlimited resources, which if wisely and unselfishly used can have a universal beneficial influence.

Whatever else may fall from his memory, the visitor is not likely to forget the warm friendship and hospitality extended to him. This is one characteristic that Americans and Egyptians seem to have in common. Amidst the impersonalness of a big city, it was good to be met by a friendly American, sometimes an elderly professor, at the airport or the railway station. One was lodged, entertained, supplied with information, introduced to many people, and generally cared for in a most generous way. The only regret I have here is that I was not able, after my return, to keep up correspondence with many kind friends whom I had the pleasure of meeting, and whose sympathy with my country's aspirations I felt I had definitely won.

The Americans strike one as a "knowledge-thirsty" nation. Everywhere there is an eagerness for information and for news, even though one cannot help but observe—despite different shades of thinking and tendencies—the same coloring of ideas, the same enthusiasms, and even the same misapprehensions, expressed from the Atlantic to the Pacific. A nationwide network of daily papers, magazines, television, and other means of quickly transmitting information seems to be effective in forming and molding American public opinion.

The topics that my hosts in the different places suggested for talks and discussions ranged from ancient to modern Arabic literature, from basic principles of the Islamic religion to its relation to contemporary life, and from ancient Egyptian history to Egypt of the Revolution and her present-day aims and attitudes. But each subject seemed to touch on some practical American interest. Everywhere the audiences seemed keen, enthusiastic, and generously appreciative. They were never ashamed to confess ignorance about the heritage of the East and its affairs. They blamed Egypt and the Arabs for not supplying the American public with adequate information about their glorious past, and sufficient explanation of their present-day problems. Many Americans expressed openly their sympathy with and appreciation of Egypt's efforts in her national reconstruction. At times, insinuating questions formed part of the picture. In most cases we Islamic visitors knew their motive and object: they were simply part of an antagonistic campaign sponsored by organizations with Zionist sympathies.

But one general question came up, in one form or another, in practically every meeting. What chance is there for Communism in Egypt? Are there any Communistic tendencies in modern Arabic literature? How do Egyptian youths look upon Communism? What is the attitude of Islam toward Communistic teachings? Would Islam favor a joint stand with Christianity against materialism? The repetition of such questions, and the earnestness with which the answers were awaited, revealed to us one of the important psychological factors in the makeup of America's international policy. Three years later this deep-rooted American concern about

Communism came to the surface to disturb the friendly attitude that America used to show toward Egypt.

Apart from this anxiety about Communism, America revealed herself to us as the land of all, and for all, races, cultures, and religious creeds. Christians, Muslims, Jews, Bahais, Free Masons, and followers of many other varieties of religions and faiths live side by side in complete freedom of belief and worship and expression. A manifestation of this freedom is the way Arab students in America exercise their rights to hold meetings, discuss their national affairs, and even criticize America for what they sometimes take to be an unfriendly attitude toward the Arab countries.

The social practice that shocked us most in the United States was color segregation, which is still adhered to in a number of Southern states. We had an idea about this color problem before visiting America. But to see it practiced before our own eyes greatly interrupted our admiration for the splendid achievements of the American civilization. The Prophet of Islam—who was an Arab—tells his followers in the most definite terms: "There is no superiority for an Arab over a non-Arab except by piety." In Islam the conception of the rights of man applies to black and white alike. Thus a Muslim, faced with color segregation in the form and magnitude it is taking now in some of the Southern states, begins to suspect that America's material progress has been achieved at the expense of spiritual values. He is driven to despair of the success of American leadership in working for international peace and justice. There is a redeeming feature in the fact that American courts have upheld the principle of integration, and that the President of the United States has gone to the extent of dispatching federal troops to a troubled area to maintain law and order and to protect individual liberty from malicious interference. But this remains one of the fields where contemporary Muslim reformers are convinced that the West can get an inspiring lead from the teachings of Islam.

Leaving aside the blemish of color prejudice in certain areas, one rejoices in the fair attributes to be found in every sphere of American life. A combination of economic wealth and scientific progress has enabled America to do wonders in the world of invention and production. Everything there is conceived and constructed on a large scale. Recently, in Egypt, we had an example of this quality of spaciousness in American endeavor. In a joint undertaking Alexandria University and the Library of Congress achieved the microfilming of a wealth of manuscripts of great historical importance and academic value, treasured in the St. Catherine Monastery of Mount Sinai; the world has now two copies of these microfilms, one in the Library of Congress and the other in the Alexandria University general library.

Graduates and scholars of Egyptian universities have always been given a genuine welcome in the American centers of learning. The several schemes of American research grants are making it possible for Egyptians to visit the States and follow the recent advances in the various fields of knowledge, both theoretical and technical. Lately a system of cultural exchange has made available to Egypt the services of American professors in her institutions, and has enabled her to send some of her own scholars as visiting professors to different American universities. American educational methods are also being carefully and critically studied, and groups of Egyptian teachers are being sent periodically to the States, to bring back practical suggestions for improvements and reform.

The same may be said of other departments of life and thought where Egypt has been seeking to benefit by the experience and success of experiments in the United States. The increasing reading public in Egypt has been introduced, by means of translation, to a number of American literary works, such as those of Edgar Allan Poe, Washington Irving, Henry James, Ernest Hemingway, Sinclair Lewis, Pearl Buck. Also in the humanities and other fields of knowledge American contributions are being translated into Arabic. A number of Egyptian writers have cooperated in preparing an Arabic condensation of six American books that appeared in the series "Twentieth Century Literature in America" and dealt with American poetry, novels, short stories, drama, criticism, and non-fiction. In introducing the book to the Arabic reader, a famous Egyptian writer and critic welcomed its appearance as a healthy sign that the Egyptian mind is beginning to seek other fields, rather than being monopolized by the cultures of England and France. This turning toward the literature, art, and philosophy of the Americans, he asserted, would help to correct the Egyptian idea about the preponderance of material over spiritual things in American life, and to show America not merely as a political, military, and

152

economic power but also as a spiritual and cultural power. America, on the other hand, cannot know other nations by simply selling them the fruits of her land and the products of her factories: she needs to study their cultures, and to enrich her life by translating the products of their minds into her own language.

II

The area extending from the Persian Gulf to the Atlantic Ocean constitutes a real geographical, historical, and cultural unity. Its 70 million citizens have the same language, Arabic, and the majority of them profess the same faith, Islam. This area is important internationally because of its intermediary position between East and West, and lately it has risen into great prominence because of its discovered economic resources. From the rise of Islam it has been the center and heart of the Muslim world. The division of this area into separate political units was a superficial accidental happening, but the area remained divided as long as foreign domination ruled over its several components. Since the withdrawal of Western colonial powers the nations have begun to seek unity again under the banner of Arab nationalism. The object of this nationalism is to seek strength through unity, to ward off the possibilities of foreign interference in the area, to cooperate in regard to the government and life of the people, and to present a harmonized and unified front in the United Nations.

The sense of oneness among the Muslims—like the sense of oneness among the Arabs—was for a long time obliterated as a result of Western colonial policies. Now many important elements in the Muslim world have won their independence. Indonesia, Pakistan, Afghanistan, Egypt, and the Muslim communities in India and China have been endeavoring to seek unity of purpose through their common heritage of belief and culture. The religion of Islam is a great unifying force. It is not merely a religion in the narrow sense, but a cultural and social system, diffusing a spirit of comradeship and brotherhood.

Arab nationalism was given a great stimulus and a successful lead by the Egyptian "Revolution of Liberation." Naturally Egypt and her sister Arab countries hoped for moral and material support from the rest of the free world, and especially from the great free New World—America. At the beginning the United States

153

showed what appeared to be genuine sympathy toward Egypt and the Arab world. But unfortunately three disturbing factors began to vitiate that policy.

The first is the biased attitude of America toward the illegitimately created state of Israel, which has proved a real menace to peace in the Near East and caused a million Arab citizens of Palestine to become homeless refugees. It broke the geographical continuity of the Arab world. It began to menace the sacred heritage and the political and economic life of Egypt and the Arab countries. It showed itself a real danger to the very existence of the whole area when it acted as a spearhead for colonial aggression against Egypt. It brought a racial consciousness into an area that has always prided itself on the fact that it never knew color, race, or religious prejudice. And America, under the pressure of influential Zionist sympathizers, began to turn the balance in favor of the million Israelites against the interest of 70 million Arabs and the sympathy of 400 million Muslims all over the world. The aid that America is supposed to have given to the Arabs, who are the other side of the conflict, is in comparison negligible: a few million dollars granted to Transjordan, and some grants to the countries of the Baghdad Pact. As things stand at present, no fair critic of international problems will blame Egypt and the Arab countries for their disappointment in American policy and their distrust of American intentions.

But a second factor in the directing of American policy toward Egypt and her neighbors has proved an even greater disturber of friendly relations than the first. In their anxiety to ward off the Communist danger to their interests, America and her allies resorted to a policy of military alliances in the Middle East. Various kinds of pressure were applied to bring Egypt and the Arab countries into line with this policy. But as part of her revolution philosophy, Egypt was convinced that, from both national and international points of view, a policy of positive neutrality for her and her Arab neighbors was best. Military alliances, she believed, would only increase the area of clashing interests between the two major rival powers of Russia and America. America, however, does not seem to appreciate this legitimate tendency on the part of the small countries. She insists on achieving her ends at all costs, applying economic pressure in various forms or making military demonstrations to intimidate the small country and those who dare to sympathize with it. The moral indignation of the countries concerned and the disapproving reaction of conscientious people all over the world lower America's prestige beyond measure, and give her adversaries a wonderful opportunity to appear as defenders of the freedom and integrity of smaller nations.

Linked with this is America's desire for power and prestige in the Near and Middle East. Every offer of aid hides a desire for infiltration and penetration. Immediate gains are sought through vulnerable points in the life of a small country. The outcome is a temporary state of chaos and confusion, but this can only be temporary. The will of the nation prevails in the end, and those who oppose it, or try to stem the tide of nationalism, finish by submitting or being removed.

America should look thoroughly and sincerely into her own motives and objectives behind her offers of economic aid. The results of an aid that hides a seeking for advantage, supremacy, or political exploitation are in many cases the reverse of what the offer is intended to achieve. I venture to suggest here that America still has a good deal to learn in human psychology. When the freedom and independence of a country are at stake, no material advantages can succeed in causing the will of that country to deviate from its determined course. Egypt and the Arab countries are quite aware of the new experiment that the West is trying in the Middle East area by replacing the old military power with the new power that uses financial potential as the bait whereby to impose its domination over the area.

There can be no real peace of the southern and eastern Mediterranean until the grievances of the million homeless Arabs of Palestine have been redressed, and the human rights of the struggling Arabs of North Africa have been recognized. The destiny of the whole area of Arab nationalism is now one organic problem, which cannot be treated in parts. And whether she wants or not, America is inextricably involved in the complicating or solving of that problem. There has been nothing in past history to mar good relations between America and Egypt, no struggle between them resulting from colonization or imperialistic aggression. To the Egyptian mind, America is in a position to give better counsels than other Western nations, and to suggest new approaches to the problems of the Middle East. The American commonwealth of independent yet closely knit states is indeed a unique organism, unlike anything in modern Europe or the ancient world, and the American system of liberty, with its Declaration of Independence and its Bill of Rights, has been and continues to be an inspiration for all freedom-loving peoples. From the logic of her history, America ought to be the world's leader of opposition to the exploitation of the small by the big countries. But recent international happenings have shown her policy to be guided by forced alliances and by gain and expediency, rather than by right and justice. They have even given rise to the suggestion that America is aspiring to oust the British and the French from their spheres of influence only to take their place as a modern colonizing power.

Humanity has reached a stage in its intellectual and moral development where every country, big or small, can contribute materially and spiritually to the well-being of the world. Egypt may be considered a small country. But she is a land of ancient culture and long history, to which world civilization owes a great deal. At the present time she is engaged in an effort of reconstruction in all departments of her life, striving to emancipate her people from poverty, ignorance, and illness. She bears no malice or hatred for any people or any country. She realizes the necessity of international peace for the success of her national endeavors, and hence working for peace is a principal issue in her general policy. Countries like Egypt are not interested in or desirous of a world domination by one power or another.

The ages of masters and slaves have gone, never to come back. There is no corner of the earth in which human beings can be content to live without their dignity and freedom. Asia and Africa are no longer open spaces for outside domination and colonization. On both continents independent nations have risen, and the other nations have become aware of their individuality and their right to live their own lives and be masters of their own destinies. To disregard this human advance, and to treat free peoples not as ends in themselves, but as means to an end, would be to push the wheel of time backward, and to contradict the true logic of history. "We hold these truths to be self-evident, that all men are created equal, that they are endowed by their Creator with certain unalienable

Rights, that among these are Life, Liberty, and the pursuit of Happiness."

There can be only one right course to take for the good of humanity: the establishment of justice and brotherhood on earth. This is the only way to harness the powers of science in the service of humanity before it is too late, the only means to achieve peace and to avoid utter destruction of mankind. The world has enough goodness and reason to guide it on the right path, more than enough of provisions and resources. The alternative is chaos, misery, factions, intrigues, secret pacts, military alliances, a race in the invention of destructive weapons—a final victory of the forces of evil, and annihilation of the powers of goodness.

from Israel

S. N. EISENSTADT

The author: born in Poland (Warsaw), 1923, and settled in Palestine in 1935; studied at the Hebrew University in Jerusalem and the London School of Economics. Dr. Eisenstadt is Head of the Department of Sociology at the Hebrew University. His writings are primarily concerned with the absorption of immigrants in Israel. He was in the United States for a year in 1955-1956 at the invitation of the Ford Foundation. The greater part of that period he spent in California, but he also lectured at the universities of Chicago, Harvard, Michigan, Minnesota, and Wisconsin, and traveled widely in other parts of the country.

I

ISRAEL's contacts with the United States have been continuous, though diverse, throughout its development. This is partly because there are few Israelis of Eastern European origin who do not have relatives or family friends in the US, and partly because many American intellectuals have had a strong interest in the cultural-national and social-humanitarian ideals of the Israeli community: on the one hand, the rejuvenation of an old language and a national culture; on the other hand, a shaping of social and economic and cultural forces in such a way as to remedy some of the ills of mass democracy and industrial society.

Since the establishment of the State of Israel in 1948, the Israelis' awareness of America and interest in it have greatly increased—with the development of more regular intergovernmental relations, the changing place of the US in world politics, the appearance of American experts and technical advisers, the great increase in the number of American tourists who visit Israel and in the number of Israeli students and professional people who visit the US. This changed perception of the US is well illustrated by a story often told in Israel: when a schoolteacher explained to his class of ten-year-olds about the wars of the Romans against the Jews in the period of the Second Temple, one of the children asked "But whose side were the Americans on?"

In considering current Israeli views about the United States

158

it is important to bear several points in mind. One is the Israeli's self-image, his interests and sensitivities: he is convinced that his country has contributed something to the problems of modern society, but at the same time he may be sensitive to its smallness, its dependence on other countries, and the fact that it has not successfully solved all social and human problems. Also, although he increasingly tends to differentiate between the United States and its people he may sometimes lump them together and accuse all Americans for what seem to him blunders of American policy. And then too, his increasing contacts with various types of Americans make him aware of differences among them, but do not necessarily prevent irritation with certain aspects of American character that he considers general. On the whole, it can be said that Israeli attitudes toward the US are much less stereotyped than formerly, and much less rigid, though several constant elements are discernible in the flux; there is also a considerable degree of ambivalence.

One of the basic images that the US evokes in Israel is of course that of bigness and wealth, technical and economic progress and productivity. There can always be found great fascination with these qualities. But to this fascination there are often added several implied criticisms. There is, for example, the idea that the US is a purely technical civilization, with emphasis on material things and on the standard of living as a goal in itself; and the idea that it has an overconcern with technical manipulations, seeming to reach even into the realm of human relations. Many reports in the Israeli newspapers tell about the great importance of the advertising industry and its manipulation of human behavior—even though the more thoughtful reports tell also about the limitations to these attempts and the resistance to them. Another criticism concerns the attitude, often encountered among American visitors, that their richness and power give them legitimate claims to human and moral superiority, and entitle them to discourse and lay down the law on all aspects of life and society, despite a lack of culture as compared with standards of classical European education.

In such criticisms the element of ambivalence is rooted in our own preoccupations with efficiency and technical progress, and our own tendency to claim superiority for the way in which we have solved so many evils of modern social life. And such irritations with

America are much less noticeable among the second generation, the younger professionals or technicians of various kinds. There we find a greater appreciation of the problems of technical advancement and the standards of technical education. Those who have studied in the US have shown great appreciation of American professional levels, and an ability to learn from them. Moreover, almost all who have had such contacts are much impressed by the friendliness of most Americans and by their readiness to help, to teach, and to learn in their professional activities.

Needless to say, the so-called American individualism, the great emphasis on individual careers and advancement, has been one of the main criticisms of the US, not only in the older type of ideological criticism but even among many of the younger Israelis, who still feel a strong identification with the community and its "collective" tasks, even though they tend to shun the ideological verbiage of their fathers. One of these, a young graduate of the University who has an important governmental position, told me after returning from the US: "It has been fascinating to be in America, and many things were wonderful. But I do not think I could live there. Here in Israel we all have the feeling that we serve some common cause, that there is some meaning for our efforts. But there you can't find anything of this kind. Everybody is for himself. This is good for a short time, for a rest. But afterward it seems empty, although they often seem to thrive on it and it spurs them to action." Here too the criticism may be a sort of defense mechanism against the critics' own emphasis on individual careers. But it is rather prevalent.

A similar pattern of attitudes can be found with respect to another aspect of American life—its democratic institutions, its ability to educate so many diverse people in the use of these institutions, its colonial past, its great efforts to amalgamate its different elements. Here—it seems to many Israelis—is a great potential affinity, both historically and in terms of current problems, between the US and Israel, despite the obvious differences of space and numbers. Many Israelis who think about these matters feel that in this sphere of common experiences and problems there are good possibilities for cooperation and mutual understanding. But here again there may be dual attitudes, especially when a claim is made concerning the superiority of the "American Way of Life." Then formalism in democracy, corruption, McCarthyism, and similar aspects of the American system are sometimes stressed, as are also instances of the hardships of generations of immigrants as compared with the care they are given in Israel.

The attitudes of the Israelis toward Americans and America have been greatly influenced by the power position of the US in the world, and its attendant problems. On the one hand are beliefs in basic similarities between the two countries in interests and institutions; memories of the help from many Americans in the struggle against the British during the last days of the Mandate; appreciation of the important part the US played in the establishment and first stages of the State of Israel. On the other hand, a certain degree of disenchantment has developed. For large parts of the Israeli public the transition from a "movement" propelled by high social ideals to an independent state that must learn to adjust itself to general international usage and diplomacy, to power politics in which it can play only a minor part, has not been easy. Thus there are frequent criticisms of American foreign policy: for what is regarded as sheer ineptitude, lack of ability to understand fully its own interests and to pursue them; and also for hypocrisy and duplicity, pretensions to moral criteria and concerns while basically pursuing narrow, egoistical interests and veritable *Realpolitik*. Israelis tend either to think that Americans and American policy are naïve or to suspect that they are Machiavellian, because nobody could be *that* naïve.

These attitudes vary, of course, in intensity. And it should be added that as contacts increase, the critical attitudes tend to be modified. It is on the concrete and personal level that mutual understanding develops, based on sympathetic attitudes toward basic differences.

II

On going to the US, in 1955, I encountered much that I expected and was told about: the fast tempo of life and intensity of daily work in the big cities, the great emphasis on material comfort and goods, the very high standard of living and preoccupation with it, the high level of productivity and efficiency. I was of course duly impressed by many of the innovations, such as the supermarkets and the "drive-in" theaters and banks, and

161

also by the hum and rush of New York, its skyscrapers and skyline, Times Square at midnight.

Perhaps even more than by all this I was astonished by northern
California, where I lived during most of the year that I stayed
in the US. To this day San Francisco has remained in my mind
as one of the loveliest cities I have ever seen, a city in which it
was simply a joy to loiter and to look around, and the "Peninsula"
as one of the loveliest sets of communities. I was struck by the
informality and "openness" of life in California, the helpfulness
and good neighborliness; and in spite of the high industrial development the pace of life there seemed to be very different from that
in other places in the US, especially the big cities. It may well be
that the base from which I "operated"—the Center for Advanced
Study in the Behavioral Sciences at Stanford—implanted in my
mind a rather rosy view of California life. The year at the Center
was in a way a dream—one of the most pleasant dreams and the
most profitable and stimulating experiences I have ever had.

This year of residence in California and many trips to the East
made me sensitive to certain aspects of American life with which
I did not expect to be preoccupied to any great extent. I knew
that I would find America a very busy country with a high intensity of life and work; I also knew that there are many social
problems in the US. But what I was not really prepared for was
to encounter a preoccupation with social and cultural problems
as a constant feature of daily American life—not in intellectual
and doctrinal terms, but in a more simple and vital way. But before elaborating this theme I shall mention some first impressions
that were later reinforced and have remained predominant in my
mind.

The strong impression of bigness and breadth is of course a
cliche. But what I mean in mentioning it is not the bigness of
buildings or enterprises or monuments—interesting as all these
may be—but the bigness of the country and the fact that it is one
country. For someone who has lived in Europe and the Middle
East this is a striking experience. It is not only that the spaces
are so great, and that going by train or flying from coast to coast
is a longer journey than one is accustomed to. The main astonishment is that on such long journeys one is still in the same country,
within the sphere of the same civilization, talking the same lan-

guage, and meeting with people of more or less similar—or so it seems on first glimpse—educational, cultural, and social backgrounds.

It takes some time to find out that beneath this similarity lie great differences, that an American from a small Midwestern city or from the South may feel more of a stranger in New York or San Francisco than the foreigner does, for whom in the beginning all such places are strange and familiar in a similar way. One begins to realize that most citizens of the US have not seen a great part of their country, have perhaps never left their own state. And it gradually becomes apparent how little, relatively speaking, one part of the country is aware of or really interested in another part, or in national and international events. To discover this it is enough to read some of the "local" newspapers, to talk with people in the train, on the bus, or even in the plane. I remember being told by a friend of mine who visited some small place in the South how shocked he was that in the local paper the news about Russia's successful explosion of the hydrogen bomb and the official US reaction to this—an item of great importance that caused great concern at the time—came last after an announcement about changing the names of the city streets and other local affairs. For the visitor who is used to a high level of interest in international affairs, such experiences may be a great shock, and he may conclude that there is nothing so provincial, self-contented, and closed as a small American city.

But all such impressions only increase one's wonder at the basic unity of this continent: how can so many groups, who are not so very much interested in one another or in national matters, form one society? I doubt whether a full answer can be given to this problem, an answer that is not an elaboration of the obvious or a flight into fantasy or mysticism. It is, of course, quite obvious that the American economy is a functioning whole, in which all the parts are interdependent to a very high degree, and that this provides a strong common framework. It is also quite obvious that the national government, the flag, the Presidency, the Congress and Supreme Court provide not only common functioning agencies but also common symbols and foci of interest. Beneath all this, however, there is a common culture and way of life, going beyond functional interrelationships or institutions. And one begins to look for common values and traditions and common ways of communication that forge so many different people and groups into one nation with a high degree of national identification.

One part of the answer may lie in the "material" aspects of American life, the great abundance of material things and the emphasis put on them. It never fails to impress one how easy it is to start a conversation with a stranger about these things. A visitor also notices how similar, all over the US, are many external aspects of this material life: everywhere the same brands of products, the same advertisements, food, eating hours. It is true that there are differences in different places, but a visitor is struck by the similarity—and by the way it facilitates communication between people.

Another common bond may exist in the realm of human relations—in the formalization, as it were, of informality. A stranger or a slight acquaintance will go out of his way to be pleasant and helpful and to show that he likes you. He may even talk to you about his family or his personal problems, things you would never dream of discussing with a relative stranger. And you find that this cult of good human relations, of "being nice" to one another, can be found everywhere—at work and in hotels, in the garage and the railroad station. People are helpful to you, and expect some such helpfulness or openness on your part.

To be sure, you may presently decide that all this is very superficial, that it is just a sham or a technique for easing personal relations and allaying internal insecurity, a means of creating a general pleasant atmosphere for the smooth going on of daily life. But the fact remains that these easy personal relations, even if facile and instrumental, are one of the great facilitators of common meeting among different groups, people, and states. Whatever their deep roots may be, in personality and cultural values—a fascinating problem on which so much has been written and so little is known—it is important to remember, I think, that they serve as a common background and a common language, and emphasize, for the Americans themselves, the national unity. This can be seen most clearly, perhaps, in the behavior of the many ethnic groups and recent immigrants, for whom the code of personal relations has been an important channel of integration and of feeling some similarity with the older groups.

In emphasizing this aspect of personal relations in the US it would be a great mistake to overlook the existence also of deep attachments and loyalties: the formal informality may be not merely instrumental but also a façade for genuine feeling. The lives of Americans are very strongly interwoven in families and groups, in friendship, in traditions of an ethnic, religious, or regional past, and in many professional and intellectual circles. The quality and nature of these relations and traditions may be different, new—but without any doubt they do exist and are very intensive.

One thing that I expected to find in the US—a great difference in cultural levels—was partly confirmed but partly contradicted. Technological knowledge, of course, is rather general: one is struck by the great technological activity, the widespread interest in technical matters and standards. But I expected a different situation in the general sphere of education and cultural interests. Here, I believed, the extremes would predominate: the very best and the lowest, with relatively little of the middle range. One knows that there are in the US first-class schools and universities, the best in the world, and on the other hand a host of schools of very low standards; in between I was prepared for relatively few ordinary middle-level institutions. Similar discrepancies I expected in styles of housing and architecture, in entertainment, and the arts. This assumption of wide cultural divergences in the US, which is corroborated in numerous ways, would explain many aspects of the American scene: some of its tensions and contradictions, the difficulties of political leaders in implementing a continuous and "planned" foreign policy, various outbreaks of the McCarthy type, the contrasts in the approaches to the problems of American life (either naïve, complacent, but not very deep self-assurance, rooted in a provincial outlook, or the most painstaking and intelligent soul-searching).

But after closer acquaintance with life in the US I found that while these extremes in cultural levels exist, there are also many "middle-range" developments in various spheres, and their number seems to be constantly increasing: many solid, good schools that draw a growing body of students; many good, informative magazines that attract a growing number of readers. The increasing attendance at discussion meetings, adult courses, and other such activities may also be a sign in this direction. It seems to me that many of the healthy aspects of American political life—like the overcoming of McCarthy—can be at least partly attributed to these tendencies, and that they are increasing and gathering strength. It may well be that they will effect great changes in the American scene. It should of course be emphasized that the mere development of various "middle" levels of cultural and intellectual orientations does not in itself solve all problems. This may easily give rise to new types of standardized culture, and to a loss of the creativity connected with the existence of an upper "extreme." But it need not be so. In any case the way in which the different levels are bridged will probably influence many of the future developments in American life and culture.

III

As I have already suggested, one of the greatest surprises I encountered in the US was a realization of how very self-appraising the American people are—I would say how very ideological. It took some time to become aware of this—especially since the American type of ideology is different from the one to which I have been accustomed. Neither is it concerned with political and collective programs nor is it couched in terms of intellectual programs of belief—such as can be found in Europe and Israel. But it is a very pervasive force, and one has the impression that it is more prevalent than its counterpart in the traditional sectors of European society. I refer to the concern of many Americans, whether defensively or critically, to evaluate continuously their own way of life, its problems and tenets, and to some extent to compare it with other ways of life. This tendency I found, on different levels, in very many places and among many people.

There seem to be certain basic elements in the American's own definition of his way of life: high productivity, high standard of living, mastery over nature, professional proficiency, high regard for moral dicta and for moral use of the technical proficiency, an interest in work and a great emphasis on its virtues. The Americans are a hard-working people who take great pride in their work. This may be part of the rags-to-riches myth or part of the Puritan or immigrant heritage, but whatever the reason, it seems to be a very important part of American life.

There is also, however, a considerable preoccupation with the problem of values beyond the external armor of a technical civilization. This problem is manifest in many tensions, in the growing interest in education, in the concern about the content of the new leisure that is being acquired by many people, perhaps most of all in the conflict between activity and passivity—mastery over the environment and independence in the social setting as against becoming a cog in the machine. This is not the place to discuss the social and historical roots of the activity-passivity conflict—such as the rise of big corporations and industries, the decline of the independent small businessman, the development of white-collar groups, probably also the burgeoning of the advertising industry and its "motivation research," its attempts to manipulate human behavior. But the resultant lessening of the individual's spontaneity and autonomy is clearly a source of anxiety to many Americans. It was surprising to find how many aspects of American life could be related to this search for spontaneity, for individuality and meaning. The "do it yourself" movement, the great proliferation of adult vocational and hobby courses and courses on personal relations, the many clubs and community organizations, the addiction to "causes" —all are at least partly related to this general search for individual and national identity in a new and mechanized age.

These preoccupations seem to me to be closely related to the problem of tradition in the US. Many people I met, those whose families had been in America for many generations as well as more recent arrivals, seemed to feel a lack of tradition. I remember an American friend I met several years ago in Europe, who had been wandering around in the old countries inhaling the breath of history and wishing he could have some such sense of continuity at home. As far as I could find, however, this feeling is most prevalent in the big cities. In many places—in the New England states, in Maryland, in the South, to some extent in the West— one has the strong impression of deeply rooted traditional ways of life, of almost distinct civilizations. Sometimes there seems to be a strong attachment to the locality, to the city, town, or village, though some uncertainty about a common culture in the whole country.

Many Americans seem to feel that they have been thrown unawares into the role of a world power—the most powerful nation and the leader of the Western world—and are still not accustomed to it. This may not be true in some of the professional groups or in those with a long tradition of political activity. But it seems to me that the greatest part of the American public is still grappling with its world role and responsibility and still feeling rather uncomfortable and insecure about it. I remember the remark once made to me by an American: "I really feel that we don't know what to do with our power, what our real responsibility is and how to behave. We want to be a 'nice guy' in the world, and to help out, and we think that therefore everybody should love us. But this is really naïve."

This attitude and feeling can be found on several different levels. Among people who do not evince any great interest in foreign affairs, who could not tell one country from another, I have often found aggressive, self-conscious assertions about the superiority of the American way of life and the good that America is doing in the world, frequently coupled with complaints about the ingratitude of others and their "mean" self-interest. On a more sophisticated level one can find a groping with the uncertainties of what to do about international affairs and of the exact role that the US is playing as a world power, mixed with some traditional feeling about the wickedness of international politics. The moralistic attitude, the self-assurance that American policy is guided only by considerations of justice and right, seems to be very widespread, perhaps because it provides some sort of anchor in a very uncertain field. There are outbursts against criticism or against any suggestion that American foreign policy too may be guided by some self-interest, and easy assertions that whatever is good for America is necessarily good also for the free world, which should take America's lead; Americans are good, serve only good causes, and therefore should be loved.

Of course there are many people who are willing to listen to dissent and to learn others' points of view. On one occasion an American, after reading about border incidents in Israel, said to me "I must tell you frankly that it does not seem to me as if the Israelis always get a clean bill of health in these matters." After some discussion about this I asked him whether he was sure that the US had a clean bill of health in all its diplomatic and international dealings. At first he seemed to be taken aback at the very possibility of such a question, although he himself was rather opposed to the current administration and was willing to admit blundering mistakes; he listened on only because of good manners. But gradually there developed a discussion from which I think we both learned a lot, and through which some of the basic prejudices of each side were weakened. Such readiness and even eagerness to learn another point of view, to listen and to discuss, I found in many circles, especially in professional and semi-professional groups, in many clubs and social gatherings.

But the fact remains that apart from certain relatively small circles there appears to be a great naïveté and self-complacency, as well as insecurity, about foreign affairs and America's place in world politics. The insecurity may sometimes become uppermost, but sometimes it may only intensify the self-complacency and the rather simple assurance about the superiority of the American way of life. In any case, all this shows that the preoccupation with foreign affairs is not a purely instrumental one: it has become to a great extent part of the "ideological search," the search for private and national self-image.

In considering for a moment the attitudes toward Israel that can be found among the American public I shall not dwell on the views of the American Jews and the attendant problems of Israel's place in Jewish religious and national feelings, but shall concentrate on the average American (if there exists such a person). This average citizen seems to be aware of Israel primarily in terms of foreign-policy problems, seeing the country as a center of international tensions or as creating them or being a victim of them: trouble brewing in the region, border incidents, threats to peace, sales of arms, these are what seem to reach him. And combined with such current impressions there are, of course, images connected with the Bible and the Holy Land. Because of all this there can be no doubt that on the whole Israel and its problems receive more attention from the American public than do many countries of larger area and population.

In personal encounters the "average" American's questions to an Israeli are directed first toward general matters—such as the nature of Israel's political and social system, its alignment in the "cold war," its customs and climate—and then toward matters concerning the particular organization, profession, or trade to which he may belong. In the intellectual circles these questions are supplemented by others about cultural activities, and about the extent to which Israel has been able to establish democratic institutions, to "conquer the desert," to cultivate the barren land, to serve as a model for "underdeveloped" countries, and to absorb waves of immigrants and mold them into one nation. There are sometimes more negative attitudes, such as the view that the Israelis have disturbed the traditional patterns of life in the Middle East by introducing modern types of technological, economic, and political organization; in support of these accusations the fate of the Arab refugees is often cited. Or one may encounter charges (sometimes rooted in "traditional" anti-Semitism) that Israel is aggressive toward its neighbors or hypocritical in foreign affairs, complaints that its high moral tones do not conform with its practical performance, perhaps even accusations of Jewish plots. But the positive attitudes toward Israel seem much more predominant than the negative, and they tend to increase with increasing knowledge and personal contacts.

These contacts, both lay and professional, do not necessarily diminish mutual irritations—irritations that may be most intensive in those areas where the two "sides" are most similar—but they do make for a more direct appreciation of each other's problems, weaken preconceived stereotypes, and help to develop a common ground. Today the development of such contacts between nations, even though they do not obliterate basic differences, is of great, perhaps crucial, importance.

from Iran

S. R. SHAFAQ

The author: born in Iran (Tabriz), 1893; studied at Robert College (in Istanbul, Turkey) and at the University of Berlin. Dr. Shafaq has taught at Tehran University since 1929. His principal publications are concerned with the literature and history of Iran, but he has also been active in political affairs. Shortly after World War II he was the Iranian delegate to a Moscow conference on oil, and during 1944-1950 he served in the lower and then the upper house of the Iranian Parliament. Meanwhile he represented his country at the United Nations' meeting in San Francisco in 1945 (his first trip to the United States), and accompanied the Shah on a tour in this country in 1949. Between 1950 and 1953 he lectured on Islam and Iranian culture at Columbia, Michigan, and McGill universities.

I

IT WAS in 1908 that I was admitted, as a young boy, to the American school in my native city, Tabriz, called "Memorial School." There I first began to think of America, and my vague mental portrait of it was vivified by a set of landscape pictures hung in the geography room. I used to sit alone sometimes, and contemplate those pictures while hearing the sweet sound of a piano gently played at Dr. Wilson's house. Dr. Wilson was the school's president, and the author of many books on Iran; he gave his life for us during the First World War, while doing relief work. Those pictures and the piano were both new to me, and helped me to form a sort of indescribably romantic view of America.

Those were revolutionary times in my country, as Iran was struggling for its national life. We schoolboys were greatly stirred, and volunteered for military training in order to share in the defense of our homeland, menaced in those days by Russians. Our young American teacher, Howard Baskerville, twenty-four years old and a Princeton graduate, undertook to train us. He led us into fighting, was shot the very first day, and died on my breast. His body rests in the American cemetery in Tabriz next to Dr. Wilson's, still visited by patriotic people. Baskerville, Dr. Wilson, and other American men and women created in our imagination the picture of

America as a country of learning, beauty, love, and humanity. Through them, and in the Memorial School, I also came to meet followers of religions different from mine—Christian Armenians of Iran and Protestants of America—and learned to tolerate other faiths (most Iranians are Muslims). I began, too, to form a political opinion of America as a country upholding the rights of small nations, a government with no colonizing policy or territorial ambition. Later the American victory in World War I, crowned by Woodrow Wilson's Fourteen Points, completely certified for us our beliefs concerning the inexhaustible resources of America, both moral and material.

I must mention, however, that I also became aware of certain factors that diminished my estimation of America as a country of sincerely freedom-loving people—for no ideal can be realized in this world. First of all, I began to feel that some of my good missionary educators rather overdid their job. It was not rare to find in them attitudes and prejudices that embarrassed me. For them the ulterior motive in all moves and conversations was to provide one with pitfalls challenging one's faith. Therefore, delighted as I was to associate with Americans and even to share their religious meetings (for every Muslim believes in Christ), I really felt embarrassed whenever I had to face a proselytizer. Another disturbing factor was that in spite of my faith in the idealistic trends of American civilization, I began to get sort of puzzled by the row raised by the critics of modern civilization and the so-called Kultur-Pessimists, with all their talk about American materialism—a characteristic that even some Americans emphasized. According to these new prophets of the decline of Western civilization, America had subordinated human values to material ones.

In 1945 the Iranian Parliament, of which I was a member, recommended me to be one of the delegates to the United Nations Organization, to meet in San Francisco. We flew overnight across the dark immense seas to come all of a sudden to a blazing sea of light. This was New York—and in two days we were in San Francisco. I was at last in America, which I had longed for so many years to see. My first general impression of the country, as I then saw it, was the hugeness, the magnitude and majesty—which I had hardly anticipated. Cities, buildings, department stores, universities, factories, cars, railways, all showed incomparable great-

172

ness. I had many times heard Hitler in his public addresses ridiculing the Americans for dealing in astronomical figures, but after I lived in the country for a few months and consulted statistics, I found out such figures were realities. Another fact that impressed me then, and still more on another visit in 1949, was the amazing advance in science and technology.

But in spite of the immense material development in America, I did not find there the materialism of which the cultural critics had spoken so much. Almost all the Americans I met were idealistic and religious. Even in business centers like New York, thousands of churches were crowded with people piously attending the services. I rarely shared any family meals that did not start with a word of grace. Also of significance to me was the democratic way of life among all the classes of the people. This cannot be easily defined; it must be observed and lived. In America I found the assertion of individualism harmoniously reconciled with the demands of society. The same person who will assert himself before the greatest potentates of the earth will obediently do his military service, willingly pay his taxes, and thoroughly obey the traffic laws. I found this to be true even in the basic unit of society, the family, where the women, for all the prominent position they enjoy, live peacefully and cordially with their men. American women are generally well educated but even among those who were professors I noticed hardly any *femmes savantes*; they usually keep their femininity.

There is still another pleasant trait of the American character that I had not known before. Wherever I was I found a sort of spontaneous inquisitiveness in all classes of people; even the most learned men and women kept asking questions about my country and other topics, in all modesty and sincerity. This characteristic is one reason why foreigners are welcomed as public speakers, if they have any talent for it; the listeners do not try to embarrass the speaker with exacting questions or remarks.

There is no need to emphasize that the qualities I observed in my own personal contacts with Americans are not enough basis for daring generalizations. Certainly there were types that looked strange to me. Even the good typical American did not always show me the same smiling face I was accustomed to expect; for instance, when it was necessary for me to go through certain red tape in order to have my status changed, so I could lecture at Columbia, I often really missed those smiling faces. But after all, behavior like this is very familiar the world over. Sometimes even the political views did not seem to be what I was inclined to believe; I met a few Americans who did not care much for the rest of the world. Already I knew, however, that such attitudes were not prevalent.

II

The majority of Iranians would more or less share the opinions I have sketched, but there are many who would consider me too optimistic in my estimation. At least in the opening decades of this century the whole of the Iranian nation hailed America as the land of liberty, justice, and humanity. We knew America through books, educators, missionaries, doctors, and philanthropic workers. But for some the two world wars and the subsequent succession of events have changed that attitude and given rise to pessimistic views about America.

In seeking the reasons for this, one can hardly emphasize enough the effect of the modern propaganda system, with its astounding techniques of publicity and broadcasting. Let us not forget that the great nations have violently attacked one another through these propaganda means for years, each laying bare the other's weak points. Never before in history has such a systematic criticism been carried out with such success. All the nations of the globe, and especially those more or less exposed to some kind of imperialistic ambition, have been listening carefully to all that the Westerners and the Communist world have had to say against each other. No wonder, therefore, if these nations have developed an incurable sense of resentment, a feeling that degenerates to a kind of hysterical nationalism and hatred of the West. Moreover, the United States, although not deserving to be called an imperialist power, remained comparatively silent for years against the propaganda charges of the Communist countries, and did not undertake any adequate clarification. It is comparatively recently that it has taken up the challenge of the cold war.

There are also concrete actions of the United States—or lack of actions—that have caused it to become unpopular among some Iranians, and have given pretexts to those whose job is subversive activities for specific political aims. These include America's post-war attitude toward the small countries; its position as an ally of the imperialists; its Palestine policy; its alleged lack of tact and diligence in foreign expenditures, with a waste of time and money in red tape and office procedures, and a spending on numerous unimportant things rather than on those that are fundamental; the suspicion that its policy is influenced by self-interested corporations; its apparent naïveté in diplomatic dealings. If the Americans do not help a country they are accused of neglecting it; when, however, a government is aided by the United States, the internal opponents of that government stimulate discontent against the benefactor.

It is well to keep in mind that international Communism has always tried, behind the scenes as well as in the open, to render the US as unpopular as possible, making use of any circumstance that might suit its purpose. Thus we have the astonishing fact that the US has spent many billions of dollars during the post-war period to help other nations and save them from subversion, and yet has received not only no gratitude but even blame. I am convinced that sooner or later the truth about the US will come to light. But this does not mean that its leaders should not seek to find out and correct their own possible mistakes.

We are living in an age of international relationship, and no true unity of nations will come about unless we try to really understand one another and know how to appreciate our different values. Considering Iran-American relations, I might say that in the first place we Iranians should work hard to acquire the science and technique so astonishingly developed in America, by sending some of our best-qualified young men to study in that country. So far, we have been doing this, but without much scrutiny as to the selection of the fittest. The problem we are facing in this matter is that many of our students in the States like to stay permanently, since better opportunity is offered to them there.

Another thing we have to learn from the US is the democratic way of life. In spite of the long history of Iran, we are not trained in a true democratic manner, which means reaching harmony between individual and social rights. This synthesis is very difficult without real democratic education.

175

One great lesson all Iranians should learn from Americans is their healthy attitude toward life, especially in the practical sense. The fact that in the United States work means real honor for every human being, irrespective of rank or position, and that idleness and vainglory are looked upon as signs not of distinction but of degeneration, sets a good example for us to follow, because our whole national life depends on our productive work. Although Iran is only one-fifth as big as the US, it is larger than Holland, Belgium, France, Spain, Portugal, Switzerland, and Italy put together. We can surely produce more than we need for our internal consumption, and thus have the possibility of exporting agricultural products. Now, however, we are actually compelled to import foodstuffs from abroad. We may not try to industrialize our country to a great extent, yet we may be able to manufacture our various raw materials according to the needs of our country.

Educational methods in America should be carefully studied by us. The fact that American education is based on actual life, and that the young men are trained to carry both individual and social duties, is a most significant matter we ought to consider for our future. The spontaneity, freedom, and initiative encouraged in American educational centers should constitute our main goal of education. Students' unions and their system of self-government are also things that we should try to adopt, in order to develop character and personality in our young generation. We should try to learn from sport activities in America, which show health, youth, and the spirit of fair play—and that is exactly what we need. We need it even more for moral than for physical reasons.

Perhaps Americans can also learn from Iran. After all, this part of the world was the cradle of human civilization. The great religions originated here. Iran established the first true world empire in history. It is not seldom that an American, otherwise a well-disposed individual, comes to us with a sort of prejudice, perhaps looking down on us and underrating our values. Possibly notions like "underdeveloped countries" prevent him from seeing things in their true light—this and the fact that he may have preformed opinions about our vices and knows nothing about our virtues. Acquaintance with the Orient might somehow induce Americans to give up, at least partly, the spirit of rush and restlessness. Iranian art and literature, especially the mystic philosophy of life, might help to bring about the quietude so needed to mitigate the relentless haste of the West.

It is surely imperative that the Muslims and Christians should come to a better understanding of each other. After all, the cardinal teachings of the two faiths are the same. Perhaps it would be appropriate if I concluded with a passage from the holy Qur'an (Chapter 111, Verse 64): "O People of the Book, come to common terms as between us and you; that we worship none but God."

from India

A. D. GORWALA

The author: born in Pakistan (Quetta, then in India), 1900; studied at the University of Bombay. Mr. Gorwala, now an independent writer and columnist, spent a quarter of a century in government service, his positions including that of Supply Commissioner in Bombay during the formative period of food control and rationing. Since his resignation in 1948 he has been chairman of several committees (Hyderabad reorganization, export promotion, stock-exchange regulation, rural credit) and has achieved special prominence for his reports on public administration and on the efficient conduct of state enterprises. His publications include works on *The Delusion of Decontrol, The Role of the Administrator*, and *India Without Illusions*. During 1946-1956 he visited the United States four times, on trips ranging from two to four months and based primarily on the East and West coasts.

I

BEFORE World War II the United States was unknown to me. I thought of it as a vast democratic country founded by liberty-loving people in search of religious and civil freedom; a country that had fought a civil war to free its slaves, but treated the descendants of the slaves very badly; that was extremely rich, energetic, machine-minded, yet could not prevent a tremendous depression; that on the whole, though with very good intentions, seemed somehow lacking in proper organization and was prone to allow the orderly processes of its life to be upset by racketeers, graft, and businessmen of the robber-baron type. I had not met any Americans, and my knowledge of American literature was limited.

It was after the United States' entry into the war that I first met some of its citizens, when a food mission led by Herbert Hoover visited Bombay. Here, it seemed, was a group of hardheaded men who knew their facts but were quite prepared to listen and question and argue. Later I met the members of an unofficial mission made up of economists, academicians, and journalists, and found most of them able and avid to learn, forthcoming and very likable; the impression they gave was that if they were representative Americans their country must be exceptionally fortunate.

178

A. D. Gorwala

This feeling was not strengthened when on two trips to the United States shortly after the war I had occasion to see Washington officialdom at close quarters; calculators and sophisters in large numbers—and such it was my misfortune mostly to meet—do not enhance the glory of any nation. These trips acquainted me, however, with the importance and uniqueness of the United States, and the need to keep in touch with happenings and opinion there. And in two further visits—in 1954 and 1956, as a private citizen—I felt that while the United States had its failures, its successes outnumbered its failures several times over and included some of the highest achievements the human spirit could reach. As the principal bulwark of freedom it was entitled to consideration from all who respected the basic human values.

On these visits the mental climate of the country seemed to me to be appropriately summed up in the lines: "How wide the limits stand, between a splendid and a happy land!" The United States was certainly "splendid." It was rich, powerful, egalitarian, providing opportunity for advancement to almost all its citizens. It had vanquished unemployment and hunger, and had taken great strides forward in the fight with disease and in the prolongation of life. But somehow the nation as a whole did not give the impression of being a "happy land," as better-integrated countries sometimes do, though poorer and less splendid.

Perhaps happiness of that nature ought not to be expected from the United States. After all, in John Dewey's words, "We are all minorities in this country. There is no majority." Consequently there has to be a great deal of amalgamation and adjustment, with all that this means in conformity and the suppression of individual impulses. By any calculation the result has been extremely good. Yet in some ways a complete national personality is not achieved. Divisions on religious lines, especially Catholic and Jewish, are common, and make themselves felt in social and political life. The country has also racial and national divisions, the most prominent being the Negro, the Irish, and the Italian. The Negro still remains in many ways a second-class citizen, even in the regions where full political rights have long been conceded to him. In other areas his position is worse, though the highest legal pronouncements have consistently gone in his favor over the last few years. In any ordinary country the situation of the Negro vis-à-vis the

179

rest of the population would perhaps be understandable, though of course it could never be justified. But in the oldest democracy in the world, dedicated to the proposition that all men are created equal, the thought cannot be avoided that after all these years the problem ought to have been solved.

These disharmonies seem to be intensified by a strange cleavage between the ordinary citizen and the intellectual. The former is inclined to regard the latter with amused contempt, often leading to a positive dislike—which provides ample ammunition for demagogues who arouse public opinion against what they term "egg-heads" and attempt to make intellectuals seem a class outside the proper American tradition. It is difficult to believe that this condition can prevail in a country where education is free, and university education the normal goal of most parents for their children. A certain arrogance and offhandedness in the intellectual, especially in the less mature type—sometimes a cause of much ill-will when his avocations take him abroad—is perhaps responsible for part of this feeling at home. Suspicion of intellectuals certainly makes the position of frank-spoken individuals among them often difficult. Conditions had improved in 1956 as compared with 1954, yet many still felt that on controversial topics discretion was the better part of valor.

A famous philosopher has classified American politicians into three groups. One third, he said, were the salt of the earth, fine, disinterested men with a real sense of the public good; one third were ordinary, decent men, who supported their parties and tried to do their best; while the remaining third were simple crooks. The proportions are probably not the same today. The last group may have dwindled somewhat; but whatever its strength, it does play an important, though often behind-the-scene, part in American public life. Graft in all its forms, from the crudest to the most polished, remains a settled feature of politics. This is not surprising when it is taken into consideration that the cost of elections is very high, that many appointments in the civil service depend on patronage, and that the bulk of the judiciary is subject to elections and political support. Some countries, it is said, are so rich that a certain amount of corruption makes very little difference to their well-being. Yet the lowering of the tone of political and administrative life caused by the presence in, and behind, politics of indi-

180

viduals of this type is a great load for any country to carry, however rich or strong. The responsible press plays a very important part in assisting the community in this matter. Its continuous exposures not only bring to book real evildoers, but also keep firmly before the people the ideal of pure and public-spirited government.

To Americans in 1956 the long-term economic situation seemed very satisfactory. It was generally assumed that in the future business fluctuations were likely to be moderate, and that the ability had been acquired to deal with inflation or deflation through monetary devices. There was also a feeling that continuing growth of population and rapid advance of technology would assure higher production, larger markets, and rising living standards over the years. But life was still not easy for the man of moderate means, especially in the larger cities. Rent was high, as was the cost of all services. The ease of instalment buying, combined with the desire to keep up with the neighbors, often brought anxiety in its train, and high-pressure advertising and salesmanship caused many people to buy things they did not really need and could very well do without.

The real hero of America seemed to be the businessman. Status and prestige were accorded him in high measure. Where else would one find a statement such as that jointly issued by the presidents of eight well-known universities, declaring that "close relations between corporations and universities are of the highest importance to the future of both"? And, continuing, "In different ways these two kinds of organizations are bulwarks of free society in this country. As a major source of new knowledge and as a training ground of many of tomorrow's leaders, the university can truthfully say that the strength of the American corporation and its own are interdependent." The American employer, especially in industry, appeared to be the best in the world. It was generally believed that he was willing to pass on to his workers a large share of his profits from the increased productivity of these times, thus making them in a sense partners in his business. Perhaps as a consequence of this, and of the fairly high minimum standard of living, there seemed to be very little shame about, or condemnation of, conspicuous consumption by those who could afford it.

From the economic point of view, and therefore from the social, which often follows the economic, the United States appeared to present the nearest approach to a classless society. Equality of opportunity for all appeared combined with fraternity, with the result that very few people felt inferior to others because of the nature of the work they did. In such a society the absence of class politics was understandable. Substantial inequalities in wealth existed, but since very few were below a minimum that covered most of the basic needs, and since there were plentiful opportunities of rising, bitterness and hatred on economic grounds seemed absent, except in special spheres and areas.

The public educational system, school and university, financed from public funds, did not seem to inspire the full confidence it should have in such an opulent and advanced country. Some parents who could ill afford it preferred the burden of sending their children to private schools, because they considered the public schools in their locality overcrowded, or the teaching there defective. A curious feature in universities, state or private-financed, was the great importance attached to the publication of books and articles by members of the teaching staff. This seemed almost to overshadow the proper function of the teacher. It was said that some extremely competent teachers were not confirmed in their appointments, or given the promotions due them, because they chose not to write.

Great as are the attainments of the American people in many spheres of human endeavor, perhaps there is even now an element of truth in Burke's view of them: "A people who are still, as it were, in the gristle and not yet hardened into the bone of mankind." A particularly engaging quality of this people is its desire to be liked and approved. As a rule strong nations, past or present, are not seriously troubled by the fact of dislike or disapproval. For them it is generally enough to be respected or even feared. The United States strikes a new note in the world's history, for its desire to be liked and approved implies also a willingness to be judged by others.

My visits of 1954 and 1956 confirmed my conclusion from previous study that the United States, the most powerful nation in the world, is in international matters the most misunderstood. To this misunderstanding its own behavior and contradictions have contributed not a little. Official, semi-official, and Congressional sources have seemed to compete with non-official sources in loud talk, boasting, the issuing of brash statements on delicate and controversial matters, and the treating of publicity almost as an end in itself. The record since at least the end of the war seems to show that what the United States wants above all else is to live and let live, but that Communist power has not permitted it to achieve this modest intention. It has been made to appear extremely aggressive and warlike. In reality it seems the least likely nation to want to start a war; it is invariably on the defensive, and time and again has put up with grave provocation. But it almost always conveys the worst motives for its actions. The contradictions that have plagued its reputation are numerous—including the ambiguities of its military policy, its equivocal position on colonialism, the political expediency that has driven it into alliances with totalitarian states, its somewhat ambivalent attitude toward world trade.

In 1956 my own conclusion was that in international affairs the United States was basically sound, standing in general for the right, generous in its endeavor to assist other countries and to alleviate hunger, misery, disease, and anxious to achieve solid and lasting peace. Its strength seemed the principal safeguard and real protection of all free nations. And yet, a sympathetic foreigner who observed the country during that summer could not but feel a certain uneasiness at the air of satisfaction and hopeful assurance he found in many circles. The keynote seemed to be a reluctance to grapple with real world problems, almost to the extent of holding that they were not there, or if they were, that they should not be considered very serious. The economic situation had been extremely satisfactory, and the bulk of the people saw no reason for a change, whatever the clamant problems of the future might be. It was difficult as one left the American scene in 1956 not to feel some apprehension at what seemed a lack of realization of essentials.

II

To the mass of the Indian people, the United States is unknown except as a rich country far away, one of the two principal protagonists in a struggle likely to engulf the world. A slightly more informed group forms its ideas of American life very largely from American films, and is attracted, on the whole, by the richness of the settings, the free play of emotion and adventure, the possibility of escape from the painful realities of its own life. Its liking for the films is sometimes carried over into admiration for the country itself, which seems so full of opportunity for ordinary people. This group is aware of the United States as one of the testers of nuclear weapons, said to pollute the atmosphere and increase the danger of disease in all parts of the world. It also knows that the United States has given aid to India and lent it wheat to enable it to meet famine and scarcity.

Indian businessmen are inclined to see in the United States their ideal. To them it appears the apotheosis of profitable laissez-faire, and they swallow wholeheartedly the free-enterprise philosophy set out by its theorists, without taking into account the considerable degree of government interference and regulation that actually prevails in American business. Even those who are aware of this often cite the United States as an example, completely neglecting the special conditions there, including the understanding of social responsibility by the majority of businessmen.

Among Indian intellectuals (who include some of the principal politicians, for there is no deep gulf in India between the intellectual and the politician) a large group is inclined to see very clearly the faults and defects of the United States and not so clearly its merits and virtues. To some of these, though perhaps not to the majority, that country has taken Britain's place as the principal imperialist power. They are inclined to equate the United States with the Soviet Union, and the fact that it is democratic rather than authoritarian makes little difference in their estimation, except that because of its democratic nature they expect from it a higher standard of behavior and substantial advances toward world peace. The idea that the international policy of the United States is much misunderstood would have no appeal to them. Their view is influenced by what they consider its specific errors, such as the refusal to admit Communist China to the United Nations, the refusal to stop atomic and hydrogen weapon tests, the failure to bring pressure on Portugal to concede Goa to India, the entering into a military pact with Pakistan, the taking of a pro-Pakistan attitude over Kashmir, and the support of colonial countries such as France.

Indian intellectuals, like their counterparts elsewhere, are not immune from thinking with their blood, and the West's general dominance over Asia for more than two hundred years has not a little to do with their suspicion of the principal Western power of the present time. This feeling is encouraged by the fact that many fellow intellectuals in the European democratic countries—countries that have benefited enormously from their recent associations with the United States—are also extremely derogatory about United States policy and culture. Indian intellectuals thus find their views confirmed and strengthened by sources they have been accustomed to treat with respect; upper-class British opinion is particularly effective in this connection.

Intellectuals of a more objective turn of mind do not accept this general opinion. They find a great deal to admire in the cultural and educational life of the United States, in the cooperative nature and the initiative and mobility of its people, in its industrial organization and high labor standards, and in the good will and courage of some of its politicians. They are also inclined to discount the interested reports put forward from time to time about the likelihood of the United States becoming aggressive and starting a global war, for they realize the nature of the people and the extent to which public opinion influences the policies of the government, even in external affairs. Some of them have attended universities in the United States, or visited the country for appreciable periods and seen various aspects of its life. But the number and position of the intellectuals who think in this way are not enough to offset the other view. And blunders in the United States, combined with blundering explanations of its policy, make it difficult for many to maintain their opinions in concrete cases. A Mc Carthy, a Little Rock, or a State Department Goa communiqué often arouses doubt and causes despondency. Even if this mood does not affect the intellectual personally, it certainly weakens his ability to argue in support of his point of view with colleagues who have always thought differently, and it correspondingly reduces such influence as he may have had.

III

To the extent that generalizations are permissible about peoples, it may be said that both Americans and Indians are hospitable, gregarious, unrestrained in their sociable moments, and fond of conversation. Deep down in their natures, however, there is in both a strong element of melancholy thoughtfulness. They are incapable, for instance, of abandoning themselves to the long periods of spontaneous gaiety that make living so charming in some countries. Both peoples subconsciously feel that there must be some meaning in life, and the need to strive toward it is sometimes expressed in the strangest places and most improbable circumstances.

Americans and Indians are almost invariably interested in persons, sometimes to the point of an embarrassing curiosity. The genuine Indian or American, if he has not allowed a veneer of refinement to make him different, is certainly poles away from the reserve of, say, the Englishman. And with his friendliness goes the desire to express an opinion. Criticism comes naturally to both peoples, and there is never much hesitation in telling somebody else, albeit perhaps gently and politely, that he is wrong and ought to do something very different from what he is doing. In international affairs this takes the form of moralizing and preaching to other nations. The assumption of world responsibilities has to a certain extent impeded, though not obliterated, this tendency in the United States government. But the government of India, unrestrained by any such policy considerations and full of the enthusiasm of its early youth, sometimes just flashes its eyes, mounts the platform, and lets fly. Hardly ever are the spokesmen of the two nations so happy as when they are reciting the faults of some other party, telling it how and where it goes wrong, and urging it to rectify its conduct.

In India and the United States alike most people are not content with merely doing a thing. They must in addition convince themselves that it is the right thing they have done. If this conviction does not come readily, they often resort to rationalization. Where rationalization is too difficult—or where the particular mind is too logical and penetrating to be satisfied with rationalization, whether its own or that of others—mental conflict and unhappiness follow. To feel right is very important. Perhaps as a result of this, conformity is greatly valued in both countries. Difference, in small things or large, causes astonishment and, when feelings are aroused, resentment.

Both nations are federations, and the ticklish problems of federal-state relationships often give anxious moments to their governments and peoples. Both have a written constitution and a supreme court that often has to be its official interpreter, though in India the constitution is more detailed, and thus the court's scope for interpretation is more limited. The judiciary is independent of the executive in both countries. Both are pledged to maintain the rule of law and all civil liberties, including the right to freedom of discussion and freedom of assembly. Indeed, so close is the resemblance in this matter that there is hardly any issue of the fortnightly publication of the Indian Civil Liberties Union that does not note and summarize relevant judgments of the American Supreme Court, often comparing the view taken in like circumstances by the Indian courts, pointing out the development of certain doctrines in the United States, and sometimes urging the acceptance of the same view in India. The law is a respected profession in both countries. Complaints about the delays and costs of legal procedure are not unknown in the United States, though they are not so common as in India. Observance of the rule that the burden of proof is on the prosecution, and that no man is guilty until he is legally proved so, is equally strict in the two countries.

The teacher holds a special place in the esteem of both peoples. Invariably poorly paid in India, and often poorly paid in the United States, he is nevertheless regarded as doing something useful beyond the ordinary. In small communities he is sometimes guide and philosopher to the adults as well as teacher to the children.

Both the United States and India include within their populations a large group of citizens who are regarded as of a lower order and treated as inferior. The distinction in the United States is based on color and race; in India on caste. The Negro and the Untouchable are reproaches to the conscience of these nations, and should serve to remind both peoples of the little right they have to the claim of being truly civilized. The Indian Untouchable may be slightly better off, in that the law accords him equality of status throughout the land and makes any citizen's refusal to accord him that equality a punishable offense, whereas in certain areas of the United States the law itself does not speak out clearly.

In both countries the fundamental belief underlying all constitutional, political, judicial, and governmental institutions is the sacredness of the individual. Everything is for the individual and because of the individual. "His life, mind, heart, perception, and soul" are important in themselves. They must not be sacrificed to some other importance, even if it be deified under the title of the

187

state and interpreted as the sum total of the true good of all individuals. The realization of this basic assumption in principle and its working out in practice make the two countries real democracies.

There are differences too, though these are not so great as some Americans believe. The name of Mahatma Gandhi is known throughout the United States, and many Americans, combining the latter-day moral approach of the Mahatma with India's reputation for religious and philosophic lore, see in India a country primarily devoted to ethics, religion, and mysticism. Accordingly, they are inclined to expect from it a higher standard of behavior than they would from a country not so endowed, and are both troubled and vexed when they find their expectations disappointed. The Vedas, Upanishads, Buddha, and Gandhi notwithstanding, Indian behavior regarding the ordinary concerns of international life is neither better nor worse than that of most other countries. India can err, can be willfully wrong and negligent, can look at problems from a selfish point of view, as much as any other country.

Nor is there anything to justify the belief that the ordinary Indian's conduct is more virtuous and less vicious that that of any other similar man elsewhere. What may perhaps be said to be different is an appreciation of unworldliness that lies in the background to the thought process of almost all Indians. The highest respect of Indian minds goes not to the great statesman or general, the successful inventor, businessman, or even social reformer, but to the wholly unworldly saint who, having nothing, coveting nothing, living extremely simply, devotes himself to the service of the people in the special way that seems best to him. This appreciation fortifies for the more serious the doctrine of detachment, and leads to the acceptance of renunciation as a worthwhile ideal. From time to time even the normally worldly aspire to rise to it, and thus it is not altogether unknown to hear of X, a man eminent in political life, or Y, a shrewd and rich businessman, suddenly giving up position, family, and wealth in order to meditate in tranquillity on the meaning and origin of things. This does not make the average Indian a spiritually enlightened being; nor does it mean that his leaders, fond as they are of appealing to the moral traditions of their land, are better than many politicians in other democratic countries.

A. D. Gorwala

During my visits in 1954 and 1956, I rarely met businessmen, bankers, economists, or publicists without their raising the question of what they termed the "socialist overtones" of the Indian economy and plan. The word socialism seemed to arouse grave distrust; it was thought to be only one remove, if that, away from Communism. There seemed to be no awareness of the fact, stressed a great deal in early American history, that the abolition of privilege is a precondition to the establishment of a democratic society, and that consequently when privilege is rampant and cannot easily be eliminated, social action and direction are important and fully justified. Few societies have been so honeycombed with privilege in various forms as India in 1947, and a great deal of it still remains to be dealt with. The Americans seemed unaware, too, that the content of the socialism in force, and proposed, in India falls far short of the actions taken well nigh universally in Western Europe and North America in order to keep the economy operating on an even keel while maintaining a fairly brisk pace—such as the provision of social-security systems, action against monopolists, action to prevent unemployment or the going to the wall of small businessmen and agriculturists, national control of public utilities, the conservation of natural resources.

As Abraham Lincoln said, governments exist to do for their peoples what they cannot do, or cannot do as well, for themselves. In some countries, especially those that are underdeveloped, there is a great deal that the people cannot do, and any government worthy of the name has to take up a large part of the burden of development. That does not make the country any the less a democracy. And in India there is a further reason for government participation in the economy: the philosophy of a competitive struggle in which some are knocked down and others march ahead successfully—while it is relevant and understandable among large masses of go-ahead immigrants operating in a land of almost unlimited opportunities—has little relevance to either the social-economic conditions or the cultural and thought background of India.

The Communist knows that his real opponent is not so much the capitalist as the democratic socialist, for the latter acts to remove the grievances and discontents that the Communist can work on and exploit. Communism and Socialism are poles apart in their basic values, and the image of an India going Socialist as a half-

189

way house to becoming Communist can be regarded only as a fantasy. It is unfortunate that Krishna Menon, in view of his intemperate behavior and his widely spread reputation as a Soviet and Communist partisan, should continue to represent India at the United Nations. But to go on from that to judge India wholly by him is clearly to do the nation grave injustice. India is much greater, far more significant, than any individual, however powerful. It would be wise for both the people and the government of the United States to regard as the reality of India the country itself and its long-term aspect, not just those temporarily in power there.

IV

Neither India nor the United States can congratulate itself on the present state of understanding between the two countries. In each there is a certain amount of knowledge about the other, but understanding means much more than knowledge. It means also sympathy, informed with sufficient sensitivity to make proper comprehension feasible. Such sympathy between two nations is scarcely possible if their leaders, especially those who influence public opinion, regard the other country coldly. In the promotion of understanding between the United States and India, leadership has undoubtedly been lacking, and individuals in prominent positions may even be said to have fostered misunderstanding. Thus the first requirement would seem to be certain changes in men, leading on to changes in attitude. A sound foundation would then have been laid, on which an edifice could be erected with the bricks and mortar of formal measures.

Many such formal measures are possible: an increase of information; the presentation of different aspects of each country's lives to audiences in the other at different levels; exchange programs; talks and entertainment by competent speakers and artists; wider exchange of news; increased facilities for learning the literatures, histories, and philosophies of the other country. Of all of them, the most valuable so far have been those whereby the citizen of one country could spend several months or years in the other country; this gives a real opportunity of seeing people and ways as they are, and therefore of coming to like them, while at the same time recognizing differences. But without change in the higher echelons, the rest cannot be effective.

190

A. D. Gorwala

From few nations can the people of India learn so much as from the United States, and one of the most important of these lessons is that of national unity. This has been a recurring problem in Indian history; on more than one occasion jealousy and disunity have brought loss of independence. For the new India of sixteen states, with their many cultures and languages, the problem has special significance and urgency. An underlying unity, based largely on the Hindu religion, joins the people of all the states, but in the past this did not suffice to keep them together. It clearly needs to be reinforced by a fresh cement—by a firm belief among the people in every part of the country that they are primarily the people of the whole country and not just of the state to which they belong. This "emotional integration" is chiefly a task of amalgamation and adjustment.

A somewhat similar development has been going on for many years in the United States with excellent results: large numbers of peoples of different stocks, speaking different languages, have been welded into the American, each child growing up with a feeling for the country as a whole. Obviously, many valuable lessons of principle and detail on this subject can be learned from the United States. The Indian problem is in a way more difficult, because here none of the cultures is held to be superior and an object of aspiration for the others. The United States' experience in keeping its units contented within a federation can be very useful to India.

Also in the whole business of economic and social development, the Indian has many lessons to learn from the United States. The American's approach to this subject is generally human and classless, combining enthusiasm with practical ability and not allowing personal considerations or prestige to come in the way. His interest in societies is not, so to speak, anthropological, but sociological, concerned less with traditions and the way in which things have evolved than with the living society today, what happens in it, why it happens, who and what are the moving forces, how something else desirable can be made to happen. The Indian, especially in dealing with rural societies, is more inclined to the anthropological approach, with results that are often unsatisfactory.

Another lesson to be learned from the American is the willingness of professional men, engineers, and other supervisors to be ready, however high their rank in an organization, to do the actual work themselves and not shrink back from manual labor. The importance of this for establishing a proper relationship with the workers on a job can scarcely be overestimated. In India even officials who may have learned this lesson during their training relapse occasionally into considering themselves brain workers pure and simple. The Indian can also learn willingness to relate blueprints to problems, rather than following the common practice of imposing an appealing idea on situations to which it cannot apply. He tends to regard the area of imagination as different from the area of action, whereas the American will often let imagination determine action when he is brought up against concrete difficulties that require divergence from previous plans.

American social mobility—which opens up the field to talent, whatever its rung in the social scale, and thus permits the less privileged to rise to positions where their knowledge and ability can benefit society as a whole—could well be an example to India, with its stratified structure, inclined to rigidity. Acceptance of the American habit of working unofficially and cooperatively for every purpose and at every level would also make a very desirable change in this country. When a few men who are interested in a particular subject come together as individuals to discuss it and take action, without formal constitution or rules, they are often able to achieve the limited objects for which they met; such small units can influence society strongly for the better, and sometimes they end up as extensive movements.

India's lesson of passive resistance without violence or hate has already been learned by some oppressed Americans, who have practiced it with signal success in their struggle against privilege. As in the India of the past, the other party to the struggle, having a tradition of liberty and the rule of law, can be made to feel ashamed; and in its emotional response a large section of the population is likely to be opposed to the oppression it practices. Therefore such measures of passive resistance, properly organized, may prove even more effective in the future. It would be different, of course, if there were no such tradition, and if the other side—the government or the group in power—were prepared, like the Nazis or the Communists, to exercise any amount of cruelty to get its own

192

way and enforce submission. Then, apart from miracles, civil dis-obedience could scarcely succeed.

One of the qualities rarest in the United States seems to be seren-ity. A serene American sounds almost like a contradiction in terms. India has nothing new to offer to Americans in the techniques and principles of business or government; but its philosophy and the example of a few of its people may perhaps assist in bringing to the average American a degree of serenity. The values of Indian thought can be a corrective to the demands and insistence of a civilization that leads human beings to

> See all sights from pole to pole
> And glance, and nod, and bustle by,
> And never once possess our soul
> Before we die.

While agreeing that great speed or large size may be useful, Indian thought does not necessarily regard it as wonderful. Nor does it hold the possession of many and varied things essential for happi-ness.

Another aspect of Indian thought, the call "to be a lamp unto thyself, relying on thyself alone," may have relevance in a land where conformity of thought is for good reason fairly entrenched. The ability not to think about situations always in an extreme form, even while realizing that they do present serious danger, is also a capacity that may have its uses in the United States. Ameri-can statesmanship, it sometimes seems, would benefit considerably from acting more often on the Gita principle of "finding full re-ward of right in doing right" and letting "right deeds be thy motive, not the fruits thereof." Its effectiveness would then be greater since it would not be disturbed and driven off course by frequent heart-burning about the ungratefulness and misunderstanding of others. Such an approach would also revolutionize the current trend of American thought on the subject of survival, which seems almost to compel the adoption, should stress arise, of the most ignoble of attitudes.

from Indonesia

MOCHTAR LUBIS

The author: born in Indonesia (Padang on Sumatra), 1922; studied there at the School for Economics. In August 1945, at the time of the Indonesian revolution against the Dutch, Mochtar Lubis joined the Indonesian news agency Antara. Late in 1949 he and a few friends founded the daily *Indonesia Raya*, which became one of the foremost newspapers in the country. His published writings include two novels, short stories, and travel books; he has received several awards for his fictional works as well as for his activities in journalism. For four months in 1951 he traveled throughout the United States, on invitation of the State Department. In 1954 he was again in this country, for a short stay in Washington and New York. Mr. Lubis is known as a strong opponent of Communism and as a vigorous crusader against government corruption. Late in 1956 he was placed under house arrest by the military police in Djakarta, and this essay was written during his long detention. Subsequently he was removed from his post as Editor-in-Chief of *Indonesia Raya*.

I

WHEN I was twelve or thirteen I received my first introduction to American life, by way of two American boys named Tom Sawyer and Huckleberry Finn. Mark Twain had been translated into the Indonesian language about thirty years before, and has always been on the list of school libraries throughout the country. My earliest childhood impression of America, gathered from this reading, was that it was a big country, with full opportunity for adventures for people with initiative and pioneering spirit.

As I grew up I read more books on America—and on its big capitalists. I was learning about the growth of capitalism in Europe, and saw reproductions of women working like beasts of burden inside the English coal mines. Capitalism became a monster to me, and I shuddered at its inhuman abuses and its exploitation of the working classes. I learned that imperialism sprang from capitalism, and in our group of young boys in our late teens or early twenties we told each other that the reason we were not free like other countries was that the Dutch capitalists had colonized our country. Our enemies were therefore all capitalists and

194

imperialists. American capitalists were also classed as "the enemy," and we deeply sympathized with the American workers.

I learned too about the American fight for freedom against England, about the philosophy of freedom as propounded by Jefferson and other leaders of the American revolution, and I felt a response welling up within me. We felt that the American heroes of revolution were our heroes; the freedoms they fought for were the freedoms we desired. A new appreciation of America grew. But the specter of the American capitalists remained. There were good men in America, but there were also those dangerous capitalists.

Then came the Second World War. Our people fell under the Japanese military occupation, which proved no less ruthless and brutal, even more so, than the old Dutch colonialism. We were more than ever convinced that we must become free. Despite all Japanese propaganda and the exhortations of even our own leaders about the glorious future awaiting us with a Japanese victory, most of us, during the darkest hours of the Japanese occupation, secretly hoped for an Allied victory. To me the war was even more close. By a stroke of luck I found work with the Japanese military radio listening post in Djakarta, with the pleasant duty of listening to and taking down notes from Allied radio stations' broadcasts. Instead of being beheaded for listening to these "enemy" radios, I was paid for listening to Radio Australia, Radio San Francisco, the BBC, and other stations.

I found great comfort in hearing how Allied radio stations and American commentators explained the ideological issues behind the big war against the totalitarian system of Hitler and Japan. Especially American radio commentators stressed and restressed that the fight was for human freedom and for democracy, for the rights of self-determination and freedom for all nations. Later, after the war, when we found out, despite all these reassurances, that we had to fight and die to win our freedom, I felt a big letdown. We saw how the Dutch came back to regain their colony, their army equipped with American weapons and uniforms. I think that my disillusionment with America, which was regarded at first as the champion of freedom and democracy, was generally felt throughout Asia. We soon found out that America was just like any other big country. It said one thing and did another. It played power politics.

So before my first visit to the United States I had many pre-conceived ideas of what America is: my childhood impression of it as a big country of adventure and pioneers, my suspicions of American capitalists, my admiration for ideas of American free-dom and revolution, my impression of America as a powerful mili-tary force based on gigantic industry, plus other impressions—de-rived from American literature, books, magazines, and movies—that it is a rich country preoccupied with living in luxury and ease, superficial, money-mad, always in a hurry, materialistic; that Amer-icans make a fetish of full-bosomed near-naked young blondes; that they are individualistic to the extreme, highly advanced in technology but without spiritual depth to speak of; and that the Negroes are second-class citizens eternally bullied by the whites. Sinclair Lewis, Upton Sinclair, Theodore Dreiser, Hemingway, Fitzgerald, John Steinbeck, and then the younger American writers, Norman Mailer, Truman Capote, Gore Vidal—all contributed to these preconceptions. The older writers confirmed the stresses in American society, while the younger ones gave a picture of an unsure generation, an inner revolt, dissatisfaction with life, a sort of disenchantment, touching the idealists and the bad, the rich and the poor.

II

I made my first visit to the United States in 1951, traveling throughout the country for four months, and I visited it for a second time in 1954. When my plane winged down from a lead-colored overcast sky in an early morning of May 1951, I had my first glimpse of New York, and a great feeling of curiosity surged within me. The huge skyscrapers on the island of Manhattan seemed to confirm my idea of a solid and dominating capitalism. After-ward, when I had checked in at my hotel and gone walking alone in the streets, I had my first feeling of utter loneliness in that city of millions. The skyscrapers towering into the sky seemed like can-yon walls, impersonal, menacing. My first weeks of travel tended to confirm my preconceived ideas about the country. And I re-ceived another impression: an illusion of uniformity and conform-ity. I use the word illusion for reasons I will make clear later.

America is a mechanical, a technical civilization, a gigantic machine monster. Machines, gadgets, buttons to push everywhere, and everywhere, and everywhere. People talk machines, use machines, work machines, control machines, are controlled by machines; already they are planning fully automatic factories where machines will produce machines. An American city is nothing like any other city on earth: the feverish atmosphere, the machines and machines, pushbuttons and pushbuttons, and the terrible haste; people everywhere are in a perpetual hurry; they do not walk but half run.

In traveling from city to city I was haunted by "Come on to my House." The blaring song, crashing through the air night and day, followed me wherever I went (it was the hit of the year). I disliked the song intensely. To me it was cheap, and tended to confirm my preconceived idea of the shallowness of American culture, its materialism, superficiality, uniformity, and conformity.

Mass advertisements in newspapers, radio, TV, billboards, for twenty-four hours a day, seven days a week, fifty-two weeks a year, year after year, telling people to go to the same places, buy the same cars, gadgets, dresses, build the same houses, read the same pulp literature, to feel the same, think the same. Through the power of the mass-communication media, the same likes and dislikes, a leveling down of taste, character, personality: uniformity, conformity. The same garish neon signs from city to city. The uniformity of food; the fine art of cooking and eating corrupted by the invention of canned foods. Uniformity even in politics. People told me they voted Republican or Democratic because they had always done so, because everybody did so family, friends, city, or state. Everybody liked Eisenhower; "he's a nice guy" was the most frequent reason.

Detroit! The Ford factory. The might of machines, the endless belt of mass production: motorcars, refrigerators, radios, television sets, machines, fountain pens, canned goods—a consumers' society. The kitchen helper at my hotel had his own automobile: incredible! Saw my first automobile graveyard: what terrible waste. And what sinful waste in restaurants—all the good food that was thrown away.

Shocked to see in the South signs "For Whites Only," "For Colored." In a New Orleans tram I deliberately broke the rule by sitting in the "for colored" section; got the biggest surprise of my life when the conductor apologized and said that I must sit up

197

front. I am brown; I am colored too. These Southern people's fine distinction of color is beyond me! In a nightclub in New Orleans a young Negro girl sang "Too Young to Remember." The guests were mostly whites. The blacks were good enough to entertain the whites and work for them, and no more. A leader of the National Association for the Advancement of Colored People told me in New Orleans that even in churches the Negroes were allowed to sit only in the rear. What an insult to God! Saw advertisements in Negro publications offering special remedies to straighten kinky hair. The whites have succeeded in instilling such a monstrous inferiority complex in the Negro that he is now ashamed of his own hair!

What a sad sight these Indian lands outside Albuquerque in New Mexico: the Indians, the orphans of America, living in orphanages called reservations, sandwiched between their old traditional life and the relentless advance of American modern technology.

Talked with an American about the increasing juvenile delinquency. Horrified to hear his stories about young people taking drugs, committing murders, robberies, assaults. Too much freedom? Parents losing control over their children?

But as I traveled on and met more and more people, the other face of America began to be discernible. I began to be able to extricate myself from the overwhelming first impressions that no first visitor could escape, and my earlier preconceived ideas of the United States were refuted one after the other by what I saw and learned.

In Washington a taxi-driver misheard my request that he take me to a certain place and we landed far away from my proper destination. When I told him it was the wrong place he apologized and took me where I originally wanted to go, but when I wanted to pay him more he refused, saying it was his fault and I should pay no more because of it. He reminded me of the kind American officer in Korea who saw me freezing in an open jeep when I was a war correspondent there in 1950, and lent me his warm coat. I began to discover that this sort of kindness and helpfulness, this human warmth, is rather a persistent quality among Americans.

I was amazed to see the amount of advertisement directed to children. A casual visitor reading American newspapers and magazines would undoubtedly think that children have quite a decisive voice in the American home—deciding what kind of cereal they want for breakfast, what they will wear, even what model of car their parents should buy this year. But I later found out that one should not take American advertising too seriously. There could never be so many people plagued by headaches, hangovers, backaches, as one would judge from the number of advertisements dedicated to tablets and pills to take as remedies; if one regarded them seriously one would think that America is a land of people with perpetual dyspepsia. The fact is that it is a consumers' paradise, and advertisers will go any length to woo prospective buyers.

I was further struck by the almost total absence of the military. To one who was used to traveling in the new independent Asian countries, where the military is present everywhere, its absence in America must be a pleasant experience. In America one tangibly feels that the civilians are in the dominant position. Eisenhower, though a real full-blooded soldier, dons civilian garb as President, while Indonesia's Sukarno, who never was a soldier, loves to wear military uniforms. The Americans do not love soldiering and war-making, as the Prussians do, for example, or the Japanese. Many Americans told me that they go into military service and to war because it is a duty they must perform for their country, but as soon as the war is finished they gladly return to normal living again. And there is little glorification of soldier-heroes. MacArthur came the nearest to being idolized in that role, but Truman cut him short, and many Americans who really admire his military prowess, and respect him for the man he is, told me that what Truman did to him was a good thing: "we don't want to have the military start saying what is good for the country and the people," they said; "it's the people who must decide that."

At first I was rather skeptical when I heard Americans telling me that they are fed up with giving aid to foreign countries; that they would like to see an end to all this business of giving away American taxpayers' money; that Americans should return to their own country, work in their own country, and die in their own country. I remember a farmer in Tennessee. When I asked him whether he approved of Marshall Aid, of the sending of American soldiers to Europe and Korea, and what he really thought about all this, he said to me: "You've seen my farm, my house. That's enough for me and my family. We'd like to continue living peacefully and happily like this. Now we must pay high taxes because the government says we have to give aid to all those foreign countries. What for? What does it mean for me? No sirree. We love our country, and we don't need other countries." While the farmer failed to understand why America should give aid to countries in Europe and Asia, because he could not see the international implications of an economic collapse of those countries, he expressed the feelings of a great number of average Americans, not only on aid but on overseas activities in general. Within the United States there is no urge for territorial expansion, because there is enough scope at home for expanding industries and economic developments; the domestic market is big enough to sustain a continued expansion of production.

Then I began to realize that what at first looked to me like sinful waste is really not waste in the ordinary sense when it is projected on the picture of this perpetually expanding economic growth: it is an inherent aspect of the rapid and colossal turnover taking place within the economic system itself. Understanding this does not mean, however, that I can accept it. To me it is still sinful waste. Americans take the bounty of their country for granted. But for one who comes from a country where the mere ownership of an automobile may make one suspected of being a capitalist, it is not easy to grasp the real potential of the US economy. It is only by slow degrees that one is able to digest impressions, facts, figures, and statistics, and see how capitalism and free enterprise have developed to their present stage in America, making it a strong democracy, politically and economically.

American capitalism is no longer recognizable as the capitalist monster of the nineteenth century. Its face and position and role have undergone a big change, completely different from the development predicted by Karl Marx. Through the power of labor unions, the antitrust laws, the federal government's power to intervene to some extent in the financial and economic sector, the diffusion of wealth among the people—with more and more people owning stocks of corporations that were once owned solely by a few individuals—capitalism in America has become unrecognizable. It is controlled capitalism—controlled by the federal government, by the unions, and by public pressures. The progress achieved by American labor has now created a situation in which labor can speak on equal terms with capital, and capital must negotiate with labor to cooperate on a mutually agreeable basis. Capitalism in America has also become enlightened. Nowhere else in the world can one find private capital establishing such gigantic foundations dedicated to noble humanitarian purposes. The efforts and achievements of these foundations, many of which extend their activities throughout the world, helping and aiding where the greatest help is needed, are things of which American capitalism may feel very proud indeed.

Thus labor in America is no longer the toiling and exploited masses of Marx's era. In fact, many an American worker would look to the people of other countries in the world today like the veritable representative of a capitalist himself. There is no cause for me or for anyone in Indonesia to pity the "poor, exploited American workers." The average worker in the United States earns more money than the highest paid government official in Indonesia. He owns his own house, his own automobile, has his refrigerator, radio, television set, carries life and health insurance, has a strong labor union, probably even owns stocks, works five days a week. Upton Sinclair's *The Jungle* is no more.

I received the impression that the American labor unions have gone far indeed. They are very rich, and wield enormous public power. They are even active outside the United States, and play a big role in international affairs and relations. For the most part they carry their responsibilities with dignity and wisdom. Nevertheless I also found some negative aspects. Gangsterism is reported to control some unions; some are outright extortion and terror organizations. This is a problem that all American labor should solve.

Not only is labor in America in such a good position that it is immune to Communist encroachment, but in general there are within the country no objective factors whatever for any success of Communist penetration. It is because of this that I felt so disgusted with the anti-Communist campaign that raged so indiscriminately while I was in the United States. The hysterics of that campaign went so far as to become a negation of the very freedoms and human rights and respect for dignity that are the basic mainstays of the American society. It is fortunate for America that this is now a thing of the past; but for some years America stood under the brand of McCarthyism, to the great discredit of her own people.

The United States has become an egalitarian society, where classes in the true sense of the word are absent. It is, I find, even more egalitarian than Soviet Russia, which boasts of having established a classless society, or than Indonesia, where traces of feudalism are still strong in many parts of the country and there is a distinct separation between the feudal classes and the common people. At first I thought that in America there is a special moneyed class, a sort of money nobility. But I found out that this is not really a class. When one can pass from one "class" to another if one has the money to buy a Cadillac, to rent an apartment on Fifth Avenue, or to dine at the Stork Club, the special privileges of belonging to a class lose their "glamor" or significance. The "money families" who once controlled banking, industry, trade, are no more. Besides, the glass of orange juice or milk, the steak or chicken, taste the same in a cafeteria or an expensive restaurant, in a Fifth Avenue apartment or the home of a worker.

The machines and their mass production have not after all systematized life and created complete conformity, as my first impressions made me believe. It must be admitted that casualties have fallen in the course of the mass manipulations of production, consumption, public opinion and taste, and even politics (or especially politics). Untold misery must have been caused in many homes and human hearts by the indiscriminate Communist "witch hunt," in which mass media of communication were used to propagandize the work of the zealous witch-hunters. No doubt it is the massive manipulation of public opinion and politics that has given the word "socialism" a bad odor in the United States. Most people there have no clear understanding of what socialism is. I was amazed to hear angry criticism leveled by Americans against the TVA projects, which have done so much for the people. Free enterprise has become a sacred symbol in the United States, and government interference with economic activities is considered bad. To most Americans the words "state planning" bring the image of a totalitarian Communist system. In dealing with other countries, especially in trying to understand the problems of the underdeveloped countries in Asia and Africa, such rigid ideas could well be fatal.

With these powerful mass manipulations, a tendency toward conformity is a natural part of the whole process of development in American society. But in spite of the fact that people eat the same food out of the same cans, read the same books and magazines, live in houses that look so much alike, ride in motorcars that also look alike, listen to the same radio or TV programs, I found out that life in the United States is after all rich in variety, and there is plenty of divergence in thoughts, opinions, attitudes and stands, likes and dislikes and taste. Some leveling down of popular taste is inevitable in such an egalitarian society with such a popular culture, but the country is so big and there is so much of everything that after you go deeper into things and meet more people you find that the first impression of uniformity is not absolutely true. A certain degree of uniformity is created by the gigantic production machine of the country itself, but for that very reason it is not too frightening: the way of life and the forms of culture are not imposed from above. And because there is free choice, which is the basis of a democracy, we can find a rich variety behind this façade of conformity.

Moreover, there is in the American people a healthy and strong inner resistance to the threat of conformity arising from mass production, mass communication, and mass culture. I met many individuals—in the labor unions, the universities, in corporations, the press, the administration—who openly see the dangers of uniformity and openly speak out against them. I also met people who have no tendency to conform whatever, who retain their individuality, and possess the fullest freedom of thinking. Once I met another visitor to America, a European, and in comparing notes he said that proportionately there are more highly cultured people and intellectuals in the United States than in any country in Europe.

I was to learn later that American intellectuals feel lonely and rather lost amidst the mass culture of America. Questioning writers and artists I met during my travels, I was astonished to learn that mostly they did not know one another, and had no social interrelationship at all. In Indonesia most writers, painters, and other artists move in the same circles, get together, discuss things, have debates. In France most of the intellectuals and artists are to be found in Paris. But in the United States there is no place where they come together. It is possible that this semi-isolation of the intellectuals makes conformity in America appear much greater than it really is.

I found many Americans who suffer from a "European culture complex" and denounce American art, literature, music as inferior to European. This is most amazing. Like many Indonesian intellectuals I once worshiped Western Europe, especially Paris, as the center of culture in this world, but now European culture seems to me to have reached its zenith a long time ago. What they have is fine. But European society and culture are established and settled. To me the new American civilization is more exciting. Especially when you come from a new nation like Indonesia, you have the feeling that in the United States you are on the threshold of the future, with room and material to build new values. One of the most important characteristics of American society is that while it is already so advanced technologically, it gives you the feeling that there are still forces working to break through new frontiers, forces that gaze into the distances of space and continue to search and research.

The progress of atomic science, the researches into space flights, the developments in medical science, all this material and scientific progress must in the end produce new spiritual values. While it is true that material wealth makes many people into crass materialists, it can also become a means toward better and finer spiritual values to ennoble man's life.

In the problem of where their material wealth and progress will lead them, the American people have nothing to fear but themselves. The loud cries and dire warnings against uniformity, against the mass man in a mass culture, are a healthy sign that such dangers, inherent in the American system, are recognized. There is awareness of their existence.

III

When I speak here about Indonesians I sometimes speak about the elite group, composed mostly of Western-educated intellectuals, familiar with modern science and thinking, sometimes about the masses of the people, some of whom may never have seen a machine or an electric-light bulb, and sometimes about both, but it is necessary never to lose sight of the basic reality that a wide gap exists between the two groups. We are trying to bridge the gap as speedily as possible, but it is there today, and must be counted as a factor in our problems. The blue lagoons, the romantic islands, eternal sunshine, and pretty Balinese girls—which are what Indonesia means to most Americans—well, all this is there, but there is more, and not all of it is pretty.

Even many Indonesians have a special idealized image of themselves, which usually tends toward self-deception; this is why many Indonesians today are so insufferably self-satisfied, and perhaps it explains to a certain extent why after a decade of freedom the country still lacks inner stability and true progress. When Indonesians talk among themselves (leaders making speeches to the people) or with foreigners (leaders giving interviews), they will say that Indonesians are basically a democratic people (which is true); that they are religious (also true) and therefore will never succumb to Communists' temptations and propaganda (not true); that they are working and fighting hard to build up their nation (not true) in an effort to become a democratic country (partly true); that in order to advance the people and the country they will accept whatever is good from the Western world (the speakers cannot specify what they mean by this), and will accept aid from and cooperate with any nation as long as there are no strings attached (not quite true); that they feel no discrimination against any nation (also not quite true); that they are *ksatrias*, or noble knights, will fight fair (not quite true), and always fight for justice and freedom (not wholly true); that they are imbued with the spirit of *gotong royong*, or working together and helping one another (not wholly true today), and prefer to solve their conflicts through *musjawarah*, or talking together (also not quite true).

Deep in the subconsciousness of every Indonesian, even those who are Western-educated, is a belief in supernatural powers, in spirits that have the power to aid or hurt mankind. Indonesian newspapers (which should know better, but do not) unblushingly publish reports of supernatural wonders, of infants who have vanished, of a small child who can do wonder healings, of ghosts attacking a house. Books on black magic, telling how to reconcile two or three wives happily in marital bliss under a single roof, how to advance one's position with the boss, how to make oneself attractive to women, or invisible, or invulnerable to knives and bullets, are advertised and sold throughout the country. Nature

205

is thought to be full of supernatural powers with which one should be at peace; it is not something to be conquered or even challenged.

The Indonesian is covered by layer upon layer of historical tradition and impressions, and each layer still reacts to each other layer and to outside influences. He is a split personality. Still anchored in his historical animism, he has also felt the diverse influences of Hinduism and Islamic and Western cultures.

Western education produced a thin layer of intellectuals who form today a small power elite, living in different worlds (materially and spiritually) from the masses of the people and nevertheless subconsciously linked with those tradition-directed masses much more than it consciously realizes or cares to admit. The Indonesian intellectual has many personalities: eager to accept modern technology to advance his country and people, he is nevertheless full of suspicions of foreign elements; his Western-learned individualism is ill-matched to the communal life that is still the basis of village society; his Western education tells him to use his reason, but his ancient tradition bends him to mystical beliefs and contemplations; though eternally dissatisfied he is plagued by attacks of self-satisfaction; he is full of inferiority complexes that he tries to hide behind attitudes of superiority.

Indonesian intellectuals were able to spark the national revolution for independence after World War II. That revolution did not lack courageous fighters, though it did not lack cowards too. But it missed a philosopher, one who could give to this specific Indonesian revolution, through which a static society leapt into the atomic age, a philosophical depth and a strong moral firmness for carrying on after the fight was won. The outer revolution of throwing off foreign bondage was not accompanied by an inner revolution, and thus power struggles kept the country in perpetual motion from crisis to crisis, and corruption became rampant, with countless officials, major and minor, grabbing money from the state as they could. The replacement of Dutch officials by Indonesians was regarded as progress, but in reality the same static society continued under the new brown masters, themselves reverting to the role of the Dutch.

The same mistake was made in the economic field. During the colonial period the simple barter economy of the masses had been completely exploited by an impinging money economy, carried on mostly by Chinese but with some Indonesians, Arabs, and others as well, and also by a credit economy under the control of Westerners. Thus the colonial period left the Indonesian people holding the weakest economic position of any group in the country: imports and exports, banking, mining, shipping, the production of rubber, tea, and the like, even most of retail trade, were in the hands of Europeans and Chinese. It was thought that if these were replaced by Indonesians the country would be also economically free, but experience has shown that few of the new Indonesian entrepreneurs are a match for the old Dutch and Chinese hands; the majority of them become "fronts" for European and Chinese capital, and the foreign entrepreneurs have grown even stronger and richer. To many thinking Indonesians the situation is full of forebodings. People have begun to realize that political freedom is not in itself enough to bring prosperity to the country.

Despite various appearances to the contrary, the Indonesian people earnestly and sincerely wish to live in a democratic society, not bossed by special-privileged leaders. They share with Americans a deep desire not only for the maintenance of world peace but also for the preservation of democracy and individual freedoms, for economic well-being and the pursuit of happiness, for the possibility of living in justice and human dignity. Ideals of American democracy and of the United Nations Declaration of Human Rights are living things to Indonesians, and quotations from Jefferson, Washington, and other American revolutionary leaders served as a clarion call in the Indonesian revolution for independence. It is easy to see, however, that there are many and basic differences between the two nations.

Thus for example the free-enterprise way of the US would not help the Indonesian people. They would simply be crushed down by it, for lack of capital, managerial and technical skill, and experience. Moreover, Indonesians in general are not competitive by nature, being more accustomed to the tradition of mutual help and collectivism on the village level. It is logical, therefore, for the government to take a hand in giving leadership and impetus to economic activities. Though state planning has to many Americans a totalitarian ring, I think it is high time to realize that there are more than two ways to economic development—not only the way of free enterprise, as in America, and the totalitarian way, as in

207

Soviet Russia. It may well be that for Indonesia a mixture of free enterprise and state planning, plus modern cooperatives—which have proved quite successful with us—would be a means toward speedy economic reconstruction with popular support and participation, without infringing on the ideals that Indonesia shares with America.

There are significant differences, too, in the personal characteristics and ways of life of the two peoples, in addition to those I have already mentioned. For one thing, there is a difference in their concepts of time and space. To the Indonesians time is aplenty. They do not hurry like the Americans, but shake their heads at the feverish haste and activity shown by Americans, twenty-four hours a day. An Indonesian will say "Your fate is in the hands of God, what's the hurry, tomorrow will be another day," while an American says "I have to finish this by five o'clock." "We are not the slaves of time" is a favorite remark of one of my Indonesian friends, Western-educated and a progressive writer, habitually late to appointments. Year after year (for whatever reasons) Indonesian cabinets have presented the government's budget to parliament long after the year has passed, and no cabinet was ever yet censored for this criminal neglect. Government departments see no importance in replying quickly to inquiries. An importer from the island of Sumatra is reported to have been kept cooling his heels in reception rooms of the Ministry for Economic Affairs in Djakarta for more than three months, waiting for his import license, losing quite a lot of money in hotel bills, taxis, and so on. Recently it was reported that teachers on one of the islands had not received their salaries for ten months.

To the American, immersed since birth in the machine age, space is continually shrinking, distances becoming shorter and shorter; today he is even contemplating the realities of flights to the moon and distant stars. To an Indonesian, distance is still distance; there are places in Indonesia that receive mail from Djakarta only once in six weeks. Thus the concept of a steadily shrinking world—necessitating better and closer understanding and cooperation among nations, in order that they may live together in peace and with a minimum of friction—is of course quite strange to most Indonesians. This is reflected in the almost nonchalant way they have governed their country since independence, as if they had unlimited time and space to go on wrangling and fighting among themselves, and as if they could live in splendid isolation and do whatever they want. The Indonesians are not haunted by the possibility that they will be left behind by a world that advances into the atomic age.

An American is eager and restless. He wants to "go places." An Indonesian lacks this quality. Even when he feels dissatisfied he does not betray his restlessness, but will wait, wait, and wait. If what he wants fails to come, he will say it was not his fate, rather than immediately finding out why he failed, and trying again. An Indonesian lacks the bull-dog tenacity to carry on and on in the face of adversity. He is easily aroused and becomes enthusiastic for new ventures, but just as easily he becomes discouraged after preliminary failures.

The Indonesian concept of a good individual is one who lives in harmony with others. To outshine others is considered not quite in good taste. An Indonesian, unlike the demonstrative American, is not quick to show his love, or his hate either. This inclination to live in harmony with others and one's surroundings is why an Indonesian does not desire to challenge or conquer nature. It is also one of the main reasons why the Indonesians are called "masters of compromise" in facing their domestic problems. Again and again events in Indonesia, which anywhere else (even in Asia) would lead to fighting and bloodbaths, have ended peacefully. In truth, however, these so-called "compromises" do not solve the real problems of the country. To compromise in Indonesia really means to do nothing, to refrain from taking a decision, to refrain from shouldering the responsibility of a decision, because nobody wants to force the issue and break the harmony.

Many foreigners feel quite annoyed with the Indonesians who readily agree to what they say and then do nothing about it; they think that the Indonesians are liars, or deliberately tried to fool them. In most cases this is not so. An Indonesian does not lack the capacity to be forthright if the occasion so demands, but in general his sense of wanting to live in harmony with the world outside himself makes him also most unwilling to hurt the feelings of others. His sense of politeness, too, makes it very difficult for him to say no, even when in his heart he really wants to. Among Indonesians one simply refrains from asking something if one senses that the other would have to say no to it. Of course foreigners cannot be expected to have so acute a sensitivity as to be able to judge the right moment to put the right questions or requests. If a visitor drops in unannounced at the very moment that an Indonesian wants to leave, the host will never tell the visitor he cannot receive him; he prefers to be late to his appointment, or even miss it completely, and if asked he will insist that he is in no hurry at all. From experience I have found that Americans like straight answers to their straight questions, whether the answer be favorable or not, good or bad.

An Indonesian is in his own way an individualist, but his individualism is deeply immersed under the tradition of the village communal life, the democratic feeling that decisions should be taken with common consent. Thus he is not very competitive. When the price of native-grown rubber fell disastrously, the Indonesian grower simply stopped tapping his rubber, and waited till good prices came back. Not long ago an association of Indonesian shopkeepers in Java protested to the government authorities about the "unfair practices" of a Chinese shopkeeper who had tried to boost sales by giving prizes (including a motorbike) to people who came to buy at his store. The Indonesian shopkeepers demanded that the authorities prohibit the Chinese from continuing his sales campaign; nobody thought of trying to compete with him by giving away better prizes or selling at lower prices. An American, on the other hand, lives and thrives on competition. The expression "may the best man win" is typical of this attitude toward life. The ideal is to reach "the top." No matter what you do, you must do it better than others. In America this attitude is fortunately accompanied by a great sense of fair play and sportsmanship, which demands that the effort be done honestly.

The Indonesian's indifference to individual competition may perhaps explain why boxing has so far not become popular; sports that lay the emphasis on individual effort and competition have not taken hold. On the other hand, playing on a team, as in soccer and basketball, is very popular. There is no village, however small, that cannot boast a soccer team; tiny tots start playing the game as soon as they learn how to run.

An Indonesian regards his head as something sacred, and the touching of somebody's head is commonly regarded as an insult.

210

Americans express friendliness and affection by a pat on the head or even by a playful tug at the hair. Similarly, an Indonesian would feel gravely insulted if you gave him anything with the left hand; even pointing out something with the left hand is felt to be very rude. To an American such uses of the left hand are natural, especially if he is busy doing something else with his right; the American uses both hands in the most practical way he can.

But despite such differences in personal characteristics, Indonesians and Americans generally come to like each other after the first difficulties of contact have been overcome and each comes to understand the peculiarities of the other. Many times deep friendship and mutual respect have blossomed out of such contacts. The Indonesian and the American find that they share the same quick sympathy, and in most cases the same sense of humor, though the American has the edge in his greater ability to laugh at himself. They possess the same warm human feelings, the same sense of hospitality, both liking their friends to come to their homes. While in America I received many such invitations from Americans; I have been several times in Paris, and I know a number of Frenchmen, but I have never yet received a single invitation to a French home.

IV

There is a lot that Indonesians can profitably learn from America. A decade or so is nothing in the history of a nation, and since Indonesia is so young as a free state, she has everything to learn: technological skill, organizational and managerial skill, public administration, business administration.

On the personal level we can learn to trust more in our own ability to reach our objectives in life, rather than putting too much in the hands of fate; and to see the real truth as it is, rather than seeing things as we would like them to be. We can learn from American practicality and pragmatism and rationality, for we could do away with a lot of our mysticism and love for symbolism, which many times impede a practical confronting of the facts of life; from the American urge to achieve better quality in material matters, to put forth one's best in order to achieve the best result, and to look for new things, to find out what's what, to seek and seek—qualities that in America result in new inventions and new findings, great and small, which all together make life better, fuller, and happier for the individual and the society. We can profit from a little bit of American individualism (but not so much as to break or destroy the present Indonesian sense of family life, which is a good thing). Indonesian intellectuals, young and old, could learn the American maxim that all labor, whether manual or intellectual, is ennobling and respectable, and that one should not look down on people who earn their living by the use of their hands. And Indonesia can profit by learning from America's mistakes. By studying the negative factors in American society today we can learn how to avoid the danger that material progress will overwhelm spiritual values.

Modern American architecture, which opens up dwellings to nature, has much to teach us. It is high time that Indonesians, whose country is blessed by God with a most benevolent and constant climate throughout the year, should leave their enclosed shells with small windows and doors called houses. We should relearn to live openly and healthily, and learn to build wisely with such materials as bamboo and wood, so plentiful in this country.

We can learn from the Americans how to use proper machines and technology in order to make work lighter and not a backbreaking and soul-destroying drudgery. Already American-introduced machines have begun to create changes in the pattern of life and thought in Indonesian fishing villages. The introduction of motorized fishing boats with the help of ICA will in the end bring many changes in these fishermen's outlook. They have always depended on the vagaries of sea and wind, and a broken mast, the dying down of the wind, could decide between a good catch and a bad one. It has been their tradition to make sacrifices each season to the spirits of the sea, living in deep superstition and fear of the mighty spirits that lurk beneath the waves, behind the clouds, and in the winds. Now finally the engine has broken their dependence on the weather. Their boats can range farther, they can run after schools of fish; the ice-hold in the boat enables them to stay out longer, and for once they are masters of the natural elements. The need to attend to the engine, the ability to range farther over the horizons, with the consequent need to learn the principles of machinery and navigation, will undoubtedly in the long run have an effect on their thinking. Once their reason starts to work, learning and asking the answers to things that were formerly enveloped in superstitional symbols, great changes are bound to come in their daily living, in their values and their attitude toward life.

Modernization of agriculture, the introduction of machinery, fertilizers, new insecticides to combat plant plagues, modern medical care, modern communication into the interior—all such technological improvements will have a strong influence on the traditional ways of life and thought. With modern implements will come new ideas, and ultimately our present static society could become a dynamic society—in one generation perhaps? In two maybe? Of course I do not overlook man's ability to use such inventions for destructive purposes as well, but this is the responsibility of man, and is not inherent in the inventions.

Since we have so much to learn ourselves I feel a little presumptuous in suggesting what Americans could learn from us. Perhaps more concern for older people, in the sense of giving greater love and care to aging fathers and mothers, rather than letting them spend the twilight of their lives in the terrible cold loneliness of homes for the aged; a return to some of the old-fashioned ideas of parents' full control over children; something of the unhurried Indonesian ways rather than the eternal feverish American haste and restlessness. Perhaps a bit of the happy serenity and peace of mind reflected in the Balinese paintings, a bit of the deep contemplation expressed by the Javanese gamelan, a bit of the sadness in the Sundanese bamboo flute, because, knowing sadness, one can enjoy happiness better. It is difficult for me to say what in the Indonesian cultural heritage could be profitably learned by the Americans, for we ourselves are still finding out what we should learn from it. And it is not for me to say what America should choose for herself. The American people have achieved an astonishing material progress. Perhaps they can now embark more consciously on a spiritual and cultural quest?

I believe that my views on America and its people are generally shared by Indonesians who have been to America themselves. But few would admit these views openly or publicly. Many people are intimidated by the anti-American propaganda of the Communists, and feel that an admission of the good and positive aspects of America would make them targets of Communist attacks. Except

213

among the Communists, however, there is ample room for better understanding and cooperation between the Indonesian and American peoples. How can this be brought about?

Information efforts carried out by the official information offices always carry the stigma of propaganda. More can be done on the level of person-to-person contacts and cultural interchange: seminars for professional people from both countries; opportunities to visit each other's country for purposes of study; reciprocal visits of responsible journalists; collaboration of universities in the two countries; "exchange of persons"; special projects to introduce each other's music, dancing, painting; the awakening of interest in America for Indonesian literature, old and new, and the easing of conditions for the translation and publication of American literature into the Indonesian language.

Perhaps the teaching of geography and history, as practiced in schools throughout the world, should be reconsidered. When our world has shrunk so much that every nation is within hours' flying distance of every other, it is imperative that we know more of one another than we do. The old history and geography lessons no longer suffice. Nations should be interpreted to each other on a more warm and human level—perhaps in lessons containing dramatic representations of how various peoples in various walks of life go about their daily living. What I want to strive for is the creation of a live and human picture of each nation, for the others to see and understand—for it is the simple truth that whatever differences there are among nations, on the human personal level people are basically the same.

It is only through cooperation, based on mutual understanding and equality, with each country giving the best and the most it has to contribute, that mankind can progress to a peaceful and happier world. And we must never forget that in order to reach that goal we have to decrease the present wide gap between the underdeveloped countries and those that are advanced and economically strong. It is really very hard to imagine genuine understanding and cooperation between the rich and the poor. The rich may be able to understand the poor, but the poor find it very difficult to understand the rich.

214

from the Philippines

PURA SANTILLAN CASTRENCE

The author: born in the Philippines (Manila), 1905; studied at the University of the Philippines and the University of Michigan. Mrs. Castrence first devoted her studies to pharmacy and chemistry, but later shifted to languages and literature. At present she is Chief of the Cultural Division in the Philippine Department of Foreign Affairs. Since 1935 she has been actively associated with Philippine education, teaching in several universities, and has also done considerable writing, both as a newspaper columnist and as a contributor to Philippine magazines. She is the mother of seven children and lives in a suburban home, where the family raises corn in the rainy season. Her graduate work in languages at the University of Michigan (1930-1933) was supplemented by a year in Europe, after which she returned to Michigan (1935) to receive her Ph.D. In those years she was best acquainted with the Midwest. She visited the United States again in 1955 on an official speaking assignment that took her throughout the world.

I

U P TO NOW it is safe to say that in general the Filipino likes the American—in spite of confusing world and local events that have disturbed Philippine-American friendship. For those of us who have been a part of this friendship there is a tendency to take present happenings in stride, with a feeling that, more likely than not, everything will turn out well in the end. Yet we are also increasingly aware that our feeling of uneasy certainty could be simply a self-propelled faith, harboring a kind of fear, a doubt about its wholeness. Our faith has not been reassured by the violence stemming from the integration problem in America, or by American attitudes in some Asiatic countries, or by America's decisions taking the side of the colonizer in his issue with the colonized. But this is anticipating the story.

It is the story of Philippine-American friendship as I witnessed it from the time I was a little girl. As a child I knew the American as the burly soldier or sailor who went around our streets with a bepainted dancing girl on his arm. He was not looked at unkindly, but he was not looked up to with much respect. It was

215

certain, and even as a child one sensed the public feeling, that the woman was despised for her attachment to the American. Her profession was bad enough, but her character was considered doubly questionable because her man was an American.

The American soldier and the American sailor, in themselves, were accepted pleasantly enough. The children particularly took to them because they were generous with pennies and candy. I recall a vivid scene (I was then about thirteen or fourteen) in which a very small Filipino girl was tugging at the hand of an American soldier, who at the moment looked to me like a tower, and saying to him in a teasing, somewhat spoiled voice: "Gimme a pi-a-no—gimme a pi-a-no." The Americano looked amused but unsurprised. Even as a youngster I sensed that the soldier must have seemed very kind to the little girl, else she would not have dared to make the outlandish demand, which to her was serious enough and more than that, possible. But I sensed too that this strange creature was different. Otherwise why did he just look big and amused? His kindness was indulgent. Later I was often to ask, is American kindness to the Filipino always indulgent?

Quite a contrast to this picture was that of our American principals and our many American teachers in high school. We liked them, and some we even hero-worshiped, but we were properly afraid of them. They looked so grand and different, and they spoke in a way not quite like that of our teachers in grade schools; the words were the same, but they came out differently. They made us feel ashamed of ourselves when we spoke the dialect around the school premises, and we paid our fines for this guiltily but willingly, for didn't we want to speak English the way these fine people did? We learned all about Washington, Jefferson, and Lincoln, all about Longfellow, Poe, Lanier, Whittier, Whitman; we knew Washington Irving well, Harriet Beecher Stowe, Horatio Alger, Louisa May Alcott; we even knew what not to read, and that was Bertha Clay and Mrs. Southworth, who wrote very romantic novels and would corrupt our young minds and morals. Very few of us then read Jose Rizal, even though he is our national hero, and none of us, I am sure, read Francisco Baltazar, author of the greatest Filipino narrative poem. We were not made to. There was no question in our young minds whether this was the way to an education that would make us aware of who we were and what

216

our country was, what the culture, the history, the traditions of our people. Only later was I to feel this lack in my education, and to work, at a panicked pace, to make up for it by filling whole areas, not merely gaps, of ignorance. The task has been well-nigh impossible.

No one can make an absolutely correct statement about the reasons behind this American way of making us see American life and institutions—whether it was impelled by the desire of the colonial power to impose its civilization on the colonized (the Spanish way was to destroy all the vestiges of indigenous culture), or whether the American wanted the Filipino to know him and what he stood for completely, and thus pave the way for the two-nation friendship. The first reason I have partially discarded, perhaps because I have been rather fortunate in my friendship with Americans; the second I have also partially discarded, because I am too old and therefore too knowing of the ways of the world to accept it totally. Between the two reasons may lie the truth.

At high-school age during my time, a young person did not sensitively take it into account that the Philippines had these soldiers, these sailors, and these teachers because his country was not free. The presence of an American Governor-General was taken for granted by him, as a circumstance of a history he was not too well briefed in. He heard his parents talk occasionally of a liberal American in that office, like Francis Burton Harrison, who encouraged the Filipinos' participation in the government, but he did not feel actively affected by either the presence or the generosity of Americans in government. Later he was to know that this same outward-going Governor-General, and an equally outward-going President of the United States, Woodrow Wilson, had offered his country independence, but that his country's leaders feared for its safety from foreign invasions and refused the offer.

In this going back to pick up the warp and woof of my early impressions of Americans, the figures that stand out are often strangely conglomerate. In contrast with Mr. Harrison's was the figure of Governor-General Wood, severe and military—militaristic I would say now, with a better hold of the nuances of the English language. President Wilson stood out too. We studied his famous Fourteen Points in class, and we believed firmly that the United States entered World War I "to make the world safe for

217

democracy." How deeply engraved those words were! Even later, when I knew better and had learned the down-to-earth reasons for any country's going into war, I never fully believed that the American entry into the first world holocaust was not purely idealistic. On such materials were the Filipino students' minds fed. No wonder we sang the "Star-Spangled Banner" lustily, while we did not even know the words of the Philippine national hymn.

There is, however, also the picture of an American couple who attempted to send my young-man brother and me (I must have been around seventeen then) out of our Carnival box because they claimed that they had a right to it, and not "these squat-faced Filipinos." Two odd phrases to string together in a young person's memory—"to make the world safe for democracy" and "these squat-faced Filipinos." Ironically enough, because the world had been saved for democracy, the squat-faced Filipinos, both products of American-fashion public schools, stood their ground and retained their Carnival box in a country ruled at the time by Americans.

The Filipinization of education was well on its way during my university days, but we still had American professors and some of these, remembered gratefully, left an imprint on my growing up. In the academic world the barrier of race and color is not patent. Outside it the Filipino was made conscious by an American motorist, businessman, politician, or wealthy neighbor of his subject role in a colonial world; in the courts of the two countries, and in the international courts, battles raged about racial discrimination. But in the university environment the prejudice was seldom seen or articulated. It was the best of all possible worlds for keeping the tenets of democracy glowing.

Thus, all along, I was being educated in the American way, the curricula, the methods, even the holidays being American. Arbor Day was a replica of the Arbor Days of American schools; Field Day was observed in the same manner, and so were student clubs, student governments, student entertainments, student jam sessions; later, student fraternities and all the other concomitants of college life. Baseball was our popular school game, basketball to come later. I was only one of millions of youngsters who were going through the same process, blissfully unconscious that we were assimilating a conglomeration of influences—no doubt, basically good—that were not ours, but imported into our country. Only later, when we were reproached and reproached ourselves about our loss of identity, were we to become uncomfortable about our individuality. At the time we knew only that we were learning, and that this acquisition of knowledge was free for all.

We insisted on speaking in English, just as my parents spoke in Spanish to their educated fellow-Filipino friends. We prayed the home prayers in Spanish and in the dialect, but when I had something to ask that was special and personal I asked it in English. Also I must already have begun partly to feel in English and to think my deepest thoughts in English (though the dialect expletives, for use when very angry, are more colorful any time than the American ones, even those that Hemingway uses).

Silent movies, in English, were being gradually replaced by the talkies, and we were beginning to see American customs and see and hear American life on the screen. I listened carefully to the way Mary Pickford and Lionel Barrymore talked, and I learned about divorces from the movies much more than from the more exact information in American sociology books or in the magazine articles that we avidly read. The movies have always been an easier way of education. They are also, of course, quite inexact, and this is perhaps especially true of American movies. We were dancing what the Americans during the days of my youth danced, the way my children are now dancing the Cha-cha and the Calypso. We were reading, we were singing, we were furnishing our homes, shaping our education in the American fashion of those times, just as now some of the relatively well-off among the Filipinos have in their homes bars and American-fashion furniture and other fixtures.

The assimilation of these foreign ways was gradual and painless and, it may be added euphemistically, gracious, and it would take much expertness in malicious persuasion to convince me that there was any intention of spiritual domination for evil purpose. What happened was the natural result of a not-too-unpleasant colonization, and that the result should be the partial Americanization of the Filipino was well-nigh unavoidable.

II

Filipino students were sent to the United States in continuous flows. They stayed in that country of promise and acquired not only book knowledge but also knowledge of a country and a people they had looked up to—and they either found their expectations fulfilled or were disappointed. I can generalize on my own experience in the first half of the 1930's, and say that my stay in the United States, and in other countries of the world, has made me aware of the essential sameness of man.

Those were years of depression in America, and I saw poverty and want such as I had never seen in my own country. I was only later to learn that in our poverty-stricken areas, especially where feudalism still prevails, people were eating only one or two meals a day and only very little rice, our staple food.

I went to the United States with the usual young eagerness for something rather unknown but pleasant, more expecting a kindly reception than something different. I was not a little afraid, of course. There was my mixed stock of memories: of the Filipino child asking for a piano, of some of my former American teachers, of why America entered World War I, of America's principle that all men are created equal; yet also the memory of my brother and me being called squat-faced Filipinos, the awareness that in my country the American did not have to wait long in offices before he was attended to, whereas the Filipino had to fight his way or patiently take his turn, even the dim knowledge that Filipinos treated the American better than they did their own fellow-countrymen.

During my trip—it was by boat—I was snubbed painfully by a group of young American students from whom I thought I would get advance knowledge of American campus life. (A trip I was to make some twenty years later gave me a very different kind of experience. World events had then changed the American view of Asia; perhaps World War II had changed also the American view of the Philippines and the Filipinos.) The chill of September met me when I landed on America's shores, but spiritually I had been prepared for it by my young companions who would have nothing to do with me. They taught me an important lesson: I resolved that henceforth I would never make any overtures to my schoolmates; every move toward friendliness had to come from them.

It was a bad beginning, but that was all. My classmates accepted me and I was part of the student body. My professors kindly (or dutifully?) invited me to their homes and showed me warm hospitality; so did my deans, the foreign-group sponsors, and the civic groups. The dormitory included me in the weenie roasts, in the pajama round-the-hearth marshmallow roasts. I went to our university games with the fullest of campus spirits. I felt part of the flesh and blood of my university, and I spent there some of the happiest years of my life.

In my heart, however, I had only a little group, to which I was not Filipino and whose members were not Americans to me, composed of a young man and two girls and their families who loved me because I was a human being in whom they found kinship of spirit. These friends of my youth, and others who came later, removed for me forever the sting of the contemptuous words "squat-faced Filipinos." My face had not changed, and they had not minded. During World War II, when in my own country we sang "God Bless America" very softly and surreptitiously, because to be heard by our Japanese conquerors meant death or imprisonment, I was singing to these friends of my university days, and to the American friends of my mature years who were in the internee camp and whom my family and I were trying to help. It is timely to state here that we were an unobtrusive part of the underground. America's cause was our cause. My husband and I had decided that if the war ended and America did not come back, or could not, we were going to leave the country. We knew, by then, only one way of living our lives, and that was the way of democracy.

I enjoyed, during my campus days, the Americans' curiosity about us, and also felt duly superior when they showed their ignorance, not knowing enough then to realize that the ignorance could mean indifference, or the littleness of the significance given to the Philippines. In my youngness, I was only too eager to correct their misinformation, as when they asked me if the Philippines was part of Hawaii or of Latin America; or to fill the gaps in their knowledge, as when they asked if we wore shoes, if our language was similar to Chinese, if we had ever heard Western music. I showed maps, I danced, I sang, I spoke, and so did all my Filipino schoolmates, for we had to show these people who and what Filipinos were. Whatever poise I have now in my talks I owe partly to my polite and appreciative American audiences. It never occurred to me to wonder if they were indulging me. I was young

221

then and very subjective. Age makes for objectivity and for looking at the world and its affairs, life and its aspects, as a whole. In maturity every issue becomes both personal and universal.

America, or my American campus, was to teach me many lessons in trust I was to learn nowhere else. I signed for articles in stores, leaving a little deposit, and the articles were delivered to me on my promise to pay the rest when my allowance came. I borrowed books from the store libraries on a ten-cent deposit, or some such trifling amount, and was allowed free time for the book and a free conscience to return it or not; the university librarians not only seemed in general more approachable than ours (who tend to be of the "closed-shelf" variety), but they trusted the students, and it never occurred to us to run off with a book we were trusted with. And of course the newspapers that were on stands with a can for coins were a complete novelty; when I bought a paper I made my own change from the coins provided. America is a rich country, was my conclusion, but the more generous thought would follow that America is also a country of trusting people. Even now, when I find an American less suspicious than the average Filipino, and more believing of the other fellow's word, I am reminded of the general trustingness I encountered during my schooldays. It is a good thing to remember.

On my American campus I learned the lesson of healthy, but sometimes shocking, irreverence to superiors. In my country there was a sharp distinction between professor and students, and while I would not say of my people that they are markedly class conscious, we are more position-conscious than the Americans. In the usual weekend games I was charmed to hear the American students make fun of the professor's incompetent batting, or his inferior volley-ball stance. Sometimes in the summer we held our classes outdoors, and I was pleasantly startled to find the professors in shirtsleeves; incidentally, we worked just as hard in the picnic atmosphere as in that of the more sedate schoolroom.

I learned in my American student days what being dedicated to work can mean in a university. Later I was to be told that American universities are more given to sports than to actual studies. I was to defend the American love of sports as part of a youngness of spirit that I had seen in no other people in the world. And I was to tell the detractors, some Europeans, some fellow-Asians and Filipinos, that American education as I found it was more thorough than Philippine education, with a more complete participation of students in class. There was no spoon-feeding, contrary to what the detractors were to tell me. The professor expected that doubts would be raised by the students; questions and answers flew back and forth, and the direction of questioning was not always from teacher to pupil. I learned in America the democratic spirit of give-and-take in class; and I witnessed, and tried to acquire, a spirit of painstaking scholarship.

To return to the subject of sports, there is no doubt that the Americans were (still are) much more sports-conscious than Filipino and, I suppose, European students. They have a joy in games, a spontaneity, a kind of childish abandon that, I feel, are purely American. I have seen universities other than American and Filipino, but in none have I found the zest in games shown by the American students and professors and, at my university, even the townspeople. In an impromptu baseball game the professor would not be different in behavior from any of my schoolmates. He was just as eager, just as clever, just as argumentative when he stole bases or caught someone stealing bases. And when our football team returned from an "invasion" of other universities the professor and the county's master-plumber might be singing the rah-rah songs together as they marched through the streets. When this ever-young American spirit is reproduced by my fellow-countrymen at home, I find it somewhat embarrassing. In Rotary meetings, for example, the American-borrowed hail-fellow-well-met gaiety of the Filipino members seems not a little put on and strained. We are usually quieter and more reserved as a people.

The American is generally more sporting of spirit than my countrymen. He will fight with his fists, but usually not with a knife, like the Filipino; and when he has had enough, or the other fellow has called it quits, he shakes hands and usually does not hold rancor against his opponent. This difference between the two peoples was a sad fact to admit. We are an extremely proud people, touchy and sensitive, and we take a defeat badly. Even in our games we show this spirit, and when we fight, almost always with a weapon, we hold the grudge even afterward, most of us even after a handshake. The American campuses could certainly teach many Filipinos lessons in good sportsmanship.

In my American university I smoked, curled my hair, used rouge and lipstick, talked the campus slang. I was not worried over the fact that I was brought up almost severely. In America I acted freely, basking in my new freedom. Perhaps I was reassured by the fact that I was really safe in my freedom. Evenings, for instance, I might go from the university library at ten o'clock to our Women's League and loaf around a bit before going back to my dormitory. I would do this without fear or compunction, because there was no danger whatever involved. One was left alone as long as one minded one's own business.

But the exaggerated expression of freedom is license, and I found on the American campus of my days not only the healthiest camaraderie between boys and girls but also a freedom in sex relations that was not altogether unshocking. In my country we were not yet prepared even to discuss the no-chaperon idea (which, incidentally, has only recently been instituted and is still not universally accepted). The double standard of morality for the two sexes was—and still is—more clearly defined in my country than in the United States. One fine American influence on us is a wholesome, matter-of-fact companionship between boy and girl classmates that has gradually found its way on our campuses, especially in the state university. An unwholesome influence is evident in the quite un-Oriental lack of shyness shown by some of our young sweethearts when they make no secret of their affection in public. Good taste is violated, and here is where un-Filipino customs do not sit well on us. Generally speaking, however, the freer behavior is still kept within the bounds of Filipino traditions and customs.

After a year of dormitory life the students were expected to live outside with the townspeople. The first summer I was away from the dormitory I had my first experience of personal prejudice since my arrival at the university. I was looking for a place to live; there were "To Let" signs against windowpanes, and I was on the lookout for just such signs. But as I approached the houses that displayed them the signs would disappear. I was not wanted, because I was brown. It took me a long time to get over the hurt. In my own land we also had our little prejudices, but we were a polite people and did not show so openly our dislike of another person. I was truly homesick then.

But there were Americans and Americans, and perhaps in the

evening of the house-hunting day I would be with my group and they would condemn with me the narrowness and crudity of their fellow-countrymen's view. There were other bitter lessons later, I am sure, but strangely enough I cannot recollect anything definite except this incident. My friends taught me, not by comforting words but by simply being themselves, that in every man's life there are people who will accept him and people who will not, and the reason need not be patent or acceptable. The person, if he would be whole, must learn, regardless of how painful the lesson, to allow to matter only those people to whom he matters. Henceforth, little by little, I schooled myself not to allow prejudice and discrimination to undignify my individuality. But even now, when I see prejudice in connection with America, and can smile over its pettiness, I cannot but reproach that country with some anger for its failure to live up to the spirit of its excellent ideals.

On that same campus where I learned American sportsmanship, the Negro students felt spiritually and socially segregated. They did not go to the weekend dances, did not chum with their white classmates. The Negro population in the town was looked down upon. Only in the grade schools did I see race democracy practiced—little white children playing happily and unconcernedly with kids who were as black and wooly as Topsy. I have always wondered, in sadness, if my own tolerance, which I feel I do possess, is not tinged by the fact that I belong to the colored and therefore still despised group of peoples.

In this matter of prejudice I reason that even in the exercise of a virtue, or in the belief in a virtue, the law of relativity holds. A Texan friend of mine, excellent, in my opinion, in every way except in his view of the Negro problem during the late thirties (I met him after I had returned from the United States), explained his prejudice in this manner: "But there's no harm in my feeling distant from the Negro. He doesn't expect me to feel close to him. He doesn't expect me to invite him for lunch, for instance, after a business talk, or even to shake hands with him. We're both comfortable as we are." But "dedicated to the proposition that all men are created equal"—that was a comfortable idea too. I couldn't understand the anomaly then. I understand it a little better now.

This understanding was to come twenty years or so after my campus days, when I was sent throughout the world by the government office where I work. I saw sights then that gladdened my heart about an America I still believed in, despite disappointments and disillusions: Negro students and white students together on American campuses; a Negro cultural officer in Italy; important Negro officials in many American offices. In that country of vast contradictions, the desegregation issue was raging violently; it still rages, to America's shame. But from the very inconsistency of events, I understood the earnest manner in which America is really trying; trying with all her might to conquer a problem bigger than all her problems put together, perhaps bigger than her spirit can cope with at this moment.

In my campus days our Negro fullback's presence on the team prevented my university from playing one in the South. Such discrimination has unquestionably diminished during the past two decades. In the old days the only American Negro in the Philippines whom I remember as holding an honored position was the leader of the Philippine Constabulary Band; today we have a Negro cultural officer in the American Embassy, very well respected by both American and Filipino communities, and a number of Negro officials in Foreign Aid Offices. I do not, however, ask about their social status when they go back to the United States, because I am not sure of what the answer would be. America's spiritual battle is still on, and it has both a Paul Robeson and a Carl T. Rowan: the one bitter against an incongruous democracy and proving his bitterness by the most violent of proofs, that of attaching himself to the enemy camp; and the other recognizing the incongruity of that democracy yet finding the means of solution within its framework because he believes in its absolute tenets. Perhaps Rowan has seen clear through the pathos of America's confusion. He must see even more clearly than I, because he is more an actor than a spectator in the drama of American prejudice. He has been more hurt, and yet he continues to believe in America.

III

In the American homes where I lived when we were allowed to stay outside the dormitory, surprises awaited me. Once my apartment was close to that of a little household in which the husband was a skilled manual worker, and the wife very well educated; apparently the contrast was striking only to me and to no one

226

else in the whole house. They spent their evenings reading, the man as greedily as the woman. I had already observed that the Americans were a much more reading people than we—and I was a literature major who had her own share of the reading habit. My Filipino friends read but little, and in my own country reading was still very much of a school chore. Even now, especially among our women, and these may be well educated, the reader is the exception, not the rule.

In one of these homes the young men, not yet married, still lived with their parents. Each had a room and paid for it; I learned later, with some shock, that they were also paying for their board. The young daughter of another landlord, at eighteen, was practically on her own, with her parents unworried about her future, which she was carving out so competently with her own hands. There was more self-reliance in this eighteen-year-old than in many much older girls in my country, where the girls, especially among the well-to-do class, were, and still are, timid, unable to take care of themselves. Could it be that there was less sweetness, however? I wondered about this rent-and-board paying for a long time, yet I could not help admiring its self-reliance. In my country it was so different. While I was a young girl I turned over all my earnings to my mother, and we all took the whole thing for granted. When I was married I did not have a bank account of my own. Would it not have been better, I wondered, if not as "nice," if I had paid my mother for my room and board and saved up a little of my earnings for later?

I decided that these are two customs of two different countries— one in which the family unit is so close that interdependence among its members is emphasized in all ways; another in which the idea of self-dependence is inculcated deeply and urgently, and as early as possible. Both customs have their beautiful and their not-so-beautiful sides. Who is to say which is better? The rugged independent spirit has become the symbol of America. The Filipino's self-determination is expressed more in a group; as an individual he is not so independent in his thinking and acting as he might be. And this is curious, for the Filipinos have always loved and sought liberty.

I have intentionally digressed somewhat to dwell on differences between the American and the Filipino in their family life, because this has always been the subject of much discussion. Thus a Filipino friend of mine in the United States was shocked when an American acquaintance casually mentioned that his mother-in-law was in the Old People's Home. My friend did not stop to wonder whether the mother-in-law was happy, whether she might prefer her life of detachment from a household that no longer needed her. What he felt, subjectively entering into the situation, was the seeming lack of sentiment in the American makeup. The American, on the other hand, can be equally shocked by an old woman living with her young daughter-in-law and quietly waiting for death in the nook of insignificance she has accepted. Maybe neither Filipino mother-in-law nor Filipino daughter-in-law thinks that the arrangement is the best and the most ideal, but both recognize it as a rule of life that in-laws, though not necessarily meant for one another's affection and approval, should bear with one another for family solidarity.

This close-knitness is gradually loosening, partly because of the Filipino woman's entry into public life, or otherwise taking up activities outside the home. The disintegration that is happening before our eyes is manifested by urgent problems like teen-age delinquency and general youth confusion. It may be that this situation is in the nature of growing pains, but also it may come partly from American influence.

As I came to know the townspeople, and to know them as people, I found them different from the movie versions of American life that my fellow-countrymen and I had. They were like us in many ways, only sometimes they were more sophisticated or more ignorant, more materialistic or more generous, the way people are. Some were exceedingly curious, others cold and indifferent. I recall Voltaire's philosophical little piece called *The World as it Goes*, in which he wanted to show that people are bad and good, foolish and wise, faithful and disloyal; in short, they possess opposite qualities that neutralize each other and make it difficult for the onlooker to either praise or condemn them completely. That was what I had learned when, irrelevant as this remark may seem, I met a poetess who was living with a man who was not her husband—and was not shocked at all. America had by then taught me to mind my own business.

I saw with young eyes many other facets of the American picture. American politeness at first charmed me, and the American's apparent appreciation of every little thing that was done for him. The Filipino is warm but not so articulate. I soon realized that the American did not mean all of his social talk—but also that he meant a promise much more than a Filipino. I saw this in the way he kept appointments, went out of the regular order of his life to make good a given word. He was not quick to say "I'll try," as the Filipino is, but when the American says it, he will really try whatever it is that needs trying. Filipinos, with their innate urbanity and that inherited from the Spaniards, and with their Malayan and Asiatic inscrutability, sometimes make polite promises that are only half meant, being blended with the general uncertainties of life. This time I cannot fence-sit. I declare most firmly that the blunt and definitive American way of dealing, whether with promises, with situations, with queries, or with requests, is a better way. The opinions or the answers given may be wrong, but the firm manner is certainly reassuring. We hem and haw too much; we hedge and beat around the bush.

More a Filipino trait than an American one is a too great concern for what the other person may think, which is a sign of thoughtfulness but perhaps also of insecurity. It can make life pretty uncomfortable. I learned a much-needed lesson from my American friends, who would not make too much of it when they had hurt me unintentionally, because there had been no planning for it, and no malice. This wholesome attitude has seeped deep into my nature and, since my return to my homeland some twenty-odd years ago, has caused not a little misunderstanding between my Filipino friends and myself. I have found making a lot of explanations a difficult and unnecessary task, and my friends have not always understood my stand. Can a second nature really change a basic, a first one? Apparently in my case it can and has. With Western peoples, especially with Americans, I feel almost completely at ease, and in some respects more comfortable than with my own people or with my fellow-Asians. This fact has saddened me, and when my Western friends tell me that I think almost like them my sadness is not assuaged at all. No split-personality individual, conscious of his condition, is happy about it.

Filipinos, as a people, are warmhearted, interested busybodies. We always want to know "all about it." Maybe we also want to talk a little about it later. Our interest in a neighbor's affairs is not at all impersonal and often leads us to help him if his "affairs" mean problems to be solved; we are generous with advice and even with material effects. The American way—again this is a generalization, and any American small-town person can belie my statement—is to let the other fellow alone. I have traveled in many countries, but America beats a number of them in this quality of respecting the privacy of the individual. At its best, the principle develops self-respect and self-containment; it observes the rule of live and let live; it establishes a feeling of individual security in oneself; it elevates the dignity of the person and his right to live his life as he sees fit. At its worst, it can mean indifference—and I must say I have found Americans almost callously indifferent to what is happening around them.

There is a curious adjunct to these opposing qualities of the Filipino and the American which can be attributed only to the strange inconsistency of man. For all his warm generosity, the Filipino does not, generally again, make common cause with others for some communal good; does not take up the cudgels for others in vicarious indignation. Along with his fellow-countrymen he will fight to the death for freedom. But civic consciousness is not his major virtue. He is an individualist. Thus the body of a cat or dog run over by a careless motorist may lie on the street and the householder will feel no urge to remove it as part of his contribution to public service; the same householder may have the neatest yard and the cleanest house in the neighborhood. Or the Filipino can watch a bully blustering his way in the bus or on the street, and will not remonstrate unless he is the victim; if he is, no one else will remonstrate for him or with him, and probably he does not expect it. And again, the Filipino can be very angry and individually indignant about some official corruption, abuse, or irregularity, and remain completely silent; he just won't be involved. The result is that we have no cogent public opinion.

The American, on the other hand, will usually not bother about you individually, but let a common good be involved, let it be something that does violence to his idea of the right, the just, or the sporting, and he is there, getting into personal trouble even when the issue involved is not personal. I know that this opinion has been contradicted by Americans themselves, who have sharply criticized American apathy to voting or to other national interests. But my own observations remain in my memory. American women leaders visiting the Philippines have told us that when grocery stores hiked their prices unreasonably, the women in the neighborhood protested by boycotting them. We have read how American congressmen have been apprised by their constituents when there were untoward conditions in the community. When a prominent person has caused public indignation to rise against him he has been made to feel the common opprobrium. I compare our own indifference in similar matters to the American interestedness, and do not feel happy about the contrast.

Yet I look deep into the warm heart of the Filipino, and realize that, because one is a Filipino, every relative is welcome to the house, and every transient will be sure of a sincere invitation to breakfast, lunch, or supper, as the case may be, if his visit happens to fall at a meal hour. The American will not, usually, give such an invitation. With us an approaching beggar will receive some little pittance because the giver is less involved in the social principle of the wrongness of open begging than in the individual necessity of giving when asked because another individual is in need.

I have emphasized the individualism of the Filipino, but this is a distinctive American trait too. Emerson, Walt Whitman, Melville, the most American of American writers, were distinct individualists. Yet (and how many times I have had to use that word!) the Americans have a uniformity about them that astounds the foreigner. That everybody should possess a car, a refrigerator, a TV, and the other condiments of living is not merely a natural reflection of prosperity and material advancement; it is an urge for sameness, for uniformity, for keeping up with the Joneses. In a way this urge means a kind of psychological insecurity. Filipino sophisticates are unfortunately catching the spirit, but the individualism of the average Filipino is too strong for a successful uniformity or homogeneity of the whole people.

The American is deeply rooted in principles and laws; rules govern his thinking, living, and doing. The Filipino, acting mostly from the heart, is more impulsive and spontaneous. America's fetish for principles, while making it more homogeneous as a people, lays it open to question again and again. How can "all men are

231

created equal" be reconciled with discrimination toward individuals and peoples and nations? Here I must pause to wonder, however, about a certain phase of American discrimination toward us. Are we perhaps guilty of fomenting it, if not actually causing it? An American friend once told me: "You Filipinos make too much of us white people. You allow us privileges, in offices, in parties, everywhere." Another said: "Do you realize that you show more discrimination toward people of a lower class than we show you?" Stated somewhat too bluntly, these facts happen to stare us in the face. And when America's critics say that America's principles look good on paper but stop there, they should remember that its insistence on principles was used for moral persuasion in United Nations' problems that could have sparked war and didn't.

Nevertheless the basic fact remains that America's incongruities, the discrepancies between its precepts and its examples, have not been its strongest selling points to people who must be convinced of its sincerity before they can be persuaded of its desirability as a friend or as a world leader. Though the Filipino needs less convincing, America confuses even the Filipino. Why these principles if they are belied by deeds? I felt that way about racial prejudice when I was in the United States, even though I did not see or feel too much of it personally. I feel that way now about the problems involved in America's keen insistence on making the hand of power and wealth felt in matters concerning the rights of nations smaller and weaker than itself.

IV

Sometimes now I wonder if in allowing American influence to impress itself on me without fighting it back, I was unintentionally cowardly, or at least weak. I felt that I came home more clearsighted about the real values in life, but I was to find out that I was not viewing things the same way as my Filipino friends and that I was often to walk a lonely path. Kipling's observation of the impossibility of meeting between the East and the West seems to be interchangeably confirmed and belied in my own personal story. There were many moments when I felt that my long stay in America had made of me too much of a divided personality for comfortable living with myself, many moments also when I felt nostalgic for my American friends who seemed to have understood me more completely than my Filipino friends were under-standing me now. Similar personal stories can be told by other Filipinos who have been to the United States, and curiously enough my own story, except perhaps for the very individual parts of it, resembles in many respects the relations between the two nations themselves.

Some parts of that story—my affection for my American friends in whose homes I ate and slept, my affection for the America where I met my husband and where a son was born to me, and for professors who molded my thinking during the most important stage of my development—I can equate with the experience of my country through the peaceful years of growing with American tu-tors, through the war years, through Bataan and Corregidor and the Death March to Capas. The equation stops there, for my con-fusion and my country's do not always follow the same line when it comes to America's show of inconsistencies, arrogance, and ma-terialism. Both my indignation and my forgiveness are personal.

The Filipino himself is full of inconsistencies, the psychological ones due mainly to his different civilizational influences. The aver-age American does not know that the Philippines has felt the ef-fects of six to eight separate waves of civilization. Dr. A. L. Kroe-ber, the well-known anthropologist, has said of these influences that they "have been super-imposed, but they have also interpene-trated one another; until today there is probably not a single per-sonality but shares in some measure in the effects of every one of the cultures." The old civilization that was to feel the Western influences was a mosaic of mixed cultures, including besides the Malay, which we may consider the basic one, those of Vedic India, Confucian China, Shintoist Japan, and Mohammedan Arabia. On this already hybrid civilization of the ancient Filipinos, Spanish and American influences made themselves felt for well-nigh four centuries and a quarter, rendering the hybrid worse, or better, hy-bridized, depending on how you want to look at it. History's hand has molded this culture, and the Filipino today cannot unmold the shape the clay has taken. We Filipinos can only admit regret that history was not kinder, or that our nature was not more stubborn and less resilient. But we make no apologies for these facts. Our outlook is mostly Western now, and our friendship for America is in general strong, not merely because of history and our nature, but because we now share deep, common ideals with America, which we are recognizing gradually but firmly as our own.

America's influence on us spans from the time of the early soldier-teachers to the time of the Fulbright-Smith-Mundt professors and the American Foreign Aid technicians who come to the Philippines now. A pervasive American spirit is unmistakably felt in our life, making us the butt of many a far-from-unmalicious dig by Europeans and fellow-Asians. We have followed American ways in almost every phase of living, although we are a number of paces behind in some matters. We have imitated, adapted, modified. We have followed the fashions, even exaggerated them. Our women, our artists, our writers, in their own living and creating, have closely followed the American urges for self-expression; our girls are becoming more and more career-minded—while, ironically enough, the American girls, according to reports, are almost ready to go back to the old-fashioned family life of kids and no outside work. We too had our time of the Elvis Presley vogue. And the yellow journalism that is now the bane of our reading existence can easily be an American importation.

Not so long ago we were writing in Spanish, and in a Spanish fine enough to rate our writers membership in the Real Academía Española. Now we have writers in English who have attracted attention in the United States and England, in Mexico and France, and painters whose works have been internationally acclaimed. The University of the Philippines, our state university, has many distinct University of Michigan characteristics—in its departmentalization and its curricula, for example. It would be safe to say, if the word can be used of a relationship between universities, that the greatest affection exists between these two institutions; after the war, which completely destroyed the University of the Philippines, the University of Michigan's first gift to it was the rehabilitation of its library.

Our customs have changed, gradually and imperceptibly, yielding place in varying degrees to the American's. But our vernacularists continue to write, some in both dialect and English, and we have publications in dialect that are sedately Oriental and floridly Filipino. Even if we are definitely not monopolized by them we have not forgotten our folk dances, our folk songs, our plaintive *kundimans*. Thus when our Asian friends say that we have lost our Asian identity and have become Western, we do not contradict them; we only modify their opinion. And when our Western friends claim that they cannot make us out because we are inscrutable and lack the candor of Western ways, we do not contradict them but only modify their opinion. We beg to be understood by both sides for what we are, not what they want us to be.

My people, like me, often have to be defenders of our mixed culture, our mixed personality. The strain of the Oriental is discoverable in the warmth, the mystery, the mysticism, also the humility of our people (especially those from the provinces), while that of the Occidental is manifested in the dynamism, the force, and the sharp coloration of our urban life. It is when the latter qualities predominate too much—and this is obvious in our cities, where the aping of the West is most apparent—that the more thoughtful Filipinos sit up and take notice. These cultural renegades are often, amusingly enough, more Western than the originals they are copying, thus making themselves ridiculous and—it is hoped—making their cause a losing one. The rest of us submit that we cannot help the fact that we often think in English, wear Western clothes, read Western books, see Western shows, at the same time that we also know and read Filipino literature written in dialect, and follow the development of the Filipino cinema, sport Philippine-made bags, and decorate our homes with Philippine mats and tablecloths.

I view this mixed culture sorrowfully, in the way that I view also my own mixed personality. My American friends do not always understand this sadness. Once I hurt one of them deeply when, speaking of Western influence on us, I said somewhat bitterly, referring to both Spain and America, "Why didn't you leave us alone?" Their country was a melting-pot too, think these American friends, yet now there is an American, a distinct, unconfused, and unconfusing personality. But there is a difference. The varied civilizations that were brought to America did not bring in their wake the problem of race. The heterogeneity was simpler. Ours carried with it the deeply painful psychological problem of color, and the superiority and inferiority involved in color. With us there is also the question of language, which again is more involved than America's: there the early settlers came from different countries but their languages shared a Latin origin, which simplified the psychological difficulties. In our case the big problem of the moment is what language the great Filipino novel will be written in. Can the Filipino faithfully depict himself and the soul of his people in a language other than his own, and so different in origin and context from his? Why, after almost four hundred years of Spanish occupation, did the Filipinos not make the grade of world literature in a work written in Spanish? Was it the inhibition of colonialism, or is there really a mystic quality in language, such as the spirit of its soil and its air, a quality that is in the flesh and blood of its people's thinking?

I did not feel all this while I was young and a student in the United States. But I was feeling it twenty years later when my American-born son decided to remain Filipino and not claim his right to become an American citizen. I was glad of his decision. I could not bear to think that my son might be subjected to humiliating discrimination by fellow-Americans because of his brown color, his Filipino accent, and his Filipino way of thinking. When we have fought the prejudice shown us by Americans even on our shores, we have done so as Filipinos. How heart-breaking it would be if we had to fight this fight as fellow-Americans! The Negro problem would always stare me in the face when I thought of the possible outcome if my son chose to become the citizen of a country that was different from mine and harbored feelings of discrimination against my people because of their color.

Yet that country, America, is one for which I bear a great love. Many of my fellow-countrymen, understanding it less, may stand more in awe of its power and wealth, but love it less. Or, understanding it less, they may see only its blatant desire to lord it over other countries by giving of its bounty and expecting in the bargain to be liked. Some violently condemn its inconsistencies in dealing with the problem of self-determination—so basic to the small peoples who are only little by little seeing their way clear to the solution of the problem and the realization of their dreams. America, the sworn idealist, the loud idealist, should not fail them, they feel. But they forget that America has to think of prestige, and of its powerful allies too, and this fact it cannot admit truthfully.

America is almost stupid, let me say here, when it wonders

236

why the Asians, even we Filipinos, do not fall over backward in gratitude for its gifts. It does not realize how needful it is to do gracious things graciously. We know that America is not playing the part of Lady Bountiful for the sheer joy of giving, but we know too that we need what it is giving, and we would show greater appreciation if it would act less condescendingly. For instance, in offices in the Philippines, housing both Filipino and American officials, the American part of the building will be air-conditioned, while the Filipino part will not be. What is involved is not a matter of affording, or of habit; it is a matter of psychology. Why can't Americans see that? In discussions involving Philippine issues, the American in our midst will be louder than the Filipino. The latter, generally less obtrusive and more reserved, and less at home in English too, will let the other talk, but will resent the fact that the American is stealing the thunder from his own thinking.

I tell my American friends something that they alone can take, because they are Americans and have the gift of being able to laugh at themselves: I tell them that I like them in spite of knowing them. That is true. True too is the fact that they laugh heartily when I say this. The laughter is neither condescending nor uneasy, but that of a friend with a friend. A Filipino friend might be insulted and withdraw into himself. Not so the American friend.

I have myself looked at life more humorously since knowing America, and I look at its funny aspects, I believe, through American eyes. Filipino humor I appreciate too, but not, I am afraid, to the extent that I enjoy American humor. The laughter of America, its clean quality, has reached the Philippines through the movies, the radio, books, and magazines. It is not improbable that exposure to such humor has helped in creating the easy relations I have mentioned among our English-speaking and English-thinking youngsters. A sense of humor is in many respects also a sense of values. The Filipino who has or acquires a sense of humor becomes less insecure as he becomes able to appraise himself and to say this is good, bad, or indifferent, this is ridiculous and laughable, and then to laugh. Who was it who said that the absence of humor is a double disaster, for those deprived of it not only are unconscious of the ridiculous but are left unarmed against the perversity of their neighbors? We Filipinos have a sense of humor, but we still do not possess the knack of laughing at ourselves.

237

If America is not careful it may lose the knack itself as a country. It is too eager to be approved, even when it cannot help being bound by the shackles of self-interest, prestige, and prejudice. When Stephen Leacock wrote his essay on Americans, ridiculing their contradictory traits, he concluded his examination by saying that the Americans knew all these defects but didn't give a damn. That was at least consistent. America now gives too much of a damn about opinion, but does not show enough attention to how it may keep the good opinion of the world, enough humility to see the separate problems of the countries it deals with not through its own eyes but through the eyes of those countries. I had always maintained, when America was so secure and could laugh at itself, that the Philippines would be less touchy when it had become secure too. The chip on the shoulder is a sign of uncertainty. Can it be that both countries are now afflicted with the illness of uncertainty?

I have liked talking about America this way. It is like talking of something I prize dearly in spite of its flaws, a cherished vase, for instance, the clay of which shows roughnesses or irregularities; or someone I like in spite of his defects, like a close friend whose big mouth is comparable only to his big heart. I believe it is not always necessary to live in a country in order to share the feelings of its people and be sympathetic with their aspirations. There is no gainsaying the fact, however, that living with a people is almost synonymous with understanding it. I feel many times, therefore, that because America has given me so much (as has France) it is my bounden duty to make the Americans (and the French) understood in my country as they are understood by me.

Conversely it is up to the Americans who have lived here to tell the American people the story of this young, growing nation, still sensitive because it does not feel secure, but extremely proud in its sensitiveness. It resents superior attitudes because it connects them with a colonialism that it accepted unwillingly and always resented. Americans who have been with us here could help future American visitors to the Philippines by telling them to accept and understand with sympathy the strong urge of the Filipinos to manifest self-determination in all its aspects. The patronizing air is felt deeply, and the strong-country bully that pulls rank is recognized immediately. I repeat that Americans must try to know us as we

238

are, half Western, half Eastern, and not as they would want to
see us. The give-and-take of friendship between equals demands
that the appraisal be like that. Besides, it is truly the only way
toward real understanding, because it is the humble, self-effacing
way.

We who know America must portray to our people who do not
know, or not too well, that America means well in spite of what
can look like bad manners; that its heart is good because its people's
hearts are good. That it is eager for prestige and approval is patent
too; therefore, what its heart gives as a natural manifestation must
also, unfortunately, be credited materially as a move for national
power and reputation. Can America be explained fully; can any
country, indeed, can any individual? The contradictions I find in
America I also find proportionately in my own hybrid nature.
America has heightened the confusion in that nature, but has also
given it the inner resources for accepting the confusion and for
straightening it out. Contrary to general belief, America has vast
inner resources, spiritual and intellectual, from which it can draw
to solve, in the American way of straightforwardness and fair dealing, the confusion it is in and into which it has thrown many
peoples on earth.

from Ghana

K. A. B. JONES-QUARTEY

The author: born in Ghana (Accra), 1913; studied in church schools in West Africa and at Lincoln and Columbia universities in the United States. Mr. Jones-Quartey is Assistant Director of Extra-Mural Studies at the University College of Ghana. As a very young man (1934-1937) he was reporter and assistant editor of the *African Morning Post* (Accra), under Nnamdi Azikiwe, now Premier of Eastern Nigeria. He is the author of three publications on the West African press, and has contributed to two anthologies of Negro poetry. His wife grew up in the United States; they are the parents of three sons. Since his student years in the United States (1937-1946) he has returned once to this country (1952), and though he has not traveled farther west than Chicago he is well acquainted with the East and parts of the South.

I

WHEN I was a child there was in my mother tongue, the Ga language, a complimentary expression that meant one had given a superlative performance in the American fashion, a piece of sheer wizardry. This standing compliment was the more surprising because forty years ago little was known in West Africa about America or Americans. But that little was, to us, much, for our "knowledge" concerned mostly a class called heroes. And doesn't this class create an excited and exciting mythology in the imagination of all people everywhere at all times, even if in some cases it is the excitement of terror?

So the individual stories of American heroes—who always were and always will be more than a fair share of the world output— these stories managed to seep through the thick blanket of our ignorance in things American, and created in West Africa an impregnable concept of wizardry, of superiority, almost of infallibility. Thirty or forty years ago the American heroes who inspired magical performances on the soccer fields of Ghana, and among jugglers, dancers, fighters, and conjurers, were—with disarming impartiality—the boxers Jack Johnson and Jack Dempsey, the saint Abraham Lincoln, and that black Messiah, Booker T. Washington. Moreover, this hero-worshiping was not just a haphazard

240

affair. It had a logical chronology of development—especially among the younger generation—with three periods, denoting three phases.

The first period was quite the most exciting. Mixed up with the fabled exploits of Jack Johnson came the sound of the heavy tread of Americans entering the First World War on the side of the Western Allies: "Over there [repeat 3 times] the Yanks are coming, the Yanks are coming, the Yanks are coming over there" —and, as it was somehow relayed to us, the Yanks came, and saw, and conquered the Kaiser. In the process President Woodrow Wilson was added to our American Valhalla, though as to his exact position there among our favorite gods we were not altogether certain.

It was soon after this, as we approached our mid-teens, that we changed the nature of our rapport with America. Now we suddenly became serious about our education, but instead of doubling our efforts at study, many of us turned for extra-human aid to a mysterious American character called "de Lawrence." His was by far the leading name among many who advertised themselves as being able to supply students as well as anybody else with supranormal powers for success in study, in business, in love, and in just about every other human activity. All this was to be accomplished through an assortment of nostrums and talismans, invocations and embrocations, passages and messages, hocus and pocus. Spiritism in African life came in to aid and abet us; the terms occult and occultism sealed our befuddled convictions; and at last we began to order out Rosicrucian literature from Berkeley, California, in the belief that it was the same thing and in the faith that this was guidance supreme in our quest for individual ascendancy.

Of course it all "got nobody nowhere." So in the end we had to give it up in sad disgust, and were then straightway catapulted into the third phase of our Americanism. Here we became aware that education was a much more serious business than some of us had so foolishly been led to believe, and that apart from the traditional source of it (England), America was very much in the picture too. It was then that we became more curious, and began to look out for more about the greatest hero of them all, Abraham Lincoln, he of the strange appearance and the incomparable eloquence; about Booker T. Washington and his hand-built Tuskegee Institute; about George Washington Carver and his peanuts and sweet potatoes. In addition, the names of America's great universities began to loom larger and larger in our consciousness—Yale, Columbia, Princeton, but in those days not so much Harvard, strangely enough (some even confused Harvard with Howard, Mordecai Johnson's imposing Negro university in Washington, D.C.).

A good many of us matched our growing enthusiasm with action, seeking confirmation for a faith now different from what we had given to de Lawrence in the funny old days. We began again to order literature from America, but this time something far removed from occult tracts and spiritualistic nonsense. We got instead things like *Great Speeches and How to Make Them* and *The Philosophy of Life*, an anthology of great little pieces of life and literature. Then more American speeches, and biographies of Lincoln, Washington, and Patrick Henry—the man who would choose liberty or, failing that, death. For good measure, we also threw in Zane Grey and his wild "Westerns."

It must be emphasized, however, that our craving for the American Way—what little we knew about it in the second and third decades of this century—was in fact only the narrower of two parallel lines. By far the broader line was the British one, along which ran the rest of our lives, at least educationally and materially if not culturally and spiritually. Some have even said culturally too. In any case it was the British line of development that counted. Alongside the comparatively few books we read on America by Americans was ranged the entire library of British books and authors that were our mentors; British heroes fiercely challenged American for our affections and loyalties. *Deeds that Won the Empire*—telling us all about Clive and Nelson, about General Wolfe and the Heights of Abraham—was a prescribed text in the middle forms of secondary school, as were *Ivanhoe, Hereward the Wake,* and *A Tale of Two Cities.* Outside of class we rested Sir Walter Scott and Charles Dickens, and turned to Edgar Wallace and the intoxicating excesses of Marie Corelli. A little later, as we advanced on *Quentin Durward* and *Childe Harold in Italy*, we became all intellectual and ambitious, and formed a literary and social club to prove it; then we became positively bold, and ordered Hall Caine and *Anna Karenina*.

It was all part of our building-up process: a section of the way leading eventually to the crossroads marked, on one side, "To England," and, on the other, "To America." The crossroads was also the point of crisis: a crisis of attitude and of choice, though we did not know that until we got there.

Before we get there, however, let us examine one more element that contributed greatly to our excitement about America. This was the famous and exclusive institution of "American millionaires." Out of the welter of hazy ideas about that country rampant among us in the early phases, the favorite one was that millionaires in the States cried second in number only to gangsters in Chicago, and that one of the ways they relieved themselves of the burden of their millions was to tour the far ends of the earth picking up derelict little "natives" and sending them off to school in the States, all found and no questions asked. Truth to tell, one or two lucky youngsters were sent for and did realize their dreams, but for the majority American millionaires and their impulsive fits of generosity were to remain just another Cinderella story to read and mope over. Well, perhaps not quite. Some of us said, "All right, if an American millionaire won't come and pick me up here, I am sure to pick one up there—if only I could find my way to the States."

Now we were approaching the crisis, although we didn't know it. For it was when some of us became serious about going to the States to study that we came up against the fact that there was a widespread though covert prejudice against American education among our elders; that an American degree was looked upon with ill-concealed contempt by both the British and their trainees, our educated fathers; that African graduates of American universities faced not only banter but a bleak future in seeking employment in their own country. The background to this prejudice is most interesting. It was a confused world of "princes" and "doctors," of ignorance of facts, and of plain propaganda based on vested interests. The "princes" were those rogues and rascals who, unknown in their own country, stole into the States under the self-created style of Prince, then came home years later with basement degrees and fake doctorates, printed on cheap paper in bad English and dog Latin. To add injury to insult, they gave personal witness of how they had "earned" their "degrees."

I recall a story told by students of a college in Sierra Leone, in the late 1920's or early 1930's, of an African graduate of American universities—anyway so he said—who sported three or four degrees and was asked one day by a student organization to address the whole college on his academic experiences in the States. Couched in stumbling, hardly literate language, the whole talk had gone to show how easy it was to acquire degrees in America, the principal method, as you would expect, being cribbing. You could copy notes onto a stiff shirt cuff, tear out sections from the texts, or indeed, take the whole damned book with you into the examination and transcribe to your heart's content. I tell you, it is great fun getting a degree, especially a doctorate, from America. . . . For a period of some thirty years or more, West Africa was afflicted, and American education bedevilled, by these stowaway "princes" and returning "doctors."

But there were also other figures in the background picture of the ill repute of American education. European traditionalists—especially British—and their African wards (the English-educated leader group, as distinct from the simple hero-worshippers, young and old) for a long time condemned American standards in almost everything, but especially in education. To prove their point they used arguments both intrinsic and extrinsic, some true, some false, some in-between. British political and economic interests in the parts of West Africa where Britain was in control, and largely still is, dictated methods of self-seeking that were less honest than they might have been. Thus the British and the African elite played down American achievements—intellectual, scientific, and cultural—and played up the looseness and massness of the American system. Apart from that, there was—and still is—profound ignorance of the form and content of the American educational system.

The results of this prejudice were disastrous to any African foolish or headstrong enough to have defied it and gone to the States for higher education. I used to know—many others used to know —a few Africans with perfectly good American degrees who literally went knocking from door to door seeking decent employment in vain—men who could teach, write, speak as well as any of their

European-trained contemporaries, and better than many. Yet Tuskegee still remained a name to conjure with, Booker T. Washington a shadowy but towering legend; Yale came up again and again in youthful, hopeful conversation; Columbia beckoned, and Chicago, California, Howard—or was it Harvard? Someday, maybe, the breach in the wall would be made and the call answered. Well, the breach *was* made, or started, in 1920 with a man called James Emman Kwegyir Aggrey.

Aggrey's story is too well known for more than the briefest summary to be needed here. He was a Fanti who had educated himself in the States; who was asked in 1920 and 1924 by the Phelps Stokes Foundation in Washington and New York to join educational commissions to West and East Africa; who promptly became the rallying point for African educational and social reform, and helped to establish and run the famous school at Achimota, Accra, one of the best in all Africa; who died prematurely in 1927 and left an imperishable memory among his countrymen, from Gambia to Kenya and from Kano to Cape Town, as well as in colonial, missionary, and educational circles in Britain and the United States. It was through Aggrey's learning, erudition, eloquence, humility, and humanity, in short his saintliness, that Africans first awoke to the suspicion that there might be some bit of quality, after all, in American education.

But Aggrey died in 1927, barely two years after the epochal founding ceremony at Achimota, and before it could be seen what he would do about American education for Africans. So the position remained pretty much the same. In spite of a now well-established excitement about the subject, very few young men left for the States to seek a degree, and hope and expectation hung precariously in abeyance—until 1934, when an equally flaming though entirely different personality returned to West Africa with an American education. First as a newspaper editor in the Gold Coast, then as press proprietor and politician in his native Nigeria, Nnamdi Azikiwe—now Premier of Eastern Nigeria—relit the Aggrey torch. Azikiwe—promptly nicknamed "Zik" in the States and now widely so called—was almost solely responsible for the great African trek to American universities and colleges. It began with a trickle, in 1935; by 1937 it had become a sizable river; and by 1950 it was a flood.

II

I left Accra on September 7, 1937, on my way to Lincoln University, Pennsylvania. I was already late for the opening of the academic year, so the seven days spent between Liverpool, Manchester, and London before boarding ship at Southampton for New York, and the nine days spent at Ellis Island as one of Uncle Sam's involuntary guests, only made matters worse. The unrequested rest-cure at Ellis Island was at first a terrifying experience, but later proved most interesting. It was my introduction to America—an unexpected extravaganza which for many has turned out to be their only experience of "God's Own Country." My stay there was the result of the fact that the vice-consul in London who issued my visa had forgotten to sign his name at the end of the long and complicated document. It seemed to me at the time a forgetful slip, but later I wondered whether it was not just a case of adroitly passing the buck: had he deliberately left out his signature so that his immigration watch-dogs in New York harbor would also scrutinize my palpably unimpressive financial status, and take what final action they thought fit, even to refusing me entry? After a while, however, I abandoned this thought as preposterous.

But I have been anticipating myself. I must return to my journey and give you an account of something—in fact, a succession of experiences. My first ship landed us at Plymouth. When we arrived the English weather was of course cold and damp; the fog was so thick you could see hardly anything. But those English people who were collected around my elbows were enthusiastic; I heard deep sighs and whispered bits of conversation—since they were English bits they had to be whispered—all tending toward the unmistakable admission that there, plainly hidden before our very eyes, was the greatest country in the world. I listened keenly, then chalked that one up for future contemplation.

Next, on the liner going from Southampton to New York, I made friends with a little ten-year-old from Greece, an orphan boy migrating to the States. One day he started talking about soldiers, uniforms, marching, and guns, and from that proceeded to tell me about a certain Greek festival at which these forces came out in glorious array and there were dancing, and singing, and eating, and fun—such as you could not imagine if you tried. The little Greek boy was quite ecstatic, and ended by assuring me very, very seriously that Greece was the greatest country in the world.

When at last we sighted the famous Statue and the even more famous skyline of New York, I was naturally excited, though slightly scared too, at the prospect before me. But my excitement was nothing compared with that of the returning Americans. They were by now out in their full numbers, and in unabashed throat were intoning almost a chant: "Look at her, just look at her— God's own country—the greatest country in the world." Now there were three, to which I firmly added Africa—all of Africa—without further hesitation or doubt.

Later, on Ellis Island, I had enough free time to reflect on the whole ludicrous matter. And, had George Orwell in 1937 already given us the sardonicism of the century, my parody would have run something like this: every country in the world is greater than every other country, but some countries are "more greater" than others. This makes England, Greece, America, Africa—and every other country—the "most greatest" in the world!

Well, they finally released me, and I arrived at Lincoln University after an all-day journey by train and bus. Philadelphia is 90 miles from New York, and Lincoln is 45 miles from "Philly"— short enough but, what with changes and waiting, it was after midnight before we stopped outside Lincoln's gateway on the Baltimore pike. As American college and university campuses go, Lincoln was, and still is, an unpretentious little place. But it is a lovely spot at all times, and in autumn, particularly, it carries a wonderful sylvan charm. In point of fact early November was no longer autumn, but there was still enough of brown leaves and green grass to give a feeling of pleasure in nature. Next morning I awoke to this feeling, and began my real American experience in earnest.

Let me at once set the proper limits to this experience, so there will be no mistake and no misunderstanding. I spent exactly nine years and two weeks in the States, from early November 1937 to mid-November 1946. Most of that time was spent in undergraduate studies at Lincoln in Pennsylvania and in postgraduate work at Columbia University, New York City. During the long summer vacations I had jobs on the Lincoln campus itself; in Atlantic City (described to me as one of America's principal playgrounds); and, between college and university, on the Pennsylvania Railroad, which took me inland to Columbus and Chicago, north to Boston and Hartford, Connecticut, and south to Washington and Atlanta, Georgia.

In addition, as a member of the Lincoln Glee Club I traveled extensively north and south during the shorter vacations, and visited several universities and colleges on student conferences and exchanges. This is of course the normal run of a student's life in the States, but I also managed to travel elsewhere on my own, with college pals, on hitch-hikes, and so on. In 1952 I visited America for the second time, with my wife and first son, then age one. On this occasion I went south as far as Fort Valley, Georgia—where I gave talks at the Negro college and kept strictly to my side of the Great Divide. To my regret I never could visit the western parts of America; my acquaintance with the Midwest was not so west as all that.

Perhaps I can illustrate the business of first impressions, for a start, with a small anecdote. Another young African student, looking out of his window on his first morning in college, turned around in great bewilderment and said to the nearest American: "Isn't this the University of So-and-So, and aren't we on its campus?" The answer came back: "Sure, sure!" Asked the African: "Then who are these people?" "These people" were only the students going to or coming from early classes. But their garb of assorted oddments—skull caps, windbreakers, slacks, sneakers, "maacassins," and a veritable forest of Joseph's coats and "saaks" (for that's how "mocassins" and "socks" sound in America to non-American ears)—this animated assortment of oddities was too much for him. When told that "these people" were to be his fellow-students from now on, his eyes opened wide in alarm. Like others before us and after us he never developed a taste for the weird attire of suburban US students. But, again like many of us, he soon became "one of the boys," and hitched his hikes with the craziest as with the quietest of them.

In college many of us never got over the shock of some aspects of student life in America, for instance foul language. There is foul language among young people everywhere, and most of us were no prudes: on occasion we could take, and in turn tell, those certain jokes equally with the boldest. But that is one thing; the "cussin' and swearin'" that assailed our sensibilities on all sides from morning to midnight was quite another. Many of us were totally unprepared for it. For me, at any rate, it was for at least two years a complete barrier to social rapport with the otherwise fine-fellows-all among whom I was to live for so long.

So this was America! Inside college the men saddened, maddened, then gladdened us; the women first excited, then baffled, then intrigued us. Outside college, life in America completely bewildered us. We had been led to expect wonders, and were nevertheless stunned by the size and speed of everything. A new arrival that one of us met near Grand Central Station in New York is reported to have said that in the state into which everything had thrown him he could no longer be surprised if he should suddenly see God walking out of that station! Gradually, however, we passed that stage, and Washington, Philadelphia, Rockefeller Plaza in New York, the Boardwalk in Atlantic City held neither surprise nor terror for us.

Atlantic City, where I worked as a bellboy for two summers, made a mixed impression on me. The magnificent sea-front hotels took my breath away as I passed and repassed their opulent entrances, barred forever, it seemed to me, to people of my color. The entertainment piers were too expensive, though when Marian Anderson came to sing in the biggest of them I went, and I went also to see for a second time the dramatization of Richard Wright's *Native Son.*

We also saw something of life as it is finely lived in millions of American homes. We saw a lot of the American worker, and some of our number even joined the big unions. They found fellowship, though there was also prejudice. On the Pennsylvania Railroad I had some of the best meals of my life, and developed the most profound respect and admiration for those wonder railroad-chefs who could toss an omelet or turn out an American steak with equal poise. In the end I learned to toss an omelet too, though not with equal poise.

But our main business in the States was getting an education. This was easy in the beginning, because on the whole our secondary education was sounder and deeper than that of our fellow-freshmen. Later on the going got much rougher, because the reading became progressively more massive and at the same time more distracting, by reason of its diffuseness. This leads me to a brief discussion of one of the differences between "them" and "us."

American education follows strictly the loose-jointed democratic ideal. There is a wide range of "optionals," even at the high-school level. Discipline, either academic or personal, is not so strict as in Europe or Britain, or even in Africa. The broadness of outlook and aim, on which the system prides itself so much, becomes in many places the cause of a superficiality disastrous to the life of the mind. From this proceeds the inevitable result that, possibly more so in the States than anywhere else in the world, only the most gifted students derive full benefit from their experience in learning. And the most gifted number no more than ten out of a hundred, if that many.

But the question is, what more do we critics from other countries want of this system? First of all, its basic difference from, say, the English system is that it agrees to train a hundred men but hopes to get only ten good ones; moreover, it gets them. The English, on the other hand, accepts only the ten from the beginning. The results-in-depth are the same. In addition the American has gained ninety more who, though admittedly not learned men, are ten times more fortunate as citizens than the ninety in Europe who never see the inside of a lecture room and cannot tell the difference between an essay on government and a paper on the chemistry of soap. And it is not as if America had no provisions at all for the naturally elite-in-mind. It is not as if to say she hadn't a Harvard, a St. John's, a Chicago, a Princeton, the specialized schools of Columbia, a Johns Hopkins, an M.I.T., where quality and depth of learning are worshiped as ardently as in the sacrosanct quadrangles of Oxford and Cambridge, in Heidelberg and Padua.

Moreover—so we argued, long into the night—every nation and every country, however it comes by it, is entitled to its own national elan, its own planned ends, as long as these do not interfere with the planned ends of other nations. We agreed that American education was effective for American civilization: that it works for the American ideal of material success in a highly technological matrix; that it is no nation's business whether another chooses materialism or culturalism as its guiding principle—quite apart from the question how this "choice" came about in the first place. We were also satisfied that, provided we knew what *we* wanted from this system and where to get the best of it, we would benefit to the full.

Meanwhile we were contributing our quota to the drive for mutual help and understanding between Americans and Africans. Meetings and conversations among the African students—many of them future leaders of their countries—resulted in the founding of the African Students Association of the United States and Canada, in New York City in 1942; the African Academy of Arts and Research; the American Council on African Education, a scholarship scheme of promise that later went awry in Nigeria itself; and several publications.

Throughout their studies and preparatory activities these young Africans received large-hearted assistance, moral and material, from the Americans: Mrs. Roosevelt and the late Wendell Willkie, two of America's biggest hearts of all; friends-of-Africa auxiliary bodies in Philadelphia, Manhattan, Brooklyn, Long Island, and elsewhere; young girls who stayed typing, proofing, and stapling practically all night—they gave of their best to Africa. High or low, black or white, it made no difference to either side. And there was also the part played by the universities—their presidents, professors, instructors, librarians, and administrative officers, in the North and in the South: Lincoln, Hampton, Tuskegee, Howard, Fisk, Atlanta, Pennsylvania, Columbia, New York, Northwestern, Otterbein, Cornell, Syracuse, Chicago, Harvard. In feeble reciprocation the African Academy organized two or three dance concerts at Carnegie Hall, which drew both large crowds and favorable press comment, though the shows were wanting here and there in precision and smooth production. We also gave innumerable talks on Africa, cooked reasonable facsimiles of African menus for some of our friends and benefactors, and participated in many American international programs.

The success later achieved by some, at least, of these citizens of a "new world a'coming" in West Africa is a measure of the gratitude felt by those who had their eyes and minds opened while studying in the United States and living among Americans. In spite of the many trying handicaps of mind and body against which we battled much of the time, we managed to fill our years with useful activity, our heads with a bit of knowledge, and our hearts with friendship.

251

III

Appraisals of national character, though highly absorbing and revealing, make little difference to the standing or the fortunes of those appraised. They may enhance or lower the prestige of the different nations described, in the eyes of a few million readers; they do little to improve, worsen, or undermine the progress of those nations. All they do is to prove the basic humanness of every people, which in any case the individual host or guest discovers for himself in a short enough time, as he studies the nationals of other countries. Moreover, many of these estimates of national character, however extreme positively or negatively, carry along somewhere their own reversals. This is my cue to say that I have found Americans to be no better and no worse than any other people I know elsewhere.

This is not an escape-clause either. I do not mean to imply that the things I liked most in the States appealed to me only as much as the things I had liked in Freetown, West Africa, or in Manchester, England; or that Americans never made me more angry or disgusted than any other people had done before. Far from it. In my nine years in the States I experienced the extremes both of anger and of pleasure with human conduct; I saw demonstrated the noblest feelings of love and compassion as well as the basest, meanest manifestations of hate and bigotry. But the point is that all nations can claim to be virtuous in many things, and against all nations can be brought a catalogue of vices and shortcomings.

I went to the States, in the first instance, with no more and no greater preconceptions than those concerning the wonderfulness of everything, the inferiority of American education, and race prejudice. I found that in fact not everything was wonderful: there was poverty and ignorance and sickness in America too; in Georgia I saw men and women, black and white, who were as wretched and degenerate-looking a cross-section of humanity as anything I had ever seen in Africa or imagined elsewhere. As for education in America I discovered, to repeat, that it was good, bad, or indifferent, in huge quantities, depending on who was being educated, what kind of education you were talking about, and where it was being given. And finally, though the color situation was even worse than I had preconceived it, there were two significant facts about it. First,

252

not only was it wrong and unlawful in the eyes of the Constitution of the United States, but the federal government itself, and most of official America, was actively and permanently committed to combating this evil—the exact opposite being true of South Africa. And second, in spite of its unavoidable evidence and influence everywhere, race discrimination in America did not and could not prevent the development of a fine community like Negro Atlanta, or of fine Negro personalities, all confidence, directness, and straightforwardness, even in their approach to the dreaded "southern white man."

And since coming back home, I have become more and more convinced of the essential mutuality of interest between man in Africa and man in America, and of the essential futility of faultfinding among peoples when this exercise has no other purpose than the direct or indirect assertion of a claim to superiority or an accusation of inferiority. In America we soon enough became aware of the complete absence of knowledge of African affairs among our hosts. In place of such information there was a skein of intractable prejudices, anthropological cliches, and ancient moving-picture stereotypes. But mutual distortions and caricatures did not long survive personal contact and social relationships.

We discovered virtues of which we stood in dire need, like the Americans' drive for efficiency and their habit of hard work. When we returned home we found that American soldiers and groundcrews had anticipated our arrival and had already gained this reputation. Our people said that for the first time in their lives they had seen white men stripped to the waist and sweating profusely under the fierce African sun, doing manual labor with the workmen they were supposed to be directing and overseeing. Our people had been most profoundly impressed. Then too we heard—we *saw*—that the Yanks had anticipated our second-hand expertise with "swing" and "jive"; that their infectious exhibitionism had accorded exactly with the African's own love of laughter, rhythm, and dancing; that chewing-gum had become a fashion among the young, and big, fast, flashy American cars an aspiration among the able.

Now, nearly a decade and a half after the end of the Second World War, which accelerated this process in the first instance, there is a real two-way traffic between America and West Africa: in trade, social intercourse, educational matters, and political and diplomatic relations. The Americans who are going to participate in this process of mutual profit, and help to make it effective and successful, are already arriving in West Africa. For a long time we have been used to American missionaries of many faiths: Roman Catholics, Episcopalians, Methodists, United Brethren, Christian Scientists, Baptists, and others. In addition, we have known teachers and doctors attached to the missions, a few businessmen, one or two official representatives of the American government, and journalists on their way in and out of brief assignments. During the war many West Africans also met American air crews and groundmen, as well as the personnel of a few visiting military missions here and there. Now, to all of these, are rapidly being added numerous diplomats and foreign-service employees, more businessmen and professionals; a husband-and-wife dental team, for example, has recently settled in Ghana, and American schoolteachers have begun to appear on short-term, temporary attachments to local schools. Very soon there will be a sizable American colony in Ghana.

When that happens, the opportunities for learning from each other will naturally increase. Children going to school together—since schooling facilities are expanding rapidly, to provide for all who need them—will naturally tend to modify each group's characteristics, thus making steadily for cultural adaptations, to the mutual benefit, we hope, of each group. But before that stage is reached, members of both communities will have discovered sharp differences in each other with regard to the approach to life and living, both generally and in specific matters.

The Americans are already discovering, for instance, that in spite of the mad rush of life in the towns of Ghana—a rush that characterizes the era of political independence in West Africa—the reflexes of Africans, especially in business matters, appear slow and time-consuming. To which the Africans are replying that therefore, for the time being at least, we exhibit fewer nervous phenomena and have fewer heart attacks than the medical reports from the States would seem to indicate about Americans. Our guest will also wonder how in the world it is possible to do any business, save any money, or have any peace, in the presence of hordes of relatives who just come and park indefinitely, straining to the limit one's resources of goods, services, and patience. To which my people will reply that their communal life has its uses as well as its abuses, and

254

that in any case modern trends like industrialization, expanding urbanization, and employment pressures will soon enough render communalism and clan life as obsolete as the hammock is now for ten-day bush treks.

Americans are appalled at the primitive conditions of sanitation, the carelessness in the processing of food, the incredible handling of babies with respect to feeding, hygiene, and so on. But here the answers are equally simple, though they do not deny the conditions or supply a palliative. It all depends on where you are standing in our twentieth-century civilization. If you were transported the few miles from Park Avenue, New York, to the Bowery at Canal Street, your reactions would be the same. And I can tell you that when I went from cellophane-wrapped and glass-caged New York to the blue flies, grimy fingers, and cracked cups of London meat stalls and restaurants, the shock was as great as that suffered by an Englishman at his first sight of an African slum compound. I also noticed, however, that although the Americans I had left behind looked every pound better fed and every inch better clothed, the English I met again after nine years were not falling down all around me from weakness or flea bites. On the contrary, bus drivers still drove in their open cabins in bitter winter weather and the girls had fresh natural complexions.

Apart from that, your Ghanaian hosts will point out that if you were to extend the impression of a messy environment, especially among the less privileged, to the question of personal cleanliness, you would fall into egregious error. Africans, particularly Ghanaians, bathe—and I do not mean "wash"—with religious regularity. No self-respecting Ga woman would leave her house for the first time in the day without a bath; she would not know how to start dressing. And with very many the national habit prescribes two baths a day. There was a long period in her younger days when my mother used to take three. The men are more modern—and shall we say more civilized? The majority of them make do with only one bath a day—plus "washes."

West Africans, on their part, are already admiring the Americans' famous technical and mechanical efficiency, their shining kitchens, their business drive, their ready wit, their irrepressible bonhomie. And there is much more that the African hosts will yet learn, like, and copy from their American guests. Meanwhile, a lot

255

of Ghanaians—at least among the older, more settled folk—are wondering why Americans want to call everybody by his first name immediately after introduction, and invite the whole world to call them by their first names too, almost before the handshake is over. Even the children are often allowed, indeed encouraged, to use first names in addressing grown-ups, an unthinkable thing in African society. The Americans would reply, presumably, that therein lies their independence of spirit, their free-speech and free-enterprise philosophy, on all of which they have built up a technological and economic marvel unparalleled in human history.

Many Ghanaians are going to be irritated at the American expectation of finding physical and psychological conditions generally the way they know them at home. Also at the wish to bring out everything from the States, and later try to replenish diminishing stocks and supplies from the same bountiful but 6,000-mile-distant source. It is quite true that many of the goods and services to which Westerners are accustomed—especially Americans—are in short supply in Africa, that pure fresh milk is unavailable, and "7-Up," and particular makes of washing machines, and other things. It is also perfectly true that we lack the standards of entertainment that are available twelve hours a day every day at the Radio City Music Hall; that we have no theater, no opera house, ballet school, great art museums, no Riverside Church, Palisades, or the rest of what makes America the exciting place it is. But there is enough food for everybody, basic foodstuffs, known to all the world, which can be prepared to suit the delicate stomachs of any visitor or foreign resident; and there is the excitement of discovering new tastes. Besides, supplies of overseas articles of every description are improving all the time, both in quantity and in quality. Just a little patience, a little ingenuity, a little trial and error, a few upsets in the beginning, are all that is required to make the satisfactory adjustment, whether the problem be food or entertainment or social contacts.

All those institutions and individuals that have done and are doing so much to bring our peoples together will pardon me, in generosity, if I single out Lincoln University, Pennsylvania, for special mention. Unless there are facts and figures of which I am unpardonably ignorant (and lots of other people too), the record of Lincoln's benefactions and altruism to Africa has been unequaled. And Lincoln is a very small institution. Many would consider it not only significant for Lincoln's preeminence but also poetically just that many of West Africa's leading political personalities today are Lincoln men, including Premier Nnamdi Azikiwe of Nigeria and Premier Kwame Nkrumah of Ghana.

The traffic between America and Ghana is gathering momentum, and the signs are extremely gratifying. The subjects include economics, political ties, education, and cultural contacts. In all of this the American national government is playing a significant role. Universities, foundations, societies, clubs, churches, and individuals without number are also engaged in showing Africans around America, giving them an education, and generally establishing good relations between the two peoples. The education we are getting from the States brings American pragmatism into balance with European intellectualism, and the results cannot but be good for Africa.

from South Africa

MORRIS BROUGHTON

The author: born in England (Colne, Lancashire), 1901, and studied at London University; moved to South Africa in 1927. Mr. Broughton has spent most of his working life in South African journalism, first in Durban, then in Johannesburg, and since 1950 in Cape Town, as Editor of *The Cape Argus*. For twelve years, up to the end of World War II, he broadcast on South African and international affairs for the BBC. His personal hobbies include astronomy and ornithology. At the end of 1956, on invitation of the State Department, he spent three months in the United States, visiting nearly two-thirds of the states and traveling from New Orleans to New Mexico and California, then through the Middle West to the East Coast.

I

IT IS a complex thing, being a South African. The very name describes a geographical area, not a people. There is no single entity "South African" in any firmly established sense, but Afrikaans-speaking and English-speaking South Africans. And these names imply not simply linguistic differences but differences in origin, outlook, development, and history that remain unreconciled. Neither an Afrikaans-speaking nor an English-speaking South African can call himself a "native" of his own land. That description belongs to the six million "Bantu," who in turn cannot officially be called "Afrikaner," the name by which the majority section of the White population wishes to be and is known; the time may come when it also includes the English-speaking Whites, but so far it definitely does not.

In order to explain South Africa at all, its inhabitants have to be broken up into White, Black, Coloured, and Indians. The Coloured people are in fact Euro-Africans, or if not that, Afro-Asians, though such ethnic terms are never used in South Africa; they would have emotional and political undertones unacceptable to the White South African. The names Native, Coloured, Indian, and Asiatic are not including but excluding definitions. They are clung to tenaciously and even with passion, because they reflect the White South African's deep belief—or fixation—that he is in South Africa

258

to establish and uphold a distinctive "White" civilization, the very distinctiveness and purity of which would be corrupted if it included "Coloured" even in thought. Thus we have White and non-White, a description by negation which lies at the roots of "apartheid"—the doctrine of complete separation of the races on every plane, social, moral, economic, political, physical, and spiritual.

And there is also a division between the two dominant White groups. This now expresses itself in cultural, linguistic, political, and religious forms but it is in origin a poverty problem. The Afrikaners are, economically speaking, a poor people. It was this that led General Smuts, that great, good, and much misunderstood man, to what I may call his "American" solution for South Africa. This did not mean the "melting pot"; far from it. Rather it meant improving the material bases of South African life to a point where there would be plenty for everybody and opportunity for all. The country could then afford democracy and the "races" would be able to sort themselves out.

What is distinctively and peculiarly American, and how can it aid South African thinking? For most White South Africans America is supremely the land where a vigorous and intrepid people, entering as strangers and pioneers, triumphantly established "European" civilization from the Atlantic to the Pacific. One does not need to be in any American city for more than a few days to find that this is an oversimplification indeed. It is probably truer to say that America has begun truly to feel herself American only in the measure that "European civilization" has been left behind.

It was the urge to escape that civilization that brought about "this nation conceived in liberty and dedicated to a proposition," and it has escaped into a civilization of its own. Why, I asked myself bewilderedly, after a few weeks of traveling from state to state, is it not written about and studied as such? Why is it always talked and written about as though Europe were the norm by which all things American were to be tested and judged, as though America were at best a deviation and at worst an intolerable freak? The European—and I talked with many of them in America—whether he is from Italy, France, Germany, the Netherlands, Scandinavia, or Britain, takes it as unquestionable that he belongs to civilization and when he visits America is moving out from it. Some of them were even convinced that in truth there was no American nation but simply a vast manifestation of juvenile delinquency, ameliorated only where backwardness was admitted and identification with Europe humbly sought or achieved.

A South African cannot make any of these assumptions. He may have the familiar screen of preconceptions and misconceptions with which most of us protect ourselves from gazing upon the blazing truth of America, but he cannot assume that he stands on a pinnacle of achieved and settled civilization; and he cannot remain unmoved by the American realization that it is up to Americans to make a new world, because that is the vast responsibility he feels he must accept himself, in Southern Africa.

Yet what is this America and Americanism I am writing about in contrast with Europe and with South Africa? Both were for me a process of revelation and conversion. I could put it more sharply than this, for my experience of America was like a series of explosions in the mind. Perhaps I had not read sufficiently of American history, or not met enough Americans, although I have had American friends nearly all my life. Yet I think now that I liked them then not because they were Americans but because they were unexpectedly and satisfyingly like myself. This, of course, touches on one of the first cliches about Americans—"Oh, they can be delightful individually, but in the mass!"

Then there were the vague general views that over the years become almost built-in. I remember a letter from a friend: "Do not go to America. Everything is painless, effortless and brainless. The children are intolerable and the grown-ups, one cannot say 'adults,' scarcely less so. It's a vortex of riches, machines, and fancy dress; a chaos of pizazz and tranquilizer pills. There is no leadership either in taste or politics." There was music and art and fine buildings— but of course "Americans can just buy anything and they do it without caring what they buy. They brag about their skyscrapers but most of their houses are rows and rows of silly little boxes, looking with their television antennae like hideous beetles painted in plastic and crawling over the countryside. Or they cluster about juke-box baroque—restaurants in bowler hats or ice-cream stands dripping plastic icicles. The ghastly thing is that they like it. . . ." In the more serious affairs of life one was taught much about the "rat race" which passes for business or for earning a living in America. Americans had done remarkable things in production and

260

they had technical "know-how," but America itself was just a man-made mess. A giant with the head of a lout.

All this is truth without understanding or completeness, and truth without completeness is not truth. I traveled more than 10,000 miles in the United States, visited thirty of her states, and was happily privileged to stay in American homes with American families in the hundred cities and towns I visited in three months of exhaustive and sometimes exhausting traveling by train, bus, motorcar, street-cars, and afoot. I went from coast to coast and from the Southern states to the North and Middle West, and the numerous strangers who became friends and took me into their homes I pestered with questions about what they regarded as peculiarly American. I studied "Americanism" in schools, colleges, factories, clubs, welfare organizations, newspapers, trade unions, and state assemblies. The critics' words disappeared and I was left alone with the American reality.

One key to this "reality" came to me in American architecture. It has beauty, audacity, and a superb sense of scale, absorbing what is best in modern architecture in Western Europe, adapting itself to American needs, scenery, and wide horizons, and yet presenting what is exciting, new, and vital. The American towers are topless. They are unfinished. They go on soaring into space like aspiration: complete but not completed, as distinct from Europe, where so many things are completed or can aspire no more. American buildings have not been built in relation to each other and yet they do not make a jumble. They make a truly typical American skyline. The architect works in freedom and according to the needs he must satisfy and the function his building must perform. It is the individual working with private enterprise, and the outcome is not anarchy but the jagged, thrusting, varied, and pinnacled pattern in space which is uniquely and unmistakably American, anchored on the earth but reaching for the sky.

The same theme with variations can be marked at more than one level. Jazz, for example, is supposed to be in some way African in origin. I have heard African music in most parts of the African continent, and none of it was jazz, except where the players had obviously borrowed or become "Europeanized." Jazz is American, but for its American quality to be appreciated it is necessary to hear it in America, preferably in New Orleans or San Francisco. This time it is not a pattern in space but a pattern in time. Yet it is woven in the same way. The general theme is stated and then, successively, the instrumentalists plunge or detonate into single, separate assertions of their own, to which the rest then become a background and a rhythmical accompaniment. At precisely the right moment the soloist will return to the movement as a whole, and then either drummer or saxophonist or pianist will take off.

Outside Columbus in Ohio there are a number of busy and prosperous and, in one or two instances, even famous factories. Columbus did not set out to industrialize itself or to the best of my knowledge even plan industrial development. A farmer found the seat on his tractor uncomfortable and set out to make a better one for himself; others liked it and now he makes them for thousands of farmers. Another became tired of his corrugated iron outbuildings and sheds constantly blowing down or gaping at the joints and letting in the rain; he designed a locking sheet that now sells in most of the states and has even stood up to atomic blast. This time it is a pattern not in space or time but in work, through which a South African, at least, sees at once a fundamental difference between American and his own or European culture. The architecture, the literature, even the higher or more intellectual forms of jazz, can be said to be part of a minority culture, but this work attitude toward life is nationwide and deep and distinctively American. In America what counts is what is done. Europe prefers to define itself in terms of culture. In South Africa we are the prisoners of a system of ideas. But to the American all this seems largely irrelevant to the needs and duties of daily life; he depends more on action than on what is thought and said.

Thus as one journeyed, the vast and varied picture began to come into focus. The preconceptions were shattered or fell away of their own inadequacy. None fitted, and, indeed, to try to fit America into any single category is like trying to pin a blanket on the sea. It is comforting to say America is "adolescent" or it is "provincial," and then either make every manifestation fit into that definition or reject it as not being typically American. One can motor, for example, from Washington to Williamsburg and deplore the billboards, posters, and stands that line the route and give one a sense of traveling through a publicity neurosis. But at the end there is a true work of restoration. Even if the eighteenth-century costumes of the inhabitants look more like fancy dress than period, much has been gained. The hideousness of the road signs falls into perspective because Williamsburg is for the many, not the few.

Perhaps it is necessary to have lived in other lands where the masses have so little, to see the significance of this aspect of American life—and prosperity—which seems to offend so many critics. It is such an emphatic escape from the constraints of class and privilege. The cars as big as small ships compel the attention not simply because of their functionless "tail fins" but because there are so many. Nowhere in the world does the mass make such an impact, such an inescapable impact, as in America. The internal combustion engine was invented in Europe, but it was in the United States that it was regarded as something that should be brought to the people. In South Africa we had a Prime Minister who held that Natives should be prohibited from having driving licenses, let alone owning a motor car. In Europe motoring was long the privilege of the few. In America mass production was invented and, almost overnight, resources that had lain idle and unexploited became a fount of riches so abundant and so widespread as to be unparalleled in the recorded history of mankind.

II

It is not from books or from the official media of communication that one can learn the dominant preoccupation of a people. In South Africa there is no politics on the radio and there is no television whatever, but in the average home with a range beyond its own domesticities the dominant topic is politics as affecting the relationships between one race and another. "What do you think is going to happen?" means in South Africa either "will a change of government ever again be possible?" or "will the Black man eventually revolt or make irresistible demands?" In Britain it generally means "will Labour get into power?" In France, Algeria. But in America it means "how is the quality of American life going to be changed?" Americans are deeply concerned about the way they live. They are searching for something that will be more meaningful than what they have at present.

The answer, for Western man, is frighteningly important. It is vital that we should try to disentangle the essential, the permanent character and values of America; the seed and kernel of the future.

America is the last great redoubt of our civilization and of a social order wherein the freedom of the individual is the basic value. It is the only land of the operative ideal. It is the only country powerful enough to defend itself for whose people the true end of civilization, although rarely articulated, is still the creation of a community of intelligently communicating individuals. For most countries order is more important than community, but for Americans it is the other way around: community is more important than order. It is this that gives confusion to the scene, a sense of sometimes wild disorder or disharmony, as when an orchestra is tuning up and each group of instruments is seeking the right note. Each note for each group may be different, but when the right ones are found they make possible the symphony that will follow. Orchestration is what America is seeking—each different group, however distinct and separate its ways, finding its place in the fuller harmony by the very fact of being itself.

This is not easy, but it is a matter of life and death to find the keynotes, the right answers and the right way. We know now that civilizations as powerful as our own, and more mature, have at a point, and sometimes at a peak, declined and crumbled, with all their wealth and might dissolved and vanished. Where now is Rome and where Byzantium? There is a sense in which it can be said that America is the Rome and Russia the Byzantium of our age, and over both the Dark Ages cast their shadow, for we can no longer count them so far away.

History, even American history, one fears, is badly taught in America. Among advanced students, for example, I found that there was an unquestioned assumption that America's history was certain to be different from all other histories, and most certainly different from Europe's. There is a very general belief that the Dark Ages came because of Europe's own weakness, silliness, or wickedness. Yet surely Americans of all people should be impressed, without necessarily reading Pirenne, by the way the decline and fall into darkness was brought about by the drying up of trade, the loss of command over raw materials and especially gold. Would the American attitude over the loan for the High Dam in Egypt have been the same if the duel for trade were seen in the deeper perspective of history? This, to many American minds, is a kind of realism that is not attractive.

264

Liberalism, in the sense of a belief that there are self-evident and unchallengeable rights of man, goes deeper than a political belief or prejudice and has become an American instinct. Many of my American Negro friends, should they ever read this, will smile, and it is indeed necessary to say at once that there is a very different emphasis in American Negro thinking. It is easier for Negroes to see that the American order may not be the last word in human organization. They can see this and yet remain within that remarkably unified body of thought and feeling which is what I mean by "Americanism." They are in it and of it, but they do not take it for granted that "progress" and opportunity for fulfillment of the best that is within a man will follow as automatically as apples grow on a well-fertilized apple tree. The Negro in many if not in most states is still struggling for these things.

The Negro is, in so many ways, the conscience and the challenge of America. In South Africa the accepted reply to any criticism on race relations that Americans may have to offer is: what about your own color bar and your treatment of the Negro? Yet here, too, "Americanism" makes it doubtful if there is any true parallel between the two. The racial conflict in the Southern states is not the same as that in South Africa. The American Negro is an American. His problem is truly as much a poverty and a White problem as it is racial. In fact, in talking to Negroes, both leaders and led, to intellectuals and laborers, to lawyers in California and field hands in Mississippi, I was struck by the likeness between their mental and emotional attitudes and those of many Afrikaners.

The point is that the Negroes of America are an advancing, aspiring, aggressive people. They are moving up from nothing as the Afrikaner moved up from nothing, and they are entering and mastering new fields of endeavor in commerce, industry, and finance, as is the Afrikaner. There are those in South Africa who want to keep the Afrikaner out, and there are those in America who want to keep the Negro out, and similar conditions produce a similar psychology, whatever the country, race, or color. There this rough parallel ends, for the Afrikaner descends from a centuries-old culture and feels himself a member of a master race. The American Negro has no other culture except American, and there will be no Black nationalism in the United States. The differences are fundamental. The White man in the Southern states feels himself being presented with a challenge on an increasingly equal footing and not, as the Afrikaner feels in South Africa, faced with a primitive tribalism that might overwhelm his own social order completely.

There is a color bar in the old South. There is a racialism of a venom and bitterness that in expression and often in sheer disregard of the law surpass anything in South Africa. Yet it still falls within the American framework and this, without in any way minimizing the seriousness, the dimensions, or the human tragedy of the problem, makes it primarily the problem of a pecking order rather than of complete racial and cultural division, as it is in South Africa. No Southern White that I spoke to but admitted at length and under pressure that the Whites were fighting a losing battle— "but we shall keep on fighting"—and that the decision for integration had really been taken. The struggle is also bound up with the assertion of states' rights, which, as Southerners point out with considerable emphasis, are guaranteed by the Constitution.

III

Stand in the foyer of a hotel in Vienna or Venice or Rome or Paris as the American visitors walk past, talking freely and confidently to each other, get into their car and drive off. The hotel page or porter or commissionaire, whoever happens to be standing there, will so often say "Americans [the "of course" is implied], they think they own everything," or, generally when untipped, "they spoil everything." Do not go here, do not go there, it is full of Americans. What does it mean? It does not mean anti-Americanism. It is a hatred of the kind of freedom that Americans unconsciously assert. It is a rejection of a kind of psychological strength which, because in truth it has but a weak philosophical basis, is positively distressing to those outside it. In this sense Americans do not think or theorize about freedom; they *are* free. It is irritating, even painful, as is a child's happiness to harassed adults who cry out "for heaven's sake be still," meaning "for heaven's sake stop enjoying yourself." People easily mistake this harassment and irritability for adulthood. It is so often an adult state. Thus all Americans become "childish" or "adolescent."

Furthermore, intelligent Americans themselves do not quite know what to do about their mass culture. It does not fit into any of the books, and most of us think that political forms come from books

266

and are to be measured by what is said in these books, not by being actually lived out. Certainly I never met a single American who, surveying his own life or that of those about him, said "this is it." Americans worry about the mass. They are troubled whether they should give it their sympathetic but critical support. It would seem that after all the revolution was not complete. There is still an aristocratic distrust of demos, or at any rate a suspicion that what is enjoyed by the many must be vulgar, questionable in taste: not something that should be allowed to place a stamp on a whole nation, a nation moreover which in its constitution gives the people freedom but then voluntarily shackles itself so that they shall not misuse it.

There does seem to be a dichotomy in American life, a vague, pervading sense that somehow democracy has not come up to expectations. America has produced and spread throughout her people standards of health, leisure, and general well-being surpassing those of any other nation in the world, even those nearest to her in living standards and material wealth. Young Americans brush this aside as something that should long ago have been taken for granted. But is it so long ago? The fact is that Americans, looking to the future to solve all problems and living most vigorously in the present, have forgotten how the majority of their fathers and certainly their grandfathers lived. They forget too that the "mass" of America is also truly young; youthful, in the best and most hopeful sense of that word.

Moreover, it is necessary to remember that in addition to its mass prosperity, which has certainly brought problems, America has also marched ahead in the things of the mind, the intellect, and the spirit. This is something hard to appreciate from abroad. Again it is perhaps necessary to be in America to see for oneself that she is now among the authorities and leaders in most of the disciplines and sciences, archaeology, music, and the classics. "We shall never do it, never," cried a Syrian student to me almost in despair, after we had been given the opportunity to see some of America's resources in the arts and sciences. "Never say never," I replied, "or you have missed the first lesson of America." Yet I sympathized. I too longed for a fraction of the American accomplishment in South Africa, and I also wondered why so little was made of this brilliant achievement and so much of the "mass." There is reason.

Materially, economically, and technologically, America is still among the dynamic nations. She is so dynamic that she has become almost completely externalized. Life in America is lived from outwards within and not from within outwards. Inwardly, America is static. The individualist striving to escape from the straitjacket of Europe has escaped. Where should he go now? America has cast out or overcome her devils of monarchy, of Europe, of tyranny, and spiritually the house is swept and garnished. She is rightly troubled that what shall take their place will not be worse than the devils she knew. Unity has been achieved. The need now is for diversity rather than singleness, for more provocative and reflective thought.

America has a problem of how to establish and maintain quality in her politics and in her society. In some countries this is done by equating quality with privilege or class or riches. In South Africa we do it by equating it with being White. I do not know if this entitles us to feel superior to America, to think that we have filled a vacuum from which she still suffers! The complaint here in South Africa is that the young people are becoming more and more "Americanized," which is another way of saying that the very distinctive culture of the masses in America irresistibly evokes responses in the masses of other countries. This is surely nothing to get angry or resentful about, either here or elsewhere. The older cultures are strong enough to assimilate these impacts without being assimilated to them.

There are disagreeable and even repellent features of American life. But they are aspects, not the whole of it. There was a time when I, too, thought they represented, nay, *were* America. Now I try to meet this charge by saying that there is also much to admire, and that neither we nor Europeans in general have the right to be patronizing. As for Americans having so much of the good things of life because they can "pay for it," I counter this by pointing out that their wealth has not been given. Americans have won it by working and sacrificing for it. They have had to wrestle with an extreme and savage climate; with nature at her most violent; and against mighty rivers that might easily have become America's sorrow rather than her highways.

America presents herself to other nations as the universal prophet of liberalism. It is a liberalism that may harmonize with American objectives of foreign policy and national security, but it does not offer a panacea for nations that have entirely different social equations to work out. On the contrary, it often seems not so much an ideal as a crude assertion of economic power. The origins of this can be seen only within America itself, where the visitor quickly marks standards of personal liberty and of comparative equality so high that there is never any need to question the principles from which these blessings flow—a questioning that could enable Americans to gain a deeper perspective first upon themselves and then upon the world outside. As it is, Americans assume almost unhesitatingly that the American outlook and American thought have a universal validity. This, it is true, is putting the matter crudely, for there are of course hundreds of Americans who criticize American thinking. But the tendency is to assume that what has proved good for the United States is good for the world.

Yet it is with nations as with all things. America has been collected from the four corners of the world and shaped by an infinity of circumstances. We cannot separate her from what she is; amid all the conflicting voices, we can be aware only that America has still the vigor of youth, is finding her way as she makes it. America can afford to make mistakes, for she can still put them right. By looking at her beginnings no man could have divined that she was working toward what she is today. We do not know what she will be, although we have a clue, or at least a faith and a hope, for there is a grace of freedom which works toward its own extension and fulfillment among those who cherish it and dedicate themselves to it.

Now that I have returned I find myself much alone in my changed view of the United States. It is as though I see America high and far-off like a beacon on a dark and distant shore, while most of those about me see it as a vast amusement park. One tends to seek the company of those who have had what I may call the American "experience," which is of strength hungering to translate itself into beauty, of conformity that yet challenges itself by most free and fearless inquiry, by the right to question and the right to disagree. Amazing material abundance most widely diffused has not brought inner development or spiritual peace. But has its lack brought these values to realization anywhere else?

269

from Canada

JAMES EAYRS

The author: born in England (London), 1926, and moved to Canada in 1933; studied at University of Toronto, Columbia University, London School of Economics. Dr. Eayrs is Assistant Professor at the University of Toronto, teaching courses in international relations and political theory. He has written a volume for the "Canada in World Affairs" series, and is working on a history of Canadian diplomacy. His sojourns in the United States, where he is a frequent visitor, have included trips in the South and West as well as his student years in New York City (1948-1950).

I

SENTIMENT in Canada toward the American people and their government has moved between the extremes of cordiality and irritation. In the past the eras of good feeling coincided roughly with periods of prosperity or economic recovery, and with the years of wartime cooperation; the periods between tended to be times of tension. In trying to account for this tension there are several ready answers that may be worth mentioning, if only because they are part of the conventional language of international relations. Whatever their weight, I do not consider any of these fully adequate as an explanation.

In the first place, there is the ambition for territorial conquest that is supposed to motivate a powerful state in relations with a weaker neighbor. It is true that the "undefended frontier," so tirelessly displayed as an example to benighted folk of other continents, is more a part of the mythology than of the history of North America, or was so at least during the nineteenth century. Even since then the two governments have occasionally assumed what Hobbes called "the posture of gladiators." In 1907 Sir Wilfrid Laurier thought that the Act of Congress creating the Militia Reserve was a threat to Canadian security; and in the 1920's there was prepared and circulated to Canadian Military Districts a top-secret "Defence Scheme No. 1," a strategic plan for use in the event of attack by the United States. But I do not think these good illustrations of

American imperialism. They are better as symptoms of Canadian paranoia. Despite the persistence of Canadian anxiety, the possibility that an American government would use force against Canada has grown increasingly remote. The only President of the present century to have considered doing so was Theodore Roosevelt, and by 1918 he had changed his mind.

But armed force is only one of several ways by which a strong state can subjugate a weak one. It may be argued that American domination of Canada has been achieved without the use of arms but no less effectively for that. There is still talk in Canada about "cultural sovereignty," or, more bluntly, about "cultural imperialism." In its usual form this notion suggests the erosion of Canada's national identity by the murrain of vulgar entertainment moving north across the forty-ninth parallel. "If the obstacle to true Canadianism was 'Downing Street,'" wrote the Governor General of Canada in 1948, "its enemy today is 'Main Street,' with all that the phrase implies." Occasionally the threat is detected not in the dregs but in the finest ferment of American culture, as in an observation in a recent report by the Royal Commission on Broadcasting that "the dangers to Canadian national identity are much greater from the good American programmes than from their poor or clumsy productions."

Some are tempted to go further. They perceive in these unwelcome cultural imports a sinister design to make Canada a "vassal state," subservient politically to Washington just as it is ruled culturally from Tin Pan Alley, Madison Avenue, and Beverly Hills. This is surely an exaggerated view. Whatever the faults of the manipulators of the communications systems, pandering to the United States government is not one. They go their own way unmindful of the feeble surveillance of the Federal Communications Commission; in their pursuit of sensationalism and profit they seem cheerfully unhampered by true patriot love. It would be hardly less incongruous to see them as bullies of the administration, forcing it to retail their shoddy wares abroad. Such a view does scant justice to the efforts of the State Department to provide foreign audiences with aspects of American culture other than horror and crime "comics," "rock 'n' roll," Mr. Mickey Spillane, and Miss Jayne Mansfield.

A similar confusion of influence with imperialism attends the charge that economic pressures have made Canada an American dependency, "the world's most northerly banana republic." Plainly, the Canadian economy is highly sensitive to changes in United States policy. R. B. Bennett once remarked that if he could set American tariff rates he could do more for Canada than as its Prime Minister; and Senators Fordney, McCumber, Smoot, and Hawley are as prominent as Senator McCarthy in the demonology of Canadian history. But sometimes forbearance goes unnoticed. Little attention was paid to President Eisenhower's rejection of the unanimous recommendation of his Tariff Commission that the rates on groundfish fillets (of which Canada is a principal supplier) be increased. It has been easier and politically more profitable to promise to keep Canada from becoming "the forty-ninth state" than to give such friendly acts their due.

Canadian concern over the vagaries of the American tariff has lately been overshadowed by apprehension at the extent of American investment. Thirty years ago such fears were dismissed by a great Canadian editor, J. W. Dafoe, as "chiefly voiced by a group of alarmists forever a-twittering with fright." Today there are few informed Canadians who do not experience what their Prime Minister has described as "an intangible sense of disquiet" when they reflect that United States investors have gained control of most of our mining and smelting, oil and pulp and paper enterprises, together with certain sectors of manufacturing industry, principally the automotive, electrical appliance, and chemical. There are of course real reasons for concern, and this wholly legitimate anxiety leads easily to the cry of "dollar imperialism." But I do not think that many Canadians, after serious reflection, would consider the United States government to be a tool of American financial and industrial interests, employed to control us politically the better to exploit us economically. At any rate it is hard to wrest this version of events from the facts. More than once the desire to maintain good relations with Canada has caused the administration in Washington to ignore the strongest pressure from the business community, most recently when the State Department persuaded the Governor of Maryland to veto legislation discriminating against a Canadian brewery.

Still another possible reason for Canadian mistrust is a belief that the United States is motivated by "enlightened self-interest," by a calculation that more is to be gained by the policy of the Good

Neighbor than by the policy of the Big Stick. Here the argument is that an amicable relationship with a weaker neighbor enables the United States to refute the charge that its foreign policy is inherently imperialistic. Canada is the world's hostage of America's good intentions. Knowing this, Americans do not harm the hostage. In return, Canadian statesmen demonstrate their gratitude by carrying to the credulous masses of Asia and elsewhere visible proof of American purity. This, it is alleged, is what Prime Minister St. Laurent was up to in February 1954, when he told the Indian Parliament that "we Canadians . . . as their close neighbors . . . have special reason to know and appreciate the qualities of the American people, which have been reflected in the fundamental outlook of their Government over the years." What foolishness for the United States to put an end to such glowing testimonials!

There may be something to this cynical interpretation. But insofar as it assumes that only a narrow calculation of self-interest restrains the United States from bringing the full weight of its power upon us, I find it only slightly more convincing than the others. It implies a taste and flair for *Realpolitik* at once alien to America's tradition and beyond its constitutional capacity.

II

To someone from Europe or Asia, or indeed from the United States, the striking thing about the two North American peoples must surely be how unnatural the border that bisects the continent, how similar the lives of those on its two sides. Both peoples have so much more than their fair share of the world's material comforts, and every prospect of becoming still wealthier. With the exception of the French-speaking Canadians, they use a common language and even a common slang. They share a European cultural tradition. Both enjoy or endure the mass culture and mass gadgetry of twentieth-century civilization. Both hold to an ethic of human brotherhood and a belief in the sanctity of the individual. Beside this common tradition of beliefs and values and institutions any recitation of differences is bound to pale.

Yet to a Canadian these differences are crucial. It is the area of distinctiveness which interests him. Indeed, it obsesses him. He wants to know what may be said to be distinctively Canadian in North America. He feels that unless his people are making some contribution to life on this continent they have little reason to go on paying the price of being Canadian, which in monetary terms is high enough. And he is of the opinion that we ought to be developing our own distinctive social, political, and economic institutions; a distinctive national character, a Canadian variant of the American Way of Life; a distinctive policy in our dealings with other nations. To what extent have we done so?

Begin with the fundamental fact of Canadian life. We are a plural community. Within the Canadian state are to be found in more or less peaceable coexistence what one of our leading historians describes as "two utterly unlike peoples, distrustful, jealous and resentful of each other." About a third of our present population of over sixteen million is French-speaking, deeply rooted in Roman Catholicism, vigilantly preserving cultural integrity. This large and distinctive cultural group, not a minority to be assimilated within a common Canadianism, still less a second-class citizenry, but a partner sharing equally in the joint project of Confederation, provides the major contrast between the two North American peoples. Its tenacious quest for *survivance*, for the preservation and enlargement of its autonomy, has been for Canada a source of strength and weakness. The variety of culture and outlook makes for a more interesting society, but it has created internal political tensions. It has slowed the growth of national identity. It has made the nation more vulnerable to the confident pull of American influence.

Since 1945 over a million "new Canadians," mostly from Europe, have arrived in Canada, raising the number of foreign-born to about three million. These new arrivals find no melting pot awaiting them. The bi-cultural state has developed few hallmarks of a common Canadianism with which to stamp them. We do not go in for oaths of allegiance. We do not celebrate "I am a Canadian" Day. We do not "pledge the flag," for we have no national flag to pledge. In contrast to American practice, which by intensive if superficial indoctrination tries to replace the traditions of the arrival's country of birth with a sense of identification with his country of adoption, we encourage the newcomer to keep his roots intact. The result may be seen in enclaves of settlement where the language, customs, and culture of the Old World are zealously preserved and propagated. It may be seen, less happily, in the resentment of some of the longer established Canadians, mainly in the cities, for those in their midst who, whatever their citizenship, remain "foreigners" by virtue of their unfamiliar tongue, their distinctive behavior, their strange names. Nevertheless, a middle and a better way between the extremes of a doctrinaire pluralism and the fierce obliterating heat of the melting pot is beginning to be sought in Canada. In the aftermath of the Hungarian revolution, when immigration regulations were set aside to receive some thirty thousand refugees, the view was widely expressed that it would be best for the newcomers and for Canada alike if they turned their back on the past and immersed themselves in the New World.

On Canadian political institutions the United States has had an important influence. It has been said that if John A. Macdonald was the father of our Confederation, Alexander Hamilton was its grandfather; and American experience suggested at least two major features of the Canadian Constitution, its federalism and the need for power at the center. But notwithstanding the initial and continuing influence of American upon Canadian government, we have managed to preserve some distinctive features. Chief among them is the parliamentary system, a heritage of British colonial days and the struggle for responsible government, which was ingeniously combined with a federal constitution. Its maintenance alongside the American Presidency is something we are very proud of and which American statesmen from Woodrow Wilson on have often envied. A further distinction is that Canada is a monarchy. This does not mean that our government is any less responsible, or any less democratic, than that of our republican neighbor. Nor does it mean that we are less able to dispense with the formal and ceremonial aspects of political life. But we are not unaware of the advantage of devolving many of those wearisome and time-consuming duties upon someone who makes their performance a full-time job.

The continuing popularity of monarchical institutions in Canada reveals also, perhaps, a distinctive political temperament. We place our faith less in formal documents and constitutional guarantees than in custom, tradition, and habit. We have not sealed the British North America Act in helium and sent it about the nation in a train—though perhaps we should. There is no Bill of Rights on the American model. We appoint our judges; and we are rather shocked that Americans elect theirs. "Political democracy in Canada," writes Professor Dennis Wrong, "is seen as an orderly and traditionally workable system of government rooted in law and precedent rather than solely as an instrument for giving expression to the will of the people. American veneration for the Constitution is paralleled by Canadian reverence for parliamentary tradition and custom."

Here, as in the United States, two major political parties, practically indistinguishable as to policy, contend for the voters' favor —as alternative administrations rather than as midwives for different social orders. Like the Democratic and Republican parties (to which, very roughly, they correspond), the Liberal and Conservative parties draw upon a wide variety of regional and economic interests for support. As a consequence the most successful of our politicians have been those most adept at compromise, not to say dissimulation. Sectional loyalties, deeply rooted in and coinciding with geographic regions of political importance, form areas of inhibition in which the Canadian politician wanders at his peril. The fear of alienating the voters of Quebec, disguised in Aesopian language as "preserving national unity," drains debate of forthrightness.

Canadian politicians are less likely than American to have served little or no apprenticeship in minor positions of public trust before attaining national prominence. This is partly a by-product of the parliamentary system, which encourages a lengthy sojourn in the House of Commons before elevation to Cabinet rank or party leadership. But it also reflects the slightly greater respectability of a professional political career. Less ambiguously than the American the Canadian regard for law and legal authority is deferential. The different emphasis has been discerned in the contrast between the popular culture heroes of westward expansion—the cowboy in the United States, the "Mountie" in Canada, the one a rugged individualist often taking the law in his own hands, the other the embodiment of established authority.

In each country the need to harness the resources of a forbidding if wealthy continent requires the participation of the state in economic life. In the United States a stronger ideological commitment to capitalism has made this an almost surreptitious process, as if the extent of the state's activity were a measure of society's

failure. An outsider, deafened by American paeans to "private enterprise" and American diatribes against "socialism," will be surprised to discover (if he ever does) how much of the economy is
run or directed by the federal government. Though no less typical,
the Tennessee Valley Authority is not so acceptable a symbol of
the American Way as is, say, the Ford Motor Company. The Canadian attitude toward public enterprise has been more pragmatic.
People being fewer, capital scarcer, climate harsher, distances and
other natural barriers even more formidable, the impulse here to
state action has been stronger. It has been reinforced by the political motive of building and sustaining a Canadian nation. These
together explain the wide range of governmental activity in a society not given to *dirigiste* solutions. The state has become an entre-
preneur, producing power, marketing wheat, running railways and
airlines. It is even in the entertainment business, furnishing, through
the Canadian Broadcasting Corporation, amusement and "uplift"
for Canadian audiences—and, we like to think, for some Americans as well.

A similar pragmatism marks our attitude toward private enterprise. We have not tried to contrive a free-enterprise ideology to
justify our free-enterprise system. The phrase "people's capitalism"
is unknown. The Stock Exchanges of Toronto and Montreal are
still seen by many as somewhat raffish institutions, a far cry from
the established respectability of the bourse in New York over which
Mr. Keith Funston presides as a kind of financial Grover Whalen.
Capitalism itself seems less secure. Canadian investors prefer bonds
to equities, and life insurance to either. A strongly Puritan streak
runs through our national life, and what has stamped us may be
the early Puritanism, with its hostility to acquisition, rather than
the later variety, in which entrepreneurial success becomes the hall-
mark of virtue. In French Canada the influence of Catholic social
theory has worked against the spread of the capitalist ethos, and
even today few French-speaking Canadians are in positions of business power. Our staple-producing economy has been more vulnerable to catastrophic depression. Deep scars and bitter memories survive the 1930's. Capitalism, even the greatly improved capitalism
arisen from the ashes, is still on trial. There persists a small but influential party of democratic socialism, unique in North America,
devoted to the creation of a Canadian society in which private enter-

prise would find no place on the "commanding heights" of big industry, big transport, and big communications.

A few impressions, finally, of the Canadian businessman. American executives who have worked in Canada often complain of the slower tempo of his activity, his devotion to bureaucratic routine, his unreceptivity to new ideas—the same complaint often made by the Canadian businessman of his counterpart in the United Kingdom. The executive in Canada is likely to remain in a single industry throughout his career, even in a single firm; American capitalism has developed the interchangeable executive, along with the interchangeable part, and it is not uncommon to find a top-flight management man shifting imperturbably and effectively from enterprise to enterprise. Recent study has disclosed a concentration of economic power in the hands of relatively few directors in Canadian corporations; but the Canadian businessman has yet to acquire that easy familiarity with his peers in government and in the military which has been seen as the distinguishing feature of the "power elite" in America. There is perhaps less total submission of his personality in his business career; he still has time (though it is shrinking fast) for other things. The "Organization Man" appears less commonly in Toronto or Winnipeg than in New York or Chicago. But he is here, and more like him are on the way.

III

Professor Daniel Boorstin of the University of Chicago has detected among his countrymen in the United States a complaint he diagnoses as "cultural hypochondria," its symptoms a morbid preoccupation with the condition of the nation's artistic and intellectual life. Canadians will recognize this ailment as one by which they are if anything more severely afflicted. Other peoples may from time to time pause briefly for cultural stock-taking; we appoint a Royal Commission. Other peoples delight in reading about their neighbors' national characteristics; we find ourselves the most fascinating subject. Introspection has become a fetish with us. Intently, usually humorlessly, we peer at our national image, hoping to discover those features of culture and of character by which we may be recognized as other than a mere projection of American traits.

What do we see? Or what do we say we see? Mr. Vincent Massey, the distinguished author of *On Being Canadian*—the title is itself revealing—claims that Canadian soldiers in London during the Second World War could be spotted as such "long before their badges could be identified. Something in their bearing told the story —a combination of qualities—. . . . a naturalness and freedom of movement, a touch of breeziness and alertness which suggested the new world." But to another observer, the Canadian historian A. R. M. Lower, "the American figure stands on its feet four square against the world: Canadian 'stance' is less decisive. Americans talk of 'the worried Canadian face.' " With such conflicting evidence it may seem wise to abandon altogether the search for the national character. Yet there is something to be said for pursuing it. Members of a distinctive political community are likely in time to develop a distinctive response to situations and events. If by "national character" we mean the dimensions of that response it may be possible to describe it without relying too much on the misleading evidence of limited experience.

Two facts of Canadian history have conditioned our national character thus understood: we have not turned upon our motherlands; nor have we turned upon ourselves. Thus we have been spared the agonies of revolution and civil war, and we know the compromises and tolerances required to work a plural society. From these facts derive many features of contemporary Canadianism. And none is more obvious, certainly none more widely discerned, than the placidity, the reserve, the caution that mark off Canadian from American behavior. Our politics are more sedate. Our millionaires are less conspicuous in their consumption. Our criminals are less violent in their crimes. Our fashions in clothes are less daring. And so, perhaps, are our fashions in ideas. We lack the vitality of our southern neighbors. Their flair, their *panache*, the reckless, raucous individuality that has carried the American nation to such dizzy heights of power and responsibility, are all strangely muted here.

To different observers this appears in different lights. Mr. Adlai Stevenson, a tactful and sympathetic visitor, once construed it as an "admirable feature of Canadian political life—I mean its stability, its tolerance and its good sense." Professor D. W. Brogan has remarked upon the more tranquil atmosphere he found after crossing from Seattle to Vancouver, where "the immunity from what was called American hysteria had admirable causes" not wholly accounted for by the lesser Canadian commitment to the Korean campaign. Canadians are less sure of themselves. While few Angry Young Men lash the national character in public, a senior Canadian historian has most scathingly deplored the smug complacency of Canadian life. "Whether we are too placid, or too insensitive, or too lethargic, or too superficial," wrote Frank Underhill a few years ago, "we are incapable of either the messianic exaltation or the existentialist agonizing of some of our contemporaries. Our limitations, in fact, make us a people incapable of tragedy."

Does it seem too farfetched to ascribe the drabber habits of the Canadian to his less violent past? A nation embroiled for better or worse in civil war or revolution engages in a fierce emotional experience. Such is the stuff of which a sense of national identity is quickly made. It brings color and excitement into the national tradition. It nourishes a legacy of hates and hopes and heroes. Just as there is nothing in Canadian history to match the Revolutionary or Civil Wars, so we have no Washington or Paine, no Lincoln or Lee, on whose exploits we bring up our young: William Lyon Mackenzie or John A. Macdonald do not quite fit the part. We need not yield to America in the daring of our explorers; but the attempt to elevate Pierre Radisson to the eminence of Davy Crockett was a humiliating failure. Of political theorists, another offspring of a revolutionary tradition, we are even more devoid. If, as has been remarked, every French Canadian is a practicing John C. Calhoun, no one has emerged to present his claims in a coherent theory of politics.

But the quiet life has its compensations. And I would place prominently among them the empirical, workaday approach to national and international problems which I think may be fairly seen as a distinctively Canadian ingredient in the North American response. If revolutions breed heroes and philosophers, they also beget doctrinaires, and that stern sense of self-righteousness which, if it sustains the weak, is not an unmixed blessing for the strong. From its revolutionary tradition stems that characteristically American belief that some swift and spectacular stroke may permanently solve problems that by their nature admit only of amelioration. The Canadian is struck by the American fondness for the "one-shot solution," for the "crash program," for "doctrines," whether they bear the name of Monroe or Stimson, Truman or Eisenhower. The American anthropologist Margaret Mead has written that if "cope" is a typically British verb, "fix" is typically American; the corresponding Canadian word, it has been suggested, is "adapt." Little has there been in our experience to encourage the delusion that injuries to society may be healed in the same fashion and with the same expectation of success as an appendix is removed or a machine repaired. Everything rather points the other way, to the need for prudence, for patience, for compromise, even for appeasement, if this word may still be used in other than a pejorative sense. We are gardeners in the field of politics, not engineers.

It will be said that the response of the democracies to the challenge of aggressive dictatorships could have done with a little more principle and resolve, a little less pragmatism and caution—a little more of the American revolutionary tradition, a little less of the Anglo-Canadian tradition of compromise. I would not deny it. But history does not often repeat itself. The lessons of the 1930's are not altogether applicable to the 1950's, when dictators have girded themselves with weapons which, if loosed, would bring to a close the history of us all.

IV

It is against this background of Canadian-American relations and differences that I would like to return now to the question of Canadian views about the United States. No one familiar with the labyrinthine discussions of recent years concerning the study of one nation's ideas about another—the doubts and misgivings about the appropriate "approach," "methodology," "scope," "focus," and "organization"—will underestimate the complexity of the problem. And if it is unscientific to think of "the average Belgian" or "the man in the street in Japan," generalization about the state of mind of the scattered and varied Canadian community is even less valid. Regional differences and the great distances between regions make systematic study of Canadian opinion costly and time-consuming; there is little data with which to test impressions. These difficulties may partly excuse whatever fuzziness and exaggeration appear in the paragraphs below.

The process by which national prejudices are formed and held was well described in the seventeenth century by Sir Thomas Browne as one "wherein by opprobrious Epithets we miscall each other, and by an uncharitable Logick, from a disposition in a few, conclude a habit in all." Anti-Americanism in Canada rests very largely on the shaky foundation of "uncharitable Logick." From our personal stock of chance encounters, from the common stock of popular mythology, we build our composite image of the "typical American." In former times this creature of our national imagination had a lean and hungry look, sly and sharp and scheming. Today he is a heftier figure, loudly dressed, wreathed in a rosary of expensive photographic equipment. But these unflattering stereotypes do not themselves explain anything. They reflect resentment; they neither cause it nor account for it. They do not tell us why we pick as symbols of America the homburged tycoon, the boisterous tourist, the windy politician, the sideburned crooner.

I have mentioned that the periods of good feeling toward the United States have tended to be periods of economic prosperity and political cooperation. This makes the last ten years of Canadian-American relations difficult to understand. Since 1949 the two countries have been for the first time linked in formal alliance. Both have enjoyed unprecedented prosperity. Yet during this past decade the Canadian nation has experienced an undercurrent of resentment for America running more strongly than at any time since the First World War, now and then welling to the surface in surges of undisguised hostility. How are we to account for this?

One reason is our increasing interdependence. The two North American members of NATO have been thrown closer together by external events not always of their own making or to their liking. A whole new range of opportunity for friction and misunderstanding has thus been opened up. Continental defense provides a good example. To build and man the radar chains that guard the northern approaches, we have admitted to remote areas of our country United States servicemen and civilians in circumstances and in numbers no sovereign nation would ordinarily allow. This has been nothing less than a condition of our survival, and we are grateful—or we should be. At the same time the presence of so many Americans in our north country, coming and going pretty much as they please, has had an unsettling effect on our public. Disturbing rumors trickle down from the northlands into parliament and the press, having a greater influence on opinion than the fine print of the "Statement of Conditions to Govern the Establishment of a Distant Early Warning System in Canadian Territory," an agreement negotiated in 1955 and made public by the government in an attempt to allay just such misgivings. This unaccustomed and uneasy interdependence, extending to a wide variety of projects, continues to worry the less powerful of the partners.

A second cause of anti-American feeling in Canada in recent years has been the *malaise* of McCarthyism. Great as its effect was in Western Europe, I believe it was even more disturbing in Canada. Most Europeans, prevented by distance and a shortage of foreign exchange from conducting investigations at firsthand, necessarily relied on the image of America that found its way across the Atlantic, often blurred and distorted in transmission. Canadians, however, had in countless ways the opportunity for more intimate assessment. We knew better than most that beneath the frothy vaporings there lay the vast reservoir of American opinion, deep and decent. And when our closer scrutiny disclosed the extent to which the pollution had spread across the great republic, our sense of shock was all the greater for having been born of better knowledge. With mounting dismay we came to fear that America's capacity for leadership was being atrophied by a frightening national paranoia that no institution or individual seemed able or willing to cure. When the movement of which Senator McCarthy was cause or symbol lost its momentum, our relief was as great as our previous concern. The most widespread outburst of popular indignation against the United States within living memory was caused by the reappearance of these un-American activities in the tragic episode of the Norman affair.

A third general explanation is less specific than either of the foregoing. Throughout our recent history Canadian leaders have tried to preserve a measure of independence and influence by playing off against each other the two great nations most intimately affecting our affairs. During the 1920's and 1930's this meant invoking the support of Washington to escape pressure from Westminster; after 1945 it meant using the United Kingdom as a makeweight in dealing with the United States. This proved difficult. The United Kingdom was triumphant but tired, no longer the lion of former years. Canadians, quick to sense the need for a substitute, looked to the Commonwealth. If its members could develop a common policy on the great issues of postwar politics the traditional balance might be restored and Canada's influence reestablished. But could they? Could Mr. Nehru make common cause with Mr. Menzies, or Mr. Bandaranaike with Mr. St. Laurent? Suez provided a chilling answer. Not only did it make it starkly clear that Britain was no longer a Great Power in the classical sense of being able to impose its will on others; it equally illuminated the impossibility of welding the members of the modern Commonwealth into a countervailing Third Force. Mr. St. Laurent could not make common cause with the Prime Minister of the United Kingdom, let alone the Prime Minister of Ceylon. Canadians were left with the unpleasant truth. "For the first time in Canada's history," wrote the Montreal journalist G. V. Ferguson, "we are faced with the full, naked force of American influence without the modifying force of any counter-pressure." This shock of recognition was apparent in a sudden surge of anti-American feeling in Canada during the weeks after the Suez War. At this juncture of our history the habit of Dulles-baiting, which had become a form of tensional outlet for Canadians, assumed the proportions of a national pastime.

I now want to say something about anti-Americanism in three sections of the Canadian community that have exhibited that sentiment more obviously than others. The first, and by far the least significant of the three, is the members of the Labor-Progressive (Communist) Party of Canada, together with those who come within its influence. With unusual consistency the party line has portrayed the LPP as the defender of true Canadianism against alien and malign forces, directed by American capital, which seek to pollute and subvert it. The party's program, adopted in 1954, rings all the changes on this theme, locating precisely enough the points of sensitivity in Canadian-American relations. While many Canadians join in the LPP propagandists' litany of grievances, it is in spite of the Communist sponsorship, not because of it. The present membership and influence of the LPP is at an all-time low. Here, as in other free nations, the triple shock of the Twentieth Congress revelations, the Polish uprising, and the brutal repression of the Hungarian revolution has administered all but the *coup de grâce* to Trojan horses fed by Moscow.

The only other group in Canada to denounce American influence in language comparable to the vocabulary of Communist abuse is

284

to be found at the other end of the ideological spectrum. It is doubtful whether one could find in the files of *Pravda* itself a more hysterical attack on American life than appeared in *Notre americanisation*, a symposium sponsored by the Dominican Order in 1936 to which both lay and ecclesiastical French Canadian leaders contributed. In culture, in sport, in finance, above all in the moral and religious life of the community, the corrupting influence of the United States is discerned with truly neurotic fervor—with all the resentment felt by the guardians of a closed society for the cosmopolitan influences of an alien world. Unrepresentative as this view is of enlightened French Canadian opinion today, it is part of a mood that reaches back into the last century of Quebec's history, and indeed still persists. It reflects the peculiar pressures to which French Canada has been exposed, the double difficulties of a society grappling with industrialization, from which it derives less benefit than English-speaking parts of Canada, while struggling for *survivance* and self-expression against formidable odds. The tensions thus generated cry for a whipping boy, and French Canada has not had far to look. "The booming, disorderly, polyglot American world," writes the American sociologist Everett Hughes, "is an all too convenient scapegoat upon which to cast the aberrations of her own people and culture."

The French Canadian community naturally resists *americanisation*. It has been encouraged in resistance by clerical leaders fearful of the decline of their influence and of the debauch of the youth, by political leaders exploiting a foreign scapegoat, and by intellectual leaders to whom the preservation of cultural integrity is a *mission civilatrice* as compelling as any that moved the founders of the French Empire. But it has been a losing battle. The jackals of the communications systems prowl the land of Maria Chapdelaine. Many of the leaders, nothing if not realistic, are changing their tactics, like St. Thomas, who, since he could not fight the Aristotelian invasion, joined it and added luster to the faith. Better, then, the Hollywood movie with French subtitles or dubbed-in soundtrack than the original reel; better "La Famille Plouffe" than "John's Other Wife," "Chacun à son métier" than "What's My Line?" The most sophisticated members of the community—and they are very sophisticated indeed—are frank to say that American culture offers much to civilization, whether on the banks of the Seine or of the

St. Lawrence. But its "elementary and often toxic products," writes the sociologist Jean-C. Falardeau of Laval University, "have changed the mentality of the mass of our population infinitely more than our elite has been influenced by the thought of a John Dewey, the *Commonweal*, or the *Partisan Review*."

A third group in which anti-American attitudes are prevalent may be described as the English-speaking intelligentsia. I use this word, for want of a better, to include all those Canadians who have read (or think they ought to read) the Report of the Royal Commission on National Development in the Arts, Letters and Sciences (the "Massey Report"), and thus it designates artists and actors as well as writers and teachers. My impressions of this somewhat diffuse community will be confined to those of its members of whom I have most experience, university teachers.

Canadian university teachers tend to judge American achievement by standards harsher than those applied to Western Europe or indeed to their own country. A Canadian recently returned from teaching in America was struck by "the tone of discussion of American institutions and culture in Canadian faculty common rooms," finding it "so violently, irrationally anti-American that an accurate transcript of the conversation would not be acceptable dialogue in a third-rate problem novel, because the credibility of the characters would be irreparably damaged." For this attitude there must be some special reason.

The academic profession has been notoriously hard-pressed by inflation. Is there a note of envy in its acerbic strictures against the power-mowered affluence and the split-leveled prosperity of the American middle class? It has experienced as well a decline in status. This has made all the sharper its reaction to the anti-intellectual forces loosed by McCarthyism. Canadian teachers visiting the United States during the early 1950's were sometimes subjected at the border to irritating and ignorant interrogation about their political beliefs; two or three distinguished scholars suffered hardship and humiliation by this practice; and our response was to indulge in our own form of guilt by association, often overlooking the vigor of those humane and liberal millions who form the mass of American society. Finally, the academic profession has some claim to be the principal guardian of a distinctively Canadian cultural tradition. Many of us, in our zeal to extend protective custody

286

over what is worthwhile in our own country, have tended to malign what is equally worthwhile in our neighbors'. The Massey Commissioners themselves express resentment at the "vast and disproportionate amount of material coming from a single alien source"— by which they mean the United States.

But there have been strong if isolated protests from within the Canadian academic community at this indiscriminate denunciation of things American. "What we need," Frank Underhill has written, "is closer contact with the finest expressions of the American mind. The fear that what will result from such contact will be our own absorption is pure defeatism. We need closer touch with the best American universities . . . and research institutions, closer touch with American experimental music and poetry and theatre and painting, closer personal touch with the men who are leaders in these activities. The Americans are now mature enough to have come through this adolescent phase of believing that the way to become mature is to cut yourself off from the older people who are more mature than you are. It is about time that we grew out of it also."

V

Many difficult problems confront us in achieving better understanding between my country and the United States. But I do not think they will be solved more easily or more effectively by tinkering with or adding to existing institutions. Perhaps I should add two qualifications. It has been suggested that some of the friction in our affairs could be removed by making continental defense a NATO rather than a North American function; no doubt the intercontinental ballistic missile has robbed this suggestion of some of its value, but it may still possess merit. Secondly, it is the hope of all Canadians cherishing good neighborhood that the United States government will always look upon its Embassy at Ottawa as among the most important of its diplomatic missions, and staff it accordingly. The main hindrance to better understanding is not, however, public law but public opinion.

Americans are often less than well informed about Canadian conditions. There was a time, perhaps not so long ago, when this might have been put more forcibly. Americans used to think of Canada, if they thought of it at all, as (to quote a popular ditty)

"the land of ice and snow, where it's ninety-nine below," as (to
quote Mr. Lester Pearson) "an enormous cold spot on the map,
inhabited by Mounties, Eskimo, trappers, Quintuplets, and Rose
Marie." But as we have come to assume more significance in their
affairs, Americans have come to have more interest in and knowledge of ours. After all, it is an American who has written most
understandingly of French Canadian life. It is an American (of
Canadian birth) who first exposed the triangular interplay of the
English-speaking nations of the North Atlantic. It is in the United
States that the only center in North America for the study of the
Commonwealth is to be found, and the only institute for the study
of Canadian-American relations. The benevolence of American phi-
lanthropy has encouraged American scholars to pursue research in
Canada, and has enabled two generations of Canadians to study
in the United States. I do not think any other nation can have expended so much effort, both governmental and private, in an attempt to understand a neighboring people.

It is about time for Canadians to increase their share in this
undertaking of understanding. Hitherto we have pleaded financial
inability; happily this excuse can no longer prevail. I hope that
some of the resources of the newly created Canada Council will
help to carry on the work so long sustained by American generosity.
I would like to see more American students and teachers spend a
year or two in Canada on Canadian fellowships, more Americans
study Canadian problems, more Canadians study American problems—especially this last. I have always doubted the assumption
that Canadians know more about the United States than Americans know about us. And if this is true, our knowledge has come
not from any greater sense of intellectual curiosity, still less from
any higher sense of citizenship, but simply from our involuntary
saturation with Americana. But even that has not added much to
our comprehension of the depth and complexity of American life.
Our judgments of men and events are often hasty and superficial;
we jump to too many two-dimensional conclusions; we have seen
too much of the United States through the eyes of Harold Ross
and Henry Luce. I am sure there is room for more knowledge on
both sides of the border.

My last word must be a plea for the preservation of that border,
and of the diversity it symbolizes. There will, of course, be moments

of crisis when sovereignty is supremely irrelevant. At such times the cultivation of national distinctiveness becomes a frivolous dissipation of effort needed to protect our common tradition from destruction. Subject to that, let us do things in our own ways. And if these diverge we should not fuss or fret, for as Lord Bryce observed many years ago, "there is already too little variety on the American continent."

from Mexico

DANIEL COSÍO VILLEGAS*

The author: born in Mexico, D.F., 1900; studied at Mexican universities, at Harvard, Wisconsin, and Cornell, and at the London School of Economics and the École Libre des Sciences Politiques. He has served in numerous teaching and governmental positions, including posts as Secretary General of the National University of Mexico and Director of the National School of Economics. In the mid-1930's he was Financial Counselor to the Mexican embassy in Washington; his country has also sent him as delegate or adviser to various international conferences, and he is now Mexico's special Ambassador to the Economic and Social Council of the United Nations. His dozen or more books, the first published in 1922, deal with sociological and historical as well as with economic problems, and he has founded and directed several journals. He is the father of a son and a daughter. Since his years of study in this country (1925-1928) he has visited the United States frequently. In 1953 he taught in the University of Texas (Institute of Latin-American Studies), but his earlier and later trips have been centered mainly in the East.

I

WHEN I visited the United States for the first time, I was twenty-five years old, and the United States was nearly thirty-five years younger than it is now. I recall that in 1925 one frequently heard it said that the United States will create —is creating—a civilization, though not really a culture. Has it been thus? What has taken place in the intellectual and artistic development of the United States during the last thirty or forty years?

Progress has been so manifest that only the ignorant can fail to recognize it or the blind deny it. I believe there is no country in the world that has won so many Nobel Prizes in science as the United States; the North American novel is translated and read in all languages, besides having created a widely imitated school; there is no region far or near where jazz music does not have its devotees and even its fanatics; the country's contributions to medicine are more important than those of any other; the North American theater now has an identity of its own and is known and ad-

---

* Translated from the Spanish by James F. Shearer.

mired in Mexico, Paris, and London; and although the cinema is not, nor will ever be, what was expected of it some years ago, at least as an industry it continues to dominate throughout the world and to exercise a definite influence, even if this is almost always a deplorable one. North American culture, as well as the automobile, the electric iron, or the refrigerator, is now exported, and successfully.

The reason for this, of course, is that the country's internal growth has been enormous. There are now at least fifty universities which, though they may not be of first rank in every department, are so in this or that branch of knowledge, and in all of them there is discipline, the stimulus to learn, and the material bases for better teaching. Now there are good professors and scholars not only in Harvard, Yale, Princeton, or California, but in the least likely universities, such as Nebraska, Iowa, or Texas. The good symphony orchestras are no longer limited to Philadelphia, Boston, and New York, but are to be found in every urban center of medium importance, and some, like that of Louisville, are excellent. Their musicians are now predominantly North Americans, and there are distinguished conductors, also North Americans. United States opera singers are regularly esteemed in Vienna, Salzburg, Milan, Bayreuth, and London. There are notable composers, and today one can view retrospective exhibitions of the work of North American painters. The journalists are also outstanding: not only the reporters but also those who launch a campaign to expose the vices of officials or of institutions, those who were in the vanguard of the Allied armies during the last war, those who become interpreters of situations, personalities, and problems of foreign countries. North American newspaper men and women have established a journalistic tradition, are imitated, and as a group are the best in the world. It is unquestionable that the North American has ceased to be simply a receiver, and that today he is a creator and transmitter of culture and art, and as deserving of this title as the national of any country in the world.

And, nevertheless . . . it strikes me that it is possible to note weaknesses in the cultural progress of the United States, and I feel sincerely that some of these may be permanent, or almost so. Perhaps the greatest is the fact that size and refinement have, from a certain moment, proved incompatible. And this is a very grave question because, for better or for worse, it does not concern only the success of the United States "experiment." It concerns the fate of all the countries of the globe, since there is not a single one of them—including at the head of the list the Soviet Union—that does not aspire to be like the United States; nor is there one of them that, in the foreseeable future, can be very different from the United States. If we were to assume that in the present struggle the Soviet Union emerged victorious, the world would doubtless be converted to Communism, but even so, it would be what the United States is and has been, and what the Soviet Union is and cannot cease to be, a civilization of masses.

The incompatibility of quantity and quality, of colossal magnitude and delicacy, has in the final analysis the simple remedy of division. But there is another weakness that I wish to refer to, more serious and basic, which seems to offer only a hope that it may some time correct itself. The universities and schools; the museums and the libraries; the orchestras and the opera; the movies, radio, television; the periodicals and the phonograph; so many countless media of cultural creation and diffusion—have they refined the artistic sense of the North American public? Not of the aristocracy, but of the common run of people? I fear very much that this is not the case, and that the situation is irremediable, as happens with the child prodigy whose talents have been wasted.

In this respect I think that the behavior of audiences is revealing. In watching a dance performance the North American public applauds to reward a physical skill or dexterity, not because of an artistic impression. When the Royal Ballet is in New York it plays to packed houses and receives cordial and sustained attention, but the applause goes to the great leaps or gyrations. Equal applause goes to the dexterity of the Rockettes, some thirty young women who dance at Radio City in a spectacle of incredible bad taste. The Bali dancers and the Indian ballet of Shanta Rao, whose performances contain very little of the acrobatic but depend primarily on an unbelievable expressiveness of face, trunk, and arms, do not attract many Americans. A North American may not applaud a man who is throwing into the air and catching five oranges; but if the juggler continues for three minutes without making a mistake he applauds like three people, if he goes ten minutes, then like ten, and if a hundred, then like a hundred—and this instead of becoming bored and leaving the theater.

The role of the intellectual in North American society is still more revealing of the fact that intelligence and culture have not penetrated very deeply into that society during the last thirty or forty years. The intellectual—the scientist, the writer, or the artist —is not, or has rarely been, an object of general public admiration in the United States. It is true, of course, that he usually enjoys a more comfortable and stable life than his equal anywhere else in the world. We Latin Americans are perhaps more aware of this than anyone else, because in our countries it has not yet occurred that a writer, for example, has been able to make a fortune with his pen. But the same thing can be said of the intellectual in the United States as of the worker or the bureaucrat: he lives better not as a result of any special dispensation, but for the simple reason that he happened to be born in a richer society, and it is inevitable that some of the national abundance should fall to his lot. The point, then, is not his income, but the general esteem accorded him—whether he is an object of admiration, whether he participates in public life, whether he has some influence in it by virtue of being an intellectual, and whether he is a hero or archetype that children and young persons propose to follow or imitate.

Of course it has been many, many years since an intellectual was chief of state. Moreover, when a Presidential candidate like Adlai Stevenson appears (who is not, strictly speaking, an intellectual), then North American society reacts by inventing the derogatory expression "egghead" to express its surprise and scorn at the arrogance of an intellectual who would try to govern it. Not only has there not for a long time been a chief of state or Cabinet member who was an intellectual, but when one has appeared in the Senate or the House of Representatives he has been the exception that proved the rule, the comet that appears every ten or fifteen years. The same can be said, and perhaps with even greater justification, of the local political scene, that of the state, cities, or small towns.

In the United States the elder statesman is Bernard Baruch, a successful businessman, not a Winston Churchill, able to occupy his leisure writing, in a remarkable style, the history of the World War or that of the English-speaking peoples; or an Alexis Léger

293

who, after serving in the Quai d'Orsay for many years, changed his name to write exquisite poetry. Not for a long time, perhaps not since the days of Jefferson, has any public figure in the United States been an object of the public veneration enjoyed by Martí in Cuba or Sarmiento and Mitre in Argentina, to mention three intellectuals who served their countries. Since the time of Franklin has there been a Paul Claudel in American diplomacy, to say nothing of a Goethe? What writer has ever occupied the place that was at one time occupied on the stage of all French life by Victor Hugo? Among the interpreters of American life has there been even one François Mauriac, Chesterton, or Ortega y Gasset? Did not Albert Einstein turn out to be a little disturbing for the United States— not, to be sure, as a physicist, but as a human being? And ultimately did not Charlie Chaplin prove too disconcerting?

It is undeniable that the archetype of North American society, the model or the hero to be imitated, is not the scholar or even the intelligent man, but the successful businessman—the man of humble origin, largely unlettered, who succeeds, through his tenacity and cleverness, in amassing a fabulous fortune. He is the ideal because his story is what actually happens in American life, and also because it occurs with much greater frequency than any other example of social success. Moreover, all education that the child receives, from his parents or in the school, is conducive to building that model. The youth spends his vacation not in rest or in intellectual self-improvement, but in earning money, selling magazines, or washing dishes and glasses in a soda fountain. I have been told that in Japan, at least in the period between the two world wars, the great lesson of life that the father wished to teach his son was that a man cannot, and should not, put his trust in any other human being, even his father. In old Spain the great moral lesson that the father spared no pains to inculcate in his children was that of loyalty, that is, fidelity to a given pledge, even though the consequences of keeping it might prove disastrous. Well, the great moral lesson that the North American father respects and teaches his children is the need for self-sufficiency, and to this end they should work, earn money, and know how to handle it wisely—in other words, handle money to earn more money.

The idealization of the businessman—like its opposite, the unconcern for the intellectual—has effects in North American political life. Of all the countries in the world the United States is the only one that has not been able to create a group of people who make public service their lifetime concern and are capable, through training and experience, of assuming major responsibility in administration and foreign affairs. In the United States it rarely happens that such dedicated "public servants" reach positions of administrative power. The rule is that administrative matters are handled at the lower levels by an inert bureaucracy, and in the upper echelons by the businessman or the professional who has lived, and will again live, for private instead of public interests.

What is important here is not simply the facts but the philosophy that underlies them. I understand that among the qualifications advanced at the time to justify the appointment of John Foster Dulles as Secretary of State was the fact that for many years he had been associated with a law firm representing the interests of large international business combines. And I recall very well that at a more recent date the Department of State published a *curriculum vitae* of Mr. Henry Holland—who had just been designated Assistant Secretary for Latin American affairs—of which the outstanding feature was the fact that Mr. Holland belonged to a law firm having interests in Mexico.

Now then, why can this and so many other similar facts have particular significance? Because in as modest a country as Mexico, not only would it be considered an inexcusable lack of tact to name as ambassador to Washington a great coffee exporter or an importer of North American machinery, but the candidate's having such interests would make the appointment absolutely impossible. Undoubtedly it is believed in the United States that having defended the commercial interests of large international combines gave Mr. John Foster Dulles the invaluable experience of discovering that the world is round, varied, and complex; and that Mr. Holland's receipt of financial benefit from Mexico predisposed him, presumably from gratitude, to love Mexico.

It is unquestionable that basically all of this arises from the American idea that the only road, or at least the most positive road, to knowledge and experience is the road of business, and not, for example, the less exposed one of books. Such a notion is not only wrong; it is harmful to the United States, because experience has shown over and over again that outside the United States it is considered axiomatic that a man closely identified with certain material interests will continue to look out for them, not only when he is in charge of them as businessman or lawyer, but also if he is temporarily in government.

The different countries of the globe can be divided in as many ways as the points of view involved in making the classification, but I use a way that strikes me as extremely interesting. My system groups the countries in two categories: those whose natives make a better impression outside the country than within it; and those whose citizens show up better at home. The Mexican, the Indian, and the Chinese of other times make a better impression abroad than within their own countries; they seem then to shake off the ballast of collective life, and without it their individuality stands out, self-sustaining and self-contained. On the other hand, the North American is attractive in his own country, but not away from it, and the same thing occurs with the Argentinean and the Spaniard and perhaps also with the Russian.

To observe the North American in a large crowd within the United States—at a World Series game or a popular football game, such as the classic contest between Army and Navy—is one of the most cheering spectacles in the world. Here we have an enormous mass of people, well balanced, attractive, determined to enjoy to the utmost an afternoon of relaxation, applauding their favorite team but without ill will or malevolence toward the adversary, on the contrary always disposed to recognize and applaud the courage and skill of the opposition. Nor is there anything more cheering than to see the North American let himself go at one of the ten or twenty or hundred thousand conventions held annually by the most varied kinds of professional or business groups: the incredible advance preparation of six, eight, or ten months during which he draws up his plans and arranges all the details of his life so that he will be, come what may, at the place of the meeting at the appointed day and hour; the seriousness with which he arrives at the registration table and records his name; the satisfaction with which he pins to the lapel of his coat the badge containing his name, place of origin, and status of his representation at the convention; the inexhaustible cordiality with which he seeks out old acquaintances and welcomes the new ones; the patient gravity with which he listens to the deep philosophy advising as to the best ways to trap the housewife and sell her this or that unnecessary and costly article; and, of course, the efficiency with which he becomes intoxicated at the social gatherings of the convention. All this gives us a picture of men and women who are well balanced and free of subterfuge; open to every new experience, even though it be frivolous; able to enjoy the old experience, even though it be for the twentieth time. These are people of a sure gregarious instinct that leads them to believe and practice the principle that society always surpasses the individual, since the latter without the former is little more than a disjointed piece, devoid in itself of any meaning or value.

Abroad, however, the North American loses the great support of the society within which he lives in his own country. Thus it is natural and inevitable that in foreign countries his limitations should appear at once and be so visible and offensive. He appears then as a noisy, stupid, meddling, inconsiderate, and childish being. And more than by his display of childishness, he impresses people by his incapacity to adapt himself to his surroundings, and consequently to understand them. This does not necessarily mean that he hates his surroundings; as a matter of fact he may like them, even more than his own, and still not understand them. Indeed, the North American abroad turns out to be so inferior to the way he appears in his own country that an extremist would advise him never to leave it, and suggest that he give all the money he spends traveling in other countries to foreigners, so that they may come to the United States. Thus he would be an object of admiration rather than one of ridicule or a cause of fear.

II

What can be the cause of what I have called the weaknesses in the cultural progress of the United States? Some might say that the North American is congenitally unfit for art, and that money and effort expended in trying to endow him with artistic sense, taste, and sensibility is so much money down the drain. This is as absurd as Hitler's racism. But the fact of limited artistic and intellectual attainment is undisputable, and I shall hazard an explanation. I think it will be substantial, even though partial.

In my opinion the United States is the only country in the world that has had a truly democratic political philosophy, the only one that preserves this in its true essence, the only one that has tried, day by day, to create a democratic society, and the only one that has attained this on a large scale. That democratic theory and practice are embraced perfectly in the formula of the English utilitarians, the greatest good for the greatest number, and in the more specifically North American formula of "equal opportunity." Thus the United States has invested its time and energy and resources in creating as high an average well-being as possible; that has been the goal. Viewed in this light, North American society is a miracle, because of the congruence of its aims and its advances in attaining them: the general average level of health, nutrition, culture, recreation—in short, well-being—is relatively high and, more important, has gone up appreciably and continues to rise year after year. In other words, there has been great progress in this respect, achieved in a relatively short space of time, and with all indications that it will suffer no eclipse in the foreseeable future.

From this point of view I would not hesitate to say that the United States, though it is not an ideal society—since nothing man does attains perfection, if for no other reason than because if it did there would be no difference between him and God—is indeed the best oriented. But then a certain conclusion is unescapable: that miracle of North American society has been achieved at the expense of something—or, as the North American puts it significantly, it has been attained at a very high price, as always occurs when something substantial is purchased. Every North American has progressed somewhat in the cultivation of his artistic and intellectual senses; but, naturally, the progress has been slight because effort and resources have been spread among everyone. If the United States did not have a democratic orientation; if its bent were aristocratic, or aristocratic and democratic; in short, if effort and resources had been concentrated on a minority or on an elite, the attainments would have been greater, but not widespread.

In pre-Franco Spain a number of intellectuals, disillusioned by the educational efforts of both the church and the state, took it upon themselves to awaken the country from the intellectual sloth in which it appeared to be submerged for all time. To accomplish this they deliberately set out to prepare an elite, and concentrated all their time, energy, and resources on that task. In France and England there may not be so deliberate a plan for creating an elite but there, too, things move toward the formation of what the French so appropriately call the *cadres*—the skeleton that supports the body of an animal, the structure of steel or concrete on which a building rests. The result is the coexistence of an intellectual aristocracy and democracy, with normal communication between the two, and mutual benefit; since there are no insurmountable barriers, it is not only possible but frequent that an individual from the lower strata, well equipped and with the will and ambition to rise, is able to do so.

In the majority of the Latin American countries, on the other hand, the situation has been, and continues to be by and large, and in every sense of the word, disadvantageous, as a matter of fact, tragic. At the top there is an aristocracy composed of a very limited number of persons (in some countries no more than twenty to fifty), possessed of such extraordinary knowledge and intellectual refinements that they are sometimes comparable with the men of the Italian Renaissance. But that intellectual elite is suspended in the air, because below it there is only a pure vacuum until the base of the pyramid is reached, formed by the enormous mass of the Indian population. At the end of the fifteenth century that population had attained an advanced, even notable, social organization, as well as high levels of cultural and artistic achievement, as in the pre-Cortés civilization of the Mayas and Toltecs. But with its own culture destroyed by the Spanish or Portuguese conquests, and not having succeeded in appropriating that of Western Europe, the Indian population is now not even a democracy, but simply a mass or heavy sheet of ignorance and disorder.

This situation, of course, is in the process of change: the possibility of ascent from the low to the high classes is now greater than it was fifty years ago. In present-day Mexico, for example, it is surprising to note that nine-tenths of those attending the best entertainments—concerts, ballets, opera, or theater—are obviously persons from the lower middle class, attending such functions for the first time in a process that will enable them to attain a stable place in the upper strata of that middle class. In the majority of the Latin American countries the most notable phenomenon is that of the self-educated individual, the man who acquires a culture outside the schools, impelled by an almost fanatic interest and lacking any other guide than his curiosity and pleasure. If today there are in Mexico two hundred historians, it can be assumed as a certainty that not more than twenty have received a formal schooling.

Well, this type of man, the self-made man, is found in great abundance in the United States, but almost always in the world of business, and very infrequently in the field of culture.

In short, it is not the English, the French, or the Germans who can best appreciate the meaning and degree of intellectual progress in North American society, but rather we Latin Americans, who find ourselves in a diametrically opposite situation. Our intellectual elite is much above the average and general level of enlightenment in the United States, but the North American level is infinitely superior to the general average obtaining in our countries.

III

I must concern myself now with the present state of relations between Mexico and the United States, and with why they are as they are. On the one hand, official government relations are good, and perhaps better than ever, but on the other hand the truth is that the average Mexican from any of the social classes dislikes the United States, its government and its people. It can be asserted that the North American has never been so unpopular in Mexico as now. The easiest way to win popularity for a cause or a person is to argue that the one will serve to protect us from the United States, and that the other is demonstrably anti-American. The surest way to ruin the political future of a Mexican is to spread the rumor that he is a friend of the United States or, as it is really put, that he has "sold out" to the United States. At the present time a Mexican seems unable to wield any moral authority unless he speaks badly of the United States, and his patriotism is measured by the degree to which he denounces that country. And this, as I have said, occurs in all social classes and groups, be they made up of students and university professors, public servants, journalists, the rich or the poor, the educated or the unlettered.

This state of affairs is not known publicly because the Mexican press does not reflect national opinion, but it can be measured negatively by a most singular fact: in Mexico today there is not a single public, open apologist of the United States, or even a man who would recommend friendship with that country, even though such a course might be advantageous to Mexico. Moreover, there are many publications, though to be sure not very important ones, that sustain themselves exclusively by explaining every national problem or difficulty as arising from the ingratitude, hypocrisy, or wickedness of the United States.

What is the reason for all this? I suppose that foreigners seeking an explanation, and certainly the majority of North American observers, would put major emphasis on certain facts of our mutual history. A little more than a century ago Mexico and the United States engaged in a war that ended not only with the complete victory of the North American army, but with the loss of more than half of Mexican territory. And then in 1914 naval forces, in 1917 land forces, occupied part of the territory still held by the Mexicans. Nevertheless, I am convinced that these events, grievous and unjustifiable as they doubtless were, have not left in the Mexican any desire for vengeance or even an enduring rancor, though naturally it was unavoidable that they should create distrust and skepticism. We cannot avoid a slight smile when we hear it said that we are now great friends, or that we shall be from tomorrow on.

The ill-will of the Mexican toward the North American comes in part from the recollection of those sad events; but in a somewhat larger measure its origin is recent, and has a marked stamp of purely irrational reaction, the ultimate basis of which, it seems to me, is to be found in the fact that while distinct, the paths of the two countries converge. Those irrational reactions are dangerous by virtue of their very irrationality; at the same time they are the most difficult to explain and combat. Some arise from trivial but real facts: the Mexican, for example, is irritated by the noisy haste of the American, and he is overwhelmed by his tendency to deal in commonplaces, one of his most lamentable characteristics. Other reactions are the result of more serious things. The Mexican, who suffers his continual presence, has come to see in the North American tourist a carefree spendthrift in a land of scarcity; and the Mexican who earns his own living is only exasperated by the fact that the destitute Mexican, through need or craftiness, resorts to flattery to get a bit of alms from the traveler.

Of course the North American, in turn, has preconceived ideas about the Mexican. There is not the least doubt, let us say, that he considers him physically, intellectually, and morally inferior. He presumes him to be of limited vitality, inconstant, and indecisive; he believes him to be not very imaginative, keen at seeing problems but stupid in finding a solution for them (apart from the fact that the problems the Mexican *sees* are not the tangible problems of physics and mechanics, but those that are vaguely and grandiloquently called "transcendental"); he views him as easygoing, with a propensity for assuming obligations that later he will either not know how or not wish to fulfill. At best the North American concedes the Mexican an undue amount of courtesy and "color," that is, attributes of the picturesque; and when he poses as a really perspicacious judge of the Mexican, he arrives at the conclusion that he is a capricious, complicated, and difficult person with whom to get along.

The truth of the matter is, of course, that the Mexican and the North American are two radically different beings, in their scales of values and in their overall attitudes toward life and the world. The North American, a fabulously rich man, is accustomed to count what he has, what he earns, and what he loses; hence his tendency to base many of his judgments of value on magnitude, on quantity. The Mexican, desperately poor, actually has nothing to count, or at best very little, and consequently the idea of size and quantity seems a little strange to him, and his judgments are based, or he tries to base them, on the concept of quality. The North American, whose country has natural resources thus far unequaled by any other (conceivably by Russia), knows from experience that he possesses the necessary means for making things, and that their attainment demands only human determination and effort. As a natural result of this, he is active and confident. Mexico is a country poor in natural resources; thus the Mexican believes that his persistence and effort are not enough in themselves, that before and above man there are certain preexistent conditions—he would call them providential—that it is very difficult or impossible to surmount. This fact renders him skeptical, distrustful of action, a believer in forces superior to himself, and rather more speculative than active. And he leaves for tomorrow many of his undertakings, not through laziness or indecision, but because the inadequacy of his means has shown him, to the point of satiety, that getting up very early doesn't bring the dawn any sooner.

This same so disproportionate disparity of means has produced another very important difference of attitude in the Mexican and the North American. Since the natural resources of Mexico are

302

limited, a good part of the country's wealth has been based on one or another form of human exploitation, to a point that the Mexican Indian has been called the country's greatest natural wealth. All the Mexican Indian civilizations previous to the Conquest rested on great masses of slaves, the only labor element, governed and exploited by two small castes: the military and the sacerdotal. This is not to mention the three long centuries of Spanish domination, during which the exploiters differed, but not the exploited. The entire century and a half of independence has been a painful effort to base wealth more on the exploitation of nature and technology than on man himself. As a result, the Mexican does not regard liberty and equality as congenital blessings; he has fought for them, and he has acquired them only in part. Thus he has not by any means given up his fear of losing them, and this accounts for the extreme zeal and distrust with which he guards and defends them: he is miserly regarding a treasure that he has been able to amass only in part.

The colonizers of the North American territory were men who fled there precisely because they were in disagreement with the restrictions of liberty in the country of their origin. They found a rich and uninhabited country, with scarcely any people to overcome or exploit. The immensity of the territory and its scant population must have given the colonist the notion of complete liberty, without even a physical obstacle to prevent its full enjoyment. This historical experience, almost unique in the world, gave the North American at the outset the idea that liberty and equality are his natural patrimony, and in the end gave him two other ideas: first, that of superiority; second, that since he has been so free in his own country he can do whatever he wishes in others. In any event it has completely incapacitated him for understanding why in Mexico liberty has made its way so slowly and at the cost of so much bloodshed; why Mexico has had such a stormy history; why the Mexican distrusts North America, which he has for a long time called, justifiably, the "colossus of the North," the greatest threat to his freedom, both individual and national.

Finally, the general atmosphere of poverty has made the Mexican a somewhat gloomy, silent, modest, and even timid being. Formerly he felt a profound sense of security in himself, a pride in his poverty. Everything about him made him a being somewhat removed from the present time: not very twentieth-century and not even very Western. He did not believe that wealth is an unmistakable sign of intelligence or virtue, for he detected therein a large measure of good luck and a little fate. I believe that until some fifty years ago the Mexican was not inordinately envious of wealth, nor was it synonymous for him with the best individual and collective goal. He did not desire it so much as freedom, so much as the repose necessary for finding his true way in life, the physical well-being to follow that road, and the seclusion to enjoy it. And he believed in God, precisely because it was only in His presence that virtue and honor seemed to count in a decisive fashion, and because He, certainly, would be able to appreciate abstraction more than ostentation.

And that poverty, that solitude, that abandonment in which the Mexican has lived has not failed to offer certain compensations, as does his ignorance, which has never prevented his developing a knowledge of the land and of man that he could not obtain from books and newspapers. A very thin-skinned individual, though his feet are cracked with so much walking barefoot among the rocks and in the mire, the Mexican possesses an artistic sense and capacity that I question has an equal among many of the peoples of the earth: he enjoys a landscape, he is enraptured by the observation of a human face or the contemplation of a religious image, color affects him, and the most distant musical note finds in him a sympathetic echo. The world in which he has lived, to say it once and for all, has been not a material universe, but vaguely spiritual and religious; that has been the only reason for his existence, the life raft he has grasped while the rest of the world, notably the United States, decided to prefer the immediate and external pleasure of the material to the more permanent and internal pleasure of the spirit.

The North American, on the other hand, has lived in luxury, which shapes or deforms the human being much more than is believed. Nowhere does he reveal the acuteness of his sensibility so much as in noticing quantitative inequality, the plus and the minus; the one who is less wealthy wants to be more and more so, to the point of losing all notion of the limit or end, all idea of repose and idleness. What has kept North America from bursting, bound as it has been to that tenacious and oppressive force of the insatiable appetite for wealth, has been not the equality of wealth—which of course has never existed—but the "equal opportunity" that all have of becoming rich. And indeed the repeated experience of North American society has been, so far, that some have been able to become rich, and that therefore all can be if they have the coarseness of the fighter. The day will come—and in fact it is not very distant—when that experience, already so restricted in occurrence, will become rarer and rarer, or clearly impossible. And then— except that it will be too late for the salvation of the Mexican—the scale of values obtaining in North America will change.

In the meantime wealth is not something to be kept in silence, but should be made manifest, displayed, caused to shine, and re- sound to the point of blinding and deafening. Hence the gaudy dis- play, the speed, the noise, and the bad odor; hence the need for the rabble to applaud, provide choral accompaniment, admire, and envy. It is not so much that the North American is a hardhearted materialist without any saving spiritual graces. For one thing he has never insisted that wealth is an end; he regards it rather as a means. But what happens is that he has been so concerned with the means, and he spends so much time in obtaining them, that they have become ends, the only end, to a degree that it is now immaterial whether one regards wealth in the one way or the other.

Because of all this the Mexican sees in the North American an intruder: a giant who erupts in his poor, quiet solitude to make himself admired and envied. And the Mexican does admire and envy him, with the rancor of one who feels obliged to abandon his placid corner and dig feverishly in the earth in search of a treas- ure that will make him worthy of a world where the password is no longer virtue and gentleness, but the rattle of a gold coin on the tavern counter.

I am not attempting to outline a general or complete picture of the psychological differences that exist between the Mexican and the North American. Only a few are being noted—to return again to the conclusion that in their mutual relations the two peoples move against a background of limited cordiality. The principal factor that estranges them is the different paths on which they are impelled—different and nevertheless convergent, among other rea- sons because of their nearness to each other.

IV

At the end of the eighteenth and beginning of the nineteenth century, Mexico seemed to be the country with the best and surest future among all those of this continent, including the United States. Its territory was then the most extensive, its population the most numerous and best settled on the land; urban concentration, so characteristic a phenomenon of the modern age, was already notable; the capital was the most populous city of America around 1800; foreign trade was attaining importance, and to a large measure this was based either on silver, a precious metal then as much coveted as gold, or on raw materials such as dye woods, as rich in industrial possibilities as were later the anilines. The territory of the United States, on the other hand, was little more than a narrow strip parallel to the Atlantic coast: thirteen independent colonies, precariously joined for the sole purpose of a military struggle, against the mother country, with origins, government, interests, and aspirations so different that they seemed difficult to conciliate.

With the two countries having such different origins, and with the auguries so favorable for Mexico, time soon revealed their different paths: for the United States a continual ascent, until today it has reached the highest peak of history; for Mexico a frank decline at the outset, then a scarcely perceptible ascent.

The United States attained its independence before Mexico, and by defeating a power that was already shining in the international firmament. The Virginia Constitution and the Articles of Confederation and Perpetual Union were political documents that did not have even a remote parallel in Mexico, and should have been taken as a strong indication that to the north a people was being born possessed of original political thought, and an uncommon capacity for social coexistence. Moreover, the United States ultimately acquired a territory that with justifiable arrogance it calls a "continent"—one that touches the two great oceans of the world and contains everything that could be longed for to construct a great modern civilization. In addition it is a well-balanced country, and as little vulnerable as is possible in a complex and necessarily universal civilization, such as that of today. It lacks nothing basic for feeding a large population with abundance, and still has large surpluses that allow it to be a most important exporter of food products; it has abundant raw materials, in general of good quality, and frequently located as though by the hand of Providence; as a result it has capital, technical skill, and an extraordinary domestic market.

With the passing of time Mexico, on the other hand, lost territory instead of winning it, lost good farm lands and mineral, water, and petroleum resources, many of them exceptional. And the territory that was left was in large measure—contrary to the prevailing legend—mediocre and difficult to exploit: torn to pieces by high, crisscrossing mountains, its narrow valleys scarcely sustaining an unstable agriculture, on lands exposed to an age-old process of erosion and badly watered by capricious rainfalls. And when, as occurs on the coast, the land is good and the rain abundant, man finds himself in a disadvantageous situation because of heat, humidity, disease, and epidemic. Communications have proved difficult and expensive and, as a result, scarce. This has greatly hindered both material and spiritual interchange, the very basis of a nationality. The country's mineral resources, extremely varied but of average quality, and almost always in moderate supply, have fallen into foreign hands through a lack of local capital, technical skill, or an immediate, rich market. A century and Mexico, economically, was to fall behind; it was not to be the most important country of the continent, or the second, or the third or fourth; in no respect was it going to attain the classification of excellent. Its modest economy scarcely suffices for it to live, and it exports more than it should, always fearful of the prices that await its articles, in order to buy abroad certain consumer goods and almost all of its capital goods.

Not only in its economy, but in its historical development, the United States is a miracle: on horseback as it were, noisily and hurriedly, leaving behind a dense cloud of dust, it galloped from the Atlantic to the Pacific, at the same time accomplishing two things difficult in themselves: the exploration and domination of an immense and unknown territory; and the constitution of a nationality, and this with human elements not always similar and at times apparently incompatible. The United States also did something else: its nation became not simply one more political community, but a model, one that essayed with boldness and consistency the greatest institutions and the best democratic forms of life known until now. And all of this it did, one might say, starting with nothing, by the sweat of its brow and accomplishing things the hard way.

Mexico, on the other hand, gained its independence under the worst possible historical conditions. The long years of struggle to attain it depleted a part of its wealth; another part, as the result of the harassment of Spaniards in Mexico, fled to Spain; what wealth was left belonged to the Catholic Church, an enemy of the new nation. Thus at birth there was unleashed in our country a conflict that was to endure in its most violent form for half a century, and for which even today there is actually no suitable, stable, and just solution. Moreover, Mexico was the offspring of a power whose vital energies had diminished almost to the point of extinction, and which, no longer capable of creating, fell necessarily into an attitude of containment, in order to preserve the great deal it had given to the world, and what in turn it had received from it. Mexico, then, like all the Spanish colonies of America, lived under a sign of conservatism and reaction and was not impelled, except in the most devious and belated manner, by the great creative forces of modern society. This was an historical accident that would have lent itself to easy solution in the seventeenth century. But the fact that Spain did not attend the drama that was to give birth to the political, economic, and philosophical revolution of liberalism was by now definitely fatal for the new Hispanic American nations; they were born in an avalanche of ideas and events foreign to them, whose real scope they were not successful in measuring. To understand them, appreciate them, and make use of them required time, effort, and what a great deal of vexation!

Thus Mexico, instead of growing throughout the nineteenth century, exhausted herself in adjusting to the world: she had not yet digested Spain when she began to swallow the modern universe. For these two principal reasons—and for so many secondary ones—Mexico too is in a certain way an historical miracle; not one, however, of fecundity, but one of survival. It is indeed a miracle that Mexico is still afoot, and even a greater one that she still has faith in her destiny.

from Chile

AMANDA LABARCA H.*

The author: born in Chile (Santiago), 1886; studied at University of Chile, at Columbia in New York, and at the Sorbonne. During her long career of public service Mrs. Labarca has been primarily interested in educational problems and in the role of women. In addition to her teaching activities she has held numerous administrative positions in Chilean educational institutions and has headed various women's organizations in Chile. She represented her country in the first General Assembly of the United Nations in 1946, and for almost two years during 1948-1949 she was in New York as Chief of the United Nations' Section on the Status of Women. Her writings include a novel, a book of lectures on women in American life, several teaching texts, nearly a score of books on educational and feminist problems, and many newspaper articles. Now a widow, she has one daughter and three grandchildren. Mrs. Labarca was in the United States ten times between 1911 and 1952, and is acquainted with all parts of the country.

I

TODAY North and South America face common dangers. Is the hand extended to us by the North that of a friend, of a master disguised as an elder brother, or of a ruthless trafficker? I have the faith that it can come to be that of a friend, provided we clear the southern mind of misunderstandings, suspicions, and grievances; provided, too, that the people of the North learn how and in what specific ways we are different, and value, at the same level as their own, our efforts to organize a kind of life consonant with our history and temperament. I hope that these pages, based on ten visits in the Land of Uncle Sam between 1911 and 1952, will promote such a friendship.

When I went to the United States for the first time, in 1911, it was to study for the doctoral degree at Columbia University. I had completed my courses in the University of Chile and—like all the youth of that period—was impressed by the books of the Uruguayan Enrique Rodó, especially by his *Ariel*, in which he passed judgment on North American culture as the exponent of a harsh, money-dominated materialism. But I had also studied for a short

* Translated from the Spanish by James F. Shearer.

time in Santiago College, an establishment of high caliber maintained in Chile by members of a Methodist mission with headquarters in New York, and there I had known generous, idealistic, and liberal teachers. My spirit vacillated, then, between my admiration for Rodó and my regard for North American professors and friends.

My first unforgettable impression of Yankeelandia was the unexpected beauty of the landscape that unfolded to my view as our boat maneuvered into New York harbor. The irregularly toothed ridge of the skyline was already familiar to me, from illustrations, postcards, prints, photographs. But I was not prepared to find—it was May when I arrived—that each of the small islands in the bay was a veritable garden. I asked myself why no one had ever commented on their beauty. The North Americans had beauty there, in most varied and opulent form, and yet they told us only of the height of their skyscrapers. Were they insensible to this beauty? The landscape was a gift, the city a victory won by their efforts. Could this be the explanation?

The country I saw at that time had attitudes and concepts that are perhaps now a thing of the past. There were a few wealthy people and some hundreds of students and university professors who crossed the ocean during vacations to learn about the world. But they were the exception. The average run of people—the storekeeper, the typist, the housewife—were supinely ignorant of cultures and customs beyond the limits of their own country. And the vast majority of the population believed that there was nothing superior to the United States.

It is a trait of the Chilean character, common to rich and poor alike, to show an aversion to boastfulness. It strikes us as the worst possible taste to brag about our own merits and possessions. We are glad when others praise them, but we are reluctant to do it ourselves. As a result, one of the psychic shocks that I experienced on my first contact with the North American masses was their tendency to consider their possessions the "greatest" or "best" in the world. It took me years to understand that what I first judged to be an unpleasant fault could in fact serve as a springboard for constant excelling; and that of the two extremes, the North American was more constructive than the Chilean. But alongside the ignorance and boastfulness there was a charming hospitality. I never

310

found myself in difficulty without someone offering to help me. It struck me that we Chileans are more courteous in words and deportment, but not always so disposed to help our neighbor. This conviction has remained unchanged over the years.

My admiration for the North American woman dates from that first trip. As yet she had not won the right of suffrage in New York, but she was most active in all branches of cultural, social, and philanthropic life. Women's clubs were unknown during those decades in the Latin countries; in the United States they numbered their followers in the thousands. Collectively women there were already a force, and individually they enjoyed a respect due not just to genteel masculine gallantry but to confidence in their own merits. One felt them to be conscious of themselves as liberated personalities and masters of their destinies, free of the prejudices and timidities that still shackled their South American sisters.

My opinions on the character of the people would have been incomplete had they been based solely on my residence in New York as a student. But during vacations, my husband and I (he was also a student at Columbia) had the good fortune to be members of a group that spent a summer in Middlebury, Vermont, and another on Deer Isle, Maine. It was during these periods that I really lived with the people and deepened my admiration and affection for them.

The jutting rock that was Deer Isle struck my husband and me as a little paradise. It was a small, wooded island, perhaps no larger than some fifty square kilometers, situated off the coast of Maine and not too far from Canada. We rented a furnished cottage and remained there about two months. The houses were scattered among the green of the meadows or on the edge of the woods, unseparated by walls or fences. There were no locks on the doors. We were told that anyone could enter any home and get himself a glass of water in the kitchen if the owners were absent. We did it more than once, not so much because we were thirsty as to make certain that this was true. People told us that a jail had been built in the cellar of the City Hall twenty years before, but that no one had yet occupied it.

At that time—I am speaking of 1912—there were neither poor nor too wealthy people on the island, no destitute old people to help. All earned a modest living, from farming or fishing, and the women who met in a club could find no more suitable project than planting flowers along the roads. The islanders—descendants of Revolutionary War veterans—had kept their Puritan faith and customs intact. It was hard to brand such people as materialistic, people guided in every one of their acts by the commandments and prescriptions of the Bible. They took it for granted that everyone told the truth, that it was not right to deceive or betray, or to question the integrity of others.

As I write this I imagine that the Latin American reader will probably think I am exaggerating or lying or was deceived—those attitudes are so far removed from ours. My husband and I frequently wondered about these traits ourselves. It seemed to us that we Chileans and South Americans, and possibly all Latins, are like those little Chinese boxes, each containing another of a smaller size: it is not simple to go through all the back rooms of our personalities; in our daily dealings we tell the truth, but not always all of it; even in our inmost heart it is difficult to reach the most recondite part of our "I." By contrast the people on Deer Isle, and in large measure all North Americans, seemed to us as simple, as free of complications, as a sheet of paper on which all sorts of things are printed, some abhorrent, others intelligent and beautiful, but no longer mysterious once the language in which they are written is understood.

In Chile the masses of the people are superstitious and devout, and in this or that region the Catholic rites are mixed with Indian practices and attitudes. The middle class oscillates between a sincere and a pretended piety—easily transgressing the commandments of God and the church, without prejudice to confessing in the end and dying with all the blessings of the church. The intelligentsia, during the first decades of this century, was inclined toward agnosticism, and opposed the political activities of the clergy. Intimate religiosity—living Christianity, the strict and voluntary observance of Christian doctrine and morality—was very much more interwoven in the existence of those people of New England than in the Catholic peoples of South America. Those with whom I lived in 1911 and 1912 observed a more sincerely pure, pious, and Christian conduct than any I had known before.

312

Amanda Labarca H.

II

My second trip to the United States coincided with the end of the First World War. The celebration of the Armistice found me in Berkeley, California, where I saw another aspect of the nation— the West. The people had felt the heavy weight of a war that, though it had seemed remote at the outset, had ultimately reached them personally, if not in their immediate homes at least in their families. I found now less boastfulness. "The best in the world" did not have, in 1918 and in the West, the same resonance as in 1911 in New York. There it had been youthful pride in what had already been accomplished; here people were looking more to the future. What did it matter if *today* it was the best in the world; the important thing was that *tomorrow* it be greater and better. The vision of the earth had widened, and thus also the task to be accomplished. It was necessary to assure democracy throughout the world, to put an end to wars and autocracies. For this and for nothing else had the soldiers of Uncle Sam sacrificed their lives on the field of battle.

Although the recent war had taught North Americans the existence of a European culture that was different from theirs but perhaps of equal or greater value, they continued to show as little interest as before in anything that had to do with Latin America. It was as though our part of the world were located on another planet. So I came from Santiago de Chile? Was that near Cuba? What state was it in? Identifying our situation with theirs, people imagined that our republics were states of a federal hemisphere. And it occurred to no one, of course, that there were bonds of solidarity between the countries of the northern and southern Americas.

I find my impressions of that period in articles that I wrote for the *Mercurio* of Santiago de Chile. I said at that time: "This is a candid people. It is not difficult to know what it thinks and feels, because it expresses this with rude and childish frankness. It is kind-hearted and optimistic; it believes that the good can and should be accomplished, and that it is in the world especially to accomplish it. It is honorable; it is tolerant; it is hard-working. Yes, it is also proud and conceited over its power, and there are not lacking among the North Americans those who share in their way the German ambition of a universal empire: in place of the Kaiser, Uncle Sam;

in place of militarism, industrialism. These are in the minority, they are the aristocrats of the Yankee oligarchy, that oligarchy of big business which, despite all its millions, has never succeeded in twisting the conscience of this people toward anything repugnant to its innate sense of freedom, democracy, and equal opportunity for all." I wrote this in 1919; my subsequent experience would lead me to revise the last sentence, and perhaps I would now say of the oligarchy of big business: "but they are influential and are to be found in all the key positions of the higher echelons of bureaucracy, business, and politics."

After finishing my work in California I visited in Burlington, Iowa, and then traveled to Cincinnati, St. Louis, Berea College in Kentucky, and finally to Hampton Institute in Virginia. I drew near, then, to the poor white and the Negro. Although I obtained no firsthand knowledge of the desperately poor Negro, what I saw in the South distressed me deeply. New England and the West, while they maintain a proud distance from the Negro, do not show a fundamental scorn, or cruelty. In my courses at Columbia I had had the opportunity of being in classes with some colored people. They had struck me as timid, self-conscious, isolated, less happy than the many Asiatics on the campus, but they seemed to be treated with equal consideration by the professors and university authorities. Nor had they been segregated on the streetcars or the subway in New York. But what I saw in the Southern states was revolting to me.

In the non-tropical regions of South America—Argentina, Uruguay, and Chile—there were relatively few Negroes during the colonial period, and those who survived the wars of independence were still fewer, a fact that perhaps contributed to their early liberation. During the nineteenth century they intermarried with mestizos (half-breeds) and whites, and the Negro problem does not exist in that part of America. Although this is not the case in Brazil, in Peru, and in regions of the Caribbean, each of these areas has found a solution for the problem. I believe there is a common denominator in this matter in all the countries descended from Iberia: a benign tolerance. When the Spaniard and the Portuguese reached America they brought with them an inheritance of race mixture, having long been accustomed to a society that included Moors and Jews.

As a Chilean woman who had not known racial prejudice, I

was shocked by what I saw of it in the southern United States. What kind of Christianity was it whose fundamental commandment, "do unto others as you would have others do unto you," was reserved for the whites, completely forgotten when it was a question of one's colored fellowmen? And what kind of democracy was it that kept them like helots? The ferocity of certain white people toward their Negro compatriots shook my esteem for the kindness, rectitude, benevolence, and Christianity of the North American democracy for the first time. I understood the demographic and historical reasons for the color line, but even so I was indignant that ethnical prejudices should cause people to see in every Negro a potential criminal, bandit, or lascivious beast, forgetting that crass ignorance and hopeless poverty deform any man and cause him to regress toward the troglodyte, be he white, yellow, or black.

III

Years later, in 1939, the University of California honored me by asking me to give two summer courses at its Berkeley branch. The circumstance of thus visiting the United States as a university professor brought me many invitations to give lectures before women's clubs, and to participate in symposia organized by other universities. In doing this I learned that it was almost impossible for the average American woman who had been born or reared in the West or the central states to accept the fact that our women are different from the type they had been told about in novels, magazines, or trivial movies. The balcony serenade, the mantilla, the high comb over the nape of the neck, the fan, the languid idleness, the siesta, and at times the uncontrollable fury of passion: these were the cliches so stereotyped in their minds that they smiled in a kindly but incredulous manner when I told them that I had never worn the mantilla or comb except at masquerade balls. I tried to make them understand that in Chile—as in various other of the southern countries—women participate in economic as well as cultural activities, but I doubt that I made them change their opinions radically.

Conversely, when I have spoken to the women of South America about those of the North, I have discovered cliches equally difficult to erase. In the opinion of our women, their northern sisters practice fidelity neither before nor after marriage; they are glamor girls, coquettes, and fortune hunters; they make no effort to establish a lasting home, and the solidly constituted and affectionate family does not exist. When I pointed out that the North American housewives of the middle and poor classes cannot afford the luxury of a regular domestic servant—that they take upon themselves the incessant and tiring labor of performing all the daily tasks, from the scrubbing of floors to the preparation of the food—the South American women would reply: "How can that be so tiring? They have so many gadgets, so many machines, so many kinds of prepared foods. It's easy for them to prepare meals and keep the house clean." To this I would answer, "Don't forget that it's easier to ring a bell." And that is what the majority of us do: ring the bell for the servant to come and take our orders.

I confess that when I arrived in the United States for the first time I was far from the convinced feminist I have been since. It was the example of the North Americans that impelled me to drive and struggle until I obtained more civil and political rights for my feminine compatriots. I believe that in all young countries, where very intense labor to create wealth is demanded of the men, women take the lead in the support of art, literature, and all that contributes to making existence more desirable. Thus in the United States it is the women who fill the concert and lecture halls, the art galleries and museums, and in Chile something similar occurs, with the benevolent consent of the men.

During this same visit I was invited by two universities of the Middle West to participate in seminars concerned with inter-American relations. In both there were gathered together, along with university professors and journalists, the magnates of enterprises having connections with Latin America. This was my first contact with big businessmen in the United States. Their mentality not only surprised me; it terrified me. No considerations of noble political aims, of continental solidarity, of the construction of a surer and more lasting peace could move them. They felt that the businessman has the duty to his stockholders, to the suppliers of the capital, to produce the highest possible profit. And if certain governments and small republics object, capital has the right—not only the right but the duty—to employ any kind of compulsion for the protection of its interests. They replied to the arguments of their own compatriots with examples of the non-fulfillment of financial contracts and with

316

well-selected (and almost always accurate) statistics on the default of payments. If these countries didn't know how to respect their obligations, what measures except those of force was it possible to turn to? The professors and some journalists among those present were aware of the unhealthiness of this intransigent attitude, and tried to combat it; but they seemed to make very little dent on the representatives of Wall Street.

IV

My service of almost two years with the United Nations, during 1948-1949, broadened considerably my knowledge of North American circles that I had previously seen only from afar: those of national and international politics. To some extent this experience confirmed my former view that the political superstructure of that great nation is inferior to its common civic virtues. Chileans had viewed it with distrust from the days of "big stick" Theodore Roosevelt and his bragging—insolent in our opinion ("I took the Isthmus"). The corruption of Tammany Hall and the gangsterism of some of its police had been the object of frequent comment in our newspapers. Those fears were quieted somewhat during the administrations of Franklin D. Roosevelt and his Good Neighbor policy. Nevertheless, my observations in the United Nations strengthened my belief that the United States, though it has an overabundance of clever politicians, has only seldom had great statesmen. It seemed to me that it had attained world supremacy before developing statesmen equal to the demands of world leadership

The North American, man or woman, does not hesitate an instant in placing himself at the service of his country when national emergency requires it. The dollar-a-year public servants performed brilliant tasks during the two world wars. In peacetime, however, the group that watches over what is done by the government—especially in the area of world politics—is very small in comparison with the nation's almost two hundred million inhabitants. Government is entrusted to politicians, and the politicians do not come from the ranks of greatest intelligence or highest culture. A great many are professionals in local political chicanery, adept in winning a political following but little equipped for the management of the involved, complicated, and turbulent world we live in. The best brains are to be found in the business world, in laboratories devoted to scientific investigation, or in the large social, cultural, or philanthropic institutions. When through urgent necessity they are moved to key positions in public life, they are slow in adapting themselves to techniques that have nothing in common with those of professorships, laboratories, or big business.

Behind the scenes at the United Nations I witnessed disagreements among the North Americans themselves over problems of international politics that demanded a firm and solidly established policy. There was a profound gulf of misunderstanding between representatives motivated by a consummate idealism and an ample conception of the rights of all peoples—there were such, and very fine ones—and those who spoke on the rostrum only to satisfy their constituents or the stockholders of some large company. More than once I asked myself if this is necessarily the fate of a democracy whose millions of industrious citizens, eager to preserve their high standard of living, are occupied from morning till night with the business of earning an honorable living, their political opinions manipulated through refined techniques of publicity and propaganda that are sometimes at the service of unknown interests.

But in spite of the defects of the political superstructure, I still believe that the social democracy of the United States is of a superior quality, exemplary and unique—except, of course, for its treatment of the Negro. Among whites, equality of opportunity is not simply a phrase: it is a fact of daily and continual occurrence. The educational system, despite its marked unevenness of quality, is on the whole an admirable instrument for the betterment of the individual, for shaping a true patriotism, for developing the virtues of industry and ambition. The generosity of the people in financing this system, and their determination to promote its daily progress, speak highly of that democracy.

On this visit, as before, I was struck by the feeling of class equality. I am referring to people in ordinary daily life, not to the plutocratic or aristocratic snobs, who constitute a very meager minority. In Chile, and I imagine in all Hispanic America, there is a very acute sense of class distinction, of social superiority. Well-to-do people show a paternal benevolence toward those who submissively accept inferiority, and a pronounced haughtiness to those who do not. A person's very type of work creates distinctions. It is rare that a craftsman, however excellent, receives the courteous treat-

318

ment accorded even an incompetent professional man. In the United States, on the other hand, I saw individuals treated with respect regardless of their origins or class, not only in my relations as an official but in those of my private life, in a small village near the seat of the United Nations.

People never speak of Yankeelandia as a classless society, but that is the way it has impressed me. Discounting a very small percentage at the two extremes—the fabulously rich plutocracy and the wretched whites and Negroes—the people appear to be on very equal terms. They harbor the deep conviction that to be a little better off or more refined is an accident, not an essential quality; they consider themselves potentially and fundamentally equal. I believe that such a conviction frees man from complexes, adds to the joy of living, and gives wings to the common man's hope that he can attain the most exalted posts or fairy-like heights of well-being. I view that sentiment of equality as one of the most fertile leavens of North American democracy.

During the time I served in the United Nations I also became aware of the pace of work in North America, a pace that was not the international one but that of Uncle Sam. During the eight-hour day people really attended to their job, and it was taken for granted that the chiefs would set an example of punctuality and dedication. Among us Chileans, and I believe also in all the Latin countries, the boss enjoys the privilege of arriving late at the office and staying away whenever he feels like it, and the employees, by the same token, can refrain from showing too much devotion to their work. What permits the intenser application to work in the United States is probably more adequate nourishment, a more regular scheduling of work, food, and rest, or deeply ingrained custom. Anyway, compared with us, the North Americans strike me as a much more powerful and better run machine. In the same amount of time they produce more. For that reason they need a week-end rest more than we do. As a matter of fact, they end the week exhausted. To what degree such intensity atrophies the imagination, or finally mechanizes the individual or makes him the victim of innumerable neuroses, I do not know.

My encounters with the press were frequent during that period. At the United Nations the corridors always overflowed with newspapermen, photographers, and the representatives of all kinds of

319

magazines. Alert, vivacious, they caught the scent of everything that could be spiced up as sensational. Every day they interviewed an infinite number of personages and, with the exception of a few truthful and honorable journalists, they would turn their reports into a spicy stew of what they themselves wanted to say or what they imagined would please the palates of their readers. The daily papers —except for four or five of the large ones, which are characterized by intelligence and vision and take seriously their role in forming public opinion—seemed to me to be mere informative devices at the service of their owners or the great advertisers who support them. They smell out and play upon the passions, the weaknesses, the hates, the prejudices, and even the hopes of the reading public.

I have the impression that radio and television, those powerful instruments for influencing the mind of the public, are still badly utilized in the United States. The broadcasting stations emulate the Spanish Golden Age dramatist, Lope de Vega, who declared that "since the public is stupid, it is correct to address it foolishly in order to please it." I am convinced, however, that if quality is given to the public, it soon pleases and interests people more than the mediocre. From the United Nations I urged more than once that the radio broadcasts beamed to Latin America be of higher quality. The stations make the mistake of supposing that in view of our high percentage of illiteracy our masses will not appreciate anything better. In Chile there may not be a gas stove in ordinary houses, but there is a radio, and within those four walls "gringo things" arouse no interest; those who listen to the rebroadcasts are people with intellectual curiosity, and they shut off the programs as soon as they discover their low level.

In our countries, everyone—young and old, rich and poor— goes to see the North American movies. And at least ninety percent believe that what they see on the screen is a truthful reflection of North American life. They imagine that in the United States the people spend their time between cocktail parties and divorces; that all the girls go scantily clad, and under only slight moral restrictions; that the boys are a mixture of Sir Galahad and Don Juan; that gangsterism is an everyday matter; and that juvenile delinquency is the plague of every household. They suppose that everyone lives in houses or hotels as sumptuous as those in the films. Our boys become eager to own all the contrivances they see there, from the latest-model automobile to the electric mixer. But how were all these things obtained? This the films do not explain. It is never suggested that a high standard of living means decades of effort and work. People see the result, but not the way it was achieved.

The animal characters of Walt Disney have won us over completely. Donald Duck and Mickey Mouse are personal friends of all the children, and their figures are replacing the traditional characters of our animal folklore. On the other hand, derision and sometimes very bitter feeling are produced by the movies that introduce Latin American characters and subjects for the amusement of the northerners. These (when they don't cause derisive laughter) are offensive because of their total disfiguration of our types and customs. They repeat the stale cliches I have mentioned, and make no attempt to correct them. Producers of such films should be advised never to export them to our countries.

An aspect of North American communication media that we often discussed at the United Nations is the tendency toward uniformity. In so incessantly repeating certain slogans, in so constantly insisting that certain procedures are necessary, that given lines of international policy are the only ones compatible with progress, that those who deviate from traditional beliefs are renegades or Communists, the North Americans are in effect solidifying differences and inhibiting original initiative; they are little by little transforming the individual into a number, collective society into a mass of robots. It would seem that variety and individualization, from which creative progress comes, are becoming scarcer and scarcer. The "robotization" of the masses, of which the Soviet is often accused— is this happening in the United States?

V

Many times in the course of lectures and classes in Chile I have tried to make my listeners share with me the affectionate admiration that I feel for the North American people. I have not attained this easily. I have had the privilege of living side by side with North Americans, of weighing at close range their fundamental kindness, their earnest desire to help, their incorruptible idealism. And probably my friendly feeling toward them is shared in greater or lesser degree by all Chileans who know them similarly: the students who go north to the universities; the individuals invited there by the

Department of State; the scholars whose work has been aided by the philanthropic, cultural, and peace-promoting foundations; the Chileans associated with the educators and technicians who have come here from the United States. But though this is a lengthy enumeration, the numbers it represents are meager in comparison with the millions who judge, as is to be expected, only by what they see and feel here. They know the North Americans only through those who come here to do business, to serve economic interests, to arrange concessions through methods not always upright and sometimes harmful to the interests of our country.

The reigning impression in enlightened Chilean circles is that two governments coexist in the United States: a visible one, whose seat is in Washington; and one that is invisible, in some ways more powerful, aggressive, and implacable, carrying on its activities sometimes with the approval and blessing of the White House and sometimes in defiance or disregard of it. The officers of this invisible government are a limited few, and do not represent the general character of the good common people. But they are the ones who give orders to those operating in our lands south of the Rio Grande. We are not ignorant of the efforts of the other North Americans who are working in these lands at cultural and idealistic tasks. Our masses, however, find it difficult to differentiate. They are inclined to believe that the latter are mere appeasers of distrust, and not essentially different from the former. It is not exclusively the Communists who clamor, "Down with Yankee imperialism." Suspicion is rooted in many who fear that these Americas will end by being only dependencies of the United States.

I believe I am not in error when I consider my views common to the enlightened classes of my country. They are not those of the extreme left, or of the ultra-nationalists, or of the half-educated public for whom the name United States is synonymous with capitalism and merciless exploitation. These groups believe that the United States' gestures of friendship are a crass hypocrisy, and that under the mantle of aid is hidden a greedy desire to get hold of our wealth or—cleverly and to its own advantage—to direct our internal policy.

Of the many lessons I learned during my service at the United Nations, I believe that one of the most valuable is that there are many ways of doing things well. Ordinarily every person, every country, believes that his way is not only the best but the only one that is good, and he is prone to impose it on others come what may. In reality, however, the different groups of human beings can attain similar objectives with different methods, consonant with their own natures. And when any people believes in the worth of its methods, as proved by experience and tradition, it resents any efforts to impose others on it. The "American way" is no doubt the best for the North Americans, but this does not imply that it is the best for others. Latin America does not revere the same values as the North. For example, "time is money" is not its favorite slogan. Triumph and great success interest it, of course, but it is less inclined than its northern neighbor to sacrifice for these the joy of its present. It adapts itself better to its mediocrity. If the attainment of a more or less stable happiness is one of the goals of the human being, the Latin tends to reach it through means fitted to the rhythm of his effort and his vital objectives, which differ from those of the Anglo-Saxon. He is able, if need be, to accelerate his pace and employ his full energies, and in a North American environment he admires and even imitates its ways. But he does these things only if they are not imposed upon him.

In the field of inter-American relations rapid decision, candor (apparent or real), and direct action fall to the part of the North; distrust, to that of the South. Neither North nor South America will change overnight. For reciprocal understanding and an appreciation of our differences, a patient and cordial process of education is required.

For such an educational effort to succeed, it must be dictated by similar interests, convictions, and ideals. As for our common interests, the United States cannot alone, despite its present colossal riches, oppose two unrelenting threats to its existence: Communist power and the poverty of great masses of people in Europe, Asia, Africa, and Latin America. It is thus to our mutual advantage that we Latin American nations be helped—and not in a spirit of charity—to raise our buying power, our standard of living. North American economic leaders learned very early that the surest means of promoting domestic prosperity is to assure the buying power of the population, the potential customers. In this period of its great economic expansion, the North could find its natural market in the southern republics, a market free of all the difficulties, threats, and intrigues of the European, and nearer than the Asiatic or the African. Then there are our common convictions. Latin America is the natural ally of the North. It has demonstrated this in times of war, when it has not hesitated to put at the disposal of the United States its potential in raw materials, or even to mortgage its future. This knowledge of shared convictions should be present in all our relations. And finally ideals: I believe we can develop the common ideal that our hemisphere come to be in truth the home of a just democracy, of a family of nations without the scourge of poverty, and therefore of a peaceful humanity.

There are very few businessmen—clever as they may be in their enterprises—who have the breadth of vision required for such a future. As long as they are the ones who manipulate, behind the scenes, the policy of the United States with respect to these nations of ours, any amount of education for harmony will fail because of the basic discrepancy between what Washington says and what Wall Street does.

An education for hemispheric harmony would have to be conducted in schools, colleges, and universities, and be aided by the press, the radio, and the cinema. In the United States its program should include knowledge not only of our languages but of our history, the development of our culture, our creations in literature and the arts. In our republics too there has to be a patient process of promoting understanding and friendship. Here there are stubborn difficulties in the path: international grudges, trifling in comparison with the importance of the future at stake; de facto governments that obstruct and impede every action directed toward solidarity. But who knows whether the difficulties might be smaller if our relations with the North were not embittered by economic crises?

The promotion of this greater hemispheric awareness—whether undertaken through foundation support or through public or private initiative—would provide insurance for both our lands. It would contribute toward the prosperity and effectiveness of the United States itself; and in Latin America it would diminish the enticement of Communism, which—holding out to the masses the illusion that justice and well-being are very soon to be attained—has now caught like wildfire, both in the depths of poverty and among idealists who consider it the most certain hope for the helpless. The only way to combat Communism is to demonstrate that democracy is capable of raising the living standard, of bringing well-being and social justice not *tomorrow* but *today*. Economic chaos, anarchy, Communism—or solidarity in a tightly united hemisphere capable of assuring the welfare of its people. This is our dilemma.

from Cuba

JORGE MAÑACH*

The author: born in Cuba (Sagua la Grande), 1898; secondary education in Spain (1908-1913) and United States (1914-1917), and university education at Harvard, Paris, and Havana. Since 1923 Dr. Mañach has been a columnist for a Havana newspaper, and since 1941 Professor of History of Philosophy at Havana University; he is also Director of the Havana "Universidad del Aire." His books include several volumes of essays and a biography of the Cuban patriot Jose Martí that has been translated into English. From time to time, however, his writing and teaching have been interrupted by political developments. During 1930-1933 he was active in one of the Cuban "revolutionary" movements, and in 1934, after the fall of the regime then current, he was made Secretary of Education. He held that position only briefly, and there followed four years of political exile, during which he supported himself by teaching Hispanic literature at Columbia University in New York. On his return to Cuba, he was elected to the Constituent Assembly (1939), and later served (1940-1944) in the Cuban Senate. In 1944 he was Secretary of State. Besides his student years in the United States (1914-1921) and his years at Columbia (1935-1939) he has been several times in this country, his acquaintance with it extending throughout the length of the East coast and over parts of the South and Midwest.

I

CUBAN opinion about the United States contains, like my own, mixed feelings of apprehension, gratitude, and critical admiration. In general, Cubans admire their northern neighbor as a nation, and have a genuine liking for its people, whose pattern of living and customs are familiar to them through close relations and frequent contacts. Few fail to admit that Cuba, even if it had attained its independence without the assistance of the United States, would have to be grateful to that nation for having made the task easier, and above all for not taking advantage of its own nearness and power to frustrate the victory. But this acknowledgment does not exclude apprehensions and reservations, at least in certain social spheres.

* Translated from the Spanish by Jose Martel.

326

The people—rural population, city laborers, minor employees—tend to judge the United States by the actions, not always open and aboveboard, of American enterprises, to which they attribute excessive profits and a connivance with venal politicians to further the aims of exploitation. The same opinion is usually held by the middle class, dependent as it is, for the most part, on trade or official bureaucracy. Among the ruling classes the view of the United States has greater variety and takes on different shades, ranging from adulation to complete condemnation.

These opinions, whether positive or negative, usually have the shortcomings of simplification and excessive generalization, for they are based on insufficient knowledge of the United States, on viewpoints centered in personal or group interest, or on preconceptions and party-line ideologies. My own opinion—coinciding in general with the informed elements of nationalist orientation—is perhaps not entirely free of some of these limitations, but I consider it better balanced, molded as it is by direct knowledge of the United States through personal experience. In order to substantiate this opinion, I would like to set forth my interpretation of the American spirit, pointing out the virtues of that nation that I have learned to love, and the defects in it that I deplore.

I think it was Santayana who first said that the American soul has been formed by two principal historical ingredients: "the frontier spirit," that is, the spirit that impelled the conquest and colonization of the whole of North America, starting from the original settlements; and Puritanism, which arrived with the Mayflower pilgrims in what would later be called New England, but did not lack religious and ethical manifestations in other regions (among the Quakers in Pennsylvania, for example). This characterization is probably true, insofar as such generalizations can be. I might add a third element to the formula, the famous melting-pot, the crucible of immigrations, except that this seems to have been absorbed by the other two primary factors in the synthesis into which the American soul tends to integrate itself. In any case, the American of today definitely reveals opposing characteristics reminiscent of that double influence.

The dominant and perhaps the most central of the characteristics deriving from the "frontier spirit" is the cult of energy, which of course does not necessarily mean the worship of force or power.

327

The youthfulness of the American people can be seen in their capacity for energy, their appreciation and enjoyment of it as a force for the realization of natural possibilities. "Rapidity of movement, the joy of adventure, and the love of change," as Maurois has expressed it—these certainly are manifestations of energy. Its elevation to a "cult" is variously revealed in features ranging from the most elementary to the complex. It is evident in a very pronounced eagerness for health and physical vigor, with a corresponding repugnance (almost surprise and unconcern) in the presence of sickness, weakness, and even death; in an almost sacramental devotion to physical exercise; in a devotion to sports, and not only as a spectacle; in a passion for athletic records; in a love of struggle ("Americans love a good fight"). The cult of energy manifests itself also in the enthusiastic dedication to work, which is looked upon not as a Biblical curse but as a sporting challenge; in the demand, so characteristically American, that man be sufficient unto himself and show himself capable of undertaking daring enterprises; and in the resulting contempt for the pusillanimous, the parasite, or the one who, capable of doing better, resigns himself to a subordinate position. Thus it is natural that the human possibilities that have the most interest for the "American" of the United States are those of action—an effort of energy intended to produce outside results—rather than mere contemplation. Even the spiritual undertakings of Americans are likely to have a missionary and fighting tendency.

Associated with the cult of energy is the pragmatic sense of values. Although this pragmatism is very well known, let us underscore certain of its manifestations. In the first place, man is not measured primarily by reference to intrinsic qualities, for example goodness or intelligence; he is weighed by deeds and by results. "To make good," "to deliver the goods," "to achieve results" are vital slogans characteristic of the North American. Energy itself must be transitive, productive. Not principles or even ultimate results are of primary importance in the average opinion, but rather the effectiveness of the effort. The shameful thing is to attempt to do something (good or bad, because we are dealing, above all, with a kind of pride in energy itself), and not to succeed. For this people strongly imbued with Protestantism, the subjective is not enough; man's salvation lies in deeds; their moral and social qualities are considered afterward. Thence the concrete and practical accents of American civilization—and the fact that it still is a civilization rather than a culture. But if this objectivation of human values works sometimes to the detriment of what is most inherent in the moral or intellectual order, it also carries with it a healthy emphasis on effort and on the generative possibilities of conduct.

All of this provides the basis for the "philosophy" of success, which so profoundly molds the life of the North American people. In the United States, to amount to something is, above all, to be successful. And the most obvious sign of success is the economic sign. Attention has often been drawn to the characteristic American expression "to be worth," which bases a person's value on how much he possesses. Such considerations are the basis of the hackneyed charge of "materialism" made against the "Yankees," but this inference calls for many reservations and specifications. Americans do not believe that human dignity or happiness "consists" in having money. What they do think, with a healthy realism, is that the possession of money is one of the objective conditions conducive to dignity and happiness. Poverty humiliates and oppresses, and of course, with its privations, it increases man's grief. Money is looked upon in the United States not as an end in itself, but as a value in exchange, and above all as a sign of energy, efficiency, and success.

Consequently, to Americans the ideal type of individual in society is not the *corteggiano* of the classical Italians, the *honnête homme*, circumspect and hard-saving, of the French, not the "gentleman," British style, or the *caballero* of the Spainsh; nor is it the scholar, the soldier, or the public official in whom the Germans seem to place their admiration. It is the businessman, the man engaged in making money, and his archetype is the millionaire. Because of the mere fact that he has earned a great deal of money, the millionaire is, in principle, admirable (we shall see with what reservations), though not always respectable. His fortune presupposes an enterprising spirit, energy, and intelligence.

But here it is fitting to consider the other aspect of the American soul, the one that proceeds from the Puritan influence. One would have a very limited picture of the North American if he were regarded only in terms of the characteristics derived from the frontier spirit—the energetic and the dynamic, the invading and the pugnacious features. William James classified consciences as "tough" and "tender." The Puritan conscience was an unusual combination of the two, though there is an excessive tendency to judge it in its historic pattern of fanatical religious nonconformity, in terms of rigid and arid austerity. Doubtless, certain limitations of the "classic" American spirit can be attributed to that discipline, just as other limitations can be imputed to the unscrupulous power drive that the frontier tended to create. But I am inclined to ascribe to the influence of Puritanism also some of the noblest and "tenderest" American qualities.

These are centered in a profound moral sanity. To be sure, it often draws on the power drive I have spoken of, but the aberrations to which this lends itself in certain marginal zones of American life—for example, "gangsterism" and other forms of delinquency or of simple moral laxity—tend to conceal from the remote observer what those of us know who have lived for a long time among Americans: that they are one of the kindest, most good-natured people into which the human species has blossomed. The average American has a natural inclination to integrity, to generosity, and to justice. Lying is repugnant to him, as a form of cowardice. He is guided not by the ideal but by what is "sensible," and yet the best-informed opinions commend his ingenuousness, his simplicity of spirit. Americans—it is said—are like big children. When they appeal to common decency as a minimum moral requirement, they are invoking what may be considered their own common denominator. When all the necessary reservations are made, there remains in the evaluation of the American soul a favorable balance that is admirable. It is only through lack of understanding that many North American attitudes (for example, certain aspects of foreign policy) are regarded as insincere, or else as calculating because of their extreme generosity.

I have already referred to the general charge of "materialism" often made against the United States. Now I should like to add that this is probably the most actively idealistic people in the world, if by "idealism" is understood not a vague sentimental disposition toward the imaginary and the ethereal, but an eagerness for a better world and a constant striving to bring it about. Keeping in mind all the relative proportions of size and wealth, one can discern in no other country so much disinterested effort in endeavors of that kind—for example, in "foundations" and societies whose aim is to promote, within and without their territory, health, culture, good social and international relations. Nowhere can you find so many endowments to universities, or such abundant help to talent, whether native or foreign. In few countries do religious and civic institutions have so much spirit of "service"—including the typically American brotherhoods of businessmen, even though at times their procedures may seem to the sophisticated glance ridiculous or childish. Americans are indeed much like big children; but the world would be better off if their candor and altruism were more widespread.

II

It is precisely the combination of the Americans' tender conscience with their cult of energy and everything derived from it that explains not only many of their external policies but also the solidity and success of American society in general and of its most characteristic institutions. The pragmatic attitude of the North American combines with his ethical tendencies to make possible in his country the supremacy of social worth—or, to be more exact, the supremacy of those values in which the individual and the social factors serve each other reciprocally.

The North American resists nothing so much as to be swallowed up by the state, or even to be excessively controlled by it—witness his protest against certain paternalistic aspects of the "New Deal" and the high praise, then current, of "rugged individualism." But this American individualism is very different from that of other peoples. It is not absolute, nor has it anything of the hermetic and "adamic," like the Spaniard's, for example. On the contrary, it seeks its own realization by integrating itself with that of other individuals. No doubt it sometimes grows at others' expense, for the "spirit of the frontier" plays its own tricks—but not without public opinion disapproving most emphatically. The public does not admire *all* evidences of energy; it does not respect those of the "gangster," for example (even though the typical American feels at heart a secret admiration for him, as is evident from the success of the films that have him as a protagonist). Public opinion does not consciously allow that only private interests are the ones that count, any more than it gives this approval to purely social ones. It holds that neither the private nor the public values can thrive alone, for the individual needs society, of whose services he is a beneficiary, and society depends for its success on those who support it. In short, we are dealing with a cooperative social individualism existing in a collectivity with a strong community sense but with no tendencies to socialize.

Thus public affairs are looked on as an enterprise—everybody's business—and its value is measured, again, by the standard of practical results. To Americans, a good society is not one that merely maintains collective discipline, but one that educates, protects health, builds roads, and so on. Nor is a society more desirable because it has certain settled or static values, such as a glorious history, an accumulated culture, noble traditions. It is admired only when it is a dynamic society, showing itself capable, above all, of providing gainful employment for its citizens and giving them a chance for the pursuit of happiness. This is why social stratification is so distasteful to the North American, as well as barriers between classes and the evaluation of an individual by his lineage and his ancestry. Thus we understand also his disdain for groups, classes, nations, or races whose present-day accomplishments are negligible, and even for those whose prestige is merely cultural or aesthetic. For a purely sentimental or lyric concept of country, Americans have substituted a functional one. The real motherland is not the country in which one was born, regardless of its illustrious traditions, but the country in which one feels freer and at the same time more assured of being able to earn a living. This attitude has contributed a great deal to the United States' assimilation of its numerous immigrants. I shall always remember the Italian barber in Cambridge who assured me, notwithstanding the literary pride with which he recited to me verses of Dante accompanied by the click of his scissors, that he would not exchange the United States for anything in the world.

If the businessman and his most prosperous representative, the millionaire, stand for the individual American ideal, they nevertheless do not constitute the *social* ideal. The latter is, rather, the good citizen—the useful worker who is law-abiding, pays his taxes, takes an interest in the community, and, in exchange for all this, demands from his official organisms (the federal, state, and municipal governments) that they live up to their obligations to safeguard the fundamental interests of the individual that he alone cannot attend to, such as public order, education, public services. This double

332

rendering of services—a citizen who fulfills and therefore exacts; a government that exacts and therefore fulfills—is the very basis of North American polity. Although this is true in greater or lesser measure of every well-organized country, in few of them does it function with such regularity.

The efficiency and continuity of this interchange are assured by a system, also double in nature, of rights and duties. The commonwealth attends to the needs of the citizenry with all of the expected services, including especially a very provident system of public education. This is not confined to elementary teaching, but aims to give the majority of the young people at least a high-school education, which is sufficient to open almost all doors. Although the schooling has generally a utilitarian emphasis, which makes it less complete than in most European countries, it never fails to inculcate respect for law and public institutions and a more or less critical appreciation of national history and achievements.

The citizen, for his part, contributes to the community the taxes and assessments of an extremely severe fiscal system, which includes direct taxes of federal and state origin. Probably in no other country is taxation more burdensome or more difficult to evade. In general, all social discipline is based on the expectation of respect for law and authority, under threat of severe penalties. Illicit influence and unwarranted immunity thrive in the United States only so long as they are not uncovered to public opinion, which is usually very alert and is assisted by a press much more independent than is sometimes supposed.

All of this is instrumented by an admirable democratic organization—admirable in spite of the blemishes of which I shall speak presently. The zeal with which the citizens exercise their right to the vote, and guard its effectiveness; the matter-of-factness with which the popular will is respected by the government and accepted by political minorities and the armed forces; the operation of a two-party political system capable of establishing and directing the great currents of opinion without too greatly smothering the differences in shading; the effectiveness of a constitutional order in which the executive, legislative, and judicial powers confine themselves to their proper functions, and remain always subject to accountability and appeal—these are characteristics of North American democracy which combine with the critical vitality of public opinion to insure that liberty in the United States is not only effective but also disciplined. Thus the country is exempt from both civil disruption and authoritarianism.

In national and international policy the most characteristic projections of this public spirit can be listed among its other virtues. Here some reservations will have to be made presently, but in general it can be said that, in the domestic field, policy is always in keeping with the public interest as seen by majority opinion within the corresponding electoral sphere. Precisely from that fact originate certain limitations and errors, derived from the quality of that majority and its judgments or its prejudices; but this in itself involves fidelity to the sovereignty of public opinion, which is the real and supreme power in the United States. While national policy sometimes appears too temporizing, because of the necessity to take into account the vast opposing interests that weigh upon it, there is no doubt that it tends to draw inspiration from the norm of the general welfare, as understood by public opinion, and not from the whims of a ruler or the preconceptions of an ideology.

On the international level, Americans—after a long period of isolation and almost of indifference to external problems—saw themselves obliged to intervene, very actively, in world affairs. Two criteria have obviously combined to guide their action: self-interest and what they consider to be the common interest of nations. In this duality we see again the two ingredients of the national make-up: the spirit of the frontier, pugnacious, utilitarian, realistic; and the Puritan spirit, proselytizing, ethical, idealistic. The combination of the two has given to American foreign policy, on the one hand, a certain economic and strategic calculation designed to assure export and import markets, to establish zones of defense, and, in recent times, to hold off the Russian peril; on the other hand, a concern, doubtless sincere, for the welfare of other peoples and the defense of Western values. Depending on whether they have chosen to look at the former aim or the latter, other nations have reacted with skepticism, sometimes ungrateful, or with gratitude and admiration. It seems to me that the balance is favorable to the United States. If it were not for that country, our world would find itself today invaded by a different "imperialism," lacking some of the defects of the Western order, but also contrary to many of its noblest traditions.

III

Not everything, however, is good and wholesome in North American life and behavior, any more than it is in any other country. After the above eulogy, which I deem to be just, I may be allowed to point out limitations and deficiencies that are no less discernible. As I have already suggested, these often stem from the virtues themselves.

The cult of energy imparts a certain crudeness and even a certain underlying brutality to North American life. Since Americans are bound to a preference for action, and above all utilitarian action, they concede little or no value to contemplative life and the spiritual predilections on which it draws. When I was a student at Harvard I almost had to apologize to the other students for my scant fondness for sports and my dedication to the arts and to books. For the average American (and let it always be borne in mind that I am referring to the semi-cultured majority, not to the well-informed minority, who are in the habit of sharpening their curiosity a great deal, precisely as a reaction to the average), the intellectual, the "egghead," is suspect, little better than an unproductive idler— in any case, unworthy to become President of the nation. Only a profound crisis like the one the United States passed through during the first administration of Franklin D. Roosevelt could have made tolerable such a team as the so-called Brain Trust.

I once heard a very distinguished North American (distinguished even though he was an intellectual) say that if it were not for the universities and similar institutions, American life would have barbaric overtones. It might be argued that the same thing would happen in any other country; but I believe what he meant was that the average North American lacks that sense of spiritual values, and that spontaneous respect for them, which in certain peoples— the Italian, for example—are almost a second nature. Thus one must not be surprised at the irony with which European countries look upon the ordinary Yankee tourist who passes through the museums and takes in the famous monuments with self-sacrificing fatigue. The cult of energy does not make for perceptiveness, and thus it breeds a certain leveling vulgarity—a characteristic of the "Babbitt" psychology, memorably denounced by Sinclair Lewis in that same United States.

I hasten to add, however, that I am one of those who believe there is not only the promise of an original American culture, but also growing and splendid realizations of it in every field. And, unless I am stretching a topic too much, I would like to suggest that in its aesthetic manifestations—whose first example in the order of time was the skyscraper—that culture shows itself always as a stylization of energy. The great American productions in the novel and the drama, which enjoy so much prestige in the world nowadays, seem to me to be a fusion of the two "consciences" I have spoken of, the "tough" and the "tender." But we must not forget what that same literature contains of reproach and protest against the most primary and general aspects of the American environment.

Let us pass now to the moral order. The great Cuban, Jose Martí, used to say that the quality of a nation can be appraised by the quality of the men and women that it produces. This moral quality is generally very high in the United States, and perhaps for that very reason it is likely to be taken for granted. But the esteem for what is external at the expense of what is intrinsic tends to produce a cheapening of the subjective qualities. The emphasis on deeds, rather than on moral substance, tends to leave the latter without support, giving stimulus to a certain disdain for the inner life; and the emptiness of that life is in turn responsible for the many forms of "escapism" that abound in North America, from fondness for the love tangles and adventures of Hollywood and for certain theatrical forms of evangelism to frenzied dancing and the excesses of alcohol and sex.

European thought is very much inclined to downgrade American pragmatism as a philosophy, and almost always does so unjustly or without much basis in fact. But there is no doubt that in its most primary manifestations the pragmatic spirit engenders a nominalism that is indifferent to the great abstractions usually considered fruitful in other nations, even if only as ideal norms. It also produces a casuistic practicalism that tends to prevail excessively over "principles." This attitude, fortified as it is by an obsession with economic success, encourages a harshly competitive and money-minded social environment that strangles all moral scruples (the so-called "go-getter"), weakens society on its most intimate levels (in the family, for example), and engenders extremely abnormal forms of delinquency. I have defended Americans from the common charge of materialism. Nevertheless, even the writings of their own most eminent social critics abound in the conviction that that great nation would benefit by an orientation less centered on economic success and more attentive to the imponderable values—on which depend, in the last analysis, the nobility of a civilization and the depth of its culture.

As I have already emphasized, the importance of social values in the United States, in many ways laudable, rests on the individual's appreciation for the advantages of what is communal. But that way also leads to an excessive exaltation of what is common or average. Since this is combined with the techniques and practices derived from mass production and automation, there results a decided standardization of North American life. Its advantages, in a practical and material sense, are quite obvious; but its disadvantages in other respects are no less visible. Standardization, which is by definition the contrary of what is unique, selective, and varied, imparts to the country a certain uniformity and surface monotony quite different from the amenities of other civilizations. Furthermore, the primacy of the average makes for routine ways of life, of thought, and even of feeling. What is general impresses its own standard on the particular. Common interest is related to common sense—and common sense is related to the plain and obvious. Common judgment tends to proscribe, at least from daily life, anything that is different or out of line. Thus we find in the average level a mistrust of outstanding personalities. Perhaps it is for this very reason that the United States is the country where eccentric attitudes and preachments are most welcome; but in general its culture is middleground, dominated by slogans and self-complacency.

This may be inevitable in such a thoroughgoing democracy. A political system based on public opinion is also one wherein majority ways of thinking, which are at times the most routine, majority ways of feeling, which are often the coarsest, and majority ways of electing, which are sometimes the most unfair, acquire overwhelming authority and public influence. The democracy of presidents who are almost always exemplary is also, on its lower levels, the democracy of political "machines" and state and municipal bosses; of vulgar, hand-shaking politicians; and of unscrupulous or fabulously enriched labor leaders.

And the same nation that is the defender of world liberty is a country of violent racial discrimination. This problem, perhaps the most serious one of American democracy, is exceedingly difficult to explain in the light of what I have said above. If the North Americans were indeed strictly pragmatic they would tend to appraise the Negro or the Spanish-speaking groups in the extreme South and the Southwest not by their race or the color of their skin but by their efficiency as workers. In the Northern states this is, in fact, the tendency. If a contrary attitude prevails in other states, it is probably because the bad habits of caste and aristocracy brought over from England weighed so heavily in their formation, and of course because so many members of the "disqualified" races live in those regions. And perhaps the fear of economic competition has some relation to that prejudice, along with apprehensions of the social and political influence that the Negro would have if freed from all restrictions. In any case, this is the most deplorable imperfection of democracy in the United States, and it lessens, to no small degree, that country's authority before the rest of the world. Yet the United States' efforts to eliminate this prejudice, even by doing violence, in the South, to respect for public opinion—the principle that molds all of its political philosophy and practice—cannot fail to do it credit.

Finally, in the United States the prevailing mental attitude toward other countries suffers from a certain provincialism that inevitably influences interrelations. This attitude is less arrogant than ingenuous. Trained in a love for the superlative ("the greatest in the world"), the American has accustomed himself to think (as formerly and for other reasons his British cousin thought) that being the richest and most powerful nation implies an all-inclusive superiority. Reflected here is the characteristic tendency of the utilitarian sense of life to infer quality from quantity. Thus whatever is foreign is likely to appear to the American as at best something too exquisite, something decorative or lacking in virility. This attitude does not, of course, extend to the well-informed classes, where we see rather a certain snobbery, perhaps a residue of the old colonial conscience; but it is fairly common in the lower and middle classes, which tend to look on the foreigner as inferior, forgetting how far the United States itself is an amalgam of foreign elements. When abroad, Americans have a tendency to find irritating or ridiculous everything that is "different." In this, as well as in other connections, the conduct of American soldiers in foreign lands has often been criticized. Of late, North American diplomacy and general foreign relations have become more refined, but this underlying feeling of superiority (sometimes in itself amply justified) cannot help but have considerable effect on the nations concerned; it shows itself in a certain rigidity that extends from incomprehension of local psychology and interests to a paternalism not always so well practiced as it is kindly inspired.

It would not be fair to conclude this general evaluation of North Americans without underscoring what, in my opinion, can be deduced from it: the conclusion that the positive qualities of that great nation far surpass the negative ones. Among the positive qualities stands an enormous capacity for historical acceleration. Let it always be remembered that only a hundred and fifty years ago the United States was still an embryonic nation. When all that is negative has been said, one must recognize that today it is one of the most noble and attractive abiding places that man has yet been able to build for himself. There is much in it that other nations can take as an example.

IV

But the fact that other countries have a good deal to learn from the United States is no reason to think that the opposite may not also be true in a greater or lesser degree. I shall undertake to explore both possibilities insofar as that part of the world from which I come is concerned—and also to point out likenesses and differences—but in doing so it will be convenient to refer not only to Cuba but to Latin America in general, so that the comparison may carry greater implications. After all, Cuba is only an element within that larger sphere.

The first thing that must be said, because it is not so obvious as it seems, is that these two great portions of the New World have many things in common. Americans of the United States tend to forget this, as is perhaps evidenced when they call their country "America," thus making it necessary for them to designate the other great portion of the hemisphere as "Latin America." Latin it is, of course, insofar as it is a cultural and, to a lesser extent, racial offspring of three great Latin nations: Spain, Portugal, and France. But this designation tends to make people forget that the essential thing about this America of ours is not its being "Latin," but its being also *American.*

America signifies above all else a *new* world, not so much in the historical sense (already becoming obsolete) of something recently discovered, but in being a world *for the new.* This, in turn, does not merely mean the land of the future, because the future may bring a mere insistence on the ways of the past. It means a *vocation for newness,* an openness for rectification and creation. The essential feature of the American spirit, in the South as well as in the North, is an attitude, at once critical and creative, of hope for a better world. On the one hand, it is a disposition to preserve from the past of the human race only those forms of culture and of life that have shown themselves fruitful for man, rejecting or rooting out everything that shackles the human spirit. On the other hand, it is a readiness to find new ways and means of promoting that spirit and its greater fulfillment.

A harbinger of this vocation for newness was the "utopianism" that was associated, even in old Europe, with the discovery of the new lands. Drawing sustenance from the Old World's fatigue and sense of frustration with regard to many of its own patterns of culture and of life, the founders of American communities, desiring to make a *new* world, immediately availed themselves of the distance, expanse, and "virginity" of these regions. Because of certain historical circumstances, this disposition was less noticeable in the Spanish colonies than in the English, but it certainly existed in the Spanish, even if more or less stifled and forced to follow indirect courses. With the coming of independence the spirit of innovation was accentuated, and in the course of this century it has made itself as evident in the America descended from Latins as in the America descended from Anglo-Saxons, although for the latter the circumstances have continued to be more favorable. Therefore all of America is "man's country," as a distinguished Colombian essayist has recently called South America—that is, a land eager to attain the best yield from human possibilities.

In concrete terms, this openness toward the future—toward a better future—carries with it a quick propensity to throw overboard all kinds of ballast. It also implies a confidence in progress, despite present-day European skepticism on that question. Increasingly,

Latin America as well as the United States—even though to a lesser degree, because it springs from a culture very much attached to "principles"—is showing a tendency toward pragmatic evaluations, toward ends rather than means, deeds rather than mere attitudes or static positions.

Thus Americans of the North and South have in common a great deal of what might be called historical psychology. This affinity has created similar attitudes toward life, similar ways of judgment, and even similar customs and institutions. Like the American of the North, the typical Ibero-American shows himself to be resourceful, enterprising, extraordinarily jealous of his personal liberty, impatient when confronted by useless conventions, and ready to welcome the new, even to the extremes of newfangled innovations. His customs, cast in the Spanish mold, struggle against that heritage, but each time they become more specifically American. This process is aided, of course, by the powerful influence of the United States, which is more effective here than in the rest of the world, as a result of relative geographic nearness and close economic relations. For example, the scruples of caste and social position—a part of the Spanish inheritance—tend to be nullified by the elimination of economic barriers. Being of humble origin no longer prevents anyone, if he has the luck and the ability, from attaining the highest position. And the Latin American, far from resisting mechanization, as often happens in Europe, welcomes it and makes use of it. In short, the old stratified and elaborated rigidity of the colonies has given way in these countries to a new fluidity, a dynamism with utilitarian overtones.

These similarities of spirit and of life are regarded as assets, and therefore they constitute *interests* that we Americans of the South and those of the North have in common. And it is hardly necessary to mention the enormous number of more concrete interests, of an economic and political nature, that bind us together. Latin America has been for a very long time the principal supplier of raw materials for the United States, one of its most important buyers of manufactured articles, the main field for the investment of its capital abroad, its most constant and loyal collaborator in the orientation of international policies, and of course, its nearest strategic point of support. If one day, through some misadventure, the rest of the world turned hostile to the United States and the latter had

341

to fall back on its own hemisphere, it could more than probably continue to rely always on the adherence and the backing of Latin America; together they could constitute a great sphere of continental self-sufficiency, dedicated to the preservation, in equal measure, of their common material interests and great human ideals.

But though we resemble each other and have much in common, we are distinct. This comes primarily from the fact that in our America the "given" reality, both natural and historical, is very different from that of the North. In our lands the physical manifestations of nature are in general harsher and more difficult: the Amazon is not the Mississippi, nor are the Andes the Rocky Mountains. Our primary social nature, too, is less manageable. The United States is a fusion of European elements, with marginal juxtapositions of relatively small Indian and Negro populations. The greater part of Latin America, on the other hand, consists of a white creole minority, mainly of Spanish origin, surrounded by an extensive indigenous population partly intermingled with Negroes that tends to imprint its character on the social whole. A relatively homogeneous people does not produce the same problems as one strained by the inevitable tensions and instabilities of racial heterogeneity.

The processes that formed these great conglomerates were so notably different that it is hardly necessary to be specific about them. The United States stems from a population that already represented a certain dissidence from the ways of continental Europe. Latin America, on the contrary, was born into the New World as an extension of a nation that was then at the apex of political and religious absolutism and had a culture of great substance, though more static than dynamic. In the North, apart from the milder physical environment and the relatively tenuous resistance of the Indian, nothing impeded the founding minorities from establishing their own types of colonies and extending the frontiers: their society was thus virtually a new creation. The South American colonies, on the other hand, subjected to the straitjacket of a rigid colonial system, were locked within themselves and forbidden to communicate with one another. When the thirteen colonies of the North achieved independence they were already largely prepared for union and political liberty. In the South an informed minority was striving toward those ideals, but it had to contend with another minority of Spanish traditionalist spirit and with a general population that was socially and politically unformed.

The result of this clash was independence of Spain, but also, subsequently, anarchy and the authoritarianism of the *caudillos*. Liberal ideas had to work hard during all of the nineteenth century to organize the new republics on democratic formulas. That they survived, even in form, as democracies is a true miracle—a result of the profound vocation I have mentioned. Many of them are not yet democracies, except in the constitutional mold, because the obstacles I have referred to have not yet been overcome. Strong residues of material and spiritual colonialism remain. The problems still confronting many of the republics are, in great measure, basic problems of social integration, political and economic development, cultural attainment. The United States was able to clear the way quickly for its national fulfillment; the Latin American republics, more impeded, find themselves still in the throes of formation, although not a few of them are showing clear signs of approaching maturity. All of this must be taken into consideration in judging them, or in dealing with their problems and aspirations.

But these nations, even within their immaturity, show certain virtues and exemplary merits, beginning with their own constant desire for improvement. In spite of the pragmatism that they share to a certain extent with the United States—as part of what I have called "historical and collective psychology"—they have a profound appreciation for the intrinsic, and this quality is more characteristically their own. It shows itself in an instinctive respect for all human dignity, whatever the race of the individual may be; in a tendency to value a person primarily for his moral or intellectual qualities; in a spiritual and sensitive projection toward life and its values. All of this, so patently derived from the Spanish character, is rooted, however, in a gentler and more extroverted temperament. I believe that in natural goodness the Latin American has nothing to envy the American of the North, while surpassing him in the capacity for tenderness and sympathetic understanding. This combination of qualities is projected into social relations (the cult of courtesy, of honor, of the family, of friendship), into customs (private and public traditions of a sentimental nature), and into a preference for a culture of ethical and aesthetic accents. As far as public life is concerned, there should be added the impassioned courage with which these nations defend their collective personality and liberty. The frequent eclipses of liberty in the field of government are likely to be the result of this very vehemence, and not of any sort of apathy.

Not a few of the Latin American characteristics I have mentioned are well worthy of esteem in the United States—among them, the sentimental cohesion of the family, the suavity of social relations and of private life in general, above all the spiritual sense of life and thorough respect for the dignity of man, especially where this is put to the hardest test, in attitudes toward other races. We Latin Americans, however, must not let our margin of superiority in such matters blind us to the defects and the excesses that limit us or to the ways of organization and conduct in which we are the ones who should learn from the United States.

In particular we should give consideration to our neighbor's public life—its civic solidarity and its disposition toward duties as well as toward rights, its respect for law, its capacity for economic organization and for disciplined liberty. Our exaggerated individualism, a heritage of the Spanish character, makes us lacking in the spirit of cooperation; our intellectual absolutism and our subjectivism frequently make us intransigent, violently emotional, undisciplined. Because they find scanty objective expression our spiritual tendencies incline us too greatly to quixotic attitudes, including an indifference toward certain forms of reality and toward practical and economic considerations. Our taste for the intellectual and aesthetic, combined with our strong sense of form, is responsible not only for a lack of balance in our culture but also for the pettifogging that has so vitiated our juridical and political life, and for a certain general tendency to sacrifice substance for the sake of appearances. Our temperament tends toward the sentimental to the detriment of the reflective, and toward the sensual to the detriment of the ethical.

If North American Puritanism has its well-known dryness and rigidity, and often hypocrisy, our moral liberalism, with pagan overtones, makes us excessively frivolous. If in the North the spirit of the frontier sometimes turns out to be harsh and unscrupulous, in the South the spirit of the courtier makes us soft, flattering, and unreliable. Using once again the language of William James, we might say that the American spirit as a whole would be well served by a fusion of the "tough conscience" of the North with the "tender conscience" of the Southern nations.

This development would be justified not only by humanity's natural desire for self-perfection but also because it would contribute greatly toward achieving good relations between the two parts of the hemisphere. In addition to our geographic proximity and our common interests a greater and higher consideration makes that result desirable: our responsibility of promoting in the world—or at least protecting from the rest of the world—that common vocation in which the essential affinity of the Americas is rooted. Not only the United States but all America is in a way a "trial experiment." Only by helping and learning from each other can we Americans of the North and the South overcome our particular defects and demonstrate that ours is indeed the promised land dedicated to the full fruition of man. This is the greater task to which we both owe ourselves.

Postscript

IN OUR TIMES the hope for better understanding among nations has become essential to our belief in a future. It is true that long before we contrived the means of annihilation, we were making efforts toward closer international bonds and stronger checks on overt hostility. Now, however, with the stakes raised to infinity, those efforts have acquired the urgency of stark necessity. In large measure they are still, as they have always been, dependent on the skill of statesmen. But in today's world the leaders and the led are interrelated, and the remarkable force known as public opinion occupies a prominent place at the council tables. The degree to which the peoples of the world understand one another is a measure of the success their statesmen can achieve in avoiding calamity. With greater appreciation of one another's values, procedures, and goals, greater awareness that attitudes taken for granted in one nation may cause surprise or even shock in another, there is more possibility that conflicts can be adjusted before they become uncontrollable.

Certainly, complete understanding is scarcely attainable in human affairs. It is a dream, a phantom—like virtue, an indispensable goal but one that lies always just beyond our grasp, whether between nations, between individuals, or even within oneself. As with virtue, however, its way-stations are what count. The farther one proceeds, the better, even though the end of the line cannot be reached. In this process, liking is helpful, though it is not essential. But knowledge is necessary—knowledge not merely of the facts but of the facts in relation to their context. What forces are at work in the building of nations' knowledge of one another?

There is no doubt that an individual, if he has the essential qualifications, can reach a considerable understanding of a culture different from his own, granted that he may misinterpret this or that aspect of character or behavior. From his vantage point as an outsider, looking at the whole with fresh vision, he may even see interrelations and explanations that are not noticed by those who live in the country and take it for granted. Such individual travelers may influence others among their countrymen, and it is probably through such personal contacts that the greatest progress can be made in

346

correcting misconceptions. Thus the more travel between countries, the better, even superficial tourist travel. International gatherings of every kind, from meetings of the United Nations to conferences of the smallest private groups; missions of international technical cooperation; trips of businessmen; scholarships for study abroad; privately or governmentally sponsored invitations to foreigners representative of various economic or cultural groups; "exchange of persons," in the numerous forms it has taken especially in recent years—everything that brings the peoples of the world face to face can help them to look upon one another with greater understanding.

Far more pervasive, of course, than individual contacts are the innumerable influences that reach into the lives of the general population at home: the press and radio, movies, international exhibits, cultural exchanges, governmental information services, the whole process of education. All such elements in the formation of public opinion are capable of working toward understanding among nations, providing an insight that goes deeper than friendly political relations or travelogue notions of picturesqueness.

All this is possible. International understanding *can* be improved by more and more international travel. It *can* be improved by education and the other factors that influence public opinion. But whether this happens is another matter. There are formidable difficulties in the process, and it would be foolish to ignore them.

Probably the greatest single deterrent to understanding among nations is sheer indifference. While this is to be deplored, it is scarcely a cause for wonder. Whatever men's hopes for a better world, their immediate concerns are personal: the well-being of themselves and their families, their effectiveness on their jobs, their relations with friends, the diversions or excitements of their leisure activities. What lies outside this circle is, for millions, perhaps for a majority of the earth's inhabitants, merely a great beyond, a matter of supreme unconcern. They don't know, and don't care. This narrow personalism would not be worth emphasizing were it not so universal an obstacle to understanding "otherness."

Further obstacles lie in the very nature of communication, which is a difficult process at best and, at worst, deliberately deceptive. All the many means by which information about other countries reaches the general public—or at least those who have any interest in it—are subject to grave deficiencies, whether their tenor is pro

347

or con: the presentation of isolated facts, without regard for context; generalizations drawn from inadequate information; emphasis on political or technical matters without reference to their human environment; concentration on the sensational and bizarre; the pull of dogmatic or ideological simplifications; out-and-out misinformation, whether provided for a purpose or unintentionally, out of ignorance. To such impediments in the path of accuracy are added others that come from memory and habit: cliches that have long since lost whatever validity they may once have had; past history, with its undertones of emotion; prejudices and notions assimilated, without examination, over a lifetime.

Many of these influences persist even when individual citizens see the other country at firsthand. They form a baggage of preconceptions. The weight of the baggage may be lessened, through diligent observation and reflection, but there is always a danger that some of the paraphernalia have come to be too essential to the traveler to be discarded. And even if the observer is determined to keep an open mind, it is not easy for him to understand a nation different from his own. Each nation has its individual character, not easily accessible to those who are not part of it. Inevitably the foreigner has his own personal predilections—likes, dislikes, interests, habits, the preconceptions he feels as a citizen of his own country. Some of these predilections may be satisfied in the country he visits; if not, he may be able deliberately to suspend them, in an effort toward objectivity, but again they may be too much a part of him to be ever fully set aside. Thus he finds what he is equipped to find, perhaps only what he is looking for.

There is also the danger, common to most travelers, of comparing unlikes: looking at the worst in the country visited in terms of the best at home, or comparing one country's middle-class groups with the other's intellectuals. And most travelers, of course, move in a public world—hotels, streets, restaurants, shops, trains, airplanes. Even when they make an effort to talk to people, and to see behind the public façade, few have an opportunity to see much of private life beyond an occasional invitation to dinner. Before they acquire a sense of the whole, an understanding of background, it is most difficult for travelers to evaluate the significance of what they see.

In any country a foreigner is not only an observer. He is also observed. Thus each in his own way contributes to his hosts' views of his own country, for there is a universal tendency to jump from the particular to the general. If all travelers or residents in other lands were representative of their countries, the generalizations they provoke—good, bad, or indifferent—would be an important addition to our knowledge of one another. But there is no true "representative" in this sense, and foreigners abroad, even when they are present in large numbers, are more likely than not to produce a misleading impression of their countries—misleading because it is partial, distorted, and out of context.

As several of these essayists have pointed out, there are particular difficulties in comprehending the essential character of the United States. In some respects it is, to be sure, an extension of Europe, and thus its observers may believe they have a point of reference. But in its basic character it is different from its "Old World," a phenomenon often baffling even to itself. The point is of such importance to the development of mutual understanding between this country and others that a brief elaboration may be worth while.

The intensity of industrialization in the United States and the mass character of its culture are a predominant concern of everyone who looks at the country. It is not difficult to see what these attributes entail—in material, psychological, social, political, intellectual terms. But they affect different people in different ways. Those from groups which hope to preserve the values of an old, established way of life tend to be most disturbed at the cultural leveling that has accompanied the headlong advances in technology and standards of living; here the United States seems to provide a vision of their own future, and the vision is looked upon with distress and dismay. On the other hand, those from groups or nations that aspire to a greater share in economic and social progress are less critical of this industrialized mass culture as such; they would be heartened to see it as a vision of their future, and they are less fearful that its cruder aspects are inescapable. In this aspect of national character, what is viewed as "typically American" is interpreted differently—though perhaps still with dismay—when it is seen as typically twentieth century.

Also in the United States' political relations with other countries there are history-dictated factors that make for difficulties of understanding, quite apart from procedural mistakes and ineptitudes. The scope of the problems the country must deal with in its new position of leadership would alone make for dissension, even if the problems were always handled wisely. An international policy that has to confront every issue with a view to its global implications cannot but baffle those who look upon that issue more narrowly. Even in a limited situation, involving one country alone, the actions of the United States are likely to be misconstrued by one faction or another. Its help is needed in many parts of the world, needed and implored, and, human nature being what it is, the need is resented, and the help as well; it is many times a question of "damned if you do and damned if you don't," and the justifications given for the damnings contribute little toward clarification. The world's understanding of United States actions in international affairs is not furthered by the country's characteristically improvising approach to problems, its deep-rooted pragmatism, which makes it difficult for others to discern a set program or a reassuring consistency.

The apparent lack of consistency goes very deep. Stark contradictions in the people's nature and behavior make it possible for any preconception, any observation, to be confirmed. "Americans" are materialistic, tending toward a quantitative or dollar measure of all values, yet they are also motivated by strong ethical principles. Resolutely competitive, yet altruistic. Addicted to the mediocre or crude or even vulgar in what they enjoy, or tolerate, but also creators of world-acclaimed works in literature, architecture, and other arts. Violent, but with a strong belief in law and justice. Conformist, almost uniform, in their behavior and values, but staunchly individualistic. The list could be indefinitely extended. A foreigner who tries to comprehend this tumultuous complexity is not at all helped by the country's own stereotypes about itself, the shibboleths that it continues to repeat without thought of their validity.

True, the "American" is recognized everywhere; people throughout the world are in substantial agreement on at least the standard-of-living implications of "the American way of life." But for those who look beyond the conspicuous external aspects, so familiar to everyone, it is difficult to find an enlightening clue to the inner meaning of it all. The difficulty is understandable, for the character of the country is still in process of formation, seeking new ways and new solutions. In the United States change is more rapid than elsewhere; the clocks run faster. Today's conclusion has to be reconsidered tomorrow. Achievements are not end-products, but stepping-stones. The dynamism of the country's character, the explosiveness

350

of its actions—more appealing to the young than to those of more settled ways—are a challenge to ideals of orderliness and stability. There appears to be only flux, blind energy—and toward what end?

It is not easy for others to comprehend how basically the character of the United States has been molded by a set of conditions leading inevitably to innovation, to divergence from the ways of older countries and older cultures. Some of these conditions are physical: enormous space for expansion, offering room enough to spread out, to move around, to try again in different circumstances; natural resources of extraordinary quantity and variety. But some come from the fact that certain values and institutions of modern civilization are the very foundation stones of the nation, with no underpinnings from a preceding indigenous tradition.

The United States represents a fresh start on new soil, carried out in a spirit of psychological revolt against old forms. It took place at a time when the whole Western world was stirring with new hopes for man's life in the social order. Equal rights to opportunity and respect; freedom of belief and expression; trust in the capacity of man to think for himself—these principles that galvanized the eighteenth century are by no means unique to the United States. But in this country, with its diverse population drawn from dozens of nations and every social stratum, they were fused with relatively little obstruction from the vested interests of those who preferred things the way they had been.

All this lies behind the familiar façade and the baffling inconsistencies. It has led to excesses, to formlessness in comparison with older civilizations. Most certainly there have been appalling aberrations from the driving ideal. But through the excesses a frame of reference is built. Out of formlessness new forms gradually emerge. And the public conscience remains watchful that its violators mend their ways with all deliberate speed. Hysterical efforts to maintain a comfortable racial separation are eroded—not alone by the unrelenting pressure of law, but also by the pressures of stubborn conscience. Outbreaks like McCarthyism wear themselves out, and each, in disappearing, leaves a tiny advance toward maturity. Undisciplined bad taste gives way to something better, learned through experience. The steps of development come from the very permissiveness of the environment. They would doubtless be surer, and go more consistently in the same direction, if they were guided by an

351

established elite, but they would then no longer culminate in that contradictory, baffling, yes-good, yes-bad amalgam that is recognizably "American," and admittedly generative.

Thus in contemplating the United States it is necessary to have genuine faith in the potentialities of freedom, faith that the better outweighs the worse when men are allowed to flex their muscles and test their full strength, each equal in worth to any other. The excesses and crudities of their trials and errors, even the degrading lapses from the principle itself, are steps in the process of learning. This is a freedom that goes beyond political institutions. In greater or lesser measure it is found in many countries. But in the United States, because of historical coincidences, it has been an impelling force from the very beginning, and hence its ramifications reach farther there than elsewhere.

The emphasis here given to the United States comes from the focus of this volume. The purpose is to point toward some of the idiosyncrasies—many of them discussed with great perception in the essays—that are disconcerting to those who try to grasp the character of this particular country. And naturally the difficulties work in both directions. These attributes cause problems for the United States too, not only in its life at home but also in its capacity to understand others.

But granted all the difficulties in international understanding, they become smaller when they are recognized. There is clear evidence too that they can be overcome when there is good will and a capacity for unbemused observation. To this the present volume is eloquent testimony. Many of its writers have shown a remarkable and enlightening comprehension of this country. A few have mirrored the deterrents that make any international communication difficult. All have contributed—each in his own way—to a knowledge of their own countries; and this is the crucial other side of the coin, because our concern is with mutual understanding. The goal is more possible now than it has ever been, for distance has been almost eliminated, and lines of communication among nations are almost as extensive as those within a single city.

In considering what is basically needed if nations are to live together more amicably, two considerations stand out from this volume that are probably essential to all others. For one thing, there has to be a greater awareness that there are many ways of living, not inferior or superior but different, each meaningful in its own context. In our age every nation has to learn from the others, but in working out its development each must go its own way, in conformance with its history and its nature. In a word, intercommunication, but also individuality.

Equally important, it must be recognized that each nation, each people, has its own kind of pride or self-confidence, essential to its existence—call it a sense of nationality, which goes beyond "nationalism" as profoundly as self-confidence goes beyond egoism. In international relations, as in interpersonal relations, there would be far less friction if there were more awareness that in some matters psychological vulnerability is universal. It takes different forms in different nations, but in every nation it is evidence of man's basic need to be respected.

F.M.J.

Appendix: National-Image Research and International Understanding

ATIONS' images of one another are unquestionably a factor in their relationships. Even though they do not, in themselves, change the course of events, they may strengthen a course determined by other causes; certainly they may be deliberately played upon for that purpose, sometimes in vicious manipulation. Thus what has come to be known as "image research"—the study of ideas and attitudes concerning other countries—has received increasing attention from social scientists since World War II. It would be impossible to summarize briefly the findings of the many image studies that have been published, each conducted in accordance with its own particular aims and procedures, but it may be useful to suggest in broad terms the kind of subject matter that is usually dealt with, and some of the difficulties that are inherent in this kind of research.

Although image studies rest ultimately on the responses of individuals, they usually address themselves to individuals in groups that are homogeneous in at least some respects. In the different studies, however, these groups vary greatly, in size and nationality as well as in personal characteristics. While some attention is paid to the attitudes of persons who have had no direct experience of the country they describe, most investigations are concerned with small specific groups of foreigners who are visiting or temporarily resident in that country, such as students and business or professional representatives.

Since image analysis is essentially an aspect of attitude and opinion research in general, the methods it uses are much the same: interviews and questionnaires, polls and surveys, and various refinements of these tools, such as audience tests, content analysis of letters and other writings, checklists of qualities, characterization of photographs, short writing assignments on given subjects. Some studies are concerned only, or primarily, with the discussion of methods, attempting to find approaches that will be at once "sensitive" and conducive to quantification.

The subject matter dealt with in the literature has been found to fall into three categories: first, the factors entering into the formation of images; second, the question of "what"—what attitudes and opinions are held, and about what; and, third, the nature and extent of any changes that are to be found. The following three paragraphs on these considerations are based on a special analysis of image studies, made at the request of the American European Foundation, sponsor of the project that led to the present book. That analysis, of some fifty pages, was conducted by Dr. Henry L. Lennard, of the Bureau of Applied Social Research at Columbia University, with the assistance of Mr. Erdman Palmore and Mrs. Corinne Kirchner. Dr. Lennard's study was concerned primarily with research on images of the United States, and for clarity of terminology it will be convenient, in abstracting it, to use the United States as point of reference. In other words, the "images" of "foreigners" refer here to the picture of this country or its citizens held by the nationals of other countries. Another nation could of course serve equally well as reference point, for the emphasis is on the process of intercultural contact rather than on its application to any particular country.

1. The factors that affect the kinds of images formed are not systematically analyzed in the research literature, but those found to be significant may be classified under four main headings: (a) personal and sociological factors characterizing the foreigner (age, sex, social-economic class, status mobility, education, occupation, political orientation); (b) psychological characteristics of the foreigner (rarely studied specifically, but assumed to include such factors as general hostility level, tolerance for ambiguity, tendency toward optimism or pessimism, toward conformism or deviance, toward introversion or extraversion, toward distance or involvement, toward rigidity or adaptability); (c) national characteristics of foreigner's own country (tempo and level of its historical development, its political relations with the United States, its cultural status in the world, the nature of its major problems); (d) "exposure" factors, that is, nature and degree of acquaintance with the United States, either from a distance (through movies, newspapers, radio, and other mass media, advertising, personal contacts at home with

traveling or resident Americans or with fellow-countrymen who profess knowledge of the United States, intercultural institutions, official organizations and publications) or through firsthand knowledge (as affected by the conditions of the visit, personal experiences during the visit, length of stay).

2. The resulting views and attitudes of foreigners concerning the United States, as found in the research studies, are usually expressed in as succinct a form as possible, often in a mere phrase or a succession of adjectives, sometimes even in a bare "favorable" or "unfavorable." While these responses cannot be systematized according to content, they may be classified according to subject matter as referring to five areas: (a) personal attributes of Americans; (b) social institutions (family life, attitudes toward sex and age, social classes, political institutions and processes, educational practices, mass media of communication, religion, economic methods and relations, racial stratification); (c) the realm of values and ideology; (d) the role of the United States in the world; (e) national symbols and "characteristic" national types.

3. As regards changes that occur in foreigners' images, the literature deals mainly with the extent and directions of change in particular images of particular groups or individuals, comparing preconceptions or first impressions with the views held after a visit.

Of course no single study could address itself to this schema as a whole in an effort to develop something like a general theory of image formation and change, comparable in usefulness, for example, to theories of capital formation. Such a theory, applicable to all peoples, could hardly be more than a broad statement of probabilities adequately suspected in advance. But much can be learned from the investigation of special circumscribed questions regarding specific groups, and all such findings, as they cumulate from study to study, can produce certain "by and large" answers regarding intercultural attitudes.

Some questions of this kind might be addressed to the material contained in this book, remembering that the personal views expressed here are those of intellectuals representing a higher-than-average level of education. For example, what degree of consistency is shown in the attributes of the United States that are here stressed? What consistencies does this book reveal about the nature of pre-visit conceptions and their sources? What are the relative weights of the various factors that are shown to enter into the formation of images, and what accounts for differences in this respect between different countries? Does there appear to be, within each individual, a tendency toward a "pattern" of images whereby ideas on one subject are integrally related to ideas on others? Can any overall conclusions be drawn regarding the images attributed to the populations at home, and their relation to specific factors? What significant changes in images do the essayists reveal, as the result of personal acquaintance with the country, and are there images that appear to be basically resistant to change?

Any effort to answer these and numerous other significant questions would reveal some of the basic difficulties that image research must cope with in its efforts to establish meaningful interrelationships. One is the problem of communication. Precise answers to "what" and "why" and "when" are difficult on any subject, and are especially difficult in regard to attitudes and opinions. The answers, when given, are easily subject to misinterpretation by the questioner, whose frame of reference may be different. The analyst has to bear in mind, too, that identical answers may have different meanings for different national or social groups, even for different individuals.

There is also the very important procedural problem of abbreviating a response into terms that will make possible a summation and comparison with other responses. Such abbreviation is essential under the aim of so formulating the "data" as to make possible their use for analysis and computation. But a foreigner's impressions, especially of a country he knows at first hand, are likely to consist of innumerable gradations of feeling and thought, mixtures of pro and con, "on the one hand" and "on the other hand," and thus they are not readily amenable to punch-card categories. This difficulty alone makes it a hazardous matter to attempt to systematize and generalize, and analysts have developed numerous methods of dealing with it. The more precise the method, however—such as lists of adjectives to be checked for relevance—the more limited are the findings ("the British are reserved, courageous, stolid," "the Americans are practical, naïve, boastful"). There is the ever-present danger of reducing a living, vital perception to a virtually meaningless truth, like summarizing Hamlet as a drama in which a son avenges the murder of his father—true, and possibly useful for some purposes, but not very revealing.

358

Then there is the problem of appraising the accuracy or justi-fiability of images. Whether this problem arises depends on the ob-jectives of the research, for in many cases the legitimate interest is only in the image itself, and not in passing judgment on it. But if the problem does arise, the analyst has to confront the fact that most meaningful observations rest on subjective values or socially dictated attitudes, and can be neither proved nor disproved. In the long continuum between truth and untruth, many statements do not fall clearly at one end of the scale or the other.

Thus image research has to cope with many pitfalls of perception, communication, appraisal, analysis. It must be ever on the alert that in its search for correlations it does not overlook the unkempt raggedness of social reality, and that in its search for scientific pre-cision it does not reduce its findings to the level of banality. But these difficulties, in greater or lesser degree, characterize every field of inquiry, especially those concerned with social processes and re-lations. And the findings of national-image research, as they cumu-late, can gradually add to the store of knowledge concerning the origins and the tenacity of the false conceptions, inaccurate stereo-types, and outworn cliches that enter so largely into one nation's views of other nations.

It was implied above that *because* national images are a factor in international understanding, the study of them can contribute to that desirable goal, and this implication is often found in the litera-ture. Whatever doubts it may raise, it can be justified when image analysis is used as a background for deliberate efforts to modify mistaken conceptions. There is scarcely a nation that does not have its information agencies and other official or pseudo-official insti-tutions that exist in large measure precisely for the improving of other nations' images of itself. Image research, directed to a defined and limited objective, can provide findings useful for this purpose. It can appraise changes in the attitudes of a specific group of for-eigners regarding specific questions; as regards a particular problem it can verify or modify assumptions based on hunch or logic; in the aggregate its "by and large" findings can provide an indication of possible relationships. In many such ways, both special and general, image analysis can be helpful to those responsible for policies and procedures in the improvement of international understanding.

But the direct contribution of image research to this aim is more

359

difficult to appraise. When national images are thus thought of as an aspect of public opinion, the term must mean the images, the views and attitudes, of the ordinary citizens, those millions of men and women who have never been in the country their images refer to, and probably never will be. Are their views materially changed by image research?

It cannot be doubted that knowledge, as such, has a certain dynamics, and ultimately percolates far beyond its original ambit. But image studies, each addressed to a circumscribed problem, hedged in by all the necessary precautions of scientific procedure, denied the dramatic flair of generalities and suggestive elaborations and final conclusions, are not an ideal bridge between scholar and public. Would a thousand studies analyzing South American views of the United States make a significant difference in South American public opinion on that subject? They would be more likely to promote North Americans' understanding of themselves. Even for this, however, the analyses would have to reach a wider audience than they are usually addressed to.

This is of course no disparagement of the image researchers' aims and findings. The point to be stressed is that there are many ways of contributing toward better understanding among nations and, of these, scientific investigations are neither the most appropriate nor the most effective. Their function is to add piece by piece to the store of knowledge; if the results are not immediately transferable to the workaday world, they ultimately become part of an inherited body of experience. But meanwhile, as regards nations' views of one another, there are other forces of change. The process of modification goes on.

It works through countless instruments, both deliberate and incidental, both constructive and destructive, ranging from the nature of schoolroom instruction to the imaginative efforts of a cultural attaché in Bangkok, from the tenor of newspaper coverage to such undertakings as the present book. In this succession of man-to-man activities, reaching throughout the public, directly approaching the interest and judgment of everyman, lie the immediate possibilities for improving understanding between nations.

ELIZABETH TODD

360